George Vere Irving

**The Upper Ward of Lanarkshire**

described and delineated - Vol. 3

George Vere Irving

**The Upper Ward of Lanarkshire**
*described and delineated - Vol. 3*

ISBN/EAN: 9783337312985

Printed in Europe, USA, Canada, Australia, Japan

Cover: Foto ©Andreas Hilbeck / pixelio.de

More available books at **www.hansebooks.com**

THE

# UPPER WARD OF LANARKSHIRE

## DESCRIBED AND DELINEATED.

THE ARCHÆOLOGICAL AND HISTORICAL SECTION

BY

GEORGE VERE IRVING, F.S.A. Scot.,

VICE-PRESIDENT OF THE BRITISH ARCHÆOLOGICAL ASSOCIATION.

THE STATISTICAL AND TOPOGRAPHICAL SECTION

BY

ALEXANDER MURRAY.

The Bower of Wandell.

VOLUME THIRD.

GLASGOW: THOMAS MURRAY AND SON.
EDINBURGH: EDMONSTON AND DOUGLAS.
LONDON: J. RUSSELL SMITH.
MDCCCLXIV.

# CONTENTS

OF

# APPENDIX VOLUME.

## ITEMS OF INQUIRY

FOR A

# Descriptive and Statistic Guide for the Upper Ward of Lanarkshire.

### CRAWFORD TO CARLUKE.

*Aim to show present in contrast with past condition of the Parishes.*

ACREAGE; extent, how and of old farmed; crops, rotation of.     *a*
AGRICULTURAL STATISTICS,—farm implements: *full.*     *b*
ANECDOTES, if locally instructive. Historical memoranda, if valuable. *c*
ANTIQUARIAN and ARCHÆOLOGICAL information.     *d*
BRIDGES, TURNPIKE TRUSTS, and PARISH ROADS.     *e*
CHURCHES—sittings, glebe, manse, stipend—value; *item of dissent.*     *f*
EMINENT INDIVIDUALS; notices of—born or connected with the parish. *g*
EXCISE; license values. Taxes levied, and parochial assessments.     *h*
FUNDS—mortified—for charitable or educational purposes.     *i*
HERITORS—resident or otherwise—given in order of "manse ratings." *j*
HOUSES—not number of—but, improving or otherwise, and how far. *k*
INNS, "publicks," how patronised, and by whom most.     *l*
LIBRARIES; No. of volumes—rates of subscription—Lectures, etc.     *m*
MANUFACTURES—of what, when started, and how prospering.     *n*
MINERALS; coal, iron, lead, limestone, marble, freestone.     *o*
MINERAL SPRINGS; where, when found, and of what value.     *p*
NATIVES; their habits, and prevailing names of the older families. *q*
ORDNANCE survey information—names of places and their import. *r*
POOR, their condition, now and of old—inspectors of.     *s*
POPULATION, increasing or decreasing, and the reasons why.     *t*
POLICE, how distributed; and their duties, how estimated.     *u*
PROPERTY; how held; and value, now and of old.     *v*
RAILWAYS; mileage in the parish; assessment and influence.     *w*
RIVERS; their angling repute; hills, mountains; woods, plantations, etc. *x*
SCHOOLS; how supported, how attended, what taught, etc.: *full.*     *y*
SITUATION, extent and natural features of the parish.     *z*
SOCIETIES; agricultural, horticultural, educational. Clubs, etc.     *aa*
VILLAGES, Burghs o' Barony and Burgh. Markets.     *bb*
WAGES, now and of old; how and what earned—and expended.     *cc*

Preliminary notice of Antiquarian and Geological matters will occupy the first pages of the Work—full and carefully classed tables of valuable figures will close it. Maps and Illustrations will be given.

*June* 30, 1859.     A. M.

# ERRATA.

At p. 291, Vol. I., reference is made to a keen dispute between the Abbot of Kelso and the Templars of Culter, etc.; the original information for that remark will be found at p. 342 of the Statistical Account of Lanarkshire—the reverend writer having confounded the *burn* of his parish with the "broad, deep, and rapid" stream of the Dee, in the north, as it flows between the parishes of Mary-Culter and Peter-Culter.

At p. 259, Vol. I., the height of Culter-fell is printed as being 5426 feet, for which read 2456, as elsewhere, and more than once, given in this Work.

At p. 259, Vol. I., reference is made to the mansion of Netherurd as being in the parish of Drummelzier, for which read the *parish of Kirkurd*.

At p. 459, Vol. I. *(the error of the Volume)*, the status of the resident in Libberton parish is given as that of a farmer; *it was that of a Norfolk landowner, of old family, great wealth, etc.*

At p. 61, Vol. III., the valuation figures (1863–4) for the parish of Covington and for that of Coulter have been transposed; *i.e.*, those for Covington should read as for Coulter, *et vice versa*.

----

In volumes dealing so largely with facts, and giving figures so profusely, other errors will be discovered; but it is hoped that the pages will give internal evidence that an earnest desire has throughout prevailed to produce the information faithfully and carefully.

A. M.

# APPENDIX.

## THE AGRICULTURE OF THE UPPER WARD.

BY

### A TENANT FARMER IN THE DISTRICT.

The ancient system of agriculture as practised in the Upper Ward of Lanarkshire differed in no respect from that pursued in other districts of Scotland at the same altitude above the level of the sea. The absence of great towns and the scantiness of the population rendered the agriculture of the past—a period dating backwards from about the year 1790—more an object of provision for the immediate wants of those engaged in it than a great manufacture of raw produce, as it has since become. The altered state of the country, and the various improvements introduced in cultivation, have produced a change in rural industry which renders it unnecessary to enter upon any description of the district further than relates to what may be styled the era of modern agriculture; and to that this sketch will be confined.

CLIMATE.—As climate is an essential condition of the growth of crops, without which a favourable soil will not avail, that of the Upper Ward will form the first subject of notice. From the small extent of the district, being little over forty miles in length, and less in breadth, it is, from the greater or lesser elevation, and their situation in reference to more mountainous tracts, that any variation in the climate of particular parishes can exist. The extremes are presented by the sunny banks on the trough of the Clyde in Carluke parish, about 400 feet above the sea, reputed one of the finest fruit-producing districts in Scotland, and the village of Leadhills, at an elevation of upwards of 1000 feet, where the cereals scarcely ever ripen, turnips seldom bulb, and the chief care-requiring agricultural, or rather horticultural productions are the early potato and the hardy Scotch red kail, whilst grass furnishes the most valuable herbage to which manure can be applied.

In Carluke parish the soil on the haughs is well adapted to the culture of wheat. These haughs, however, are of very limited extent.

*a*

The remainder of the parish rises rather abruptly from the river, so that the greater part of even this, the lowest of the Upper Ward, is confined to the cultivation of oats and barley, and has the greater part of its surface in grass as the most profitable crop.

The great and abrupt rise in the elevation of the valley of the Clyde, occasioned by the falls of the river in the neighbourhood of Lanark, renders the rest of the Upper Ward unfit for the growth of wheat. Being situated near, and in a great measure consisting of, elevated mountains, the climate is generally rather variable, and the rainfall, although not so great as in some districts farther west, is yet very considerable on the whole. Thus it becomes more profitable to devote the greater extent of arable land to grass rather than to the growth of corn, and a large portion of the cultivated land being more or less steep, the expense of working it, combined with the fickleness of the climate, renders the practice still more common. Wheat was certainly more extensively cultivated of old than at present, notwithstanding all the modern improved modes of agriculture, but this is easily explained. In former times, any good land might be profitably employed in the growth of this grain for home use, at a time when roads were few and bad, and the difficulty of procuring supplies from the more favoured districts operated as a sufficient counterpoise to the variable yield, or the general inferiority of the sample. Now, owing to the improvements of the roads, and the more recent introduction of railways, it can be supplied with greater advantage from the lower districts of the country. Indeed, the growth of grain in the district has become subservient to the dairy and the fattening of stock.

TERMS BY WHICH LAND IS HELD.—The terms on which land is held have a most important bearing on its agricultural prosperity. In this particular there is little variation throughout the district, the general custom being to grant leases of nineteen years' duration for both sheep and arable farms. About the conclusion of the American War of Independence, in consequence of dull trade and general financial depression, many of the tenants in this district, as well as elsewhere, obtained from their landlords leases of three nineteens, as the phrase was, at a low annual rent, to induce them to take the land at all. Of such as availed themselves of this opportunity, a few realised considerable wealth, either from their greater original capital, which enabled them to hold out through the bad times, to the high prices of the last French war period, or from their possessing greater sagacity and energy than their neighbours.

SIZE OF FARMS.—The size of arable farms in the Upper Ward of Lanarkshire varies from about 100 to 500 acres; many ranging from 100 to 200 acres—an extent which enables the farmer personally not only to undertake the superintendence, but also to overlook, as far as practicable, the *minutiæ* of out-door labour, of the barn, and of the treatment and feeding of the live stock, whilst the labours of the dairy and the kitchen are under the active charge of his wife; a considerable part of the labour in this department being often shared by her. The number of cows kept seldom exceeds 25 or 30.

Although the system of dairy farming is that which in general characterises the agriculture of the Upper Ward, there are instances where very few cows are kept, beyond those necessary for the family, and where the main object is the rearing and feeding of cattle, or more frequently of sheep. Such farms are generally of the largest size, and composed of soils particularly adapted for turnip cultivation.

The average rent of the old cultivated or croft land may be stated at present at about £2 10s per Scotch acre; the outfield land, which has been later subjected to the process of green cropping, at £1 10s; while that lately lying in comparatively unproductive pasture cannot be set down as on the average above 10s. The smaller farms, having less of the latter kind of land, and being more easily wrought, from having been more frequently subjected to the plough, have generally commanded more per acre than similar soils on those of larger size. The latter class of farms, from their extent and the improvements now thought desirable by landlords, require so much more capital, and entail so much greater risk, that there have been in general fewer competitors for them than for the smaller holdings. It may be remarked, however, that from the increase of capital, a more generally-diffused spirit of enterprise, the introduction of a higher class of implements and machinery, and an altered system of farm management more especially adapted to large farms, they now command proportionately larger rents than formerly.

CAPITAL.—The capital required for the smaller farms may range from £500 to £1000; for the larger, from £1000 to £2000, and upwards. But probably the largest part of the arable land is held by tenants whose capital will average about £750 or £800, embarked chiefly in dairy cows and young cattle, and the horses required for the labours of the farm, with a few young ones annually reared. To give a clearer idea of this matter, we may remark that capital to the extent of about four and a half years' rental is requisite for the stocking of both sheep and arable farms.

Of exclusively sheep farms there are not many in the Upper Ward. In most of the parishes there are, however, a number of farms where sheep husbandry forms the most important department, at the same time that considerable attention is also paid to the dairy and cropping. In these cases, from 10 to 15 cows are frequently kept, and have equal care bestowed upon them with the sheep. On some, where the land suited to milk-cows can be spared from that appropriated to the sheep stock, it has become a custom of late years, to let from 20 to 40 cows to a "Booer," who is said to "boo" or rent them; and who pays for each cow a stipulated amount, either in cheese or money. In such cases the farmer himself keeps no more cows than are sufficient to supply dairy produce for family use, except the small quantity required in spring for the lambs whose dams are unable to provide for them. In such farms fewer servants are kept; the cows having oftener a proportion of natural pasture, and deriving more of their winter food from meadows, in the form of hay, which require less labour than where turnips and straw are their chief support.

From the ease with which a large extent of sheep land can be superintended by one master, a general practice has prevailed, for the last eighty years, of one tenant holding two or more farms. The wild nature of these "led" farms, having ordinarily no land at a low enough elevation for the growth of grain or green crops, has caused them to be consigned to the care of shepherds, who are only visited by their masters at the principal handlings. Many of them, from their high situation, are peculiarly liable to storms, and to the loss, in bad years, of the greater part of the stock, circumstances which not only lead to the smallness of the rent, but tend to keep them in the hands of men of large capital.

The practice of holding led farms prevails less extensively in Lanarkshire than in some other parts of Scotland; neither are so many of the Lanarkshire store farmers holders of land elsewhere. This, however, has rather been on the increase of late, and a few of them hold very extensively in the north.

FARM IMPLEMENTS.—Of these, one by which the extension of modern agriculture has been much aided, is the thrashing machine. In the Upper Ward it has almost superseded the flail, except in the case of crofters and villagers cultivating small patches of land, where the labour of old men once used to it can be had cheaply. Instances of machines for one horse even are not uncommon on small occupancies where only one is kept, and where the operations of ploughing and such as require two horses are carried on by two such occupiers conjointly. The accounts of the dates of the *first* erection of thrashing mills in several parishes vary from 1790 to 1805, but they had become pretty general by 1810. Since that date several individuals have established themselves as millwrights, whose chief employment is in connection with these machines. Of late, many farmers employ the English portable steam machines, which thrash and partly dress from 70 to 100 bolls per day.

The mills in general use separate the chaff from the corn, but do not prepare it for the market, so that the finishing part of the operation is performed by manual labour, partly by means of the riddle or *ree*, and partly by the hand-fanners. The latter seems to have been common in the district for a considerable period before the introduction of the mill. Many barns still exist with the doors placed opposite each other, for the purpose of carrying away the chaff by the draught thereby occasioned on a blowy day when the corn and the chaff were tossed or shovelled up before it. The prejudice against the first introduction of fanners seems to have been great. They were often styled "The Devil's Wind."

In probably one-half of the mills water power is employed, which, from the nature of the district, both as to rainfall and inequality of surface, is to a great extent available without much expense; and steam power is used in little more than a dozen cases in the whole district. The remainder are driven by horses.

Shortly before the introduction of thrashing machines, an improvement took place which was productive of a scarcely less saving of labour. This was the substitution of ploughs with two horses for those drawn by three or four. This change was contemporaneous with, and perhaps originated in, the use of iron instead of wood in the manufacture of the plough. These iron ploughs have now universally superseded the older implement, although the latter for a long time continued to hold its ground. Many gave a preference to it from the idea that the iron one had a tendency, by its greater weight acting on the bottom of the furrow, to cause a greater consolidation of the subsoil. The chief recommendation of the wooden plough was its cheapness—the average price being about 13s 6d—less than a fourth of that of an iron plough. On the other hand, the iron implement can be formed with much greater ease and certainty on any pattern, and, above all, possesses the great advantage of durability. The saving produced by the introduction of the two-horse plough, performing as much work in the day as the older ones with three or four horses, consists not only in the smaller number of horses now used, but in enabling the farmer to dispense with the services of the gaudsman or boy who formerly assisted the ploughman. The plough in general use is identical with, or similar to, that commonly known as "Gray's Plough," so called from the manufacturers, at Uddingstone, near Glasgow, and it is considered as fully sufficient for the requirements of the district when in the hands of an experienced ploughman. In some districts there has arisen a feeling in favour of the attachment of wheels to the ploughs. The greater ease with which the wheeled plough is held enables a boy, or "hafflin," to perform satisfactory work, which is a consideration in the scarcity of hands and rise in the price of labour. There is no doubt, too, that, from the increased cultivation of farms, apart from the comparative merits of these two classes of ploughs, the land is now much better adapted for the wheeled plough than it was formerly. Turnips and potatoes are drilled up with the double plough, which is well suited for the free moulds of the Upper Ward.

Within the last ten or twelve years a most important implement in the cultivation of green crops has been introduced, viz., the grubber. This was, until lately, generally of the kind known in East Lothian as "Finlayson's Triangular," with a wheel at each angle, and drawn by three or four horses. A lighter grubber, somewhat similar to "Tennant's Patent," and suitable for two horses on well-cultivated farms, has now much superseded Finlayson's. The grubber has almost entirely abolished the use of the plough in spring, for turnip and potato land; the practice being to plough the land in autumn with a strong furrow, in some cases with three horses, where the soil is strong enough, and the subsoil such as to warrant the practice. Besides overtaking more work than the plough, the grubber does not expose the soil to the influence of drought, which in very dry seasons, such as that of 1859, is especially advantageous. It is also superior to the plough in freeing the soil of couch grass, or *wrack* as it is called, and must be considered as altogether a *sine qua non* of advanced turnip husbandry, especially on light lands.

The harrows in general use are the wooden rhomboidal, with iron teeth, which seem to hold their ground against the superior zig-zag patent iron harrow, probably from the general character of the soils—stiff clay seldom occurring. They are equally used for covering the grain seed and harrowing turnip land. Another kind, well known as the brake or break harrow—a name very significant of its use—is employed for the latter purpose in cases where the land has been recently broken up or is peculiarly foul.

Besides the grubber for general cultivation, the drill-grubber may be particularised as an important auxiliary in the cultivation of green crops. This implement is of only recent introduction, and not yet generally employed. The drill-harrow, or *hurkle*, has long been in use, probably since the introduction of turnip husbandry, about the beginning of the century. On all average-sized farms, the double-drill turnip-sowing machine is in general use, and probably few new single ones are now ordered, the saving of labour being of so much importance at the season of sowing.

Another important change, occurring within a comparatively recent period, has been the universal substitution of the scythe for the reaping-hook. The scythe, except for hay, had no place as a harvest implement till about twenty years ago. About ten years previously, the toothed or serrated hook or sickle had been superseded by the scythe-hook, which may be said to have paved the way for the introduction of the scythe. Shearing with the scythe-hook, as practised by the Irish—who seem to have been the medium of its introduction into the district—so far resembles mowing, as it is a mowing and gathering at the same time by one individual. Mowing appears now to have become universal in the district, the long-established practice of stooking the mown rye-grass for seed, perhaps making the change easier than otherwise it might have been, as the one operation so far resembles the other. The only difference is that, in the case of grain, the swathe is laid to the standing corn, whilst, with the hay, it is laid away from the uncut grass. The change was also recommended by the greater ease with which three good mowers could be got than a dozen good shearers. It also provided a much fitter employment for the women than the hook. In harvest, the ploughmen generally wield the scythe. On the larger farms some extra hands may be employed. The bandsters are generally hired for the harvest, although "hafflins," or half-grown lads, engaged for the whole summer, may, to some extent, perform this work. The female servants, and occasionally an additional woman or two, are employed lifting to the mowers, whilst boys and girls are employed in raking and making bands. There are a few reaping machines, but as the crops are generally oats, and not, in most seasons, so strong as to be unsuitable for the scythe, the latter seems well adapted for most of the district, and so long as extra hands can readily enough be got for harvest labour, will probably remain so. Reaping machines, however, are, on the whole, rather unmanageable in a country so undulating as the greater part of the Upper Ward; and, fifteen hands being needed to work the machine to profit, few farms, in the upper districts particularly, can muster that number.

As to grain-sowing, the implement most in use is the broad-cast machine, which is considered advantageous in distributing the seed more regularly than by the hand, effecting a saving of seed, besides the great saving of skilled labour at such an important season.

FENCING AND DRAINING.—The existence of fences was, to a very recent period, the exception rather than the rule, even in the agricultural parts of the Upper Ward. The stock, consisting almost entirely of cattle, were divided into two *hirsels*—the milch cows and the young cattle or *yeild beasts*, each lot under the care of a herd-boy or girl. The croft land in grass, and any good natural pasture, fell to the share of the milch cows, whilst the outfield, or moorland pasture, was grazed by the others; and, fences seldom separating these herds from the patches of corn that occurred here and there, all depended on the watchfulness of the attendant and the collie dog; and carelessness or want of skill on the part of the herd resulted, not only in damage to the crops, but in injury to the cattle of which they had the charge. Farmers now avail themselves of fences, where they can be had, on payment of a remunerative interest on the money expended by the landlord in their erection.

The fences in the agricultural districts, erected eighty or ninety years ago, consist of an earthen dyke formed from a ditch running alongside of it, on the summit of which a thorn-hedge was planted; or, in other cases, of two hedges planted on the edge of a dyke, formed from two ditches, one running along each side. The dyke in this case was about five feet wide at the top, and with the ditches, took up about twelve feet altogether. In the latter case hard-wood trees were often planted between the hedgerows, and in the former at intervals among the thorns. These trees, however, were seldom planted where thorns were likely to thrive well and grow to a good height. Had it been totally omitted, these fences might, with ordinary care, have continued good till the present day, but the trees have, in most cases, smothered the hedges, and however advantageous as shelter, they now serve but little purpose as fences. These fences seem also to have been, in many instances, intended to serve as drains for cutting through springs, and consequently were planned according to the nature of the surface, so that the enclosures were often very small in size and irregular in outline. Thorn-hedges in single rows, with or without a ditch, as the land was wet or dry, have all along been planted to some extent, but are not very common. Dry stone dykes, except in the moorlands, where sheep husbandry prevailed, were seldom used, and then chiefly as marches or fences between different farms. In fact, the greatest portion of even the agricultural districts continued almost without fences till very recently. In some places a considerable extent of hedges has been recently planted, but within the last ten or twelve years by far the greatest part of the fences erected have been of stobs and wire. In the pastoral districts stone dykes still continue to be the main kind of fence, and having the advantage of considerable shelter in themselves, will hold their ground wherever materials of good quality can be readily obtained. Where these are scarce, or the situation, by its difficulty of access or extreme steepness, is ill suited for this class of wall, wire fences have been introduced, in many instances, with great success.

As already remarked, the old fence of hedge and ditch usually served the purpose of draining the field to some extent. These, with cross ditches cutting up the land into small subdivisions in proportion to its wetness, seem to have been the only kind of drains known at the time these fences were formed, which, from the age of the hedge-row timber, appears to have been about eighty years ago. This leads to the belief that under-drainage was not then practised in the district. Since that period, drains formed of the stones gathered from the land, without any apparent regard to their size, have been executed to a considerable extent for carrying away spring water, or cutting between the wet and the dry on a declivity. Wherever such drains had really any considerable perennial run of water, they have been permanent advantages to the land, serving the purpose intended even to the present day. In other cases, they have generally become choked with earth. They were generally conducted, wherever practicable, across the field to the nearest point of the fence ditch, instead of running straight up and down the declivity, according to the most approved method of modern drainage.

This appears to have been almost the only drainage generally practised till the opening up of the country by the Caledonian Railway, in October, 1847, gave facilities for procuring tiles. The only other mode of covered drainage seems to have been the wedge draining on deep peat bogs, where a firm wedge of peat in a dry state was introduced into the bottom of the drain, leaving below it sufficient space for a water-run. When well executed, such drains will serve all purposes of the tenant farmer on such soils.

The system of thorough draining, by running parallel drains, filled with broken stones, up and down a field at a distance proportioned to the nature of the subsoil, appears not to have been practised to any great extent in this district, although introduced by Smith of Deanston, and extensively carried on in more favoured localities. The expense of this system appears to have been so great that it prevented any attempt at draining those wild moorlands which have more recently been reclaimed. Liming, indeed, could have been resorted to, and to any extent, but in most cases the distance from a market and the comparatively low prices of many kinds of farm produce, offered no inducement for such operations. It was only after the general introduction of guano that such an improvement could be profitably adopted, by means of which the price of live stock has been so much increased, from the great addition to the supply of food produced throughout the country generally. As to the beneficial effects of draining throughout the Upper Ward, it is not going too far to say that the produce of a great proportion of the soil has been doubled, besides the additional land brought into the rotation, which had formerly been seldom cropped, and then little to the benefit of the subsequent pasture.

We must not omit to notice the improvements made by embankments against the overflow of the Clyde or its tributaries. Considerable breadths of valuable land, that formerly were very precarious as arable land, have been rendered secure even in wet seasons. This operation has been assisted to a considerable extent by improved drainage, which has deepened the bed of the river by increasing the rapidity of the current. The most extensive operations in this way have been carried on in the higher part of the arable district, chiefly in the parishes of Coulter and Lamington, where the harvests are in general so early as to warrant considerable outlay for arable purposes. On one or two estates in that locality, land to the extent of some hundreds of acres has been thus embanked, and is now good arable land, excepting a few spots, consisting of old back ponds or hollows of stagnant water, incapable of being drained. Formerly, these lands were generally completely overgrown with rushes which no mowing could extirpate, and which could be kept down only by the plough. Now green crops can be grown upon them equally with other land without the soil being liable to be swept away in winter, or the crop itself in summer and autumn.

Irrigation has not been carried on to any extent. Whenever the surface is conveniently available for tillage, and of such an extent as to be thought of consequence, meadows situated on the banks of burns or small rivulets are usually cropped. Water in general, though greatly advantageous to the growth of the coarser kinds of herbage, does not seem to be equally conducive in ordinary seasons, at least, to the growth of the finer grasses. Indeed, rivulets that have their source in, or flow through, extensive mossy tracts, are found to be hurtful to vegetation. It is only in particular cases, where the liquid manure of the farm-yard, or the waste water of villages can be applied, that irrigation can be said to be of any benefit.

In such cases the results are often remarkable, and render the land so treated much more profitable than it otherwise would be.

Mr Sim of Coulter, who has always been deeply interested in the progress of agriculture, some years ago erected apparatus for distributing liquid manure, but this only to land in the immediate vicinity of the manure tank. The expense of laying down the metal pipes seems to prevent the general extension of the system.

Mr Brown of Libberton Mains farm has also been at the expense of building large tanks, and erecting a steam engine, for the purpose of making use of the surplus liquid rejected by the dung-heap. He inclines to think that about six acres of land in grass, near to the farm-steading, is sufficient to absorb beneficially all the liquid manure of his farm, of about 700 acres, on which the whole of the straw and turnip crop are consumed. Mr Brown is no advocate for using all the straw as fodder, and thinks it important to have such a quantity used as bedding or litter as will secure a comfortable lair to the animals; and so far, therefore, he is opposed to the extreme advocates of the liquid system, who would have the cattle lying on bare boards or cocoa-nut matting, and apply the whole of the manure in a fluid state.

As to the present modes of cropping, it has been already stated that at least one-half of the arable land is devoted to pasture, or clover and rye-grass for hay. The almost universal practice of the district now is to sow oats on the land ploughed out of lea, to follow that by turnips or potatoes, the latter crop seldom exceeding a fourth part of that devoted to the former. These crops are generally followed by oats, only a little barley being sown, bearing, probably, about the same proportion to the oats that the potatoes do to the turnips. Grass and clover seeds are universally sown at the same period with the oats or barley succeeding the green crop. Red clover, from its liability to failure of late years, and the great success with which the Alsike has been used, is now much less frequently sown; indeed, Alsike is likely soon to supersede it entirely. White clover will stand its ground. Timothy-grass may also be considered of importance for strong or mossy soils, especially where sheep are kept. However, rye-grass will remain the most important kind of grass for general use. Italian rye-grass is often sown where the situation is favourable for irrigation by gravitation. Otherwise, a crop of tares is considered as more profitable for soiling or the house-feeding of cattle, to which both of these crops are always applied. The crop of young grass was, at one time, always cut for hay, but it has become very common to pasture it in summer. Owing to the greater quantities of turnips grown, this hay is of much less consequence as winter food for cattle; the supply of other fodder having been, by the assistance of this root, rendered sufficient. Besides, by the application of from one and a-half to two and a-half cwts., per acre, of nitrate of soda or sulphate of ammonia, as much rye-grass hay can be procured from one acre as from two or three where this top-dressing is not used. This enables the cows to be much better kept and the stock increased; and, in many cases, although the winter stock may not be added to, it has made the custom more prevalent of grazing the young stock at home, a practice which can be carried out without any additional house accommodation; whilst, at the same time, the permanent stock of cattle kept on the farm is actually increased.

The oat crop, on the land ploughed from lea, is frequently top-dressed with two or three cwts. of Peruvian guano per Scotch acre, a practice which increases about one-third the yield of both grain and straw, and in most cases is found profitable; the average of soils not being of such a nature as to lodge the crop under such a mode of treatment. Turnips in general have an allowance of guano, ground or dissolved bones, or of some compound wherein bones form one of the principal constituents. This is applied, with the farm-yard manure, in the drill, so far as the latter will go. When it fails, the remainder of the turnips are manured with the portable materials alone, at an expense of from £3 to £7 per acre, and, though the latter sum may seem an extravagant outlay, its advantages to the subsequent crops, especially to the pasture, are such as to make it highly remunerative. Potatoes have not been, to such a considerable extent, aided by these manures, farm-yard manure alone being generally used for their growth. Their cultivation, according to the modern method, seems to have been generally introduced about the close of last century, as was also that of turnips, to such an extent at least, as to enable the farmers, in some cases, to fatten a number of cattle and sheep; yet the land under turnips cannot, in any case, have been more, at that time, than about a seventh of that now devoted to it, while the bulk of crop per acre was probably not above one-half of what it now is. The present average is about 25 tons per Scotch acre, although as many as 45 have been produced.

Any other crops cultivated cannot be said to be of much consequence. Mangold-wurzel has been tried, and, in favourable situations, produced a fair amount of bulbs, but never such as to pay for the greater quantity of manure required for its cultivation. Carrots, from the greater trouble connected with them, have never been cultivated to any great extent. The Swedish turnip has succeeded well, however, both as to growth and quality of produce, where the soil is strong enough. Cabbage, where a piece of superior soil can be applied to its cultivation, may be expected to be grown to some extent in future, as, where it has been tried, it has succeeded pretty fairly; and as a food for dairy cows it is peculiarly valuable. Rape, also, is grown to some extent as a forage plant on the larger farms, having a great breadth of dry soil; but this is only practised when the turnip sowing cannot be accomplished so early in the season as to insure a full crop, or in the breaking up of steep lands.

PERIODS OF SOWING AND REAPING.—Both of these are considerably earlier since drainage and improved farming became prevalent. Seed-time is, on the average, from the 28th March to 4th April, and harvest about the beginning of September. In former times harvest often extended till November. Crops have become earlier by the increased facilities for procuring a change of seed from warmer districts, and the introduction of earlier varieties of oats, which the land can now carry so as to produce an abundance of fodder, where formerly that could be raised only by using the later varieties.

CATTLE.—The cattle generally kept in the Upper Ward have the characteristics, more or less, of the Ayrshire breed, and, indeed, there are many pure Ayrshire stocks of superior excellence. For forty or fifty years back, large numbers of Ayrshire cows, chiefly bred in the Middle Ward of the county, have been introduced through the Fairs of Carluke, Lanark, Carnwath, and Biggar; these Fairs at the same time serving, especially of late, as the medium of a considerable export trade to Dumfriesshire and the north-western counties of England. A very large proportion of the cows are now bred in the district; the practice on most farms being to rear at least as many quey-calves as keep up the stock, and in many cases considerable numbers of young cattle are annually disposed of as queys in calf. This has been brought about, partly from the greater risk of purchasing since the prevalence of *pleura pneumonia*, and partly from their enhanced value. The general custom is to have the queys calving at three years old, and to dispose of the old cows at from seven to eleven years. The latter in general go to the dairies of Edinburgh and Glasgow as milkers, where they are milked and fattened at the same time, and never again produce offspring. Their price varies according to the season of selling, as well as their size and apparent milking qualities. In March, when there is an abundant supply, they average about £10 a head, whilst in November, and for a period before and after, they bring about £13. Good calving queys, in the month of May, fetch about £12. Many prize animals, however, both male and female, have been purchased at prices averaging from £18 to £40, and in several instances for exportation to the Continent.

In a few instances, Ayrshire cows are kept principally for rearing feeding stock. They are put to a short horn bull, and the progeny, both male and female, carefully reared, and sometimes fed off at the age of two years, but more frequently kept till rising three. In these cases more than fifteen cows are seldom kept, and more frequently about twelve. The calves get a full supply of sweet milk for three or four months, after which cheese and butter are generally made.

On some of the higher haughs of the Clyde numbers of Highland cattle are wintered in the open air with the assistance of a little hay, and are fed off the following summer on the same land. A few inferior Highland cattle are grazed occasionally in the moorland parts of Carnwath parish, but, in general, only so as to be resold, still lean, at a farther stage of their growth. More generally the rough natural pasture of that district is grazed in summer by two-year-old yell Ayrshire queys, frequently bred in the district, but in many cases sent from a distance by farmers who rent finer lands, and think it more advantageous to devote their own pastures to their milch cows.

The cows which the Ayrshire breed displaced in the Upper Ward, excelled them, both in weight of carcase and quantity of produce, and to some individuals might appear more valuable animals. Judging from the few still remaining, which, however, have a cross of the Ayrshire, they appear to have been flat-sided and deep-ribbed, without that compactness of form and roundness of barrel which is characteristic of the latter breed. They must, in consequence, have been great consumers in proportion to their produce. The Ayrshire Association gives the points indicated in the subjoined note as the characteristics of the Ayrshire breed. They seem also to have been better suited to the rough natural pasture, formerly so prevalent on most farms, than to the shorter, though more nutritive, bite of the grass on tilled land.*

The dairies in the Upper Ward during the last twenty or thirty years have been chiefly devoted to the manufacture of full milk cheese, made almost universally after the Dunlop method. In a few instances the Somersetshire system has been introduced. In many cases, however, skim-milk cheeses and butter are made. The latter is sometimes sent fresh to Edinburgh and Glasgow. When it is powdered, it is sold to the west country manufacturing districts, where alone there is a demand for it. In other cases it is full salted and kept over till the end of autumn. This system is mostly practised in the smaller dairies. It has also become common to send sweet milk by railway to Glasgow.

* The points indicating excellence in Ayrshire cows are as follows:—Head, short; forehead, wide; nose, fine, between the muzzle and eyes: muzzle, moderately large; eyes, full and lively; horns, wide set on, inclining upwards and curving slightly inwards; neck, long and straight from the head to the top of the shoulder, free from loose skin on the under side, fine at its junction with the head, and the muscles symmetrically enlarging towards the shoulders; shoulders, thin at the top; brisket, light; the whole fore-quarters thin in front, and gradually increasing in depth and width backwards; back, short and straight; spine, well defined, especially at the shoulders; short ribs, arched; the body deep at the flanks, and the milk-veins well developed; pelvis, long, broad, and straight; hook-bones (*illium*), wide apart, and not much overlaid with fat; thighs, deep and broad; tail, long and slender, and set on level with the back; milk-vessel, capacious and extending well forward; hinder part, broad and firmly attached to the body; the sole or under surface, nearly level; the teats, from two to two and a-half inches in length, equal in thickness, and hanging perpendicularly, their distance apart at the sides should be equal to about one-third of the length of the vessel, and across to about one-half of the breadth; legs, short, the bones fine and the joints firm; skin, soft and elastic, and covered with soft, close, woolly hair. The colours preferred are brown or brown and white, the colours being distinctly defined. Weight of the animal, when fatted, about forty imperial stones, sinking offal.

In conclusion, we may remark that the Ayrshire breed was moulded into its present form chiefly amongst tenant farmers, whose principal dependence lay on the produce of their dairies, and we cannot believe that merely fancy characteristics, as some suppose, had much sway with them. They have, indeed, produced an animal eminently graceful and well-proportioned; but this beauty of form is the result of the combination of particular features, each of which has been sought for and prized as indications of some practical excellency. Thus, the strong loins, the round barrel, and well-carried milk vessel, are so many signs of durability and productiveness. An animal so constituted will yield, weight for weight, a more valuable carcase than a lanker and coarser one, besides being much more easily fed. As to the yield per acre on the general soils of this district, the Ayrshire, at least as a dairy breed, is that which is the most profitable.

The sheep stock generally kept was, until twenty years ago, almost entirely the black-faced. In the Old Statistical Account of Scotland there is no mention of any Cheviot sheep in the County of Lanark, except in the parish of Lamington. A few stocks had, however, before the date of that publication, become Cheviot, either by purchasing young stock or by the use of Cheviot rams; but the change does not seem to have spread to any extent, the very severe winter of 1797 being probably the chief cause of this. Within the last twenty years, however, more than one-half of the sheep stock of the Upper Ward have assumed, more or less, the characteristics of pure Cheviots. The system of crossing and re-crossing with the Cheviot ram has been carried on so long that many stocks are now essentially Cheviot, as to quality of wool and weight of carcase, while the wether lambs bring equally high prices with the pure Cheviot. Probably, however, had it not been for the great extension of the turnip husbandry, this change in the breed would not have been found profitable. So, the introduction of portable manures has had a great influence on sheep farming, as well as on that of the arable districts. It has also led to considerable alteration in the periods when this stock is disposed of. Formerly, large numbers of the wether lambs, mostly black-faced, were wintered on the farms where they were bred. These were sold at Linton (a market now transferred to Lanark), in the following June, where they were purchased by storemasters from the Highlands; while the *shots* of the ewe lambs were disposed of to farmers in the neighbouring arable districts, by whom they were wintered and sold, at the same time with the wethers—the larger number going into Yorkshire for breeding purposes. Now, store farmers, whether having black-faced or Cheviot sheep, sell off the whole of their wether lambs and the casts of their ewe lambs in the beginning of August, either to the arable farmer of the district or to the market at Lockerbie or Lanark. This leaves room for a considerable addition to the ewe stock, and the throwing into the general run of a portion of the best of the land formerly reserved for the hoggs, must, in many cases, have gone far of itself to afford grounds for the change of a black-faced stock to a Cheviot one. Previous to the general use of guano and bone manure, few Cheviot hoggs were wintered on arable farms in the Upper Ward. The general practice in Lanarkshire, where Cheviot hoggs are wintered, is to keep them on grass, with a moderate allowance of turnips, sometimes carted to the pastures, and sometimes eaten where they grow, the sheep being confined on them with flakes or hurdles during the night or a few hours of the day. They are then grazed during summer on good pasture. In October they are again put on turnips, and in some cases allowed, in addition, a portion of corn or cake, and made ready for the fat market. They are sold from January to April, according to their previous condition, or the views of the farmer, at prices ranging from 34s to 46s. In general, they are supplied with straw or hay, more frequently the former, placed in a rack, especially when they are constantly confined to the turnips. In very severe winters, particularly towards the spring months, the hoggs, under good management, receive an allowance of oil-cake or oats, the latter being generally preferred, as more readily eaten by them. The allowance for each hogg is from a quarter to a pound of oats, according to the supply of other keep. During the severe weather here, in the winter of 1860-1, owing to the general destruction by frost, as well as the original deficiency of the turnip crops, feeding substances seldom before used in the district were resorted to, such as rape-cake, alone or mixed with locust beans. As there is good reason to believe the rape-cake to be almost equal to oats in nutritive properties, while it is a great deal cheaper, the use of it is likely to become considerable in subsequent winters.

Besides the total change of the characteristics of permanent stocks by the use of Cheviot rams, crossing with the Leicester ram, for the purpose of raising stock for feeding, has also been put into practice with both Cheviot and black-faced ewes. The employment of other breeds has also been attempted, but although unattended by any practical results, they serve to show that enterprise and energy were not wanting before the most beneficial system was hit upon.

We may here notice the means by which farmers now consider that the fleece can be benefited. Since the introduction of the Cheviot ram, smearing with tar and butter has been gradually going out of practice, the tar being much more detrimental to the Cheviot wool than to the black-faced, which is of so much less value and used for many purposes wherein the stain of the tar is of little consequence. Even many holders of black-faced stock have given up the practice of smearing. Others smear only every alternate year. The black-faced wintered in the district, on farms partially arable, are smeared chiefly from a regard to a prejudice amongst the buyers from upland districts against those unsmeared, the idea being that the white hoggs must have been wintered in too low a climate, and become unfitted for an Alpine home.

Dipping has now become a prevalent mode of dealing with the fleece. Previous to its introduction, *pouring* had been for some time in practice. But it is probable that before long dipping will entirely supersede it. In both cases, the composition deemed suitable for hill sheep contains, besides some poisonous ingredient for the destruction of vermin, a considerable proportion of some kind of oil. Many experienced storemasters, who had been in the habit of using arsenic, are now averse to its use, believing that it has an injurious effect on the skin and wool, damaging the latter in quality, and reducing its weight, besides, of consequence, hurting the health of the animal. They recommend the use, rather, of hellebore or tobacco, neither of which have the corrosive nature of mineral poisons. After the dipping, the sheep stand till thoroughly dripped, on a platform whence the liquid runs again back into the trough in a way now well known and described in our latest agricultural dictionaries. The *pouring* is performed on a stool made for the purpose, such as was used for smearing, and shearing the sheep, and the fleece requires to be divided into sheds for the introduction of the liquid. The oil generally used for Cheviot sheep is olive, or, as it is more commonly styled from one of its chief places of shipment, Gallipoli oil. Castor, rape, and whale oils are also used—the latter, however, seldom or ever for Cheviots. We may notice here that, although almost every improvement in the management of the sheep stock has emanated from the eastern districts, the Upper Ward of Clydesdale has the credit of introducing successfully the system of adding from half to three-quarters of a pound of oil to the plunge, with as profitable results as when applied with the pouring bath.

The increasing value of sheep stock has given rise to many improvements in the managements of sheep grazings, by which a great addition of valuable pasturage from tracts formerly comparatively worthless has been effected by open or *sheep drains*, on which large sums have been expended. By means of these, palatable and nourishing pasture is produced, where formerly grew only herbage of the coarsest description. Of late years a great improvement has been made in these drains by placing them parallel to each other, in the same manner as covered drains on arable land, and in a few instances covered drainage has been practised to some extent, in which cases it is found advisable to follow up this improvement by liming on the unbroken surface. Among the other modes of improvement of sheep pasturage may be mentioned the burning of the heather in proper rotations, and the extirpating of breckens, or ferns, by repeated mowing. The first practice, unfortunately, is to some extent interfered with from its being thought prejudicial to the grouse. But preservers of game are beginning to think the grouse are thereby as much benefited as the sheep by having young

heath to feed upon, and, in consequence, a judicious system of burning portions in rotation, alike advantageous to the sheep and the game, has been sanctioned by all well-informed sportsmen.

The horses generally kept in the district for agricultural purposes are favourable specimens of the famed Clydesdale breed. Breeding does not, however, seem to be carried on so largely since the extension of the turnip husbandry. The disuse of the four-horse plough had of itself been previously a cause of fewer young horses being bred. The stock kept is composed chiefly of mares, and where breeding is practised the colts are generally disposed of.

The kind of horse generally used in the Upper Ward may seem rather of a lighter description than in some districts farther west, where the soils are heavier, and many of the horses are geldings, which frequently grow larger than the mares, although many of these very animals are the produce of the Upper Ward, where the absence of this greater weight is preferred, as the soils are in general so friable as to be easily ploughed by slighter horses; and speed in stepping is of considerable importance for the expeditious overtaking of the turnip-culture. For the grubber, and cases of plouging of a particularly severe kind, three horses can usually be provided, without purchasing any additional or laying idle any one on account of its fellow being so occupied. It is a remarkable peculiarity of the Clydesdale breed, as at present existing, that few of them, considered as purely belonging to it, are not possessed of one or more white feet; and we believe that it can be proved that many of the best specimens of the breed trace their pedigree to a horse having this peculiarity, bred within the present century.

As to other kinds of stock, swine may be set down as of considerable importance in a dairy district, where so much of the waste produce is available for their support. Kindly-feeding varieties are now most commonly sought after, whereas indications of growth were formerly the principal qualification of the young pig. Some of the finest English varieties have been introduced from some of the most distinguished breeders, and will, no doubt, have a beneficial influence on those bred in the district. The increased value of potatoes, since the opening of the Caledonian Railway, has, no doubt, been a chief cause of this increase in the attention paid to the breeding or selection of pigs. By the transit presented by that railway to the southern markets, the value of pork has been greatly enhanced. A strong prejudice is known to have existed, at no very distant period, against the use of swine's flesh over a great part of Scotland. As a striking instance of the rareness of this kind of stock at the time of Sir John Sinclair's Survey, about 1790, in one parish of the Upper Ward, where now the number lately amounted to 77, then it was only 7—certainly a curious example of the extent to which the habits of a people may be changed in a comparatively short period.

FARM-STEADINGS.—The farm-steadings in the Upper Ward are,

on the whole, mostly below the requirements of the age and the accommodation demanded in accordance with modern improvements. In new leases this matter is fully appreciated by the tenants in general. Many landlords, also, are now anxious to give accommodation of a superior kind, or such as the tenant considers necessary and desirable. In some cases, farm-steadings of the most perfect description have been erected. The importance of looking to the comfort of the servants tending the cattle, as well as to that of the animals themselves, has become greater from the increased value of labour, and in the newest kind of farm-steading, the whole is contained under one roof, so that the servant, during the performance of necessary duties, remains quite independent of the state of the weather without. At Libberton Mains there has been erected one of the most noteworthy combinations of this kind at present existing, and which may be considered the model of a farm-steading.

As far as we are aware, there exists in the Upper Ward only two instances of steam-power being used for the purpose of applying the liquid manure of the farm-yard, the one at the home farm of Coulter Mains, the other at the farm of Libberton Mains. In both of these cases, however, as we have formerly remarked, this pertains chiefly to the surplus liquid or drainage from the dunghill, there being no effort made to convert a large proportion of the animal excrements into a liquid state; and the application extends only to the irrigation of a small proportion of grass to be cut for soiling, and does not aim at any farther extension of the system.

FARM SERVANTS.—It is the universal custom in the Upper Ward to board the unmarried servants, male and female, in the farm-house; the women having their sleeping rooms adjoining or over the kitchen, and the men in an apartment adjoining or over the stable. The married men live in cottages near the farm-steading, and in general board themselves; and in such cases frequently have either the keep for a cow or the produce of one as part of their wages, besides being allowed to keep a pig; and are allowed as wages from £18 to £24, with board or privileges equivalent. The wages of shepherds are generally better than what is given to ploughmen, and formerly were almost entirely paid from the produce of from forty-two to fifty-five sheep; of late they are usually paid in money terms.

We may here remark that the farm servants in the Upper Ward of Lanarkshire will compare favourably, in their social life and habits, with their class in any other part of Scotland. Marriages are frequent —for which careful provision is made, and in no respect does the treatment of them tend to demoralisation. This subject has been engaging the attention of the philanthropist, and let us hope that nothing may be neglected to secure to us what we have enjoyed in times past—

> "A virtuous peasantry to rise the while,
> And stand a wall of fire around our much-loved Isle."

D. T.

## HISTORY OF JOHN TAYLOR—LEADHILLS.

JOHN TAYLOR, son of Bernard or Barnabas Taylor (he calls him Barny), by his wife, Agnes Watson, was born in Garry Gill, in the parish of Alston, in Cumberland. His father came from Westmoreland, was a miner, and died when John was only four years old, leaving two daughters older and a son younger to the care of their mother, who lived many years after. His eldest sister (Agnes) went to the south of England, unmarried, and never returned; the other (Mary) married one William Hoggard (or Haggard?), a miller at Penrith, whose children were alive there not many years ago. His brother (Thomas) went to Flanders as a soldier under King William, and never returned. John was, at the age of nine years, set to dressing of lead ore, which he followed for two years, at 2d per day; he then went to work below ground, and had been employed in assisting the miners in removing the ore and rubbish, at the rate of 4d a-day, for three or four years, when the great solar eclipse called Mirk Monday happened; for he says he was at that time at the bottom of a shaft or pit, and was desired by the man at the top to call those below to come out, because a great cloud had darkened the sun, so that the birds were falling to the earth. This event, which he has always told with the same circumstances, is the only era from which to reckon his age. He continued to work in the mines at Alston till about twenty-six years of age, when he went to the lead mines at Black Hall, in the Bishoprick of Durham, where he wrought some eight or nine years, and was then sent by one Doubledays, a Quaker, to view and make a report of some mines in the island of Islay. Some time after his return he went back to Islay, where he remained as a kind of overseer for a year or more. But for some years after this his history appears a little dark, as he wrought at different mines in the south of Scotland and north of England, in an ambulatory manner, without being able to ascertain the time he remained in any one place. He and all his family have always asserted that he lived twenty-eight years in Islay, whereas, by what is formerly asserted and what follows, which is ascertained by proper certificates in his own possession, we have only twenty-two years of his residence there. Be that as it will, in 1707 he was employed by Lord Lauderdale, at the Mint in Edinburgh, coining the Scots money into British. In 1709 he married his only wife in Islay, being then, as he says, upwards of sixty. He wrought there as a miner till 1730, when he came to Glasgow, and, leaving his family there, went to the mines at Strontian, in Argyleshire, and returned to Glasgow about two years after. He wrought at Glasgow as a day-labourer till 1733, when he came to Leadhills, where he wrought regularly as a miner till 1752. He was always a thin, spare man, about 5½ feet high, black-haired, ruddy-faced, and long-visaged. He had always a good appetite, and when he was obliged to go to work (as the miners are at all hours), found no difficulty in making as hearty a meal at midnight as at mid-day; his diet was chiefly flesh, and always the best he could procure: his drink, malt liquor, and although he could never be called a drunkard, he says he never refused a good fellow. He never remembers to have been sick (for the small-pox he had in his infancy), till about 1724, when he was seized in Islay with a bloody flux. At Strontian he was seized (in common with the rest of the miners) with the scurvy, occasioned by drinking spirits and feeding on salt provisions, and afterwards with a fever. The only circumstance remarkable attending this last was that, having been let blood, the wound broke out, and before it was discovered the blood had run through the bed and floor to a lower room. In February, 1758, his wife died; and he having got cold, was seized with a looseness, attended with feverish symptoms, which brought him very low, but since his recovery he has not had the least complaint. At present his appetite is still good, but finds a glass of brandy necessary to warm his stomach, twice or thrice a-day. He has a very antiquated look, but although the hair on his eye-brows and beard are perfectly white, that on his head is not more grey than of most men at fifty. He lies much a-bed in the cold weather, but in warm days he walks out with a stick, and is not greatly bowed down. In last October he walked from his own house to Leadhills (a computed mile), and having entertained his children and grandchildren in a public-house, returned the same day on foot. His wife bore him nine children, of which four died young. The eldest (a daughter) was born in 1710—was married and died in 1744. Two sons and two daughters are still alive at Leadhills, and all married except his youngest child, a son aged about thirty-six. He is not yet, nor ever was, a great sleeper, and always used a great deal of exercise. Till within these few years he used to divert himself, while the season answered, with fishing (trouts) with a rod.—*14th March, 1767.*

[In No. 126, Aug. 21, 1852, an article appears in *Household Words*, entitled "News from an Old Place," and locally attributed to the pen of Miss Martineau, from which paragraphs referring to John Taylor are given as below.—A. M.]

There is a tombstone in the cemetery, which is shown with pride to the stranger, recording as it does the death of a man, a miner, who had lived one hundred and thirty-seven years. He must have been a brave old fellow; for he used to go a-fishing among the hills, all alone, when he was one hundred and twenty years old. What a strange meditation must his have been in such a solitude!—supposing him to have retained his faculties, which he seems to have done. As he walked slowly along, playing his line, as men do in those mountain streams, was he tired of life, looking back on a succession of generations, with whom he ought, in natural course, to have gone to the grave? Did he fear in his heart, as an aged woman once did openly, that God had forgotten him? Or did it seem to him, as it does to some who have outlived all they once knew, a perfectly natural thing that they should have died, and that he should be there to tell the history of their deaths? Did he think of the armies that had come that way, marching over the hills with music and shouts, every man of whom had become dust? What did he think of the greybeards of the village getting past their work, when he remembered that he had dandled some of them as infants after he himself had reached three-score years and ten? The everlasting hills, with their inexhaustible streams, were the same as ever; and he probably thought himself the same as ever. But what a mere procession he must have considered all the rest of human life—a procession of companies; now a set of proprietors of the mines, and a chaplain, and an Earl of Hopetoun, and a population of grandparents, working-men and women, and children; and presently another set of proprietors, another chaplain, another Earl of Hopetoun, another population of old, middle-aged, and young; and he, at first walking with them in the procession, but long ago standing by to see them pass, as naturally as if it was his business to observe them, and theirs to pass on towards their graves!

Perhaps it was all less striking to him than to us, the grass, and the rocks, and the sky, being what he had already known them, and the fish leaping to his bait as they had done in his youth. One day, when he was one hundred and twenty years old, the snows came upon him when he was up in the hills, and blocked up his way on every side. He gave himself up for lost. Perhaps he felt it hard to be thus cut off untimely, instead of dying in his bed. He stuck his fishing-rod upright in the snow, and made another struggle for life. He struggled through to a place where he was found. When he had recovered, he went back, plucked his rod out of the snow, and returned to begin his new lease of seventeen years of life.

Old as he lived to be, John Taylor had been a miner—had worked under ground. In his day, as now, the gallows-like apparatus erected over the shafts of the mines stood up against the sky, on a ridge here, on the summit of a knoll there. Down the ladders he went, fathoms deep, to a resting-place; and then, turning aside a little, down many more—ten times as many—to where he had to work six hours a-day, hewing away at the vein of ore, sending up the rubbish, sending up the ore, toiling in darkness, heat, damp, and often up to the knees in the turbid water of the mine.

[Old as John Taylor lived, his sons were men of worth and merit, one of them having become the "Baillie" or overseer of the works at Leadhills; and from his stock came also Taylor who, in conjunction with Symington, first solved the problem of steam navigation.—A. M.]

## THE OLD BRIDGE OF CLYDESHOLM, LANARK.

At p. 347, Vol. II. of this Work, reference is made to an Act of Parliament obtained in 1649, which appears in the Records of the Presbytery of Lanark as follows: *March 29.*—"It is ordained that the Act granted in favours of the town of Lanark, for a general collection throughout the kingdom, for building a bridge at Clydesholm—a work of great necessity and public concernment—be represented to the Synod, that we may have the help and advice of the Synod for the furtherance of the work." *April 19, 1649.*—"The brethren, after return from the Synod, report to the bailies of Lanark, being then present, how willing all the brethren of the Synod were to further the work of building a bridge at Clydesholm, by a contribution of their several paroches, and desires the bailies not to neglect to go on speedily with the work, which the Presbytery will further all they can."

Davidson, in his History of Lanark, p. 96, states that "the whole sum collected by private subscription and public parochial collections, amounted to only fifty-six pounds eleven shillings and sevenpence; at which time mason's wages were only one penny, or a peck of meal a-day."

In 1694 (May 16) an Act of Council was obtained to rebuild the bridge of Clydesholm, and as the items "of Disbursements on the Work," and the "Accompt of Money receaved by Archibald Simpson, Merchant in Lanark, by Publick Collection and otherwayes," are quaintly and minutely given, they are reported here *in extenso*—the items being instructive as to the habits of the people, and suggestive as to the relative liberality of the districts whence the moneys were drawn.　　　　　　　　　　　　　　　　　　　　　　　　A. M.

*Ane Accompt of Archibald Simpson's Disbursements in Building the Bridge of Clydsholm, by Act of Councill, dated May 16, 1694.*

*Imprimis*—Expences for Baillie Hunter, Clerk Stoddhart, and myself, for going Ed$^r$, ilk two days, £12; It.—When Baillie Hunter and I went to Ed$^r$ to extract the Act, sex days, £24; It.—Wee went to gett Town Councill's Act for a volunter contribution from door-to-door, sex days, £24; It.—Wee went to Glasgow for the Councill's consent for a collection, three days, £12; It.—Ffrom thence myself to Air and Irbing Presbitries, eleven days, £22; It.—When I went to Ed$^r$ for lifting the collections, four days, £8; It.—From thence to Kelso and Dunce, four days, £8; It.—One day to Lithgow, another to Peebles, £4, - - - - £114　0　0

It.—Fifteen days at Glasgow, when the collection went throu the toun, £15; It.—Giben Mr Laqwhor for his advice, 5 dollars—£14 10s; It.—Giben S$^r$ Gilbert

Elliot when petition was giben in, £14 8s; It.—Payed
John Lawqhor for his wages, £146; It.—More wages
to Mr Laqhor, £76, - - - - - - £265 18 0
It.—Ffor four quair paper for Thomas Stodhart to write
letters to the gentlemen of the shire, £1 6s 8d; It.—
Ffor printing the accounts, £14 4s, - - - 15 10 8
It.—Ffor three men going through ilk quarter of the toun
scall times, £12; It.—For myself going to Birkenshaw
and Carstairs, £1; It.—Payed a man that came from
the south, three days, 12s; It.—Payed at Ed<sup>r</sup>, as per
William Brown's subcribed accompt, £28 16s 10d;
It.—Payed £2 18s; It.—Ffor payed William Libingstone for going to ilk minister att Ed<sup>r</sup> with acts to
intimate the Sabbath before collection, £2 18s; It.—Ffr
Will Libingstone's goeing to Strathaben for collection,
6s; It.—Expences sending a man from Glasgow to
Renfrew with acts to the seal ministers, ilk a letter,
£2 16s; It.—Payed for writing the letters and sending
acts to Stirling, 10s 6d; It.—To Alex. for goeing two
times to Laqhor with a horse, £1 2s; It.—To John
Muir for goeing to Hamiltoune for him, 6s, - 53 5 4
It.—Spent with John Loqwhor and the Magistrates, agreing
for his day's wages at the Whinbuss, 14s 6d; It.—Spent
with the Magistrates and Clerk at Boathill, agreeing with
Alex. Telfer for bringing home the osler, 9 pints ale,
14p., 6d of ernest, £1 12s 6d; It.—Spent with the
men that went to the Head's Craig to mend the way at
Clydsholm, 16s; It.—Spent agreeing for arch bow, £2
3s 6d; It.—To Alex. Telfer, 8 pynts ale, qr was not
payed at setting up the first couin, 18s 8d; It.—Earnest,
14s 6d, spent 5s 6d, inde, 20s; It.—Ffor meat and
drink at begining to the lymen, 24s; It.—Spent with
the Cringers at payment and agrement, 16s; It.—Daid
ernest, 10s; spent at Culbins, 81s; It.—Agreing with
carrier, 8s; It.—Spent with Laqwhor when the draft
of the bridge was altered, and others, 24s; It.—When
he came to make the shabes, with others, 24s; It.—Of
Daid ernest, 14s 6d; It.—Spent with Laqhor when he
went away from making the shabes, and others, 28s;
It.—When the carters brought up the last stones, 5
pynts ale, 11s 8d; It.—Spent with Carvel Blair and
others when I gabe him commission to collect the south,
12s; It.—With Laqhor when he came to lay the ground-
stone, 9s; It.—Spent with Loqhor when he took up his
chamber, 7s; It.—Spent with the masons, 4 pints ale, 8s, 21 2 4
It.—Giben John Fforest and James Douglas for cutting a
1000 eslar at the Hard's Craig, £50; It.—Payed

John Buckles for 60 great stone for the pens, out of
Newmayne's Burn, £30; It.—Payed Robert Hastic for
cutting and hewing a 1000 eslar, with 14s 6d earnest,
and 6d spent,    -    -    -    -    -    -  £267  13  10
It.—For bringing them fort the cart, £40; It.—For
bringing them to the Holm, £200; It.—Paid masons,
slaidsmen, borrowmen, as per particular accompt
weekly, £1187 1s 4d; It.—For lyme, sand, and
wages to masons, borrowmen, and others, as per
accompt, £1079 8s 6d; It.—For lyme, sand, stones,
loading, bigging dyke, and filling up of the ends of
the bridge, as by particular accompt, £591; It.—Payed
for lyme, being 148 loads at Craigenhill, payable
(141) at 4s 6d per load, £31 14s 6d; It.—For
carrying it to the Holm, 2s per load, inde, £14 16s;
It.—131 load of lyme, payable at 4s 6d per load, is
£29 9s 6d; It.—For carriage, 2s per load, £13 2s;
It.—For carrying the 1000 eslar to the carts, £40;
It.—Payed William Duncan for two days cutting stone,
14s; It.—Seven weeks' wages paid to masons in presence of Deacon Hamilton, before I sett the bows at a
pennie, as per accompt, £195; It.—Payed seberals for
bringing 1000 eslars to the Holm, £200; It.—For
carrying 600 stones from Nemphlar Craig, £20; It.—
Payed Deacon Hamilton for hewing 1000 eslar, at £11
the 100, £110; It.—Payed John Buckles younger and
Stephen Howieson, for one penn of the bridge readie at
the Holm, 800 merks, with a dollar of ernest and three
lib. to reed the Craig, £539 4s 8d; It.—Payed John
and James Hamiltoun for a bow readie, with a dollar
and crown, £472 11s 4d; It.—Payed John and Dabid
Semples for making out the last bow at 800 merks,
deducing what I paid of former dayes, there remains
£361 2s 8d; It.—Payed of addition 30 lib. per bow,
£90; It.—To James Lockhart for filling up the holes
between the bows, £58; It.—Payed John Thomson for
the masons, £2; It.—8 score 19 loads lyme at 4s 6d
per load, £40 15s 6d; It.—73 load riddled, at 5s per
load, £18 5s; It.—For carriage to the Holm, £25 4s;
It.—10 score 16 loads lyme from Craigenhill, £47 5s;
It.—4 score a loads lyme lifted, at 5s a load, £20;
It.—For 91 loads, at 4s 6d per load, £19 9s 6d; It.—
For carriage of these three parills, 2s per load, is £38
2s; It.—10 score 10 load, at 4s 6d per score, is £47
5s; It.—26 ditto sifted, 6s 10d; It.—For carrying these
two parcells, £23 12s; It.—From Watsheill, 27 load
at 5s per load, £6 15s; It.—Carriage 40d per load, £4

10s; It.—87 at 4s 6d per load is £19 11s 6d; It.—To
Robert Turner for 1168 load of sand to the foresaid
lyme, £58 8s; It.—To Alex. Telfer for bringing mortar
and sand from the Inch to this syde, £2; 1t.—Payed
Ralph Howieson and his neighbour for seeking penn-
stone at the Raking, ilk six days, £4 13s 4d,    -   £5724 17  2
It.—For cutting timber at Clydsholm, £3 6s 8d; It.—
Payed James Simpson and Alex. Harbie for dressing
the timber, ilk thirteen days, £13; It.—Ffor 12 great
trees from the Laird of Lee, £27; It.—Ffrom James
Hamiltoun, 63 trees, £60; It.—Ffor bringing them to
the Holm, 3s the draght, £20 13s; It.—To James
Hamiltoun for sex-score sex birk trees, 58 cutting and
bringing out, and spent 4 lib. 6s, £62 6s; It.—Bringing them to the Holm, 3s per piece, £18 18s; It.—For
5 alder trees, £4 14s 6d; It.—Ffor bringing them to
the Holm, £5 8s; It.—To James Thomson at Stonebyres, 6 trees, £6; It.—For bringing them to the
Holm, £1 4s; It.—To James Lindsay for 7 Quaking-
esps, £14; It.—Ffor bringing them to the Holm, £6;
It.—Payed Buckles and Howieson for making the
shabes, £200; It.—For daills furnished as per accompt,
£582 9s 8d,   -    -    -    -    -    -    -    1024  1  3
It.—Payed Thomas Brown for a mell rolling, 10s.; It.—
Ffor 3 shobell and clasps for shafts, 16s.; It.—For 6
shobells bought at Hamilton, with carriage, 2l. 14s.;
It.—Payed Arthur Tutop for cutting trees at Clydsholm for nuts to let of the water, 1l. 6s. 8d.; It.—
Payed to James for making tresses, bakeds, and wheel-
borrows, 8l.; 1t.—For his nex nutes, 1l.; It.—For
two ridles and sibe to the Holm, 1l.; It.—For a stand
and a tub for water, 2l.; It.—To James Simpson for
four days, making ten car, and a three-stilted borrow,
and foot-gang, 1l. 12s.; It.—To Alex. Telfer for bringing timber from St John's Wood and Clydsholm to the
bridge, 5l.; It.—To Deacon Hamiltoune for mending
the bridge beyond the Lee, and a borrow, 13s.; It.—
Payed for bringing trees and daills back that went
down the water, 2l. 8s.; It.—To Arthur Tutop for eight
days, making sex cars, and a day at Holmhead cutting
timber, 3l.; It.—To James Ballantyne for taking sundrie
one of the cart wheels, putting new spakes, new knaves,
and new Lurdie, 2l.; It.—To John Buckles for two
spars to the body, and knave for daills to it, 2l. 6s. 8d.;
1t.—For shoeing one wheel with a clasp and nails, 1l.
4s.; It.—For rolling a mell, 10s.; It.—To Deacon Hamiltoune for additional wages, 64 days, 3l. 4s.; It.—

*d*

Payed Thomas Brown for batts, garens, double plenis-
ing, as stands in his accompt, 215*l.* 4*s.* 2*d.*; It.—Payed
sex carters for helping the way with the carts, with 2
pynts ales, 1*l.* 14*s.* 8*d.*; It.—For 2 iron mells at 7*l.*
16*s.*, for carriage, 8*s.*—8*l.* 4*s.*; It.—For ane dozen
shobells, with carriage, 10*l.* 19*s.*; It.—For the loan of
Ralph's mells, 6*l.* 8*s.*,  - - - - -    £275 12 10
It.—Payed Arthur Tutop and other two for reding the
way at Baillie Weir, as by accompt, 1*l.* 1*s.* 8*d.*;
It.—Ffor two cart sadles, rig-woodies, greeses ffor
the carts, as per accompt, 7*l.* 18*s.* 8*d.*; It.—To
James Watson, as per accompt, 1*l.* 16*s.*; It.—To ditto
for cutting the great mell, 1*l.* 4*s.*; It.—Ffor two
daills for a wheelborrow at Newmaynes, 1*l.* 10*s.*; It.
—To John Clyd for rowing a mell, 14*s.*; It.—To
John Scott for six quaking esps, 9*l.*; It.—To Alexander Telfer, 7½ P^d iron, and making 4 carter nails,
1*l.* 4*s.*; It.—Two axell-trees and 2 borrows, with
home-bringing, with ale, 1*l.* 16*s.*; It.—For sharp-
ing their irons, 1 stone of iron, 1*l.* 12*s.*; It.—Payed
Ralph Howieson, and another man, looking for stane,
four days, 6*s.* 8*d.* a-day ilk, 2*l.* 13*s.* 4*d.*; It.—Two
men's wages mending the way at Clydsholm, 8*s.*; It.—
Payed James Lockhart and George Aitken, three dayes,
for mending the cart wayes, 1*l.* 10*s.*; It.—To John
Dowglass and John Fforest, for cutting a stone for cart
way, 3*s.* 6*d.*; It.—Att the agreement at Clydsholm, and
for Robert Rogers minding stanes at Braxland, 2*l.*;
It.—Giben Ralp Howieson, in earnest, 14*s.* 6*d.*; It.—
Ffor 2 carts, as per accompt, 66*l.* 13*s.* 4*d.*; It.—Payed
James Watsone for upholding the wadges, pikes, and
iron, so long as the bridge was building, 66*l.* 13*s.* 4*d.*.
It.—Payed John Thomsone for shafts to pikes and mells,
pynts ale at agreeing during the whole work, 4*l.* 6*s.* 0*d.*;
It.—Payed James Hamiltons, 3 stout borrows, 15*s.*;
It.—Ffor 8 fathoms 12-threed cord for tree theats, 16*s.*;
It.—To William Vessie, for mending cartwayes, two
dayes, 10*s.*; It.—Payed James Watsone for small neces-
sars and garrens, 6*l.* 13*s.* 4*d.*; It.—Payed Baillie Weir,
for naills, cords, and iron, 6*l.* 11*s.* 4*d.*; It.—To Decon
Thomson, ½ 1000 naills, 15*s.*; It.—13 st. 3 pd. iron
James Watsone got for wadges, pikes, at 32*s.* per stone,
21*l.* 12*s.*; It.—A great daill sawen in roons, to meet the
water at the bowes, 19*s.*; It.—Payed for sawen, dight-
ing, and making, 24*s.*: It.—Ffor 34 stone, and for
batts, at 2 marks per stone, 45*l.* 6*s.* 8*d.*; It.—To
Andrew Weir for bringing timber to and from Clyds-

holm, 12s.; It.—To as stone pitch for the bridge batts,
16s.; It.—Ffor timber to John Buckles the younger for
making sincars and other necessarias, 38l. 18s.; It.—
Ffor 7 ell 12-threed cord, 8s. 6d.; It.—Ffor 60 fathom
12-threed cord, at 2s. per fathom, 6l.; It.—Ffor butter
and soap to the gin, 18s.; It.—Ffrom myself 1.400 naills,
at 8s. per 100, 5l. 12s.; It.—To John Buckles (elder),
12 hundees, 4l. 4s.; It.—For girding them, and tub
and barrel, 28s.; It.—For sex fork shaftes, 6s.; It.—
Two trees for a cart bodie, 12s.; It.—Ffor bars to the
cart, 4s.; It.—To William Libingstone, being pricker
46 dayes at 8s. per day, 18l. 18s.; It.—For upshotts to
sec cars, 20s.; It.—For 8 stone laid, at 2 marks per
stone, 10l. 13s. 4d.; It.—More payed Thomas Brown
for cuts, and naills, and garrens, and other work, 97l.;
It.—For sex shoebells from Ed$^r$, with carriage, 5l.;
It.—More paid James Lockhart for filling, 2l. 18s.,   £453  8  6

*Ane Accompt of Money received by Archbald Simpson, Merchant in
Lanark, by Publick Collection and otherwayes, for Building a
Bridge at Clydsholm, by Act of Councill, dated May 16, 1694.*

|  | Lib. | B. | D. |
|---|---|---|---|
| *Imprimis*—From Edg$^r$, - - - - - | 521 | 13 | 08 |
| It.—Receabed at Lanark when wee went throw, - | 177 | 16 | 02 |
| It.—Ffrom John Baillie, by the Shire's order, - | 300 | 00 | 00 |
| It.—Ffrom Clelland, by the same order, - - | 333 | 06 | 08 |
| It.—Ffrom the Guildrie of Lanark, - - - | 200 | 00 | 00 |
| It.—Ffrom Lanark Session, by Collection, - - | 024 | 00 | 00 |
| It.—Receabed from John Jack, in part of the Collections | | | |
| for the lands of Nemphlar which was in his hands, | 007 | 10 | 00 |
| It.—Ffrom James Gray for Crawfurd-John, - - | 007 | 01 | 00 |
| It.—Ffrom Cobingtoun, - - - - | 006 | 13 | 00 |
| It.—Ffrom the Deacons, a band, dated Mart, 99, - | 066 | 13 | 04 |
| It.—Ffrom Mr Scott att Carlouk, - - - | 015 | 00 | 00 |
| It.—Ffrom Mr Bryce for Crawfurd-John, - - | 002 | 00 | 00 |
| It.—Ffrom Mr Good at Carnwath, - - - | 028 | 09 | 08 |
| It.—Ffrom Sir James Carmichaell, - - - | 100 | 00 | 00 |
| It.—Ffrom Mr Duncan at Dunsyre, - - - | 010 | 03 | 00 |
| It.—Ffrom Mr Linning at Lesmahagow, - - | 065 | 18 | 00 |
| It.—More from Lesmahagow, - - - - | 006 | 15 | 00 |
| It.—Ffor a cart sold to John Hamiltoun in Lesmahagow, | 022 | 00 | 00 |
| It.—Ffrom Mr Braidfoot, Pettinain, - - - | 013 | 00 | 00 |
| It.—Ffrom Mr Ballantyne for Aberdeen, - - | 054 | 03 | 00 |
| It.—Ffrom y$^e$ Paroches in Air Presbytrie, - - | 024 | 00 | 00 |
| It.—Ffour ounces twelve drops bullion, - - - | 014 | 04 | 00 |
| It.—Ffrom Mr Robert Law for some Parochs in Argyle, | 021 | 19 | 00 |
| It.—Ffrom Mr William Thomsone for Couper Presbytry, | 027 | 13 | 04 |

|  |  | Lib. | B. | D. |
|---|---|---|---|---|

It.—More from Mr Veach at Dumfreis, - - - 016 12 06
It.—Ffrom Gabin Wood in part of Glasgow, Paisley, and
    Renfrew Presbitries, - - - - - 064 07 00
It.—Ffrom Mathew Hopkin for Irbing Presbytry, - 089 06 10
It.—Ffrom Jeremiah Hunter for part of Lithgow
    Presbytrie, - - - - - - 062 18 00
It.—Ffrom John Lanerk, 17 Guineas for vacent stipends, 241 08 00
It.—Candlemas, 1700.—Receabed for a Bond agreed
    with Cors Mitchell for vacent stipends, - 166 13 04
It.—Ffrom this Presbyterie, that the Councill hath giben
    Band for to refound if required, - - - 091 15 00
It.—Ffrom William Whyte, in po dean for Lochmaben
    Presbytry, and aplebie with loss of money, - 017 10 00
It.—Ffrom Muirkirk Paroch, - - - - 005 04 00
It.—Ffrom the Borrows, - - - - 866 13 04
It.—Ffrom the Burrows att Glasgow, when the 3 B. was
    laid on this toun, - - - - - 072 00 00
It.—Ffrom Mr Veach for Dumfriestown, - - 048 00 00
It.—Receabed at Glasgow, 4 Quarters, - - - 131 14 00
It.—Ffrom Toun and Paroch of Hamiltoun, - - 100 00 00
It.—Ffrom Port-Glasgow and Kilenam, - - - 007 10 00
It.—Ffrom Proviost Tuddie at Peebles, - - - 008 05 00
It.—Ffrom Auchtiefardell, - - - - 029 00 00
It.—Ffrom Blackwood younger, - - - - 028 00 00
It.—Ffrom Mr Ballantyne for Mr John Veach, - 030 00 00
It.—Ffrom Cumnock Paroch, - - - - 003 00 00
It.—Ffrom Robert Clerksone, Chamberland, - - 042 00 00
It.—Ffrom William Cowan, - - - - - 003 00 00
It.—Ffrom Baillie Hamiltoun for Mr William Selkirk, 009 04 08
It.—Ffrom James Lithgow, Paper-maker, - - 002 18 00
It.—Ffrom Lickprivick, Fouler, - - - - 000 09 00
It.—Ffrom William Sommerbell of Harperfield, - 005 16 00
It.—Ffrom Stonebyres, - - - - - 066 13 04
It.—Ffrom Commissar Wilkie, - - - - 003 14 00
It.—Ffrom Baillie Weir, - - - - - 014 04 00
It.—Ffrom Cambusnethan, 3 lib. 11 p. 06d.; Blanter,
    1 lib. 10—is, - - - - - - 010 01 06
It.—Ffrom Cambuslang, - - - - - 002 18 00
It.—Ffrom Culross, - - - - - 005 00 00
It.—Ffrom Kirkbryd, - - - - - 010 00 00
It.—Ffrom Mr Ballantyne for Gladshields, - - 020 03 00
It.—Ffrom Longdreghorn Paroch, - - - 001 01 00
It.—Ffrom Dalserff 9lib.6p.; Stonehouse 6lib. 13p. 4d—is, 015 19 04
It.—From Mr Naper at Straben, - - - 001 12 06
It.—More from Gabin Wood for forsaid places, - 003 07 08
It.—Ffor Profite of the Customes, our part 10 Guineas,
    at 14 lib. 04 p., - - - - - 142 00 00

|  | Lib. | B. | D. |
|---|---|---|---|
| It.—Ffrom Borroustouness, - - - - - | 014 | 00 | 00 |
| It.—Ffrom Robert Thomsone for Edin<sup>r</sup>shire, - - | 284 | 17 | 06 |
| It.—Ffrom him for the Cannongate, 22 lib. 15 p. 04d., | | | |
| cliped money, weighing, - - - - | 014 | 08 | 00 |
| It.—Ffrom Baillie Hamiltoun for parts in Ffife, - | 044 | 16 | 00 |
| It.—Ffrom Mr John Fforest for Hadingtounshire, - | 065 | 11 | 00 |
| It.—Ffrom Robert Thomsone for Leith, - - | 028 | 00 | 00 |
| It.—Ffrom William Callendar for Stirling Presbitrie, | 032 | 13 | 04 |
| It.—Ffrom Carmichaell Paroch, - - - - | 008 | 00 | 00 |
| It.—Ffrom Mr Ballantyne for the Merns, - - | 001 | 17 | 00 |
| It.—Ffrom Old Monkland Paroch, - - - | 006 | 00 | 00 |
| It.—Ffrom Mr Ballantyne for Melros Paroch, - - | 016 | 00 | 00 |
| It.—Ffrom John Thomsoue for the Bonnitoun Quarter, | 011 | 09 | 00 |
| It.—What was collected for a man here, the lyke being | | | |
| for us with him, - - - - - | 002 | 00 | 00 |
| It.—By some old work rooped at the Bridge, as per | | | |
| Accompt, - - - - - - - | 279 | 18 | 10 |

RICHARD DICK, *Witness.*     ARCHBALD SIMPSON.
THOMAS SUMERS, *Witness.*

*1695.—A ne Accompt of Archbald Simpsone's Debursements in Building the Bridge of Clydsholm, by Act of Councill, dated May 16, 1694.*

| | | | |
|---|---|---|---|
| The totall of the charge is fybe thousand two hundred | | | |
| nyntie-nyne pound, eight shills, sex pennies, - | 5999 | 08 | 06 |
| Totall of the discharge is eight thousand two hundred | | | |
| and fourty-sebeu pound, fifteen shills, eight pennies, | 8247 | 15 | 08 |
| The discharge exceeds the charge in the soume of two | | | |
| thousand nyne hundred and fourty-eight pound, | | | |
| sebeu shillings, and two pennies, - - - | 2948 | 07 | 02 |

RICHARD DICK, *Witness.*     ARCHBALD SIMPSONE.
THOMAS SUMERS, *Witness.*

---

COPY ACT OF PARLIAMENT.—Anno Decimo Geo. II. Regis.

*An Act to enable the Magistrates and Town Council of the Burgh of Lanark to Repair and Maintain their Bridge over the River Clyd, at Clydsholm, in the shire of Lanark.*

Whereas, by an Act passed in the Parliament of Scotland, the Thirtieth Day of June, in the Year of our Lord One Thousand Seven Hundred and Three, intituled, "An Act in Favours of the Burgh of Lanark," reciting that the Burgh of Lanark had been at a vast expence in building a Bridge over the River Clyd, and that by reason of the great repair, and the violent current of the water, it would require frequent Reparations, which the Magistrates of the said Burgh were unable to do, it was enacted: That for enabling the said Magistrates to maintain the said Bridge, the several tolls therein mentioned should be granted to the Magistrates of the said Burgh for the space of Nineteen Years; and whereas the said Bridge hath been, and still is, of so great use and service to the neighbouring country in general, that, notwithstanding the term granted by the said Act expired in the year One Thousand Seven Hundred and Twenty-two, yet the said tolls have been voluntarily paid, till of late that some persons have refused to pay the same; and whereas the annual expence of keeping the said Bridge in repair exceeds the yearly income of the tolls granted by the said Act, and the maintaining and keeping in repair the said Bridge will be attended with a constant charge and expence to the said Town; and whereas the Magistrates of the said Burgh of Lanark are unable to repair and support the same (their debts being already so large, and the circumstances of the community so low), unless the said former Act be revived, and the term and tolls thereby granted continued and enlarged: May it therefore please your Most Excellent Majesty, upon the humble petition of the Magistrates and Town Council of the said Burgh of Lanark, that it may be enacted, and be it enacted by the King's Most Excellent Majesty, by and with the advice and consent of the Lords Spiritual and Temporal, and Commons, in this present Parliament assembled, and by the authority of the same, That for the better enabling the Magistrates and Town Council of Lanark for the time being, to repair and keep in repair the said Bridge, there shall be paid to the said Magistrates and Town Council of the said Burgh of Lanark, and their successors, or to such person or persons as they shall from time to time nominate and appoint, for pontage, or in name of toll, before any passage over the said Bridge shall be permitted, the several sums following, videlicet:—

For every Coach or Chariot drawn by Four or more Horses, Six Pence Sterling. For every Cart, Car, or other Wheel Carriage, Two Pence Sterling. For every Sledge, and for every Horse loaded or unloaded, One Penny Sterling. For every Ox, Cow, or Bull, Two-third Parts of a Penny Sterling. For every Calf, Hog, Sheep, or Lamb, One-sixth Part of a Penny Sterling. For every Foot Passenger, One-Sixth Part of a Penny Sterling.

Which said respective sums of money shall and may, by the authority of this present Act, be demanded and taken in name of pontage, or as a toll or duty, before any Coach, Chariot, Cart, Car, Wheel Carriage, Sledge, Horse, Ox, Cow, Bull, Hog, Sheep, Lamb, or Passenger, be permitted to pass over the said Bridge; and the monies so to be taken and received as aforesaid, are hereby vested in the Magistrates and Town Council of Lanark; and the same and every part thereof shall be from time to time paid, applied, and disposed of (the reasonable charge expended in or about the obtaining or passing this Act being first deducted) for and towards amending and repairing and keeping in repair the said Bridge, as aforesaid; and the Magistrates and Town Council, and their successors, and the Collector or Collectors, to be by them appointed, are hereby authorized and empowered to hinder all Coaches, Chariots, Carts, Cars, etc.

And be it further enacted, by the authority aforesaid, That this Act, and all the tolls hereby laid and made payable, and the powers hereby given and granted, shall take place and have continuance from and after the Second Day of August, One Thousand Seven Hundred and Thirty-seven, for and during the term of Thirty-one Years.

And be it further enacted, by the authority aforesaid, That this Act shall be adjudged, deemed, and taken to be a Publick Act, and be judicially taken notice of as such by all the Judges, Justices, and other Persons whatsoever, without specially pleading the same.

---

## THE CLYDESDALE UPPER WARD SOCIETY

Was formed in Glasgow in October, 1785; has been of much service to those connected with it, and continues "undissolved"—still in prosperous activity.

The preamble is, that, Whereas it is agreeable both to the laws of God and man to provide for the relief of the poor and necessitous, etc., we, of the "Clydesdale Upper Ward," have agreed to join ourselves for the mutual support of one another, and of such as may hereafter join us, in order to prevent, as far as in us lies, any of our brethren from being reduced to want, or being a burden to town, county, or sessions; and for this purpose we commence a fund for the relief of our members, to be regulated and distributed according to the following Articles, thirty in number, entitled, 1. Erection of the Society. 2. Members—their age and qualification: "to be above fourteen and below forty years of age, a Protestant, and of good moral character, etc." 3. Notice before entering—given "four days before the annual election of office-bearers, etc." 4. Immorality, how checked: "Any member found guilty of swearing, blaspheming, or profaning the Sabbath-day, to be reproved first, then fined 6d, again, 1s; if persisting, to be expelled. Further, if any member be convicted of adultery or theft, his name to be erased, and all interest forfeited." 5. Entry money and quarter accounts: "On admission 5s 6d, of which 5s goes to the funds, 4d to the clerk, and 2d to the officer; the annual payment 2s, or 6d quarterly, besides one penny for officers' wages." 6. Exemption from quarter accounts gained by paying 30s on entry on admission; if three years a member, 20s sterling. 7. Office-bearers or managers to be elected annually, etc. 8. The Preses to preside at all meetings, transact in all affairs, have a casting vote, etc. 9. Treasurer to receive and deposit the moneys, legacies, benefactions, etc., bonds, etc., in the box or charter-chest, and be ready, within a fortnight after the annual election to give off his accounts to the Preses and Masters, etc. 11. That there be twelve Masters or Directors, five of whom, including the Preses, to be a quorum, and all office-bearers to serve gratis. 12. The Treasurer to be elected from a leet of three members, etc. 13. Election of Masters: The former Preses and Treasurer are directors, *ex officio*, for one year; the old Preses chooses two from the old council, and the new Preses three, either from the old council or the Society, as *he thinks* proper, etc. 14. County members, described as residing in Shettleston, Pollokshaws, Paisley, etc., may choose a director among themselves, who must attend all the Preses' meetings if desired, etc. 15. The clerk to be allowed the sum of 25s per annum of salary, over and above the perquisites arising from entry money. 16. The Society to pay their officer 15s yearly, besides his chance of entries. 17. Members' funerals: "It is expected that the Society, on all funeral occasions, will, for their own credit, turn well out, and as decently dressed as possible. 18. Proxy lines taken from members living above a mile from the city, etc. 19. Members declining to act as Preses or Treasurer fined 5s. 20. The box or charter-chest to be kept in house of the Preses, in the city of Glasgow, in a convenient house and secure apartment. 21. Directors to be fined 6d if half-an-hour late for meetings. 22. Members two years in arrears to be struck off the list, etc. 23. Money or stock of the Society to be invested; if by bill, in name of the Preses. Meetings to be held in November, February, May, and August; and all entertainments of eating and drinking are expressly prohibited and discharged. 24. A member guilty of embezzling the funds of the Society, must indemnify, and be for ever deprived of all privileges, both for himself and family. 25. Any member coming to meetings of the Society drunk, disposed to fight, abuse or vilipend any of the managers, to be fined 6d for the first offence, 1s for the second, then expelled, etc. 26. Complaint, to be held relevant, must be laid before the Preses, etc.; and if any member upbraid another for having received supply when in trouble or straits, to be fined 1s for the first, 2s for the second offence, then expelled, etc. 27. Members three years connected with the Society, if disabled through old age, sickness, or distress, to be allowed 3s per week if not confined to bed, or 5s per week if bedfast; but no member who by quarrelling, fighting, drunkenness, or any other dissolute practices, brings distress on himself, will be allowed any aliment. 28. When an indigent member dies, the Society to see him decently interred at the expense of two pounds sterling, etc.; and if deceased member have no heirs, his goods and effects shall belong to the Society, and the Preses carry his head. The widow to be allowed 20s, etc. 29. If any member propose to break open the box and share the stock, he shall be expelled, etc. 30. It is agreed that if any three members abide by the foregoing established Articles, to them and their adherents only shall appertain and belong the whole power and properties of the box, money, writs, etc.; and no Act hereafter made shall be valid which tends to weaken the strength of this Article. Articles subscribed at Glasgow, December 26, 1785.

*Preses*, JOHN CHRISTIE.          *Clerk*, WILLIAM FISHER.

# PARISH OF CRAWFORD.

[The corrected version referred to in note at foot of p. 85, Vol. I., and produced here to save the cancel of two sheets of the work.—A. M.]

for £360 Scots (*Ibid*, VII., 422). The capital conviction of Mr Lawrie, the tutor of Blackwood, in the year 1683, on the ground that he had harboured a person who had been in rebellion, but had never been marked out by process or proclamation, created great alarm among the gentlemen of the western counties. A number of them, of whom Weir of Newton was one, proceeded to London with the view of negotiating "the settlement of ane Scots collonie in Carolina." They there entered into communication with the Earl of Shaftesbury, Lord William Russell, and the other leaders of the liberal party in England, as well as with the Scotch refugees in Holland. There can be little doubt that in the course of their consultations the chances of an insurrection in the north were discussed. The discovery of the Rye House Plot gave the Government a clue to this intrigue. Weir and his associates were arrested and sent to Scotland; Baillie of Jerviswood was executed, but John Weir was reprieved through the intercession of his friends. The tradition of the family as to the manner in which it was obtained, is, that he had a sister who was married to a cadet of the Irvings of Saphock, and that the latter was usher to the Privy Council. By his connivance his wife obtained access to the Council Chamber when her brother was under examination, and implored the Lords to grant a pardon. At first in vain. Being, however, near her confinement, her agitation brought on the pains of labour. She nevertheless refused to be removed, and continued her frantic entreaties for mercy until the Chancellor exclaimed, "Take away the woman, and make out a remission for life and limb." Upon which Weir swore that, were the bairn lad or lass, it should inherit his lands, as its coming had saved his life. The tradition appears confirmed by a deed executed by him about this date, by which he conveys his estate to his sister and her husband, on condition that they should take the name and arms of Vere. Although his life was spared, the process against John Weir was remitted by Parliament to the Court of Justiciary, where a decree was pronounced forfeiting his property (*Ibid*, VIII., 490; *App.*, 39, 40). This was rescinded in 1690 by the General Act remitting all fines and forefaultures since the year 1665 (*Ibid*, IX., 164; *App.*, 94). He was appointed one of the Commissioners of Supply for the county in the years 1689, 1690, and 1704 (*Ibid*, IX., 70, 138; XI., 141). The farms of Harthope and Raeclough were held by branches of the Johnstone family, that of Crimperamp by the Tintos, and afterwards by the Bertrams of Nisbet; while the lands of Ellershaw, Troloss, and part of those of South Shortcleugh were possessed by other sub-vassals.

*e*

Blind Harry (*B. V., l.* 1057, *et seq.*) states that the castle of Crawford was surprised, dismantled (spoyled), burnt, and its walls partially thrown down in the spring of 1297. This author, as we will hereafter have on more than one occasion to demonstrate, is no reliable authority, unless in those parts of his narrative where he is corroborated by more trustworthy historians or authentic documents. In the present instance we were at first inclined to think that this was the case. He informs us that

> "A squier then rewllyt, that Lordschip haill,
> Of Cumnerland born, his name was Martyndaill;"

and it is remarkable that this could only have occurred at the very time at which, according to his narrative, this event took place. We have purposely abstained from giving in detail the pedigree of the Lindisay family in full, as it is given with great accuracy in the well known work recently published by their descendant Lord Lindesay. In explanation of the present subject, we may, however, mention that the Alice, the heiress of the elder branch of the Lindesays, married Sir Henry Pinkeney, an English knight. Their grandson, Sir Robert de Pinkeney, inherited the barony of Crawford, and died about the year 1296, when he was succeeded by his brother Henry. Robert the Bruce deprived the latter of these lands, and bestowed them on the representative of the male line of the Lindesays, who had adhered to the patriotic cause. There was, however, an interval between the death of Sir Robert and the time when his brother obtained possession, as Edward I., on the 24th October, 1296, issued a letter, directing that the lands of Sir Robert should be kept by the Earl de Warrene, Governor of Scotland, *for the King.* On the 18th of the following February, Henry Pinkeney, having duly paid his homage, the King sent an order to Warrene to infeft him (*Rot. Scot*, I., 36, 38). This interval is the precise period in which Blind Harry places the surprise of the castle. On examining more carefully the details of the Minstrel's narrative, we, however, found it to contain such a mass of improbabilities that we became convinced that what we had at first supposed to be a corroboration from the authentic records in the *Rotuli Scotiæ,* was a mere *accidental* coincidence, and that no credence can be given to the Minstrel's account of the matter. His tale is: That Sir William Wallace, after surprising the castle of Lochmaben, retired to Corehead, which lies at the head of the Annan, and is the house which is situated nearest the head of that river. Starting from this, he and Sir John Graham, with "fourtye off men with armes cleir," marched through Crawford Muir till they came to Crawfordjohn village. In doing this they must have passed within a short distance, if not in sight, of Crawford Castle. Although "on Ingliss(men) thar mynd remanyt ay," no attack is made upon it. From Crawfordjohn

" The water (Duncaton) downe thai ryd,
Ner hand the nycht thai lychtyt upon Clyde."

Then, when they are at the distance of more than six miles from the place, Wallace, for the *first time*, proposes that they should turn back and try an assault on the castle of Crawford. On approaching the village, that the English garrison, although they have received information of the surprise of Lochmaben, "that gerris them be full wa," had, to a man, crossed the river, and were carousing in a hostelry or tavern, leaving the castle in charge of some women. Nor is this the only astounding piece of imprudence they are supposed to have committed, for we are informed that they had also entirely neglected to take the precaution of supplying the castle with provisions in case of attack, as after it was taken Wallace and his men had to content themselves with a scanty allowance brought from the hostelry.                                                     G. V. I.

## LEADHILLS.

[In "Pennant's Tour in Scotland," Vol. II., page 129, appears the subjoined account of Leadhills, at the close of last century; and it is correct now, as it was then.—A. M.]

" THE little village of Leadhills consists of numbers of mean houses, inhabited by about fifteen hundred souls, supported by the mines; for five hundred are employed in the rich *sous terrains* of this tract. Nothing can equal the barren and gloomy appearance of the country round; neither tree, nor shrub, nor verdure, nor picturesque rock, appear to amuse the eye; the spectator must plunge into the bowels of these mountains for entertainment, or please himself with the idea of the good that is done by the well-bestowed treasures drawn from these inexhaustible mines, that are still rich, baffling the efforts of two centuries. The space that has yielded ore is little more than a mile square, and is a flat or pass among the mountains; the veins of lead run north and south, vary, as in other places, in their depth, and are from two to four feet thick; some have been found filled with ore within two fathoms of the surface, others sink to the depth of ninety fathoms.

" The ore yields in general about seventy pounds of lead from a hundred and twelve of ore, but affords very little silver; the varieties are the common-plated ore, vulgarly called potters': the small or steel-grained ore, and the curious white ores, lamellated and fibrous, so much searched after for the cabinets of the curious. The last yields from fifty-eight to sixty-eight pounds from the hundred, but the working of this species is much more pernicious to the health of the workmen than the common. The ores are smelted in hearthes, blown by a great bellows, and fluxed with lime. The lead is sent to Leith in small carts, that carry about seven hundred-weight, and exported free from duty.

" The miners and smelters are subject here, as in other places, to the lead distemper, or *mill-reek*, as it is called here, which brings on palsies, and sometimes madness, terminating in death in about ten days. Yet, about two years ago, died, at this place, a person of primæval longevity, one John Taylor, miner, who worked at his business till he was a hundred and twelve; he did not marry till he was sixty, and had nine children; he saw to the last without spectacles; had excellent teeth till within six years before his death, having left off tobacco, to which he attributed their preservation; at length, in 1770, he yielded to fate, after having completed his hundred and thirty-second year.

"Native gold has been frequently found in this tract, in the gravel beneath the peat, from which it was washed by rains, and collected in the gullies by persons who at different times have employed themselves in search of this precious metal; but of late years these adventurers have scarce been able to procure a livelihood. I find in a little book printed in 1710, called *Miscellanea Scotica*, that in old times much gold was collected in different parts of Scotland. In the reign of James IV. the Scots did separate the gold from the sand by washing. In the following, the Germans found gold there, which afforded the King great sums; 300 men were employed for several summers, and about £100,000 sterling procured. They did not dispose of it in Scotland, but carried it into Germany. The same writer says that the Laird of Marcheston got gold in Pentland Hills; that some was found in Langham-waters, fourteen miles from Leadhill House; in Meggot-waters, twelve miles; and Phinland, sixteen miles. He adds that pieces of gold, mixed with spar and other substances, that weighed thirty ounces, were found; but the largest piece I have heard of does not exceed an ounce and a-half, and is in possession of Lord Hopetoun, the owner of these mines.

"Continue my journey through dreary glens or melancholy hills, yet not without seeing numbers of sheep. Near the small village of Crawfordjohn procured a guide over five miles of almost pathless moors, and descend into Douglasdale, watered by the river that gives the name; a valley distinguished by the residence of the family of Douglas, a race of turbulent heroes, celebrated throughout Europe for deeds of arms; the glory, yet the scourge of their country; the terror of their princes; the pride of the northern annals of chivalry."

---

## NEWS OF AN OLD PLACE.

[Slightly abridged from an article in *"Household Words"* for August, 1852, locally attributed to the pen of Miss Martineau; that gifted writer having, about that time, visited the district.—A. M.]

IF any friend of ours be sad and sorry, and desire to improve the occasion by solemn meditation on human life amidst vast rural solitudes, we advise him to take a journey by the Caledonian Railway, from Carlisle to Edinburgh. We have seen no tracts so unpeopled since we emerged from the deserts of Arabia. The banks of the Nile in Nubia, the valleys of the Lebanon, the plain of Damascus, are populous in comparison. There is something very striking in being carried, easily and rapidly, through that great district of green hills, almost bare of trees, and quite bare of houses for miles together. There is something striking in seeing wide tracts of oats, barley, and turnips spreading in the levels, without discovering who can have sown them, or who in the world is to reap them. Here and there the angle of a house-roof peeps out from behind the profile of a hill. Now and then, when there is a long vista into the mountains, a small dark island is to be seen, far away amidst the ocean of green—an oasis in this verdant desert, in which are collected the little kirk and manse, a farmstead, and half-a-dozen cottages, under the cover of as many trees. Where people are seen at work, awaiting the ripening of their barley and oats, it is a rather piteous kind of work. There is hay in nooks, and on any strip otherwise useless; and such hay!— over-ripe, long ago, yet never mellowed by true ripening—with sour water standing in among the clumps, and so many weeds, that the grass-part can hardly be seen. In some of these dank and dreary enclosures (one wonders why they were ever enclosed), three or four men are mowing (one wonders why in the world they mow) their bog hay, rushes, and ragwort, and all together, and tie up the crop in sheaves, and set up the sheaves in shocks—just as if they were the finest wheat grown in the Lincolnshire beds. On the top of the railway banks stand large cocks of this hay, which looks like damp straw. The stranger wonders what species of animal is to eat it. If he inquire, he is told that it is a welcome and needful resource for the sheep in time of snow-drifts. One is glad that the sheep have something better to eat now. There they are, clean from a late shearing, scattered over the brown and purple fells, or thrusting themselves into any hand's-breadth of shade that may be afforded by a broken sand-bank, or any little quarry on the hill-side. There are patches of vivid green among the purple heather, where ewes and lambs are browsing tranquilly to-day, without a thought of the snow-drifts which, six months hence, will doom them to emaciation on the coarse fodder which is in preparation for them below. Here and there a few cattle are seen, and a young horse, in some distant field, may fling up his heels at the train. A group of bare-headed and bare-footed children may be at play on some tiny bridge over a pretence of a burn or rivulet, and a hen and her chickens may scratch up the sand below in defiance of the intrusion of the strangers from the south, with their steam and their noise. But this is nearly all that is seen between station and station, unless where the hills have been laid open for stone, slate, or ore.

The most obvious thought suggested by this scene—so strange in our busy islands—is, that it will not long be to be seen. If our capitalists and labourers are emigrating to new lands for the sake of more space, a district of this extent will not remain so scantily peopled. Along the railway, at least, there will be a fringe of producers and traffickers, who will essentially alter the character of the landscape. The next consideration which will occur to most people is, that they here see—what is not a very common thing to see—a large district which must be, in the main, very much like what it was hundreds or thousands of years ago. One of the railway stations is at Abington, a rather pretty hamlet, with one or two good houses near; and more wood, more cultivation, a more modern aspect than many of the stations before and after it. From this place a valley runs up among the hills, away from the sound of the railway whistle, and of the din of human life altogether. In this valley the Romans certainly were, once upon a time. A military road of theirs passes near; and in, and near this valley, are the tokens of their encampment. Whether the valley was wooded then and cleared by them, we cannot undertake to say, but the probability seems to be, that it must have looked to the Roman eye, on entering, much as it now looks to the eye of any modern foreigner. Its hills, green and bare, with metallic indications showing themselves in places, with heather on the higher slopes, and bog in the bottoms—these features appear to be about as primitive as any natural scenery can well be. That it was much like what it now is, midway between the Roman period and ours, is known.

At the time when Edward the Third of England was watching his son, the Black Prince, winning his spurs, or was trying to make his way safely out of some very difficult and dangerous valleys in France —at the time when Scotland was mourning her David Bruce, a prisoner in the Tower; or, perhaps, rejoicing at the sight of him, returned on his parole—at that time, when the nations were so busy with war as not to be able to look closely after what lay round about them at home—a foreigner was poking about in this valley to see what he could find. A German, named Bulmer, was looking for gold amidst these Scottish hills; and he came into this valley, and found something else besides gold. He found LEAD; and the fate of the valley has been ruled by that discovery of his ever since. The valley we speak of is that which contains the curious village of Leadhills at its highest end—a settlement six miles from Abington, and as wild a place as can well be seen in our islands.

Having a fancy to see so odd a place, and having heard much, twenty years ago, of the intelligence and other good qualities of the inhabitants, we recently determined to go. At Abington, a carriage was to have met us; but there was a mistake about it, and no carriage was forthcoming. The morning was hot, and the hours were precious, so that we were glad to obtain any sort of vehicle that would save our strength and our time. The vehicle proposed was a cart—such as had probably conveyed in its day more pigs and calves than human beings. It was half filled with straw, on which was laid a bolster, and over the bolster was laid a clean plaid. Off we went, under the care of an intelligent labourer, whose Scotch dialect was of so moderate a character that conversation would have been easy, but for the slow trot of the horse, which made our words come out like puffs of steam from the engine which had just left us behind. By a gradual ascent, on a good road, we penetrated the recesses of the hills, seeing nobody but two men eating oat-cake and drinking milk at the mouth of their little quarry, and two women at the cottage beside the toll-bar where the carts of coke pay toll on their way up to the mines. During the journey of six miles we saw three trees; one in a field on the upland, looking rather sad, all by itself, and two more down in a field at the bottom, marking the spot where Bulmer found his gold five hundred years ago. A woman, down in the bog, had her arms full of what appeared to be rushes; and a solitary man, high up on the steep, was cutting heather—no doubt to mend his own or some neighbour's thatch. Grass, and groundsel, and hemlock grew to the height of a foot along the ridge, and down the sides of two or three of the first cottages we saw. We inquired why, as slate was quarried (under the name of edge-metal), in this very valley, the cottages were so wretchedly roofed. The answer was, that there had never been any thought of using so good a material as even this very poor slate.

From far below we had seen smoke hanging about an opening before us. This was from the smelting-houses, the driver informed us; and the village lay a mile and a-half farther on. The road crossed the valley near the smelting-houses; and they lay below us on the right—the turbid little stream oozing away from the works, and men and boys, with hoes, spades, and scrapers, washing the soil, on stage below stage, so that what escaped from one set of channels might run into the one below. It seemed a piece of unnecessary toil to place the square tower of the smelting-house—the tower whence the smoke belched forth—so high up the steep and stony breast of the hill. It afterwards appeared that nobody had occasion to go up there. The smoke was driven, by the blast of the furnace, through the interior of the hill, to issue forth from a chimney, which looks like a tower from below.

A succeeding ascent hid from us what we were now looking for with some anxiety, as our ride had occupied nearly an hour and three-quarters, and we had been churned enough for one day. The village, we were told, was "just behind there," and there it was—the strangest of British villages. The valley suddenly opens out into an area of undulating character, bounded by more distant hills. Rows of cottages stand on all available platforms, turned in all directions. Beside one may be a roof just fresh thatched with heather; and on the other hand may be a roof bristling with weeds, and with grass that sways in the wind. Scattered about, amidst the wild vegetation of the moorland, up and down, turned this way and that, are little oblong patches of cabbages, turnips, or potatoes. Formerly the miners were allowed to appropriate from the moorland as much as they could cultivate with the spade in over-hours. This is no longer permitted; but the ground under tillage is about 400 acres.

Glancing over the neighbouring slopes, we saw a man mowing some most unpromising grass. Another was coming up from a boggy place with an enormous bundle of rushes on his head. High up on a ridge, a man's figure was seen, digging peat. Three sheep were within sight, and several cows. It was a comfort to see so good a supply of cows for the number of persons.

There are some old books on the shelves of the agent's office, which give the information that in the early half of the last century the population at Leadhills amounted to upwards of fourteen hundred. Twenty years ago it was about eleven hundred; it is now between eight and nine hundred. Of these, one hundred and ten are able-bodied men. There are some old men able to do some work or none. Such as these were formerly maintained by their sons; but under the present rate of wages (which average nine shillings per week) the reluctance to look to the parish for an ultimate support is fast diminishing. There is a baker in the place, of course; and there are no less than three tailors. Some few men are employed in blanket-weaving. Here and there we saw some old men sitting in the sun, smoking and chatting; and one or two were returning from their morning's task, who were still capable, at the age of seventy and upwards, of doing some hours' work in the day at washing the ore. But a man who can do this at such an age, may be safely supposed not to have worked under ground in his earlier days. There are no less than from eighty to ninety cows in this village—a very large proportion for the number of people. It is explained by the fact that the customary diet of the population is that which we saw the two quarrymen enjoying by the roadside—oat-cake and milk. Meat is an almost unknown luxury, even in the form of bacon. We had not before, nor have we now, a high opinion of the wholesomeness of oatmeal diet; but it is certainly the fact, that the people of Leadhills, living on a poor soil, in the midst of metallic works, at a height of one thousand two hundred and eighty-six feet above the level of the sea, have a remarkably healthy appearance, notwithstanding the presence of the fumes of the smelting, and the absence of a meat diet.

The men work, as in Cornwall, on tribute—sharing the success or failure of their enterprises with the proprietors. They change the name of a mine, quaintly enough, according to their approbation or displeasure towards it. We saw one which had, till lately, been called the "Labour-in-vain Vein." After a lucky turn which disclosed new riches (more lead with a little gold), it was called "California," which is its present title—a title, by the way, which shows that some tidings from the world without reach this secluded spot. The residents say, that even fewer strangers come now than before the opening of the Caledonian Railway; but, on the other hand, we find reason to believe that there has been enough of intercourse with the navvies of that railway, to work anything but good to the habits of

Leadhills Village

the miners, who must be very like children in their impressibleness, and in the precarious character of the innocence which has been maintained in the absence of temptation. One other kind of intercourse is provided by the annual arrival of Lord Hopetoun, or his sporting friends, in August and onwards. We saw an elegant moor-hen moving tamely on in the heather, not far from the smelting-houses; and this game so abounds on the hills, that the sportsmen come home to dinner at "the Ha'" with their thirty or forty brace each. Looking round on the very small cabbage patches of the miners, remembering their oatmeal diet, without even a smell of bacon to their bread, pondering also the average of nine shillings a-week, which leaves so many with only six, we inquired whether poaching could, in such a wild scene, be kept within bounds. The answer was, that poaching is a thing never heard of; and the reason given was, that the poacher would forfeit everything if detected. It is wonderful, and must be the result of strong compulsion of circumstance, that hungering men can see wild creatures fluttering in the herbage on far-spreading moors, away from every human eye but their own, and can abstain from taking what can hardly appear like property.

Perhaps we should not say that the labourer has no sport, for we heard of a novelty in that way having been lately introduced—an occasional game at quoits. There is a library, supported by seventy miners, paying two shillings a-year each. The works seemed to be chiefly Scotch divinity, with a very few voyages, and a volume of narrative, or fiction, here and there. What a blessing it would be to these people, if some kind person would send them a good assortment, and a plentiful one, of works of fiction! What a new world it would open to them during the long snows of winter, and in the light evenings of summer, when the men are exhausted by their hot toil under ground, or at the furnaces; and the women and girls are stooping over their "handsewing," and wearing their eyes out, ay, even little children, with embroidering for twelve hours every day!

There is a school, where the boys and girls looked thoroughly healthy; the room was airy, and the master intelligent-looking and kind, though his appearance did not lessen our impression of the poverty of the place. The members of the school have fallen off sadly, more than in proportion to the diminished population of the place. The average attendance is eighty in summer, and one hundred in winter. The scholars pay from one shilling and sixpence to two shillings and sixpence per quarter; and it is a proof of the value that the parents set upon education that, out of a population which falls short of nine hundred, earning, on an average, nine shillings per week, there should be one hundred children paying for their schooling at this rate. Some of the oldest boys could show arithmetical exercises which justify their hopes of getting to be clerks in Glasgow warehouses, and two have learned a little Latin—that darling pride of the humble Scotch! They think, and talk of Allan Ramsay, who was a native of these hills; and somebody has painted outside the

*f*

library something which is called a portrait of the poet. Whatever
may be the taste of the painting, we like the taste of putting it
there—*(it is now removed, the miners' arms, in very questionable taste,
replacing it).*

At the very top of the settlement, when we have passed all the
cottages, and "the Ha'," and the potato patches, and the heaps of
lead ore, we come to a place which takes all strangers by surprise:
a charming house, embowered in trees, with honeysuckle hanging
about its walls, flowers in its parterres, and a respectable kitchen
garden, where the boast is that currants can be induced to ripen, and
that apples have been known to form, and grow to a certain size,
though not to ripen. This is the agent's house, and here are the
offices of the Mining Company. The plantation is really wonderful
at such an elevation above the sea; and it is a refreshing sight to the
stranger arriving from below. There may be seen, growing in a
perfect thicket, beech, ash, mountain ash, elm, plane, and larch,
shading grass-plats, and enclosed walks, so fresh and green that, on
a hot day, one might fancy oneself in a meadow garden, near some
ample river. In this abode there is a carriage, and a servant in
livery—a great sight, no doubt, to the people, who can hardly have
seen any other, except when sportsmen come to "the Ha'," with all
their apparatus of locomotion and pleasure. In connection with this
abode is the office of the Company, where the books are preserved as
far back as 1736. There may be seen specimens of the ores found
in the valley; and among other curiosities, a small phial of water,
about half-filled with gold from the Californian vein before-mentioned.
There it is, in rough morsels, just like the specimens from California
and Australia, which may be seen everywhere now. The water in
the phial is to make the gold look brighter; and for the same purpose, the owner lays it upon some dark surface—as the sleeve of a
coat—that strangers may see it to the best advantage. Here is about
ten pounds' worth; so there is no fear of choosing the wrong casket,
out of the three placed before them.

Our cart had been dismissed long ago; and we were to return to
Abington in the carriage, and driven by the servant in whom the
worldly splendour of the place is concentrated. We were to stop by
the way and see the smelting; and we saw it accordingly. Descend-
ing from the successive platforms where the bruised ore is washed,
till it is almost pure dust of lead, we put our heads into the noisy
vault, where the great water-wheel was revolving and letting fall a
drip which filled the place with the sound of mighty splashings.
The blast of the furnaces roared under our feet, and all around about
us, every light substance, such as coal dust and shreds of peat, was
blown about like chaff. At the furnace were men, enduring the
blaze of the red heat on this sultry day. They work for five or six
hours; but only for five days in the week. They were piling up the
glowing coals upon the bruised and washed ore in its receptacle in
the furnace; and from under the front of the fire we saw the molten

lead running down its little channels into its own reservoir, leaving behind the less heavy dross, which was afterwards to be cast out in a heap in the yard. The mould for the pig stood close by, at a convenient height from the floor. We waited till there was lead enough in the reservoir to make a pig. One man ladled out the molten metal into the mould, while another skimmed off the ashes and scum with two pieces of wood. It was curious to see this substance, which looked exactly like quicksilver, treated like soup. It was curious to see the process of cooling begin from the edges, and the film spreading slowly towards the centre, till all was solid. It was curious to see the pigs set on end against the wall, looking light and moveable from their lustre, when just out of the mould, and to remember that one might as well try to lift up the opposite mountain as to move one of them unaided.

---

## LEADHILLS.

THE village of Leadhills, formerly named Hopetoun, from which the Earls of Hopetoun derive their title, is situated in an open area of undulating character, at the head of the valley through which the Glengonar-water flows on its way to the Clyde, and is within one mile of the southern extremity of Lanarkshire. It is distant seven and five miles respectively from the Abington and Elvanfoot Stations of the Caledonian Railway, forty-six miles from Edinburgh, and forty-four from Glasgow. This village is the highest in Scotland, being 1307 feet above the level of the sea. The aspect of the surrounding country is bleak and barren, consisting of hills above hills clothed with scanty herbage or heather. Elevated though it may be, the village is well sheltered, being surrounded on the east, west, and south sides by hills, having an average elevation of 1800 feet above the level of the sea; whilst, farther south, the Lowthers, a bleak, lofty range, tower to the height of 3150 feet. The view from this latter point is truly magnificent, embracing on the south the ample sweep of the Solway Frith, the Isle of Man, and beyond, the mountains of Hellvellyn and Skiddaw in Cumberland; whilst on the west the eye ranges over Ailsa Craig, the serrated peaks of the isle of Arran, the lofty Ben-lomond, and the Paps of Jura.

There are no records to accurately determine the antiquity of this village, but in all probability it did not exist until about the beginning of the sixteenth century, when the attention of adventurers was more particularly drawn to the place in search of the precious metals. As these pursuits, however, were irregular, and the parties employed principally foreigners, it is not unlikely that it would then only consist of a few rude huts, occupied during the summer months. Towards the middle of that century it appears that the search for lead, as well as for gold, was more systematic and successful, and it is therefore natural to suppose that the village would then become of some importance, as there were upwards of 300 workmen employed; yet in all likelihood the population would be unsettled until about the year 1590, when Thomas Foulis purchased the lands in which his mines were situated. From that time—the works being carried on with great spirit and success—the population rapidly increased, so much so, that about the middle of the eighteenth century it amounted to upwards of 1400. The population then remained stationary until the beginning of the nineteenth century, when it began to decline, till the year 1861, when the number of inhabitants, according to the census returns, was only 896. Since that time, however, owing to the vigour with which the lead mines are being wrought, the number has considerably increased, being now upwards of 1100.

The village, consisting of 224 houses, is principally built in rows, without any regard to architecture or proper sites, which are, generally speaking, ill-chosen, thus giving it a scattered and irregular appearance. Formerly the houses were nearly all covered with thatch, which is now, however, being rapidly replaced by Welsh slate.

The principal buildings are the Hall, to which the church is attached, and the houses and offices of the mining company. One of these, the residence of the manager of the mines, from its size and conveniences, may be termed a mansion. It is situated on an eminence overlooking the village, surrounded by a plantation of fine old trees, of a size seldom seen at such an elevation. Within this belt of wood are gardens, terraces, and walks, laid out with great taste, forming a pleasant contrast to the bare scenery around.

The Hall, the residence of the Earls of Hopetoun and their friends during the shooting season, is plainly but substantially built. It stands in the centre of the village, and, with the small plantation behind it, greatly improves the appearance of the place. The church, which has galleries, contains 500 sittings, and is well attended, the usual congregation being about 300.

There are schools for the instruction of the children in the place, in which 76 boys and 71 girls are taught daily by a schoolmaster, assisted by two pupil teachers, and a schoolmistress, whose salaries are partly paid by quarter-pence, and partly by subscriptions from the Earl of Hopetoun and the Mining Company.

So early as 1741, a library was established at Leadhills, being one of the first circulating libraries in Scotland, which now numbers 2348 volumes. The number of ordinary members who pay 2s yearly is 80, whilst that of the honorary is 15.

A post-office was established at this place in 1760, but then with only one delivery a week, the post starting from Edinburgh each Monday, passing through Linton, Leadhills, Sanquhar, Drumlanrig, Minnyhive, to New Galloway, and returning by the same route to Edinburgh on the Saturdays. At present there is a daily post from Abington, arriving at 9 a.m. and leaving at 4 p.m. The post-office grants money orders, and has recently been made a savings bank under Government regulations.

There is a benefit society in connection with the works, from which each member receives 8s per week during illness; also a doctor's fund, which all the workmen contribute to, each householder paying 1s 9d, and single men 1s 3d per quarter. The Earl of Hopetoun and the lessees subscribe also, as well as to the minister's stipend.

By the beneficence of the Earls of Hopetoun, portions of land have been granted from time to time rent free to the miners, who have reclaimed upwards of 300 acres of land around the village. This land has been brought into a high state of cultivation, and produces excellent crops of grass, which enables each occupier to keep one or more cows. This privilege, with their houses (built by themselves) and kail-yards rent free, combined with the liberal wages they are now receiving, viz., 15s per week, make the mining population of Leadhills much more comfortable than the generality of workmen in other districts. Although only two cows were kept in the village in 1740, there are now 105, besides 18 horses, and 75 sheep. The cows during the summer months are depastured on the hills, outside the cultivated ground, in three separate herds; and, as there are no fences to keep them in their proper hirsels, they are watched by boys during the day, and brought in at night. The horses are chiefly employed about the works.

Through the liberality of the Earl of Hopetoun, who contributed one-third of the cost, a plentiful supply of pure water has recently been brought into the village from a considerable distance; and several handsome drinking fountains erected, the gift of a number of ladies and gentlemen interested in the place.

The inhabitants, who are entirely dependent on the mines for their support, are very intelligent, being, generally speaking, better educated than the population in many other mining districts; and in point of moral worth are fully equal, if not superior, to the working-classes in large towns. Having, through the nature of their employment, a good deal of leisure time, and every facility being afforded them for improvement, they are well aware of what is going on in the busy world beyond; and, whilst nestling in their bleak mountain homes, contrive to make themselves comfortable and happy in the pursuit of knowledge, and the practice of industry.

The soil being porous, and the air light, Leadhills is exceedingly healthy, it being no uncommon circumstance that miners upwards of seventy years of age are able to follow their usual employments, and are, generally speaking, quite as strong as lead-miners are in many other places at the age of fifty. Indeed, it may truly be said that the inhabitants of this village are a long-lived race, in proof of which it is only necessary to mention that a Leadhills miner, John Taylor, attained the ripe old age of 137 years.

This mountainous region, with the facilities afforded by the Caledonian and South-Western Railways, is now much more accessible than formerly, being brought within a few hours' travelling of the principal towns in the south of Scotland. Consequently, during the summer months, it is frequently visited by tourists, intent on viewing the far-famed passes of Mennoch, Enterken, and Dalveen, which are all within a few miles of the village.                              J. N.

---

## LEADHILLS AND ITS LEAD MINES.

THE whole of these lead mines were let in 1861 to a company of Scotch gentlemen (of which the principal partner is William Muir, Esq., Leith), who, under the name of the Leadhills Mining Company, are now prosecuting them with a vigour hitherto unknown in lead-mining in Scotland. The mining field extends over about ten square miles, but the principal workings are in and around the village of Leadhills, where, within an extent of four square miles, there are upwards of forty veins, the majority of which run in a north-easterly and south-westerly direction; but these again are intersected by others whose bearings differ. All the veins in this district are more or less productive of lead ore, and in many of them, according to old records, six feet wide of solid galena was often met with, whilst in more than one vein ore has been found in a solid mass, varying from ten to fourteen feet in width. These large "knots" or "bunches" of ore did not extend, however, to a length of more than a few fathoms, nor continue to any great depth, and were therefore soon wrought out.

The rocks in the district are of the inferior stratified series, below the transition or grauwacke group, and consist principally of gneiss, mica, and clay-slate, through the close texture of which it is difficult to penetrate. The veins vary much in thickness, being frequently as many feet as in other places they are inches wide, and have generally a considerable underlie, sometimes at an angle of thirty degrees. The walls are principally composed of iron pyrites, and their contents, as is the case with other mineral veins, differ much. In some places galena alone is found, in others galena mixed with sulphate of baryta and quartz; whilst in other places again the sole contents are either sulphate of baryta or mineral soil. Perhaps in no other mining district is there such a variety of lead ores as is found here. Besides galena, no less than seven species occur in phosphates, carbonates, sulphates, and their compounds. Copper ore is also found; but the quality being poor, and the quantity obtained small, it will not pay working. A vein of antimony is also known to exist, but is not considered rich enough to pay the cost of exploration.

These mines are to a certain extent drained by two adit levels, the higher of which extends over the greater part of the mining field, and is about fifty fathoms or 300 feet below the surface at its extremity. The lower adit level is not yet driven much farther than the village, which is about the centre of the principal workings, but is now being continued as part of the underground railway hereafter described, and when it reaches the extent of the mines already opened out, will be about eighty fathoms from the surface. The former lessees, it appears, have not availed themselves of the facilities these adit levels afford of bringing the work to bank by an underground railway, but have carried on their operations by means of shafts, of which there are great numbers. The cost of sinking these shafts would amount to no inconsiderable item in the expenditure, as the total depth of the same is fully equal to the distances between them. This being the case, the courses of the principal veins are clearly delineated on the surface by the lines of shafts, which, with the refuse heaped up about them, produce a very unpicturesque effect, and add much to the barren appearance of the district. From these adit levels to the surface, nearly all the veins have been wrought out, and have yielded a considerable quantity of lead ore; but, through neglect, these old workings, as well as the adit levels, were nearly all closed, so that when the present lessees commenced operations in 1861 more than three-fourths of the mines were inaccessible and abandoned. Since then great exertions have been made to re-open the whole, and more particularly the adit levels, so as to drain off the water; which levels are being extended throughout the whole of the mining field. Although these mines have been wrought for upwards of 300 years, yet it is only in two of the principal veins that operations have been carried to any great depth below the lower adit level. In prosecuting these workings, steam and hydraulic power were employed to draw the water and work. These workings are again being resumed, and it is intended to carry them to a still lower depth, when more powerful machinery will be required than has hitherto been employed for pumping purposes, as they were formerly abandoned for the want of sufficient power to draw the water.

At present the lessees of these mines are forming an underground railway, so as to bring the whole of the work excavated to a central depot and washing-place at the surface. This railway is at the lowest point accessible, namely, at the lower adit level; will be carried throughout the whole of the works, and will be at least five miles in length when completed. It is being laid with malleable iron rails, 40 lbs. per yard, on which it is intended that a locomotive, of twelve horse power, should run, with waggons attached; thus bringing out the whole of the work produced at a much cheaper rate than by any other means that could be adopted. The excavation for this underground railway is seven feet in height, by four and a-half feet in width, and being principally driven in hard rock—the cost of which will probably average £10 per fathom—the expense of completing the same will be about £45,000. It would have taken at least twenty years to finish, but shafts are being sunk on the line of this railway, from which it is intended to drive both right and left, so as to get it completed with as little delay as possible. When this level or underground railway is carried out to the extent proposed, the facilities for working these mines to advantage will be equal, if not superior, to any other mine in Great Britain.

In order to have sufficient power for driving their hydraulic and other engines, the present lessees have constructed a series of reservoirs. One of them covers upwards of thirteen acres of land, and contains about 60,000,000 gallons of water, the embankment being forty feet in height. The different water races from these reservoirs to the works are upwards of eight miles in length, and are being laid with clay pipes, spigot and faucet joints, some of which are twenty inches in diameter, costing about £650 per mile.

For working these mines water power alone is now employed, and at present there are 4 hydraulic engines for pumping, 1 hydraulic engine and 4 water wheels for drawing work, 1 water wheel for crushing and dressing the ores, and 1 ditto for driving the blasts at smelting works—the united horse-power of which is upwards of 550. One of these hydraulic engines, recently erected, is the largest in Scotland, having a 2 feet cylinder and 10 feet stroke, with a pressure of water of 216 feet; and, when double-acting, is equal to 139 horses. Other two of these powerful engines will shortly be erected, when the available horse-power at the mines will be greatly increased.

The present washing floors and mode of conducting the washing operations, are, like the previous working of the mine, capable of great improvement, the machinery being old and antiquated. Preparations are therefore being made to construct a new washing floor at the terminus of the underground railway, when all the recent improvements in crushing and dressing lead ores will be introduced, and covered over, so that operations may be carried on, independent of the weather, at all times of the year. From this washing floor a railway will be laid to the smelting works, which are on the Glengonar-Water, 2 miles below the village of Leadhills.

These smelting works consist of 2 roasting furnaces, one reverberatory furnace, 4 ore-hearths, and 1 slag-hearth, and are capable of smelting 50 tons of lead per week. The blast for the hearths is given by a water wheel, working two air cylinders in connection with an air cistern or reservoir, from which the air is conducted in pipes to the hearths. In consequence of the ores not containing much silver, namely, only about five oz. per ton—desilverization, or the extraction of the silver from the lead, has not been practised at these works; but as four oz. per ton will pay the cost, and a great improvement in the quality of the lead is made thereby, buildings are being erected to carry out the process. At present there is only a short chimney flue from these works, in which not more than two per cent. of the fumes from the hearths are collected, and as fully ten per cent. of the lead ore smelted escapes in fumes, the loss is considerable. In order to remedy this, new flues are being commenced with, the dimensions of which are nine feet in width by six feet in height, and will be carried to the distance of at least 1000 yards, where apparatus for condensing the remaining fume will be erected.

J. N.

# PREFATORY NOTES ON ORDNANCE SURVEY RESULTS.

ACCEPTING, as valuable, the figures recently produced by the ORDNANCE SURVEY OF LANARKSHIRE, some labour has been expended in analysing, extracting, and summing up the amounts, and reporting them, in classed and condensed form, as on this and pages 52 to 57.

The Survey "nomenclature" has been adhered to, although often not over-applicable; but where so, free comment thereon will be found made in the topographic pages of this Work.

The "Survey Results" being given here in line, over the twenty parishes forming the Upper Ward of Lanarkshire, will facilitate comparison, and prove the more instructive.

On page 50 will be found noted the heights of thirty of those mountains, in the "Southern Highlands of Scotland," which affect the water-flow, or are landmarks in the district.

On page 51 are given the "course and length" of the more important of the streams in Upper Clydesdale, grouped as they flow, singly or absorbed, into the CLYDE—properly designated in the Ordnance Survey as the RIVER; and which—bisecting Crawford, whence it springs—forms part boundary for all the other parishes in the district it drains, those of Dolphinton, Dunsyre, Walston, and Douglas excepted.

In estimating the length of the streams, allowance has been made for their windings; and the figures to the right of their names denote the heights they rise from.

| ORDNANCE SURVEY RESULTS. 1860. | Land. | Roads. | Vil- lages. | Water. | Rail- ways. | TOTAL. | Sheets. | Book. | Pages. |
|---|---|---|---|---|---|---|---|---|---|
| Biggar,........... | 7166¹⁹⁸ | 69⁴⁴⁹ | 35⁹⁰⁹ | 16⁹¹⁸ | ... | 7288⁴⁷³ | 15 | 6/ | 24 |
| Carluke,......... | 15002⁴⁵⁰ | 208⁶¹⁶ | 87⁰⁸⁶ | 65¹⁹⁶ | 46⁷⁹³ | 15410¹⁴¹ | 24 | 3/ | 51 |
| Carmichael,..... | 11227⁴⁶⁵ | 75⁹⁹⁷ | 10⁸⁴⁰ | 59⁴⁵³ | ... | 11373⁷⁵⁵ | 20 | 4/ | 19 |
| Carnwath,..... | 30147⁶³² | 219²⁶¹ | ... | 118⁷⁹³ | 79²⁵⁸ | 30564⁹⁴⁴ | 43 | 2/6 | 45 |
| Carstairs,....... | 9664³⁹⁷ | 90⁹⁴⁸ | 17¹⁷³ | 79⁸⁹⁴ | 47⁰⁷⁷ | 9899⁴⁸⁹ | 17 | 1/6 | 18 |
| Coulter,......... | 10136⁶⁸¹ | 38²⁶⁷ | ... | 44³³⁷ | ... | 10219⁴⁸⁵ | 7 | 1/ | 11 |
| Covington,..... | 5033¹⁵⁴ | 44⁷⁸⁸ | ... | 53¹¹³ | 36³²³ | 5167³⁷⁸ | 10 | 4/ | 9 |
| Crawford, ...... | 68222⁴⁹³ | 172³⁵¹ | ... | 313¹⁹⁶ | 131⁴⁰² | 68839⁴⁴² | 22 | 2/ | 12 |
| Crawfordjohn,.. | 26251²³³ | 105⁷⁸² | ... | 103²⁷² | ... | 26460²⁹⁷ | 19 | 1/6 | 12 |
| Dolphinton,..... | 3543⁰⁹⁶ | 29²⁹³ | 1⁵⁰¹ | 7⁵⁴³ | ... | 3581⁴³³ | 9 | 4/ | 9 |
| Douglas,......... | 34031⁷⁹¹ | 89¹⁶⁵ | 15⁵⁹⁶ | 180⁶⁶⁶ | ... | 34317⁴²⁸ | 19 | 2/ | 16 |
| Dunsyre, ........ | 10713⁰¹¹ | 23⁴⁶⁵ | 7⁰⁰⁷ | 16⁰⁶⁷ | ... | 10759³⁵⁰ | 11 | 1/6 | 6 |
| Lamington,..... | 12738⁸⁹⁸ | 38¹⁴⁹ | ... | 98⁶⁴³ | 42⁹⁸⁴ | 12918⁶⁶³ | 9 | 1/ | 8 |
| Lanark,......... | 10192⁶⁶⁵ | 142⁰³⁵ | 297⁰²¹ | 175¹⁰⁵ | 50²⁴⁶ | 10560⁰⁵¹ | 19 | 8/ | 38 |
| Lesmahagow,... | 40842⁸³⁴ | 375⁷⁸⁴ | ... | 234⁸⁴⁴ | 80⁰⁸⁷ | 41533⁵⁴⁹ | 55 | 4/ | 92 |
| Libberton,....... | 8155³⁴⁴ | 68³²¹ | 7⁵⁵⁵ | 88⁷⁰⁰ | ... | 8319⁹²⁰ | 15 | 6/ | 19 |
| Pettinain,....... | 3848⁰⁶⁵ | 33⁹²⁵ | ... | 98⁰⁶⁴ | 17⁶⁷⁴ | 3997⁷²⁸ | 9 | 4/ | 9 |
| Symington,..... | 3436¹⁴⁸ | 36⁰²⁷ | 9¹⁶³ | 46⁰⁰⁷ | 22³⁹⁶ | 3549⁸³¹ | 8 | 4/ | 10 |
| Walston,......... | 4310³³³ | 37³⁰⁹ | 13⁶⁰⁶ | 49⁵⁸ | ... | 4366²⁰⁶ | 10 | 1/ | 7 |
| Wiston,......... | 13041¹⁷¹ | 84²⁵⁸ | ... | 70⁰⁰⁵ | 14³⁴⁷ | 13209⁷⁸¹ | 21 | 1/ | 12 |

FIGURES—designate acres, or 1000 fractions thereof. SHEETS—costing 2s 6d each—are the number of those containing the Ordnance Survey areas, on the 25³⁴⁴ inch scale to the mile. BOOK—is the cost of that containing the areas referred to. PAGES—showing that 427 have been occupied with the items, the result of nearly all which are reported here.

NOTE.—*Items of statistical information are marked with numbers on margin; given in consecutive order to economise space in the topographic pages of this Work.*

| MOUNTAIN HEIGHTS. | Situation | Biggar | Carluke | Carmichael | Carnwath | Carstairs | Covington | Coulter | Crawford | Crawford-john | Dolphinton | Douglas | Dunsyre | Lamington | Lanark | Lesmahagow | Libberton | Pettinain | Symington | Walston | Wiston |
|---|---|---|---|---|---|---|---|---|---|---|---|---|---|---|---|---|---|---|---|---|---|
| 1 Auchensaugh, | S.E. | | | | | | | | | | | | | | | 1609 | | | | | |
| 2 Auchensilloch, | S.W. | | | | | | | | | | | | | | | | | | | | |
| 3 Cairnkinney, | W. | | | | | | | | | | | | | | | | | | | | 1675 |
| 4 CAIRNTABLE, | W. | | | | | | | | | | | | | | | | | | | | |
| 5 Comb-Dod, | E. | | | | | | | | 2082 | 1616 | | 1286 | | | | | | | | | |
| 6 Comb-Law, | W. | | | | | | | | 2107 | | | 1942 | | | | | | | | | |
| 7 Commonhill, | S.E. | | | | | | | | | | | | | | | | | | | | |
| 8 COULTER FELL, | S. | | | | | | | 2456 | | 1370 | | | | | | | | | | | |
| 9 Coulter-stane hill, | | | | | | | | 1801 | | | | | | | | | | | | | |
| 10 Dungavel, | S.W. | | | | | | | | | | | | | | | | | | | | |
| 11 FIVE-CAIRN LOUTHER, | S.W. | | | | | | | | 2377 | | | | | | | | | | | | |
| 12 Gana hill, | W. | | | | | | | | 2125 | | | | | | | | | | | | |
| 13 Green Louther, | W. | | | | | | | | 2403 | | | | | | | | | | | | |
| 14 LEADHILLS, | W. | | | | | | | | 1280 | | | | | | | | | | | | |
| 15 Mine hill, | W. | | | | | | | | 1831 | 1567 | | | | | | | | | | | |
| 16 Mount-Stuart, | E. | | | | | | | | | | | | | | | 1712 | | | | | |
| 17 Nutberry, | S. | | | | | | | | | | | | | | | | | | | | |
| 18 Pinstane, | W. | | | | | | | | 1605 | | | | | | | | | | | | |
| 19 QUEENSBERRY, | N.E. | | | | | | | | 2285 | | | | | | | | 1097 | | | | |
| 20 Quothquhan Law, | S.W. | | | | | | | | | | | | | | | | | | | | |
| 21 Rome hill, | S.W. | | | | | | | | | | | | | | | | | | | | |
| 22 SCALD LAW, | S. | | | | | | | | 1852 | | | | | | | | | | | | |
| 23 Serjeant Law, | S. | | | | | | | 1874 | 2166 | | | | | | | | | | | | |
| 24 Snow Gill hill, | W. | | | | | | | | 2257 | 1784 | | | | | | | | | | | |
| 25 Sowen-Dod, | N.E. | | | | | | | | | | | | | | | | | | | | |
| 26 Start-up hill, | S. | | | | | | | | | | | | | | | | | | | | |
| 27 Tewsgill, | W. | | | | | | | | 1867 | | | | | | | | | | | | |
| 28 TINTO, | N.E. | | | 2350 | | | | | | | | | | 1399 | | | | | | | |
| 29 Wedder Law, | W. | | | | | | | | 2185 | | | | | | | | | | | | |
| 30 Welhill, | W. | | | | | | | | 1987 | | | | | | | | | | | | |

| No. | Affluents of the Clyde | Course | Biggar | Carluke | Carmichael | Carnwath | Carstairs | Covington | Coulter | Crawford | Crawfordjohn | Dolphinton | Douglas | Dunsyre | Lamington | Lanark | Lesmahagow | Libberton | Pettinain | Symington | Walston | Wishton |
|---|---|---|---|---|---|---|---|---|---|---|---|---|---|---|---|---|---|---|---|---|---|---|
| 31 | Crook-burn, (23, 19) | N. | | | | | | | | 7 | | | | | | | | | | | | |
| 32 | DAER-WATER, (11, 22, 28) | N. | | | | | | | | 14 | | | | | | | | | | | | |
| 33 | Pitrenick-burn, (10,12) | E. | | | | | | | | 4 | | | | | | | | | | | | |
| 34 | POWTRAIL-WATER, (22,29) | N. | | | | | | | | 8 | | | | | | | | | | | | |
| 35 | Clyde-burn, (17) | W. | | | | | | | | 5½ | | | | | | | | | | | | |
| 36 | Shortcleuch-burn, (12) | N.E. | | | | | | | | 1⅓ | | | | | | | | | | | | |
| 37 | Elvan-water, | E. | | | | | | | | 6 | | | | | | | | | | | | |
| 38 | Midloch-water, (5) | W. | | | | | | | | 4 | | | | | | | | | | | | |
| 39 | Grains-burn, (24) | S.W. | | | | | | | | 6½ | | | | | | | | | | | | |
| 40 | Camps-water, (21, 26) | W. | | | | | | | | 8 | | | | | | | | | | | | |
| 41 | Glengonnar, (14) | N.E. | | | | | | | | | 6 | | | | | | | | | | | |
| 42 | Snar-water, (25) | N. | | | | | | | | | 4½ | | | | | | | | | | | |
| 43 | Black-burn, (1) | S. | | | | | | | | | 17 | | | | | | | | | | | |
| 44 | DUNEATON, (4, 15) | S.E. | | | | | | | 8 | | | | | | 3 | | | | | | | 5 |
| 45 | Roberton-burn, (10) | E. | | | | | | | | | | | | | | | | | | | | 6 |
| 46 | Garf-water, | E. | | | | | | | | | | | | | | | | | | | | |
| 47 | Lamington-burn, | N.W. | | | | | | | | | | | | | | | | | | | | |
| 48 | Culter-water, (8) | N.W. | | | | | | | | | | | | | | | | | | | 8 | |
| 49 | MEDWIN, South, | S.W. | | | | | | | | | | | | | | | | | | | | |
| 50 | Do. North, | S.W. | | | | | | | | | | | | | | | | | | | | |
| 51 | Dippool-burn, (2) | S.W. | | | | | | | | | | | | | | | | | | | | |
| 52 | MOUSE-WATER, (7) | S.E. | | | | 11 | | | | | | | | 9 | | | | 10 | | | | |
| 53 | Monks-burn, (16) | N. | | | | | | | | | | | | | | | | | | | | |
| 54 | Glespin-burn, | N.E. | | | | | | | | | | | 3 | | | | 8 | | | | | |
| 55 | Poniel-water, (4) | E. | | | | | | | | | | | 5 | | | | 6 | | | | | |
| 56 | DOUGLAS-WATER, | N.E. | | | | | | | | | | | 16 | | | | 13 | | | | | |
| 57 | Logan-water, (16) | N.E. | | | | | | | | | | | | | | | | | | | | |
| 58 | Nethan-water, | N.W. | | 5 | | | | | | | | | | | | | | | | | | |
| 59 | Garion, | N.W. | | 5 | | | | | | | | | | | | | | | | | | |
| 60 | The Clyde, | | ¼ | 5 | 3 | 2½ | 4 | 5 | 31½ | 10 | 3½ | | 16 | | 9 | 12 | 10 | 8 | 8 | 7 | 8 | 6 |

| Ordnance Survey Figures. | Biggar. | Carluke. | Car-michael. | Carnwath. | Carstairs. | Coving-ton. | Coulter. | Crawford. | Crawford-john. | Dolphin-ton. | Total. |
|---|---|---|---|---|---|---|---|---|---|---|---|
| 61 Marsh, | 359 | 315 | 6385 | 3041 | 2743 | 121 | ... | ... | 327 | ... | 7011 |
| 62 Moss, | 5346 | 257230 | ... | ... | 831297 | ... | ... | 2146 | ... | ... | 1163319 |
| 63 Do., and Rough Pasture, | ... | ... | ... | 435746 | ... | ... | ... | ... | ... | ... | 435746 |
| 64 Meadow, | 1247 | 71579 | 6429 | 84138 | ... | ... | 4296 | 5018 | 1859 | ... | 291426 |
| 65 Arable, | 5290388 | 10312215 | 6374879 | 16526301 | 6009918 | 2895358 | 261874 | 1291935 | 4137340 | 1975433 | 57435295 |
| 66 Moorland, | 377982 | 296399 | 1019409 | 3117291 | ... | ... | ... | ... | ... | 618463 | 914462 |
| 67 Heathy Pasture, | ... | 1342996 | ... | ... | ... | 1950231 | ... | ... | 8323857 | ... | 12838939 |
| 68 Do. and Rough Pasture, | 4126306 | 589018 | 3914122 | 4066293 | 1857762 | ... | 6789181 | 6421278 | 12538662 | 194727 | 3293327 |
| 69 Rough Pasture, | 47286 | 454152 | 140291 | 299001 | 12230 | 3137 | 112324 | 1812020 | 961427 | 67114 | 94574 |
| 70 Pasture, | 439 | 253032 | ... | 1236 | 2969 | ... | ... | ... | 1292 | ... | 3909304 |
| 71 Do., strip of, | ... | ... | ... | 7342 | 52236 | 7074 | ... | ... | ... | ... | 5407 |
| 72 Grass Park, etc., | ... | 8130 | 386 | ... | ... | ... | ... | ... | ... | ... | 313319 |
| 73 Furze, | ... | 22350 | 2423 | ... | 1003 | ... | ... | 171968 | ... | ... | 7470 |
| 74 Whins, | ... | ... | ... | ... | ... | ... | ... | ... | ... | ... | 8360 |
| 75 Brushwood, | ... | ... | ... | ... | 595758 | ... | 5316 | 5793 | ... | ... | 25578 |
| 76 Fir, | 855852 | 762503 | 624409 | 1296704 | 6958 | 126105 | 406389 | ... | 223420 | 624113 | 578559 |
| 77 Plantation, | 361 | 5991 | 2181 | 11423 | 1601 | 321 | 331 | ... | 4369 | 1784 | 5109464 |
| 78 Wood, | 3533 | 24892 | 2954 | ... | ... | ... | ... | ... | ... | ... | 8533 |
| 79 Shrubbery, | 1749 | 106615 | ... | ... | ... | ... | ... | ... | ... | 673 | 6732 |
| 80 Garden, | ... | ... | ... | ... | ... | ... | ... | ... | ... | ... | 106946 |
| 81 Orchard, | ... | 72541 | ... | ... | 180 | ... | 455 | ... | ... | ... | 4953 |
| 82 Nursery, | ... | ... | ... | ... | ... | ... | ... | ... | ... | ... | ... |
| 83 Glen, | ... | 190 | ... | 1377 | ... | ... | ... | ... | ... | ... | 7231 |
| 84 Do. Wooded, | ... | 734 | ... | 973 | ... | ... | ... | ... | ... | ... | 1347 |
| 85 Wooded Slope, | ... | ... | ... | ... | ... | ... | ... | ... | ... | ... | 1707 |
| 86 Green, | ... | ... | ... | ... | ... | ... | ... | ... | ... | ... | 457 |
| 87 Lane, | ... | ... | ... | ... | ... | ... | ... | ... | ... | ... | ... |
| 88 Footpath, | ... | ... | ... | ... | ... | ... | ... | ... | ... | ... | ... |
| 89 Walk, | ... | ... | ... | ... | ... | ... | ... | ... | ... | ... | ... |
| 90 Bowling Green, | ... | ... | ... | ... | ... | ... | ... | ... | ... | ... | ... |

| Ordnance Survey Figures. | Douglas. | Dunsyre. | Lamington. | Lanark. | Lesmahagow. | Libberton. | Pettinain. | Symington. | Walston. | Wiston. | Sum Total. |
|---|---|---|---|---|---|---|---|---|---|---|---|
| 61 Marsh, | $6^{22}$ | ... | ... | $39^{695}$ | 631 | $2^{222}$ | $2^{357}$ | ... | $7^{18}$ | ... | $116^{356}$ |
| 62 Moss, | ... | $79^{081}$ | ... | $9^{151}$ | $1103^{347}$ | ... | ... | $12^{489}$ | ... | ... | $2457^{987}$ |
| 63 Do. and Rough Pasture, | ... | ... | $12^{402}$ | ... | ... | ... | ... | ... | $43^{58}$ | ... | $4401^{004}$ |
| 64 Meadow, | $9^{609}$ | $7^{684}$ | ... | $11^{322}$ | $668^{496}$ | ... | $1^{070}$ | $2^{416}$ | ... | ... | $1004^{355}$ |
| 65 Arable, | $5405^{771}$ | $2701^{386}$ | $2186^{180}$ | $7053^{025}$ | $23887^{354}$ | $6158^{976}$ | $2434^{989}$ | $2274^{186}$ | $2806^{500}$ | $4605^{624}$ | $116949^{016}$ |
| 66 Moorland, | $25413^{289}$ | ... | ... | ... | ... | ... | ... | ... | $525^{372}$ | ... | $26863^{523}$ |
| 67 Heathy Pasture, | $166^{247}$ | ... | ... | $524^{860}$ | $2190^{082}$ | $14^{761}$ | $739^{315}$ | $674^{371}$ | $7^{20}$ | $38^{283}$ | $24395^{539}$ |
| 68 Do. and Rough Pasture, | $648^{010}$ | $433^{266}$ | $10215^{833}$ | $62961^{2}$ | $1449^{133}$ | $7^{100}$ | $241^{382}$ | $227^{335}$ | $793^{705}$ | $7975^{584}$ | $3533^{474}$ |
| 69 Rough Pasture, | $7^{622}$ | $49^{384}$ | $69^{057}$ | $230^{59}$ | $1247^{664}$ | $66^{066}$ | $124^{274}$ | $20^{968}$ | $36^{408}$ | $32^{347}$ | $117188^{800}$ |
| 70 Pasture, | $20^{27}$ | ... | ... | ... | $1^{838}$ | $2^{730}$ | ... | ... | ... | $1^{71}$ | $5655^{533}$ |
| 71 Do., strip of, | 254 | ... | ... | ... | $25^{195}$ | $1^{524}$ | ... | ... | ... | ... | $9^{377}$ |
| 72 Grass Park, etc. | ... | ... | ... | ... | $40^{550}$ | ... | ... | ... | ... | ... | $343^{399}$ |
| 73 Furze, | ... | ... | ... | ... | $1^{053}$ | ... | ... | ... | ... | ... | $49^{544}$ |
| 74 Whins, | $21^{091}$ | ... | ... | $24^{078}$ | $95^{622}$ | ... | ... | ... | ... | ... | $9^{373}$ |
| 75 Brushwood, | ... | ... | ... | ... | $350^{480}$ | ... | ... | ... | ... | ... | $166^{769}$ |
| 76 Fir, | ... | ... | $137^{196}$ | ... | ... | ... | ... | ... | ... | ... | $350^{480}$ |
| 77 Plantation, | $2039^{029}$ | $44^{646}$ | ... | $1220^{065}$ | $2265^{062}$ | $1075^{922}$ | $257^{319}$ | $192^{759}$ | $6^{2868}$ | $316^{410}$ | $12583^{592}$ |
| 78 Wood, | ... | ... | ... | $1^{226}$ | $15^{220}$ | ... | ... | 138 | ... | ... | $21^{979}$ |
| 79 Shrubbery, | $4^{744}$ | $7^{79}$ | $3^{361}$ | $231^{29}$ | $354^{42}$ | $4^{339}$ | $1^{704}$ | ... | $0^{67}$ | $2^{302}$ | $143^{490}$ |
| 80 Garden, | ... | ... | ... | $29^{495}$ | $55^{463}$ | ... | ... | ... | ... | ... | $191^{906}$ |
| 81 Orchard, | ... | ... | ... | $10^{193}$ | $1^{478}$ | ... | ... | ... | ... | ... | $15^{594}$ |
| 82 Nursery, | ... | ... | ... | ... | $2^{714}$ | ... | ... | ... | ... | ... | $2^{714}$ |
| 83 Glen, | ... | ... | ... | $43^{031}$ | ... | ... | ... | ... | ... | ... | $115^{572}$ |
| 84 Do., Wooded, | ... | ... | ... | $2^{556}$ | $6^{43}$ | $3^{824}$ | ... | ... | ... | ... | $6^{093}$ |
| 85 Wooded Slope, | $1^{667}$ | ... | ... | ... | ... | $2^{25}$ | ... | $7^{26}$ | ... | ... | $10^{735}$ |
| 86 Green, | ... | ... | ... | ... | ... | ... | ... | ... | ... | ... | $1^{707}$ |
| 87 Lane, | ... | ... | ... | $11^{05}$ | ... | ... | ... | ... | ... | ... | $1^{562}$ |
| 88 Footpath, | ... | ... | ... | $4^{32}$ | ... | ... | ... | ... | ... | $7^{26}$ | $1^{138}$ |
| 89 Walk, | ... | ... | ... | $4^{14}$ | ... | ... | ... | ... | ... | ... | 444 |
| 90 Bowling Green, | ... | ... | ... | ... | ... | ... | ... | ... | ... | ... | ... |

| Ordnance Survey Figures. | Biggar. | Carluke. | Carmichael. | Carnwath. | Carstairs. | Covington. | Coulter. | Crawford. | Crawfordjohn. | Dolphinton. | Total. |
|---|---|---|---|---|---|---|---|---|---|---|---|
| 91 River Clyde, | 775 | 43080 | 29540 | 23780 | 30055 | 4935 | 21370 | 96940 | 16691 | … | 311046 |
| 92 Water, | … | … | 12534 | 24526 | 29543 | … | 2103 | 211534 | 86203 | 2021 | 369063 |
| 93 Stream, | … | … | … | 24334 | … | 794 | … | … | … | 2634 | 2712 |
| 94 Burn, | … | 11116 | 10933 | … | 3569 | … | 415 | … | … | … | 25734 |
| 95 Dam, | … | 441 | 158 | 485 | 120 | … | 180 | 1331 | 242 | … | 3707 |
| 96 Mill Stream, | … | … | 437 | … | … | 698 | … | … | … | … | 1135 |
| 97 Pool, | … | 649 | 2437 | 1613 | 429 | … | … | … | … | … | 5510 |
| 98 Pond, | 9764 | 5032 | 2888 | 6971 | 12061 | 2396 | 342 | 191 | … | 2455 | 42041 |
| 99 Do., Curling, | 6379 | 4430 | 1726 | 1864 | 5047 | … | … | 2910 | 373 | 178 | 17009 |
| 100 Loch, | … | … | … | 3464 | … | … | … | … | … | … | 39949 |
| 101 Lake, | … | … | … | … | … | … | … | … | … | … | … |
| 102 Island, | … | … | … | … | … | … | … | … | … | … | 1104 |
| 103 Embankment, | … | … | 1104 | … | … | … | … | … | … | … | 648 |
| 104 Ferry-House, | … | … | … | 645 | … | … | … | … | … | … | … |
| 105 Bridge, | 4160 | 3992 | 776 | 4729 | 711 | 174 | 2934 | 9561 | … | 716 | 34843 |
| 106 Road, Old, | … | … | … | … | … | … | … | … | … | … | … |
| 107 Do., Old, | 41012 | … | 157 | 64822 | 41162 | 12490 | 15274 | 43780 | 61039 | … | 77468 |
| 108 Do., County, | 25916 | 152939 | 49586 | 126519 | 49786 | 31318 | 20979 | 98780 | 41743 | 15306 | 581305 |
| 109 Do., Parish, | 23135 | 36237 | 26314 | 27920 | … | 2304 | … | 3351 | 768 | 1387 | 343576 |
| 110 Do., Turnpike, Old, | … | … | … | … | … | … | … | … | … | … | 4919 |
| 111 Do., Do., Old, | … | … | … | … | … | … | 4603 | 684 | 114 | 459 | 139642 |
| 112 Do., Occupation, | … | 43095 | 9560 | 32746 | 12452 | 2514 | … | … | … | … | 2704 |
| 113 Do., Farm, | 1850 | 1850 | … | 2704 | … | … | … | … | … | … | 5747 |
| 114 Do., Cart, | 283 | … | … | 2430 | 1511 | … | … | … | … | … | 283 |
| 115 Do., Track, | … | 536 | … | … | … | … | … | … | … | … | 4418 |
| 116 Do., Private, | … | … | 2931 | … | … | … | … | … | 945 | … | 4302 |
| 117 Tramway, | … | 4382 | … | … | … | … | … | … | … | … | … |
| 118 Railway, | … | 46793 | … | 87228 | 43139 | 36323 | … | 131192 | … | … | 344814 |
| 119 Do. Station, | … | 926 | … | … | … | … | … | … | … | … | 956 |
| 120 Race-Course, | … | … | … | … | … | … | … | … | … | … | … |

| Ordnance Survey Figures. | Douglas. | Dunsyro. | Lamington. | Lanark. | Lesmahagow. | Libberton. | Pettinain. | Symington. | Walston. | Wiston. | Sum Total. |
|---|---|---|---|---|---|---|---|---|---|---|---|
| 91 River Clyde, | $79^{916}$ | | $83^{913}$ | $114^{768}$ | $159^{666}$ | $78^{099}$ | $95^{433}$ | $36^{528}$ | | $56^{119}$ | $935^{512}$ |
| 92 Water, | $1^{089}$ | $10^{947}$ | $5^{24}$ | $25^{564}$ | $35^{208}$ | | | | $4^{608}$ | $4^{090}$ | $529^{402}$ |
| 93 Stream, | $27^{751}$ | | $4^{772}$ | $1^{290}$ | $16^{791}$ | | | | | $3^{399}$ | $46^{296}$ |
| 94 Burn, | $156$ | $2^{228}$ | | $168$ | $213$ | $406$ | | $6^{49}$ | | $557$ | $62^{344}$ |
| 95 Dam, | | | | | | | $345$ | | | | $7^{938}$ |
| 96 Mill Stream, | $153$ | | $1^{922}$ | $647$ | $876$ | $1^{442}$ | $638$ | $073$ | | | $2^{762}$ |
| 97 Pool, | $127$ | $1^{377}$ | $4^{905}$ | $6^{574}$ | $2^{228}$ | $2^{221}$ | $1^{648}$ | $8^{847}$ | $450$ | $3^{029}$ | $12^{613}$ |
| 98 Do., Curling, | $5^{955}$ | $1^{295}$ | $2^{660}$ | $096$ | $12^{125}$ | $3^{203}$ | | | | $2^{221}$ | $83^{544}$ |
| 99 Do., Curling, | | | | $25^{989}$ | $3^{060}$ | | | | | | $34^{204}$ |
| 100 Loch, | $15^{971}$ | | | | $5^{079}$ | | | | | | $72^{212}$ |
| 101 Lake, | $1^{017}$ | | | $3^{685}$ | $1^{013}$ | | | | | | $15^{571}$ |
| 102 Island, | | | | | | | | | | | $5^{715}$ |
| 103 Embankment, | | | | | | | | | | | $1^{164}$ |
| 104 Ferry-House, | | | | $220$ | $619$ | | $039$ | | | | $^{878}$ |
| 105 Bridge, | $3^{843}$ | $3^{123}$ | $5^{681}$ | $20^{073}$ | $28^{878}$ | $4^{945}$ | $8^{374}$ | $8^{459}$ | $8^{555}$ | $449$ | $109^{309}$ |
| 106 Road, | | | | $1^{456}$ | $8^{46}$ | | | | | | $10^{281}$ |
| 107 Do., Old, | $28^{233}$ | $15^{437}$ | $8^{612}$ | $69^{437}$ | $318^{314}$ | | $27^{979}$ | $18^{321}$ | $22^{061}$ | $37^{068}$ | $9^{474}$ |
| 108 Do., County, | $27^{736}$ | $9^{028}$ | $23^{680}$ | $50^{270}$ | $44^{677}$ | $65^{201}$ | $5^{946}$ | $9^{047}$ | $15^{248}$ | $40^{390}$ | $119^{288}$ |
| 109 Do., Parish, | $1^{040}$ | | $127$ | | | | | | | | $583^{798}$ |
| 110 Do., Turnpike, | $14^{170}$ | $5^{272}$ | $959$ | $45^{521}$ | $88^{247}$ | $14^{046}$ | $4^{126}$ | $2^{065}$ | $1^{159}$ | $9^{452}$ | $5^{186}$ |
| 111 Do., Do., Old, | | | | | | | | | | | $324^{629}$ |
| 112 Do., Occupation, | | | | | | | | | | | $2^{704}$ |
| 113 Do., Farm, | | | | | $8^{108}$ | | | | | $1^{333}$ | $5^{747}$ |
| 114 Do., Cart, | | | | | $7^{971}$ | | | | | $2^{298}$ | $9^{704}$ |
| 115 Do., Track, | | | | $4^{876}$ | $2^{562}$ | | | | | | $19^{973}$ |
| 116 Do., Private, | | | | | $80^{087}$ | | | | $3^{216}$ | | $10^{141}$ |
| 117 Tramway, | | | $42^{994}$ | $50^{240}$ | | | $17^{764}$ | $22^{396}$ | | $14^{347}$ | $572^{968}$ |
| 118 Railway, | | | | | | | | | | $194$ | $1^{150}$ |
| 119 Do., Station, | | | | $4^{660}$ | | | | | | | $4^{669}$ |
| 120 Race-Course, | | | | | | | | | | | |

| Ordnance Survey Figures. | Biggar. | Carluke. | Car-michael. | Carnwath. | Carstairs. | Coving-ton. | Coulter. | Crawford. | Crawford-john. | Dolphin-ton. | Total. |
|---|---|---|---|---|---|---|---|---|---|---|---|
| 121 Avenue, | 304 | $2^{683}$ | | | $25^{237}$ | | $161^{134}$ | $7^{931}$ | $27^{150}$ | $31^{919}$ | $28^{223}$ |
| 122 Ornamental Ground, | $8^{736}$ | $12^{626}$ | 529 | $8^{214}$ | $173^{027}$ | | | | | | $431^{266}$ |
| 123 Do. Park, | | $11^{040}$ | | | | | | | | | $14^{040}$ |
| 124 Pleasure Ground, | | | | | | | | | | | |
| 125 Lodge, | 534 | 460 | $6^{823}$ | | 125 | | 060 | 018 | | | $8^{020}$ |
| 126 Mansion, | 798 | $3^{166}$ | $3^{24}$ | | $5^{516}$ | | 878 | 373 | 393 | | $11^{448}$ |
| 127 Offices, | | 792 | 664 | | | | $4^{916}$ | 501 | | | $5^{973}$ |
| 128 Stables, | | 681 | | | | | | | | | 684 |
| 129 Kennel, | | 710 | | | | | | | | | 710 |
| 130 Camp, | $3^{032}$ $3$ | | | 801 | 379 | $2^{034}$ | | $1^{732}$ | | | $67^{98}$ |
| 131 Ruins, | | | 014 | | 110 | | | | | | $1^{180}$ |
| 132 Tomb, | | | | | | | | | | | 124 |
| 133 Castle, | | 631 | | | | 669 | | 142 | $1^{720}$ | 503 | 773 |
| 134 Church, | | $1^{256}$ | 759 | 649 | 573 | | | | | | $6^{398}$ |
| 135 Manse, | | $2^{52}$ | | | 748 | 730 | 407 | | | | $26^{53}$ |
| 136 Graveyard, | | $1^{096}$ | | 933 | | | | | | | $27^{39}$ |
| 137 Chapel, | | | | | | | | | | 305 | 305 |
| 138 Burial-Ground, | | | | | | | | $20^{49}$ | | | $20^{49}$ |
| 139 School, | | 239 | | | | | 359 | 293 | | | $13^{65}$ |
| 140 Playground, | | | | | | | | | | | |
| 141 Hamlet, | | | | | | | | | | | |
| 142 Village, | | | | | | | | | | 474 | |
| 143 Town, | | $6^{578}$ | | | 855 | $36^{298}$ | | $1^{786}$ | | | $5^{327}$ |
| 144 Houses, | $84^{680}$ | $142^{968}$ | $60^{902}$ | $113^{679}$ | $50^{969}$ | | $3^{458}$ | | 677 | $23^{751}$ | $7^{436}$ |
| 145 Do., Front of, | | | 275 | | | | | $190^{75}$ | | | $515^{700}$ |
| 146 Do. and Garden, | | $6^{434}$ | | $80^{922}$ | $8^{798}$ | | $2^{473}$ | $4^{090}$ | $88^{926}$ | | $265^{053}$ |
| 147 Cottage and do., | | $4^{295}$ | | | | | | | 286 | | $11^{144}$ |
| 148 Washing-House, | | | | | 534 | | | | | | 534 |
| 149 Bleaching-Green, | | | | $1^{207}$ | | | | | | | $1^{207}$ |
| 150 Cot-Houses, | | $6^{832}$ | | | | | | | | | $6^{832}$ |

| Ordnance Survey Figures. | Douglas. | Dunsyre. | Lamington. | Lanark. | Lesmahagow. | Libberton. | Pettinain. | Symington. | Walston. | Wiston. | Sum Total. |
|---|---|---|---|---|---|---|---|---|---|---|---|
| 121 Avenue, | $1^{743}$ | | | | $5^{776}$ | | 378 | | | $1^{227}$ | $36^{120}$ |
| 122 Ornamental Ground, | $106^{139}$ | | $29^{960}$ | $227^{640}$ | $21^{996}$ | $5^{473}$ | | | | | $823^{601}$ |
| 123 Do. Park, | | | | | | | | | | | $14^{940}$ |
| 124 Pleasure Ground, | $1^{326}$ | | | $4^{140}$ | $85^{251}$ | | | | | $2^{83}$ | $89^{391}$ |
| 125 Lodge, | | | $2^{41}$ | | | | | | | | $9^{870}$ |
| 126 Mansion, | $3^{567}$ | | $3^{40}$ | $2^{069}$ | $2^{418}$ | $8^{03}$ | | | | $1^{340}$ | $20^{645}$ |
| 127 Offices, | | | $3^{05}$ | $1^{222}$ | $4^{717}$ | 489 | | | | | $14^{046}$ |
| 128 Stables, | | | | | | | | | | | 684 |
| 129 Kennel, | | | | | | | | | | | 710 |
| 130 Camp, | | | | | | $1^{282}$ | | $9^{26}$ | $1^{339}$ | | $10^{345}$ |
| 131 Ruins, | | | | | $2^{93}$ | | | | | | $1^{180}$ |
| 132 Tomb, | | | | $2^{90}$ | | | | 621 | | | 124 |
| 133 Castle, | 596 | | $4^{32}$ | $1^{178}$ | | | | | 826 | $1^{051}$ | $1^{887}$ |
| 134 Church, | | | 661 | | | | 768 | | | | $11^{349}$ |
| 135 Manse, | $1^{908}$ | | | $2^{431}$ | | 379 | | | $2^{499}$ | | $8^{811}$ |
| 136 Graveyard, | | | | | | | | | | $3^{09}$ | $5^{946}$ |
| 137 Chapel, | | | $5^{19}$ | | | | | | | | 824 |
| 138 Burial-Ground, | | $4^{14}$ | | | 454 | | | | $3^{46}$ | $5^{10}$ | $2^{049}$ |
| 139 School, | 843 | | $2^{52}$ | | | | | | | | $4^{134}$ |
| 140 Playground, | $4^{217}$ | | | | | | | | | $5^{77}$ | 577 |
| 141 Hamlet, | $15^{823}$ | | | | | $5^{206}$ | | | | | $4^{217}$ |
| 142 Village, | | | | | $2^{957}$ | | | | | | $26^{556}$ |
| 143 Town, | | | | $232^{370}$ | | | | $38^{384}$ | | | $10^{493}$ |
| 144 Houses, | $12^{579}$ | | $1^{90}$ | | $46^{306}$ | $58^{170}$ | | | $14^{902}$ | | $906^{722}$ |
| 145 Do. Front of, | | $2^{510}$ | | | $220^{996}$ | | $30^{432}$ | | $17^{239}$ | | $251^{703}$ |
| 146 Do. and Garden, | | $0^{61}$ | $5^{555}$ | | $136^{369}$ | | | | | $25^{965}$ | $466^{170}$ |
| 147 Cottage and do., | | | | | | | | | | | $11^{205}$ |
| 148 Washing-House, | | | | | $1^{022}$ | | | | | | 534 |
| 149 Bleaching-Green, | | | $2^{77}$ | | | | | | | | $2^{506}$ |
| 150 Cot-Houses, | $5^{732}$ | | $1^{737}$ | | 208 | | | | | | $14^{529}$ |

h

| Ordnance Survey Figures. | Biggar. | Carluke. | Carmichael. | Carnwath. | Carstairs. | Covington. | Coulter. | Crawford. | Crawford-john. | Dolphinton. | Total. |
|---|---|---|---|---|---|---|---|---|---|---|---|
| 151 Farm Steading, | 1^608 | | | | 1^131 | | 15^981 | 21^527 | 34^100 | 293 | 73^376 |
| 152 Stack Yard, | | | 195 | 2^105 | | | | | | | 3^724 |
| 153 Thrashing Mill, | | | 0^682 | | | | | | | | ... |
| 154 Shed, | | | 194 | | | | | | | 0^089 | 220 |
| 155 Sheep Fold, | | | | | | | | | | | 901 |
| 156 Lead Mines, Old, | | | | | | | | 138 | 263 | | 1^075 |
| 157 Do., Old, | | | | | | | | 355 | | | 2^909 |
| 158 Smelting Mill, | | | | | | | | 1^075 | | | 430 |
| 159 Coal Pit, Old, | | 10^940 | | | | | | 2^809 | | | 10^940 |
| 160 Do., Old, | | 1^925 | | | | | | 490 | | | 1^925 |
| 161 Do. Yard, | | | | | | | | | | | ... |
| 162 Ironstone Pit, | | 46^055 | | 1^106 | | | | | | | 46^055 |
| 163 Reservoir, | | 194 | | | | | | | | | 1^214 |
| 164 Iron Works, | | 1^389 | | | | | | | | | 1^389 |
| 165 Limestone Pit, | | 19^645 | | 5^788 | | | | | | | 19^645 |
| 166 Lime Work, | | 919 | | | | | | | 5^916 | | 12^623 |
| 167 Clay Field, | | | | | | | | | | | ... |
| 168 Brick Work, | | 5^556 | | 5^913 | | | | | | | 5^913 |
| 169 Tile Work, | | 268 | | | 358 | | 268 | | | | 5^556 |
| 170 Coke Work, | | 8^738 | | | | 1^165 | | | | | 268 |
| 171 Refuse Heap, | 1^836 | 13^873 | | 6^687 | | | | 631 | | 7^22 | 8^738 |
| 172 Quarry, Old, | 617 | 13^675 | | | | | | | | | 25^540 |
| 173 Do., Old, | | | | | | 504 | | 132 | | | 14^292 |
| 174 Gravel Pit, | | 5^933 | | | | 1^975 | | | | | ... |
| 175 Mills, | | 978 | | | | | | | 600 | | 7^369 |
| 176 Gas Work, | | 1^823 | | | | | | | | | 2^953 |
| 177 Smithy, | | | | | | | | | | | 1^823 |
| 178 Wood Yard, | | 491 | | | | | | 325 | | | ... |
| 179 Shingle and Water Course, | | | 698 | | | | | | | | 514 |
| 180 Waste, | | 39^943 | | 23^092 | | | | 15^686 | | | 79^621 |

| Ordnance Survey Figures. | Douglas. | Dunsyre. | Lamington. | Lanark. | Lesmahagow. | Libberton. | Pettinain. | Symington. | Walston. | Wiston. | Sum Total. |
|---|---|---|---|---|---|---|---|---|---|---|---|
| 151 Farm Steading, | $74^{811}$ | $16^{588}$ | $11^{173}$ | | $2^{958}$ | | | | | $21^{998}$ | $198^{296}$ |
| 152 Stack Yard, | | | $2^{123}$ | | | | | | $615$ | | $9^{120}$ |
| 153 Thrashing Mill, | | | | | | | $079$ | $060$ | | | $069$ |
| 154 Shed, | | $071$ | | | | | | | | | $299$ |
| 155 Sheep Fold, | | | | | $261$ | | | | | $334$ | $1^{567}$ |
| 156 Lead Mines, | | | | | | | | | | | $1^{075}$ |
| 157 Do., Old, | | | | | | | | | | | $2^{809}$ |
| 158 Smelting Mill, | $482$ | | | | | | | | | | $490$ |
| 159 Coal Pit, | | | | | $11^{246}$ | | | | | | $22^{608}$ |
| 160 Do., Old, | | | | | | | | | | | $1^{925}$ |
| 161 Do., Yard, | | | | | $835$ | | | | | | $835$ |
| 162 Ironstone Pit, | $28^{159}$ | | | | | | | | | | $46^{955}$ |
| 163 Reservoir, | | | | | | | | | | | $29^{373}$ |
| 164 Iron Works, | | | | | | | | | | | $1^{380}$ |
| 165 Limestone Pit, | | | | | | | | | | | $19^{645}$ |
| 166 Lime Work, | | | | | | | | | | | $12^{023}$ |
| 167 Clay Field, | $902$ | | | | $3^{967}$ | | | | | | $4^{869}$ |
| 168 Brick Work, | | | | | $2^{159}$ | | | | | | $5^{913}$ |
| 169 Tile Work, | $2^{350}$ | | | | | | | | | | $10^{065}$ |
| 170 Coke Work, | | | | | | | | | | | $268$ |
| 171 Refuse Heap, | | | | | | | $660$ | | | | $8^{738}$ |
| 172 Quarry, | $2^{735}$ | | | $6^{158}$ | $15^{360}$ | $1^{087}$ | $630$ | | $492$ | $2^{611}$ | $54^{643}$ |
| 173 Do., Old, | | | | $480$ | $212$ | | | | | | $15^{614}$ |
| 174 Gravel Pit, | | | | $656$ | $168$ | | | | | | $824$ |
| 175 Mills, | $2^{201}$ | $063$ | | | $943$ | $239$ | $566$ | | $832$ | | $12^{284}$ |
| 176 Gas Work, | $428$ | | | | | | $040$ | | | $071$ | $3^{421}$ |
| 177 Smithy, | | | | | $397$ | | | | | | $2^{220}$ |
| 178 Wood Yard, | | | | | $474$ | | | | | | $474$ |
| 179 Shingle and Water Course, | | | | | | $3^{327}$ | | | | | $4^{241}$ |
| 180 Waste, | | | $179$ | | $32^{977}$ | | | | | $523$ | $113^{300}$ |

The Census figures for 1755 were collected by Dr Webster; for 1791, are those given in the "Sinclair" Statistical Account of Scotland; those given for 1801 to 1861, are as officially reported at the decennial dates designated. In the topographic pages of this Work, the causes of "Increase" and "Decrease" have been adverted to at the proper places.

POPULATION—1755-1861.

| | Biggar | Carluke | Carmichael | Carnwath | Carstairs | Covington | Conltor | Crawford | Crawfordjohn | Dolphinton | Douglas | Dunsyre | Lamington | Lanark | Lesmahagow | Libberton | Pettinain | Symington | Walston | Wiston |
|---|---|---|---|---|---|---|---|---|---|---|---|---|---|---|---|---|---|---|---|---|
| 181. Census —1755, | 1098 | 1159 | 899 | 2300 | 845 | 521 | 422 | 2009 | 765 | 302 | 2009 | 359 | 599 | 2294 | 3996 | 730 | 330 | 264 | 479 | 876 |
| 182. Do. —1791, | 937 | 1730 | 781 | 3000 | 924 | 609 | 326 | 1490 | 599 | 200 | 1715 | 360 | 417 | 4751 | 2810 | 750 | 336 | 307 | 427 | 740 |
| 183. Do. —1801, | 1216 | 1756 | 832 | 2650 | 899 | 456 | 369 | 1671 | 712 | 231 | 1730 | 352 | 375 | 4492 | 3070 | 706 | 430 | 308 | 383 | 757 |
| 184. Do. —1811, | 1276 | 2311 | 926 | 3759 | 875 | 438 | 415 | 1773 | 858 | 268 | 1873 | 345 | 356 | 5667 | 4464 | 749 | 401 | 364 | 377 | 836 |
| 185. Do. —1821, | 1727 | 2925 | 963 | 2888 | 937 | 526 | 467 | 1914 | 971 | 236 | 2195 | 290 | 359 | 7085 | 5592 | 785 | 461 | 472 | 392 | 927 |
| 186. Do. —1831, | 1915 | 3288 | 956 | 3501 | 981 | 521 | 497 | 1850 | 991 | 302 | 2542 | 335 | 382 | 7672 | 6409 | 773 | 416 | 489 | 429 | 940 |
| 187. Do. —1841, | 1865 | 4802 | 874 | 3550 | 950 | 523 | 536 | 1684 | 993 | 306 | 2467 | 288 | 358 | 7679 | 6902 | 796 | 428 | 488 | 493 | 929 |
| 188. Do. —1851, | 2049 | 6283 | 805 | 3551 | 1066 | 548 | 472 | 1670 | 1111 | 305 | 2611 | 312 | 369 | 8243 | 7746 | 800 | 407 | 536 | 497 | 839 |
| 189. Do. —1861, | 1999 | 6176 | 836 | 3554 | 1345 | 532 | 484 | 1590 | 980 | 260 | 2490 | 312 | 380 | 7891 | 9266 | 836 | 407 | 528 | 480 | 786 |
| 190. Increase, 1775-1861, | 901 | 5017 | | 1194 | 500 | 11 | 62 | | 215 | | 491 | | | 5597 | 5270 | 106 | 77 | 264 | 1 | |
| Decrease, do., | | | 63 | | | | | 419 | | 42 | | 47 | 219 | | | | | | | 110 |

Lanark is a burgh; Biggar, Carluke, & Douglas, burghs of barony; Abbeygreen & Turfholm, the parochial village of Lesmahagow; Coulter, Crawford, etc., have no place, as villages, in the enumeration of the Census last taken.

| NAME. | PARISH. | 1841. | 1861. |
|---|---|---|---|
| 191 Abbeygreen & Turf- | Lesmahagow | 881 | 1136 |
| 192 Abington, ...[holm, | Crawfordjohn | 135 | |
| 193 Biggar, | Biggar | 1395 | 1448 |
| 194 Carluke, | Carluke | 2090 | 3111 |
| 195 Carnwath, | Carnwath | 766 | 895 |
| 196 Douglas, | Douglas | 1313 | 1426 |
| 197 Lanark, | Lanark | 4831 | 5834 |
| 198 Carstairs, | Carstairs | 350 | 450 |
| 199 Coulter, | Coulter | 197 | |
| 200 Crawford, | Crawford | 236 | |

| NAME. | PARISH. | 1841. | 1861. |
|---|---|---|---|
| 201 Crawfordjohn, | Crawfordjohn | 137 | |
| 202 Dunsyre, | Dunsyre | 68 | |
| 203 Lamington, | Lamington | 122 | |
| 204 Libberton, | Libberton | 117 | |
| 205 Pettinain, | Pettinain | 80 | |
| 206 Synington, | Synington | 213 | |
| 207 Walston, | Walston | 101 | |
| 208 Wiston, | Wiston | 141 | |
| 209 Braehead, | Carnwath | 312 | 350 |
| 210 Crossford, | Lesmahagow | 431 | 530 |

| NAME. | PARISH. | 1841. | 1861. |
|---|---|---|---|
| 211 Ellsrickle, | Walston | 211 | |
| 212 Leadhills, | Crawford | 950 | 842 |
| 213 Roberton, | Wiston | 201 | |
| 214 Braidwood, | Carluke | 234 | |
| 215 Kirkfieldbank, | Lesmahagow | 1023 | 1212 |
| 216 Kirkmuirhill, | Do., | 242 | 371 |
| 217 Newbigging, | Carnwath | 217 | |
| 218 New-Lanark, | Lanark | 1642 | 1396 |
| 219 Quothquhan, | Libberton | 160 | |
| 220 Thankerton, | Covington | 113 | |

## PREFATORY NOTES ON VALUATION ROLL PAGES.

HAVING obtained copies of the Valuation Rolls for the twenty parishes (that of the burgh of Lanark excepted) forming the Upper Ward of Lanarkshire, the information they afford, as to the distribution of property, etc., has been produced, and reproduced, in such form as may interest those seeking instruction from figures carefully collected and faithfully reported.

The sums appearing for 1791, are those reported by the reverend contributors to the Sinclair (the Old Statistical) Account of Scotland.

For 1815 and 1842-3, the amounts are those reported to Parliament as the assessed value of the parishes at these dates.

For 1858-9 and 1863-4, the values are those entered in the rolls now annually made up for parochial objects. The Railways, as valued for 1862-3, contribute largely to the local assessments; where no entry appears, no railway yet exists.

There are few reliable figures, which can be had ready access to, which will not be embodied in these statistical tables, if they throw light on the material and social arrangements of the Ward—special attention being given to those of clerical or educational importance.

As the increase in value of farms, between 1858-9 and 1863-4, has been considerable, two pages will be allotted, to show the more important of such in detail, giving the former and the present rental, and the names of owners and occupants at both periods.

| VALUE OF PROPERTY. | 1791. | 1815. | 1842-3. | | | 1858-9. | | | 1863-4. | | | RAILWAYS, 1862-3. | | |
|---|---|---|---|---|---|---|---|---|---|---|---|---|---|---|
| | £ | £ | £ | s. | D. | £ | s. | D. | £ | s. | D. | £ | s. | D. |
| 221 Biggar, ........ | ... | 4017 | 7359 | 4 | 2 | 8566 | 18 | 0 | 9919 | 14 | 0 | 2543 | 6 | 6 |
| 222 Carluke, ....... | ... | 8553 | 13436 | 13 | 9 | 20939 | 0 | 3 | 23260 | 11 | 0 | 6459 | 0 | 6 |
| 223 Carmichael,... | ... | 4326 | 5279 | 11 | 6 | 5215 | 4 | 11 | 5836 | 8 | 0 | ... | | |
| 224 Carnwath,..... | 5000 | 10384 | 14206 | 0 | 0 | 17022 | 2 | 5 | 22026 | 5 | 0 | 15268 | 0 | 6 |
| 225 Carstairs, ..... | 2150 | 4022 | 6464 | 15 | 6 | 6732 | 3 | 8 | 7733 | 8 | 0 | 6189 | 15 | 0 |
| 226 Coulter,........ | 1600 | 2769 | 5230 | 18 | 6 | 4766 | 18 | 0 | 3918 | 0 | 0 | 5296 | 5 | 0 |
| 227 Covington,.... | 920 | 1720 | 2880 | 5 | 6 | 2967 | 5 | 3 | 5085 | 0 | 0 | 1194 | 5 | 0 |
| 228 Crawford, ..... | 3400 | 16016 | 12341 | 4 | 11 | 11250 | 4 | 3 | 12049 | 9 | 0 | 16563 | 13 | 0 |
| 229 Crawfordjohn, | 2500 | 5014 | 6328 | 10 | 1 | 7326 | 4 | 2 | 8360 | 2 | 0 | ... | | |
| 230 Dolphinton,... | 600 | 1301 | 1989 | 4 | 6 | 2364 | 10 | 7 | 2450 | 2 | 0 | ... | | |
| 231 Douglas, ...... | ... | 7538 | 11012 | 17 | 7 | 10990 | 9 | 7 | 12715 | 7 | 0 | ... | | |
| 232 Dunsyre,...... | 1000 | 2000 | 2623 | 14 | 9 | 2951 | 6 | 1 | 3441 | 4 | 0 | ... | | |
| 233 Lamington, | 1500 | 3335 | 3667 | 19 | 0 | 3768 | 18 | 4 | 4482 | 1 | 0 | 6382 | 12 | 0 |
| 234 Lanark, ....... | 3000 | 9715 | 17780 | 4 | 5 | 21306 | 5 | 3 | 23314 | 14 | 4 | 7972 | 6 | 6 |
| 235 Lesmahagow, | 7000 | 17481 | 27055 | 15 | 5 | 43475 | 1 | 8 | 43173 | 14 | 0 | 16398 | 19 | 0 |
| 236 Libberton,... | 1189 | 3790 | 4730 | 8 | 7 | 5721 | 7 | 11 | 6727 | 14 | 0 | ... | | |
| 237 Pettinain,..... | 900 | 2082 | 3234 | 15 | 6 | 3216 | 3 | 6 | 3610 | 5 | 0 | 2260 | 13 | 6 |
| 238 Symington, .. | 700 | 1984 | 2384 | 11 | 8 | 2437 | 13 | 9 | 2872 | 18 | 0 | 6230 | 18 | 6 |
| 239 Walston,...... | 700 | 1730 | 2137 | 2 | 0 | 2399 | 13 | 9 | 2894 | 10 | 0 | ... | | |
| 240 Wiston,........ | ... | 4162 | 4952 | 10 | 11 | 4964 | 14 | 11 | 6125 | 5 | 0 | 2365 | 10 | 6 |

The ministers of Biggar, Carluke, Carmichael, Douglas, and Wiston gave no estimate of the rental of their parishes; while those reported have, in some cases, the qualifying phrase "about" added. Crawford, in 1791, may be taken as rental of land.
The mines at Leadhills are, at present, comparatively inactive; costly and extensive operations at present proceeding to ensure large increase of production.

NOTE.—*In those pages, where the names of "farmers and tenants" are given, the "inner" figures designate the "estates" they may be on.*

| VALUATION ROLL—1858-9. (Pence omitted.) | Biggar. | | Carnluke. | | Carmichael. | | Carnwath. | | Carstairs. | | Covington. | | Coulter. | | Crawford. | | Crawfordjohn. | | Dolphinton. | |
|---|---|---|---|---|---|---|---|---|---|---|---|---|---|---|---|---|---|---|---|---|
| | £ | s. | £ | s. | £ | s. | £ | s. | £ | s. | £ | s. | £ | s. | £ | s. | £ | s. | £ | s. |
| 241 HOME, COUNTESS OF, .... | | | | | | | | | | | | | | | | | | | | |
| 242 Montague, Lady, .... | | | | | 1701 | 15 | | | | | | | | | | | | | | |
| 243 Douglas, Lord A., late,.. | | | 738 | 0 | | | | | | | | | | | 619 | 0 | 1832 | 0 | | |
| 244 Lockhart, Sir N. M'D.,.. | | | 1326 | 13 | | | 4820 | 5 | 166 | 10 | 1366 | 0 | | | | | | | | |
| 245 Lockhart, A. E.,.... | | | | | | | | | 758 | 6 | | | | | | | | | | |
| 246 Lockhart, L., D.D.,.... | | | 1486 | 14 | | | | | 10 | 10 | | | | | | | | | | |
| 247 Anstruther, Sir W. C.,.. | | | 471 | 9 | | | | | | | 1314 | 3 | | | | | | | | |
| 248 Carmichael, M. T.,.... | | | | | 2761 | 13 | | | | | 105 | 0 | | | | | | | | |
| 249 Cochrane, A. B.,.... | | | | | 635 | 0 | | | | | | | | | | | | | | |
| 250 Ross, Sir W. C.,.... | | | 1086 | 0 | | | | | | | | | | | | | | | | |
| 251 HAMILTON, DUKE OF,.. | | | | | | | | | | | | | | | | | | | | |
| 252 Buccleuch, Duke of,.... | | | | | | | | | | | | | | | 706 | 0 | 343 | 5 | | |
| 253 Hopetoun, Earl of,.... | | | | | | | | | | | | | | | 3962 | 6 | 160 | 0 | | |
| 254 Vere Hope, W. E.,.... | | | | | | | | | | | | | | | | | | | | |
| 255 Colebrooke, Sir T. E.,.. | | | | | | | | | | | | | 1510 | 0 | 3015 | 13 | 3441 | 4 | | |
| 256 Irving, G. V.,.... | | | | | | | | | | | | | 1629 | 4 | 869 | 7 | 285 | 0 | | |
| 257 Sim, Adam,.... | | | | | | | | | | | | | 352 | 0 | | | | | | |
| 258 Bailley, R. C.,.... | | | | | | | | | | | | | | | 485 | 0 | | | | |
| 259 Bertram, W.,.... | | | | | | | 895 | 7 | 4173 | 17 | | | | | | | | | | |
| 260 Chancellor, J. G.,.... | | | | | | | | | | | | | | | | | | | | |
| 261 MONTEITH, R.,.... | | | | | | | | | | | | | | | | | | | 1846 | 5 |
| 262 Mackenzie, J. O.,.... | | | | | | | | | | | | | | | | | | | | |
| 263 Cranstoun, Miss E.,.... | | | | | | | | | | | | | | | | | | | | |
| 264 Brown, Laurence,.... | 1010 | 0 | | | | | | | | | | | | | | | | | | |
| 265 M'Kirdy, J. G.,.... | | | 738 | 6 | | | | | | | | | | | | | | | | |
| 266 Brown, J. T.,.... | | | | | | | | | | | | | | | | | | | | |
| 267 Alston, J. W.,.... | | | | | | | | | | | | | | | | | | | | |
| 268 Coltness Iron Co.,.... | | | | | | | | | | | | | | | | | | | | |
| 269 Shotts Iron Co.,.... | | | 1098 | 13 | | | | | | | | | | | | | | | | |
| 270 Walker & Co.,.... | | | 1689 | 5 | | | | | | | | | | | | | | | | |
| TOTAL FOR PARISH,.. | 8566 | 18 | 20942 | 0 | 5215 | 4 | 20560 | 13 | 6732 | 3 | 2967 | 5 | 4766 | 18 | 11256 | 4 | 7326 | 4 | 2364 | 10 |

| No. | Valuation Roll—1858-9. (Pence omitted.) | Douglas £ s. | Dunsyre £ s. | Lamington £ s. | Lanark £ s. | Lesmahagow £ s. | Libberton £ s. | Pottinain £ s. | Symington £ s. | Walston £ s. | Wiston £ s. | Total £ s. d. |
|---|---|---|---|---|---|---|---|---|---|---|---|---|
| 241 | Douglas Castle, | 8931 15 | | 1169 12 | | | | | | | | 10101 7 4 |
| 242 | Do., | | | | | 2126 13 | | | | | 1802 12 | 7463 1 2 |
| 243 | Do., | | | 500 0 | | | | | | | 30 0 | 1887 0 0 |
| 244 | Lee and Carnwath, | | 2706 6 | | 2891 13 | | 2077 11 | | | 1092 0 | | 16447 0 6 |
| 245 | Cleghorn, | | | | 1189 9 | | | | | | | 2974 4 8 |
| 246 | Milton-Lockhart, | | | | | | | | | | | 1497 0 0 |
| 247 | Westraw & Carmichael, | | | | | | | 2909 3 | | | 1026 5 | 7456 9 1 |
| 248 | East-end, | | | | | | | | 880 2 | | | 1620 2 0 |
| 249 | Lamington, | | | 2037 1 | | | | | | | | 3701 5 4 |
| 250 | Bonnington, | | | | 1379 15 | | | | | | | 1379 15 4 |
| 251 | And Brandon, | | | | | 9883 19 | | | | | | 9833 19 3 |
| 252 | And Queensberry, | | | | | | | | | | | 1049 5 0 |
| 253 | Hopetoun, | | | | | | | | | | 578 3 | 4122 6 8 |
| 254 | Blackwood, | | | | | 8555 1 | | | | | | 8555 1 0 |
| 255 | Crawford, | | | | | | | | | | | 6456 17 9 |
| 256 | Newton, | | | | | | | | | | | 1154 7 0 |
| 257 | Coulter-Maynes, | | | | | | | | | | | 1510 0 0 |
| 258 | Coulter-Allers, | | | | | | | | | | | 1629 4 0 |
| 259 | Kersewell, | | | | | | | | | | | 1732 7 0 |
| 260 | Shieldhill, | | | | | | 1470 12 | | | | | 1470 12 0 |
| 261 | Carstairs, | | | | | | | | | | | 4173 13 8 |
| 262 | Dolphinton, | | | | | | | | | | | 1846 5 7 |
| 263 | Corehouse, | | | | | 1813 2 | | | | | | 1813 2 6 |
| 264 | Edmonstone, | | | | 277 5 | 702 19 | | | | | | 1010 0 0 |
| 265 | Birkwood, | | | | | | | | | | | 1718 11 0 |
| 266 | Auchlochan, | | | | | 2167 10 | | | | | | 2167 10 0 |
| 267 | Stockbriggs, | | | | | 1273 5 | | | | | | 1273 5 3 |
| 268 | Birkfield, | | | | | | | | | | | 1098 13 0 |
| 269 | Castlehill, | | | | 1622 2 | | | | | | | 1689 5 0 |
| 270 | New Lanark Mills, | | | | | 105 15 | | | | | | 1727 17 4 |
| | Total for Parish, | 10284 9 | 2051 6 | 3768 7 | 13190 7 | 46106 1 | 6001 11 | 5217 9 | 2437 13 | 2399 13 | 4964 11 | ... |

| Valuation Roll—1858-9 | Name. | Biggar. | Car-luke. | Carn-wath. | Car-stairs. | Coulter. | Craw-ford. | Dolph-inton. | Doug-las. | Lanark. | Lesma-hagow. | Libber-ton. | Syming-ton. | Wal-ston. | Wis-ton. | Properties. |
|---|---|---|---|---|---|---|---|---|---|---|---|---|---|---|---|---|
| 271 | Brown, James,.... | | 848 10 | | | | | | | | | | | | | Orchard. |
| 272 | Dickson, D.,...... | | | | | | | | | | | | 186 17 | | | Hartree. |
| 273 | Douglas, Miss,... | | | | | | | | | | | | | | | Brads. |
| 274 | Ewart, Robert,... | | | 814 0 | | 434 14 | 782 10 | | | | | | | | | Ellarshaw. |
| 275 | Gillespie, A., late, | | | | | | | | | | | | | | | Sunnyside. |
| 276 | Lorraine, W. S.,.. | 123 12 | | | | | | | | | | 836 12 | | | | Loaningdale. |
| 277 | M'Queen, Robert, | | | 710 0 | | | | | | 161 0 | | | | | 696 | Hardington. |
| 278 | Mitchell, W. G.,.. | 918 15 | | | | | | | | 225 0 | | | | | | Caerwood. |
| 279 | Monteath, Doug. | | | | | | | | 712 | | 940 4 | | | | | Stonebyres. |
| 280 | Paterson, Alex.,.. | | | | | | | | | | | | | | | Cornacoup. |
| 281 | Souter, D. R.,.... | | | 733 14 | | | | | | | | | | | | Lawhead. |
| 282 | Wilson, John,.... | | | 829 0 | | | | 52 0 | | | | | | | | Westsidewood. |
| 283 | Woddrop, W. H., | | | | 396 10 | | | | | | | | | | | Garvaldfoot. |
| 284 | Buchanan, R. C., | | | 185 0 | | | | | | | | | | 886 9 | 107 | Drumpellier. |
| 285 | Gibson, Thos.,.. | 120 0 | | 348 5 | | | | | | | | | | | | Toftcombs. |
| 286 | Hamilton, J.,..... | | 552 19 | | | | | | | | 698 10 | | | | | Fairholm. |
| 287 | Hozier, James,... | | 589 12 | | | | | | | | 707 0 | | | | | Mauldslie. |
| 288 | Inglis, John,..... | | | | | | | | | | | | | | | Verehills. |
| 289 | Mossman, Hugh, | | | | | | | | | | | | | | | Auchtyfardle. |
| 290 | Stainton, E.,..... | 710 0 | | | | | | | | | | | | | | Biggar Shiels. |
| 291 | Steel, Samuel,... | | 699 4 | 691 3 | | | | | | | | | | | | WAYGATESHAW. |
| 292 | Tennant, J.,....... | | | | | | | | | 431 10 | | | | | | Pool. |
| 293 | Baillie, G.,........ | | | | | | | | | | 440 10 | | | | | Jerviswood. |
| 294 | Gillespie, A.,..... | 529 8 | | | | | | | | | | | | | | Biggar Park. |
| 295 | Greenshields, J.,.. | | | | | | | | | | | | 555 19 | | | Kerse. |
| 296 | M'Pherson, A.,... | | | | | | | | | | 461 0 | | | | | Symington Lodge. |
| 297 | Marshall, J.,...... | | | | | | | | | | 497 16 | | | | | Cumberhead, Nor |
| 298 | Stein, J.,.......... | | | | | | | | | | | | | | | Kirkfield. |
| 299 | Stevenson, N.,.... | | 489 19 | | | | | | | | | | | | | Braidwood. |
| 300 | Thomson, J.,...... | | | | | | | | | | 511 10 | | | | | Birkenhead. |

| VALUATION ROLL—1858-9. | NAME. | Biggar £ | s. | Car-luke £ | s. | Carn-wath £ | s. | Car-stairs £ | s. | Coulter £ | s. | Craw-ford £ | s. | Craw-ford-john £ | s. | Dol-phin-ton £ | s. | Lanark £ | s. | Lesma-hagow £ | s. | Libber-ton £ | s. | Wal-ston £ | s. | Wiston £ | s. | PROPERTIES. |
|---|---|---|---|---|---|---|---|---|---|---|---|---|---|---|---|---|---|---|---|---|---|---|---|---|---|---|---|---|
| 301 | ANDERSON, S., | | | | | | | | | | | | | | | | | 307 | 12 | 45 | 0 | | | | | | | CARFIN. |
| 302 | Birrell, Lieut.-Col., | | | | | | | | | | | | | | | | | | | 353 | 8 | | | | | | | Cumberhead, So. |
| 303 | Cunningham, A., | | | | | | | | | | | | | | | | | | | | | | | | | | | Newholm. |
| 304 | Howieson, Dr, late, | | | | | | | | | | | | | | | 389 | 5 | | | | | | | | | 341 | 0 | Hillend. |
| 305 | Johnstone, P. & J., | | | | | | | | | | | | | 395 | 0 | | | | | | | | | | | | | Snar. |
| 306 | Kirkland, Sir J., | | | | | | | | | | | | | | | | | | | | | | | | | | | Clarty. |
| 307 | Logan, Miss, | | | | | 368 | 19 | | | | | | | | | | | | | | | | | | | | | New Mains. |
| 308 | Rowatt, J., late, | | | | | 350 | 0 | | | | | | | | | | | | | | | | | 403 | 0 | | | Falla. |
| 309 | Somerville, J., late, | | | | | 368 | 8 | | | | | | | | | | | | | | | | | | | | | Greenfield. |
| 310 | Wilson, Brothers, | | | | | | | | | | | 400 | 0 | | | | | | | | | | | | | | | Troloss. |
| 311 | THOWN, Mrs, | 296 | 0 | | | | | | | | | | | | | | | | | | | | | | | | | LINDSAYLANDS. |
| 312 | Gilchrist, J., | | | 314 | 10 | | | | | | | | | | | | | | | | | | | | | | | Gilfoot. |
| 313 | Gordon, Col. W., | | | | | | | | | | | | | | | | | | | 295 | 15 | | | | | | | Harperfield. |
| 314 | Haggart, J. C., | | | | | 339 | 16 | | | | | | | | | | | | | | | | | | | | | Craigenburn. |
| 315 | Hamilton, J.C., | | | | | | | 323 | 0 | | | | | | | | | | | | | | | | | | | Birniehill. |
| 316 | Handyside, W., | | | | | | | | | 321 | 15 | | | | | | | | | | | | | | | | | Cornhill. |
| 317 | Hastie, A., M.P., | | | | | | | | | | | | | | | | | | | 315 | 0 | | | | | | | Bankhead. |
| 318 | Leighton, W., late, | | | | | | | | | | | | | | | | | | | 312 | 0 | | | | | | | Bankend. |
| 319 | Murray, T., | 314 | 10 | | | | | | | | | | | | | | | | | | | | | | | | | Heaviside. |
| 320 | Robertson, G., | | | | | 331 | 19 | | | | | | | | | | | | | | | | | | | | | Auchengray. |
| 321 | HOWIESON, A., | | | | | | | | | | | | | | | | | 281 | 5 | | | | | | | | | HYNDFORD. |
| 322 | Logan, J., | | | | | 286 | 0 | | | | | | | | | | | | | | | | | | | | | East Shields. |
| 323 | Mather, J., | | | | | | | 246 | 12 | | | | | | | | | | | | | | | | | | | Westbank. |
| 324 | Murray, J. W., | | | | | 249 | 17 | | | | | | | | | | | | | | | | | | | | | Leamside. |
| 325 | Paterson, Robt., | | | | | | | | | 289 | 0 | | | | | | | | | | | | | | | | | Birthwood. |
| 326 | Pearson, W., | | | 275 | 0 | | | | | | | | | | | | | | | | | | | | | | | Springfield. |
| 327 | Robertson, Misses, | | | 265 | 11 | | | | | | | | | | | | | | | | | | | | | | | Hallcraig. |
| 328 | Somerville, R., | | | | | | | | | | | | | | | | | | | | | 286 | 0 | | | | | Cormistone. |
| 329 | Somerville, S., M.D., | | | | | 234 | 10 | | | | | | | | | | | | | | | 236 | 5 | | | | | Amperlaw. |
| 330 | Stark, J.M., M.D., | | | | | | | | | | | | | | | | | | | | | | | | | | | Huntfield. |

*i*

| VALUATION ROLL—1858-9. NAME. | Biggar £ s. | Carnluke £ s. | Carnwath £ s. | Carstairs £ s. | Covington £ s. | Crawfordjohn £ s. | Lanark £ s. | Lesmahagow £ s. | Libberton £ s. | Pettinain £ s. | Symington £ s. | Walston £ s. | PROPERTIES. |
|---|---|---|---|---|---|---|---|---|---|---|---|---|---|
| 331 COLLYER, W. D., | | | | | | | | | 229 10 | | | | CORMISTON-TOWERS. |
| 332 Dickson, W. J., | | | | | | 240 0 | | | | | | | Glentewan. |
| 333 Harvie, W., | | 244 0 | | | | | | | | | | | Brownlie. |
| 334 Logan, R., | | | | | | | | | | | | | Corramore. |
| 335 Murray, Lord, late, | 238 17 | | | | | | | | | | | | Langlee. |
| 336 Ramsay, Mrs C., | | | 240 0 | | | | | 230 0 | | | | | Falla. |
| 337 Smith, H., | | | | | | | | | | | | | West-town. |
| 338 Thomson, J., | | | | | | | | 224 0 | | 260 0 | | | Kirkbank. |
| 339 White, W., | | 245 6 | 220 0 | | | | | | | | | | Blackcastle. |
| 340 Wilson, J., | | 193 0 | | | | | | | | | | | Turf-foot. |
| 341 BELL, A., | | | 194 18 | | | | | 204 0 | | | | | WESTER-HOUSE. |
| 342 Logan, Rev. J., | | | | | | | | | | | | | Newmains. |
| 343 M'Ghie, R., | | | | | | | | | | | | | Stonehill. |
| 344 Murray, W., | | | | | | | | | | | | | Spittal. |
| 345 Robertson, G., | 200 0 | | | | | | 216 10 | | | | | | Baronald. |
| 346 Smith, J., | | | | | | | | 214 17 | | | | | Fauldhouses. |
| 347 Stewart, A., | | 213 10 | | | | | | | | | | | Brownlie. |
| 348 Todd & Sutherland, | | | | | | | | 200 0 | | | 109 0 | | Carpet-Works. |
| 349 Waugh, J., | | | | | 100 0 | | | | | | | | St John's Kirk. |
| 350 Wyld, A., | 99 10 | | | | | | | | | | | 112 0 | Lanmerlaw. |
| 351 BLACKWOOD, T. J., | | | | | | | 174 0 | 190 0 | | | | | LEELAW. |
| 352 Carmichael, Miss, | | | | | | | 179 0 | 181 10 | | | | | Smylum Park. |
| 353 Ferguson, J., | | | | | | | | | | | | | Ellenbank. |
| 354 Gillespie, W., | | | 173 0 | | | | | 192 10 | | | | | Huntlyhill. |
| 355 Goldie, W., W.S., | | | | | | | | 173 15 | | | | | Heathland. |
| 356 Hamilton, G., | | | | | | | | 186 0 | | | | | Auldton. |
| 357 Hamilton, G., | | | | | | | | | | | | | Gill. |
| 358 Newbigging, J., | | | | | | | | | | | 175 0 | | Netherton. |
| 359 Somerville, W., | | | | | | | | | | | | | Gowanbill. |
| 360 Somerville, W., | | | | 191 0 | | | | | | | | | Wyndale. |

| VALUATION ROLL—1858-9. Name. | Biggar. £ s. D. | Carluke. £ s. D. | Carnwath. £ s. D. | Coulter. £ s. D. | Crawford-john. £ s. D. | Douglas. £ s. D. | Lanark. £ s. D. | Lesmahagow. £ s. D. | Lilberton. £ s. D. | Wiston. £ s. D. | Properties. |
|---|---|---|---|---|---|---|---|---|---|---|---|
| 361 Douglas, J. C.,... | 170 0 0 | | | | | 154 0 0 | | | | | POLMOUKSHEAD. |
| 362 Edmonstone, Capt., [late, | | | | | | | | | | | Hillend. |
| 363 Forrest, W., [late, | | 158 10 0 | | | | 157 0 0 | | | | | Gills. |
| 364 Gillespie, R.,... | | | | | | | | 163 0 0 | | | Springhill. |
| 365 Jackson, Mrs,... | | | | | | | | | | | Newick. |
| 366 Lean, W.,... | | 160 0 0 | | | | | | | | | Middlehouse. |
| 367 Martin, J.,... | | 152 10 0 | | | | | | | | | Saw-Mills. |
| 368 Steel, J.,... | | | | | | | | 156 0 0 | | | Skellyhill. |
| 369 Wrightson, F.,... | | | | | | | | | 160 0 0 | | Corniston. |
| 370 Wyndham, J., late, | | | 153 0 0 | | | | | | | | Greenfield. |
| 371 Bain, Messrs,... | | | | | | | | 136 0 0 | | 136 0 0 | MOAT. |
| 372 Dickson, J. R.,... | | | | | | | | 139 0 0 | 137 1 3 | | Priorhill. |
| 373 Haddow, A. C.,... | | | | | | | | | | | Little Galla. |
| 374 Johnstone, P.,... | | | | | | | | | | | Ogg's Castle. |
| 375 Lithgow, R.,... | | | | | | | 133 1 0 | | | | Stanmore. |
| 376 Orr, Capt.,... | | 148 12 0 | | | | | | | | | Catcraigs. |
| 377 Steel, D.,... | | | | | | | | 140 0 0 | | | Teath. |
| 378 Todd, W.,... | | | | | | | | 140 0 0 | | | Logan. |
| 379 White, J.,... | | | | 149 0 0 | | | | | | | Coulterhall. |
| 380 Whyte, A. C.,... | | | 148 17 0 | | | | | | | | Rowantreehill. |
| 381 Elder, J.,... | | | 130 0 0 | | | | | | | | GILLHOUSE. |
| 382 Gillespie, R.,... | 125 0 0 | | | | | | | 130 0 0 | | | Cambuswallace. |
| 383 Hamilton, T.,... | | 129 10 0 | | | | | | | | | Scorryholm. |
| 384 Hamilton, W.,... | | | | | | | | | | | Brackenhill. |
| 385 Lang, T.,... | | | | | | | | 127 0 0 | | | Crossford. |
| 386 Lockhart, W.,... | | | | | | | 129 0 0 | | | | Nemphlar. |
| 387 Reid, J.,... | | 131 18 0 | | | | | | | | | Nellfield. |
| 388 Semple, W.,... | | | | | 131 0 0 | | | 130 0 0 | | | Greenridge. |
| 389 Thomson, Capt. J., | | | | | 125 0 0 | | | | | | Glendovran. |
| 390 Williamson, W. B., | | | | | | | | | | | Strancleugh. |

| VALUATION ROLL—1858-9. | Name | Biggar £ s. d. | Carluke £ s. d. | Carnwath £ s. d. | Coulter £ s. d. | Crawford £ s. d. | Douglas £ s. d. | Lanark £ s. d. | Lesmahagow £ s. d. | Libberton £ s. d. | Wiston £ s. d. | Properties |
|---|---|---|---|---|---|---|---|---|---|---|---|---|
| 391 | CARMICHAEL, T., | 119 10 0 | | | | | | | | | | KING'S INN. |
| 392 | Cuthbertson, M., | | | 120 0 0 | | | | | | | | Lindsaylands W. |
| 393 | Davidson, T., | 117 18 3 | | | | | | | | | | Bellfield. |
| 394 | Gillespie, Mrs, | | | | | | | | | | | Biggar Park. |
| 395 | Hamilton, A., | | | | | | | 120 0 0 | | | | Springbank. |
| 396 | Lockhart, W., | | | | | | | | 122 0 0 | | | Nemphlar. |
| 397 | Meikle, R., | | | | | | | | 119 0 0 | | | Auchren. |
| 398 | Pagau, J., M.D., | | | | | | | | 122 2 0 | | | Boghill & Rigbead. |
| 399 | Watson, W., | 120 0 0 | | | | | | | 131 0 0 | | | Midtoftcombs. |
| 400 | Wilson, J., | | | | | | | | 122 0 0 | | | Bellfield. |
| 401 | Dyce, J. N., | | | | | | | 96 0 0 | | | | CASTLEBANK. |
| 402 | Hamilton, Heirs of, | | | | | | | | | | | Tanhill. |
| 403 | Howieson, Lt.-Col., | | | | | | | 104 0 0 | 100 0 0 | | | Holmfoot. |
| 404 | M'Lagran, D., M.D, | 105 0 0 | | | | | | | | | | Stane. |
| 405 | Newbigging, W., | | | 104 2 4 | | | | | | | | Girdwoodend. |
| 406 | Liddell, P., | | | 119 0 0 | | | | | | | | Midhinshelwood. |
| 407 | Selkirk, A. & J., | | 119 0 0 | | | | | | | | | Minerals. |
| 408 | Semple, W., | | | | | | | | 113 0 0 | | | Letham. |
| 409 | Symington, W., | | | | | | | | 114 0 0 | | | Netherburn. |
| 410 | Todd, J., | | | | | | | | 163 0 0 | | | Birthwood. |
| 411 | ALLAN, A., | | | | | | | | | | | HILLHEAD. |
| 412 | Craig, W. C., | 97 7 9 | 98 0 0 | | | | | | | | | Burgh Lands. |
| 413 | Douglas, J., | 95 0 0 | | | | | | | | | | Auchmedan. |
| 414 | Forrest, J., | | | | | | | | 95 0 0 | | | East-tofts. |
| 415 | French, T., | | | 96 5 0 | | | | | | | | Garngower. |
| 416 | Kidd, Professor, | | | | | | | | 95 10 0 | | | Hinshelwood. |
| 417 | Orr, Capt. E. M., | | 100 0 0 | | | | | | | | | Catcraig. |
| 418 | Somerville, W., | | | | | | | | | | | Westermorshot. |
| 419 | Wilson, J. L., | | | 108 18 0 | | | | | | | | Nemplar, West. |
| 420 | Wilson, W., | | | 96 0 0 | | | | 101 0 0 | | | | Oldtown. |

| No. | Name | Biggar | Carluke | Carnwath | Crawford | Crawford-john | Douglas | Lanark | Lesmahagow | Walston | Wiston | Properties or Occupations |
|---|---|---|---|---|---|---|---|---|---|---|---|---|
| | VALUATION ROLL—1858-9. | £ s. d. | £ s. d. | £ s. d. | £ s. d. | £ s. d. | £ s. d. | £ s. d. | £ s. d. | £ s. d. | £ s. d. | |
| 421 | Dykes, A., | | 91 9 0 | | | | | | 92 0 | | | Ladeshead. |
| 422 | Forrest, A., | | | | | | | | 87 2 0 | | | Yeildshields. |
| 423 | Frame, R., M.D., | | | | | | | | 100 0 0 | | | Abbeygreen. |
| 424 | Hamilton, W., | | 85 10 0 | | | | | | | | | Loganbank. |
| 425 | Jack, J., | | | | | | | | 90 0 0 | | | Draper. |
| 426 | Lamb, J., | | | | | | | | | | | Boreland. |
| 427 | Logan, Mrs A., | | 99 0 0 | 91 10 0 | | | | | | | | Browshot. |
| 428 | Martin, J., Heirs of, | | 90 0 0 | | | | | | | | | Inn, Houses, etc. |
| 429 | Walker, J., late, | | | | | | | | | | | Eastquarter. |
| 430 | Wyld, Mrs, | 92 5 6 | | | | | | | | | | Merchant. |
| 431 | Allan, J., late, | | 85 0 0 | | | | | | | | | Tanhill. |
| 432 | Cadzow, W., | | 82 0 0 | | | | | | 85 0 0 | | | Craighead. |
| 433 | Hamilton, Capt. N., | | | | | 80 0 0 | | | | | | Kypeswaterhead. |
| 434 | Jack, W., | | | | | | | | | | | Carluke? |
| 435 | Lorimer, G., late, | | | | | | | | | | | Holmhead. |
| 436 | Mitchell, Rev. G., | | | | 80 0 0 | | | | | | | Throughburn. |
| 437 | Menzies, Jos., | | | | | | | | | | | Bellfield. |
| 438 | Semple, A., | | | 80 0 0 | | | | | 80 0 0 | | | Greenhill. |
| 439 | Simpson, J., | | | | | | | | | | | Browshot. |
| 440 | Thomson, M., | | 74 0 0 | | | | | | 80 0 0 | | | Whiteside. |
| 441 | Belhaven, Lord, | | | 81 0 0 | | | | | | | | Tupenhill. |
| 442 | Brown, W., | | | | | | 73 0 0 | | 73 19 0 | | | Abbeygreen. |
| 443 | Howieson, Mrs, | | | | | | | | | | | Crossburn. |
| 444 | Rowe, J., | | | | | | | | 74 2 0 | | | Weaving Agent. |
| 445 | Scott, J., | | | | | | | 75 0 0 | | | | Bellfield. |
| 446 | Semple, T., | | | | | | | | 78 7 6 | | | Darnfillan. |
| 447 | Tennent, J., | | | | | | | | 75 14 0 | | | Clydegrove. |
| 448 | Weir, C. S., | | | | | | | 73 5 0 | | | | Stanmore, North. |
| 449 | White, W., | | | | | | | | | 79 0 0 | | Blackcastle. |
| 450 | Wilson, A., late, | 75 0 0 | | | | | | | | | | Inn—Biggar. |

| VALUATION ROLL—1858-9. Name | Properties or Occupations | Biggar £ s. d. | Carluke £ s. d. | Carnwath £ s. d. | Carstairs £ s. d. | Crawford £ s. d. | Douglas £ s. d. | Lanark £ s. d. | Lesmahagow £ s. d. | Pettinain £ s. d. | Walston £ s. d. |
|---|---|---|---|---|---|---|---|---|---|---|---|
| 451 Brown, Rev. A., | Bereholm. | | 72 0 0 | | 70 0 0 | | | | 71 12 0 | | |
| 452 Gilchrist, R., | Stockwell. | | | | | | | | | | |
| 453 Grossart, W., | Newmains. | | 70 0 0 | 71 4 | | | | | 71 10 0 | | |
| 454 Hamilton, T., | Burnfoot. | | 70 0 0 | | | | | | 69 15 0 | | |
| 455 Henderson, J., | Crossford. | | 71 0 0 | | | | | | | | |
| 456 M'Glie, T., | Moatyett. | | 69 15 0 | | | | | | | | |
| 457 Marshall, W., | Tile-Works. | | 61 15 0 | | | | | | | | |
| 458 Rankine, A., | Shoemaker. | | 68 5 0 | 63 0 | | | | 68 6 0 | | | |
| 459 Ross, J., | Gowanside. | | 66 15 0 | | | | | 66 7 | | | |
| 460 Tudhope, J., | Heathlands. | | 66 15 0 | | | | | | 71 12 0 | | |
| 461 Barr, J. & T., | Law Colliery. | | | | | | | 68 6 0 | 68 0 0 | | |
| 462 Cassells, A., | Carrier. | | | | | | | | | | |
| 463 Cassells, J., | Carter. | | | | | | | | 64 0 0 | | |
| 464 Dixon, W., | Wilsontown. | | | | | | | | | | |
| 465 Easson, J., | Baker. | | | | | | | | | | |
| 466 Forrest, R., | Miller. | | | | | | | | | | |
| 467 Gray, D. M'Q., | Croftonhill. | | 61 15 0 | | | | | | | | |
| 468 Gray, S., | Mansefield. | | | | | | | | 0 0 | | |
| 469 Stein, J., | Kirkfieldbank. | | 60 0 0 | | | | | | 0 0 | | |
| 470 Thomson, Rev. V., | Castleyett. | | 60 10 0 | | | | | | | | |
| 471 Brown, T., | Kilnulls. | | | | | | | 65 11 | | | |
| 472 Brownlie, J., | Smith. | | | | | | | | | | |
| 473 Duncan, T., | Weaving Agent. | | | | | | | | | | |
| 474 Frame, Mrs J., | Easterseat. | | | | | | 64 7 | 62 10 | | | |
| 475 Gray, J., | Coldstream. | | | | | | | | 0 | | |
| 476 Lithgow, W., | Stanmore. | 62 11 0 | | | | | | | | | |
| 477 M'Gowran, W., | Oxgate. | | | | | | | 65 0 | 66 2 0 | | |
| 478 Stoddart, H., | Mousebank. | | | | | | | 62 10 | 60 10 0 | | |
| 479 Taylor, S., | Kirkfieldbank. | | | | | | | | | | |
| 480 Tudhope, J., | Midgarngour. | | | | | | | | | | |

| No. | VALUATION ROLL—1858-9.<br>NAME. | Biggar | | | Carluke | | | Carnwath | | | Carstairs | | | Douglas | | | Lamington | | | Lanark | | | Lesmahagow | | | Libberton | | | Wiston | | | Properties or Occupations. |
|---|---|---|---|---|---|---|---|---|---|---|---|---|---|---|---|---|---|---|---|---|---|---|---|---|---|---|---|---|---|---|---|---|---|---|
| | | £ | s | d | £ | s | d | £ | s | d | £ | s | d | £ | s | d | £ | s | d | £ | s | d | £ | s | d | £ | s | d | £ | s | d | |
| 481 | ARCHIBALD, J., | 55 | 12 | 0 | | | | | | | | | | | | | | | | | | | | | | | | | | | | | MERCHANT. |
| 482 | Gairns, A., | 57 | 10 | 0 | | | | | | | | | | | | | | | | | | | | | | | | | | | | | Skirling. |
| 483 | Gall, H., | 55 | 15 | | | | | | | | | | | | | | | | | | | | | | | | | | | | | | Milltown. |
| 484 | Gibson, R., | | | | 57 | 0 | 0 | | | | | | | | | | | | | | | | | | | | | | | | | | Lamington. |
| 485 | Grierson, Mrs, | | | | 60 | 0 | 0 | | | | | | | | | | | | | | | | | | | | | | | | | | Glasgow. |
| 486 | Hamilton, J., | | | | | | | | | | | | | | | | | | | | | | 55 | 0 | | | | | | | | | Easterseat. |
| 487 | M'Ghie, J., | | | | 55 | 0 | 0 | | | | | | | | | | | | | | | | | | | | | | | | | | Montyett. |
| 488 | Miller, J., | | | | 59 | 17 | 0 | | | | | | | | | | | | | | | | | | | | | | | | | | Claddenhill. |
| 489 | Selkirk, J., | | | | | | | | | | | | | | | | | | | | | | 56 | 0 | | | | | | | | | Beanshields. |
| 490 | Sinclair, J., Heirs of, | | | | | | | | | | | | | 52 | 17 | 0 | | | | | | | | | | | | | | | | | Whiteside. |
| 491 | BRADFUTE, CAPT., | | | | | | | 52 | 0 | 0 | | | | | | | | | | | | | | | | | | | | | | | LONDON. |
| 492 | Carmichael, T., | | | | | | | 50 | 0 | 0 | | | | | | | | | | | | | | | | | | | | | | | Craigiehall. |
| 493 | Carmichael, W., | | | | | | | | | | | | | | | | | | | 54 | 0 | 4 | | | | | | | | | | | Greenshield. |
| 494 | Gladstone, J., | 54 | | 0 | | | | | | | | | | | | | | | | | | | | | | | | | | | | | Dalerig. |
| 495 | Hastie, J., | | | | 52 | 14 | 0 | | | | | | | | | | | | | | | | | | | | | | | | | | Wright. |
| 496 | Marr, Rev. J. L., | | | | | | | | | | | | | 51 | 15 | 0 | | | | | | | | | | | | | | | | | Gallowhill. |
| 497 | Robinson, J., | | | | | | | | | | | | | | | | | | | 50 | 0 | 0 | | | | | | | | | | | Slater. |
| 498 | Selkirk, A., M.D., | | | | 50 | 15 | 0 | | | | | | | | | | | | | | | | | | | | | | | | | | Physician. |
| 499 | Shirlaw, J., | | | | 52 | 10 | 0 | | | | | | | | | | | | | | | | | | | | | | | | | | Auctioneer. |
| 500 | Vallance, Mrs, | 51 | | 0 | | | | | | | | | | | | | | | | | | | | | | | | | | | | | Stane. |
| 501 | CAPIE, J., | | | | 49 | 2 | 0 | | | | | | | | | | | | | | | | | | | | | | | | | | CATTLE-DEALER. |
| 502 | Cullen, W., M.D., | | | | | | | | | | | | | | | | | | | | | | 47 | 0 | | | | | | | | | Physician. |
| 503 | Frame, J., | | | | | | | | | | | | | | | | | | | | | | | | | | | | | | | | Birkhill. |
| 504 | Maxwell, T., | | | | | | | | | | | | | 48 | 18 | | | | | | | | | | | | | | | | | | Draper. |
| 505 | Meikle, R., | | | | | | | | | | | | | 49 | 12 | | | | | | | | | | | | | | | | | | Surgeon. |
| 506 | Nielson, J., | | | | 48 | 0 | 0 | | | | | | | | | | | | | | | | | | | | | | | | | | Castlehill. |
| 507 | Robertson, J., | 50 | | 0 | | | | | | | | | | | | | | | | | | | | | | | | | | | | | Builder. |
| 508 | Steel, T., | | | | | | | | | | | | | | | | | | | | | | 50 | 0 | | | | | | | | | Brae. |
| 509 | Steel, W., | | | | | | | | | | | | | | | | | | | | | | 50 | 0 | | | | | | | | | Riddoch Brae. |
| 510 | Tudhope, J., | | | | | | | | | | | | | | | | | | | | | | 50 | 0 | | | | | | | | | Whitesidehill. |

| Valuation Roll—1858-9. Name. | Biggar. £ s. d. | Carluke. £ s. d. | Carmichael. £ s. d. | Carnwath. £ s. d. | Coulter. £ s. d. | Crawford. £ s. d. | Lanark. £ s. d. | Lesmahagow. £ s. d. | Symington. £ s. d. | Wiston. £ s. d. | Properties or Occupations. |
|---|---|---|---|---|---|---|---|---|---|---|---|
| 511 Craig, Mrs C., | 48 0 | ... | ... | ... | ... | ... | ... | ... | ... | ... | Netherwell. |
| 512 Forrest, J., | ... | 46 0 0 | ... | ... | ... | ... | ... | ... | ... | ... | Kilcadzow. |
| 513 Gibson, W., | 45 0 0 | ... | ... | ... | ... | ... | ... | ... | ... | ... | Edinburgh. |
| 514 Gray, J., | ... | 47 0 0 | ... | ... | ... | ... | ... | ... | ... | ... | Coldstream. |
| 515 Hamilton, J., | ... | 48 0 0 | ... | ... | ... | ... | ... | ... | ... | ... | Mavisbank. |
| 516 Leggett, J., | ... | 46 12 6 | ... | ... | ... | ... | ... | ... | ... | ... | Wishaw. |
| 517 M'Ghie, Misses, | ... | ... | ... | ... | ... | 44 5 0 | ... | ... | ... | ... | Craighead. |
| 518 Murray, D., | ... | ... | ... | ... | ... | ... | ... | 45 0 0 | ... | ... | Crawfordlaird. |
| 519 Somerville, W., | ... | 45 0 0 | ... | ... | ... | ... | ... | ... | ... | ... | Coldstream. |
| 520 Waugh, S., | ... | ... | ... | ... | ... | ... | ... | ... | ... | ... | Tutoside. |
| 521 Donald, W., | ... | 43 0 0 | ... | ... | ... | ... | ... | ... | ... | ... | Waterside. |
| 522 Fraser, R., | ... | ... | ... | ... | ... | 43 0 0 | ... | ... | ... | ... | Gallagreen. |
| 523 Goodfellow, A., | ... | 44 12 0 | ... | ... | ... | ... | ... | ... | ... | ... | Crawfordlaird. |
| 524 Martin, W., | ... | ... | ... | ... | ... | 42 0 0 | ... | ... | ... | ... | Newknowe. |
| 525 Morrison, W., | ... | ... | ... | ... | ... | ... | ... | 44 0 0 | ... | ... | Calcutta. |
| 526 Shirlaw, S., | ... | 44 0 6 | ... | ... | ... | ... | ... | ... | ... | ... | Auctioneer. |
| 527 Somerville, J., | ... | 42 0 6 | ... | ... | ... | ... | ... | ... | ... | ... | Craighend. |
| 528 Steel, W., | 42 0 0 | ... | ... | ... | ... | ... | ... | ... | ... | ... | Vet.-Surgeon. |
| 529 Tait, M., | 41 10 0 | ... | ... | ... | ... | ... | ... | ... | ... | ... | Grocer. |
| 530 Young, J., | ... | ... | ... | ... | ... | ... | ... | ... | ... | ... | Rosehill. |
| 531 Alexander, M., | ... | ... | ... | ... | ... | ... | ... | 43 0 0 | ... | ... | Ironmonger. |
| 532 Cringan, R., | ... | 41 1 0 | ... | ... | ... | ... | ... | 41 5 0 | ... | ... | Broker. |
| 533 Kelly, J., | ... | ... | ... | ... | ... | ... | ... | 41 10 0 | ... | ... | Shoemaker. |
| 534 Lockhart, J., | ... | ... | ... | ... | ... | ... | 40 0 0 | ... | ... | ... | Nemplar. |
| 535 Murdoch, J., | ... | ... | ... | ... | ... | ... | ... | 41 1 0 | ... | ... | Kirkfieldbank. |
| 536 Ross, J., late, | ... | ... | ... | 41 0 0 | ... | ... | ... | ... | ... | ... | Houses, etc. |
| 537 Somerville, J., | ... | ... | ... | ... | ... | ... | 41 10 0 | ... | ... | ... | Carluke. |
| 538 Stewart, R., | ... | ... | ... | ... | ... | ... | ... | 40 0 0 | ... | ... | Orchardville. |
| 539 Waugh, Dr., | ... | ... | ... | ... | ... | ... | ... | ... | 45 0 0 | ... | Hazelbank. |
| 540 Wilson, J., | ... | 40 0 0 | ... | ... | ... | ... | ... | ... | ... | ... | Quarrier. |

| Valuation Roll—1858-9. | Name. | Biggar. | | | Carluke. | | | Crawford. | | | Carnwath. | | | Douglas. | | | Lanark. | | | Lesmahagow. | | | Libberton. | | | Symington. | | | Wiston. | | | Properties or Occupations. |
|---|---|---|---|---|---|---|---|---|---|---|---|---|---|---|---|---|---|---|---|---|---|---|---|---|---|---|---|---|---|---|---|---|---|
| | | £ | s. | d. | £ | s. | d. | £ | s. | d. | £ | s. | d. | £ | s. | d. | £ | s. | d. | £ | s. | d. | £ | s. | d. | £ | s. | d. | £ | s. | d. | |
| 541 | Brocket, A., | 38 | 0 | 0 | | | | | | | | | | | | | | | | 38 | 0 | 0 | | | | | | | | | | NETHERFAULD. |
| 542 | Brown, J., | | | | | | | | | | | | | | | | | | | 40 | 0 | 0 | | | | | | | | | | Middlemains. |
| 543 | Burton, T., | | | | | | | | | | | | | | | | | | | | | | | | | | | | | | | Hawksland. |
| 544 | Dick, W., | | | | 39 | 17 | 0 | | | | | | | | | | | | | | | | | | | | | | | | | Miller. |
| 545 | Dick, J., | | | | 38 | 10 | 0 | | | | | | | | | | | | | | | | | | | | | | | | | Houses. |
| 546 | Hunter & Co., | | | | | | | 40 | 0 | 0 | | | | | | | | | | | | | | | | | | | | | | Woollen Mill. |
| 547 | Marshall, P., | | | | 38 | 1 | 0 | | | | | | | | | | | | | 40 | 0 | 0 | | | | | | | | | | Contractor. |
| 548 | Monkland Iron Co., | | | | | | | | | | | | | | | | | | | | | | | | | | | | | | | Collier Houses. |
| 549 | Pairman, R., | 39 | 0 | 0 | | | | | | | | | | | | | | | | | | | | | | | | | | | | Collector of Taxes. |
| 550 | Turnbull, M., | 38 | 6 | 0 | | | | | | | | | | | | | | | | 40 | 0 | 0 | | | | | | | | | | Eastfield. |
| 551 | Baur, R., | | | | 36 | 0 | 0 | | | | | | | 36 | 11 | 0 | | | | | | | | | | | | | | | | TAILOR. |
| 552 | Hunter, J., | 36 | 0 | 0 | | | | | | | | | | | | | | | | | | | | | | | | | | | | Merchant. |
| 553 | Hunter, W., | | | | | | | | | | | | | | | | | | | | | | | | | | | | | | | Baker. |
| 554 | Johnstone, R., | 35 | 15 | 0 | | | | | | | | | | | | | | | | 35 | 8 | 0 | | | | | | | | | | Portobello. |
| 555 | Johnstone, W., | 36 | 0 | 0 | | | | | | | | | | | | | | | | | | | | | | | | | | | | Merchant. |
| 556 | Paterson, W., | | | | | | | | | | | | | | | | | | | | | | | | | | | | | | | Kirkfieldbank. |
| 557 | Pettigrew, J., | | | | 36 | 17 | 0 | | | | | | | | | | | | | | | | | | | | | | | | | Houses. |
| 558 | Reid, J., | 36 | 0 | 0 | | | | | | | | | | | | | | | | 37 | 11 | 6 | | | | | | | | | | Burgh Lands. |
| 559 | Shaw, W., | | | | | | | | | | | | | | | | | | | 36 | 0 | 0 | | | | | | | | | | Newton. |
| 560 | Smith, A., | 35 | 0 | 0 | | | | | | | | | | | | | | | | | | | | | | | | | | | | Factor. |
| 561 | Bell, J., | | | | | | | | | | | | | | | | | | | | | | | | | | | | | | | FULLBURN. |
| 562 | Cadzow, J., | | | | | | | | | | 35 | 0 | 0 | | | | | | | 35 | 0 | 0 | | | | | | | | | | Burnfoot. |
| 563 | Harvey, W., | | | | | | | | | | | | | | | | | | | 34 | 10 | 0 | | | | | | | | | | Kirkfield. |
| 564 | Liddell, A., | | | | 35 | 0 | 0 | | | | | | | | | | | | | | | | | | | | | | | | | Innkeeper. |
| 565 | Lightbody, J., | | | | | | | | | | | | | | | | | | | | | | | | | | | | | | | Drums. |
| 566 | M'Gowran, M., | 35 | 0 | 0 | | | | | | | | | | | | | | | | | | | | | | | | | | | | Baukhouses. |
| 567 | Pairman, A., | | | | | | | | | | | | | | | | | | | 34 | 9 | 8 | | | | | | | | | | Draper. |
| 568 | Ross, J., | | | | 34 | 10 | 0 | | | | 34 | 0 | 0 | | | | | | | | | | | | | | | | | | | Quebec. |
| 569 | Stewart, G., | | | | | | | | | | | | | | | | | | | | | | | | | | | | | | | Hinshelwood. |
| 570 | Telfer, J., | | | | | | | | | | | | | | | | | | | 36 | 10 | 0 | | | | | | | | | | Sun Inn. |

k

| Valuation Roll—1858-9. Name. | Biggar £ s. d. | Carluke £ s. d. | Carnwath £ s. d. | Crawford £ s. d. | Douglas £ s. d. | Lamington £ s. d. | Lanark £ s. d. | Lesmahagow £ s. d. | Symington £ s. d. | Wiston £ s. d. | Properties or Occupations. |
|---|---|---|---|---|---|---|---|---|---|---|---|
| 571 Baxter, J., | | 32 18 0 | 32 15 0 | | | | | | | | Houses. |
| 572 Brown, Miss C., | | | 32 — 0 | | | | | | | | Braehead. |
| 573 Cuthbertson, Mrs, | | | | | | | | | | | Cannend. |
| 574 Meikle, J., | | 33 2 0 | | | | | | 32 — 0 | | | Baker. |
| 575 Pettigrew, W., | | | | | | | | | | | Late Innkeeper. |
| 576 Rae, J., | 32 — 0 | | | | | | | | | | Weaver. |
| 577 Shand, W. A., | | 34 0 0 | | | | | 32 — 0 | | | | Peasehill. |
| 578 Shaw, J., | | | | | | | 33 — 6 | | | | Braidwood. |
| 579 Todd, J., | | | | | | | | | | | Logan. |
| 580 Wilson, A., | | 31 17 0 | | | | | | 31 — 0 | | | Wright. |
| 581 Baird, M., | | 32 0 0 | | | | | | | | | House, etc. |
| 582 Burns, J., | | | | | | | | 31 5 | | | Highcross. |
| 583 Field, J., | | | | | | | 32 — 0 | | | | Brooklands. |
| 584 Graham, J., | 31 15 | | | | | | | 30 14 0 | | | Baker. |
| 585 Kean, J., | | | | | | | | | | | Baker. |
| 586 Reid, R., | | 31 19 0 | | | | | | 32 0 0 | | | Shoemaker. |
| 587 Scott, Mrs, | | | | | | | | 31 17 0 | | | Abbeygreen. |
| 588 Stewart, A., | 32 0 0 | | | | | | | | | | Mason. |
| 589 Vallance, J., | 31 10 0 | | | | | | | 30 0 0 | | | Saddler. |
| 590 Wilson, J., | 30 0 0 | | | | | | | 30 0 0 | | | Houses. |
| 591 Ballantyne, J., | | | | | | | | 30 18 0 | | | Houses. |
| 592 Barr, T., | | | | | | | | | | | Park. |
| 593 Brown, W., | | | | | | | | 30 10 0 | | | Graystone. |
| 594 Easton, Mrs, | | | | | | | | | | | Crossford. |
| 595 Gibson, T., | 30 0 0 | | | | | | | 30 10 0 | | | Stonehead-park. |
| 596 Hamilton, D., | | | | | | | | | | | North Belfield. |
| 597 Hastie, M., | | 30 0 0 | | | | | | | | | Muirfoot. |
| 598 Morton, J., | | | | | | | | | | | Kirkmuirhill. |
| 599 Somerville, M., | | 30 0 0 | 30 3 0 | | | | | | | | Houses. |
| 600 Spence, G., | | 30 0 0 | | | | | | | | | Thornlie Muir. |

| No. | Valuation Roll—1858-9. NAME. | Biggar (£ s. d.) | Carluke (£ s. d.) | Carnwath (£ s. d.) | Carstairs (£ s. d.) | Crawford-john (£ s. d.) | Douglas (£ s. d.) | Dunsyre (£ s. d.) | Lanark (£ s. d.) | Lesmahagow (£ s. d.) | Walston (£ s. d.) | Properties or Occupations. |
|---|---|---|---|---|---|---|---|---|---|---|---|---|
| 601 | Donald, R., | | 30 0 0 | | | | 30 · 0 | | | 30 0 0 | | CAPEHALL. |
| 602 | Lean, S., | | | | | | | | | 30 0 0 | | Greystone. |
| 603 | Scott, T. R., M.D., | | | | 30 0 0 | | | | | | | City Glasgow Bank. |
| 604 | Smellie, W., | | | 30 3 0 | | | | | | | | Flesher. |
| 605 | Somerville, M., | | | | | | | | | 30 0 0 | | Edinburgh. |
| 606 | Somerville, Mrs., | | | | | | | | | 30 0 0 | | Strawfrank. |
| 607 | Templeton, W., | | 30 0 0 | | | | | | | | | Crossford. |
| 608 | Thomson, J., | | | | | | | | | 30 0 0 | | Netherfauld House. |
| 609 | Weir, J., | | | | | | | | | 30 0 0 | | Eastside. |
| 610 | Wilson, J., | | | | | | | | | 29 0 0 | | Crossford. |
| 611 | Burton, W., | | 28 0 0 | | | | | | | 28 19 0 | | BANKHEAD. |
| 612 | Frame, J., | | 29 16 0 | | | | | | | | | Smith. |
| 613 | Gilchrist, J., | | 28 0 0 | | | | | | | | | Clothier. |
| 614 | Hamilton, T., | | | | | | | | | 29 10 0 | | Scoular Hall. |
| 615 | Lang, M., | | | | | | | | | | | Houses. |
| 616 | Leiper, J., | | | | | | | | | | | Baker. |
| 617 | Rae, J., | | | | | | | | 29 15 | 28 10 0 | | Towhead. |
| 618 | Reid, A., | | | | | | 29 12 0 | | | | | Bereholmmill. |
| 619 | Watson or Smith, | | | | | | | | | | 28 0 0 | Kilncroft. |
| 620 | White, J., | | | | | | | | | | | Nether Urd. |
| 621 | Anderson, Mrs, | | | 26 15 0 | 27 12 0 | | | | | | | INNKEEPER. |
| 622 | Boyd, F., | | 27 5 0 | | | | | | | 27 · 5 | | Labourer. |
| 623 | Carmichael, J., | | 27 12 6 | 28 · · | | | | | | | | Shoemaker. |
| 624 | Graham, A., | | 28 0 0 | | | | | | | | | Millroad. |
| 625 | Hamilton, R., | | | | | | | | | | | Mason. |
| 626 | Lang, Mrs, | | | | | | | | | | | Houses. |
| 627 | Stewart, G., | | | | | | | | | 26 10 0 | | Stobwood-dyke. |
| 628 | Twaddle, W., | | | | | | | | | 27 10 0 | | Mason. |
| 629 | Wharrie, J., | | | | | | | | | | | Pathhead House. |
| 630 | Wilson, A., | 27 11 0 | | | | | | | | | | Wright. |

| No. | Name | Biggar £ s. d. | Carluke £ s. d. | Carnwath £ s. d. | Carstairs £ s. d. | Crawford-john £ s. d. | Douglas £ s. d. | Dunsyre £ s. d. | Lanark £ s. d. | Lesma-hagow £ s. d. | Syming-ton £ s. d. | Properties or Occupations. |
|---|---|---|---|---|---|---|---|---|---|---|---|---|
| 631 | Aitken, J., | … | … | … | … | … | … | … | … | … | … | Miller. |
| 632 | Cassels, J., | … | 26 0 0 | … | … | … | … | … | … | … | … | Houses. |
| 633 | Clark, J. & G., | 26 0 0 | … | 26 6 0 | … | … | … | … | … | … | … | Houses. |
| 634 | Forrest, J., | … | 26 0 0 | … | … | … | 26 10 0 | … | … | … | … | Rosemount. |
| 635 | Goldie, Mrs J., | … | … | … | … | … | … | … | 26 0 0 | … | … | Houses. |
| 636 | Jack, G., | … | 26 0 0 | … | … | … | … | … | … | … | … | Boreland. |
| 637 | Lockhart, Misses, | … | 26 0 0 | … | … | … | … | … | … | … | … | Nemphlar. |
| 638 | M'Min, H., | … | 26 0 0 | … | … | … | … | … | … | … | … | Ironmonger. |
| 639 | Orr, Capt., | … | 26 0 0 | … | … | … | … | … | … | … | … | Burnbank. |
| 640 | Stoddart, A., | 26 0 0 | … | … | … | … | … | … | … | … | … | Hillhead. |
| 641 | Browslie, P., | … | 25 0 0 | 25 0 0 | … | … | … | … | … | … | … | Shoemaker. |
| 642 | Elder, J., | … | 25 15 0 | 0 | … | … | … | … | … | … | … | Westyard-houses. |
| 643 | Ferguson, S., | … | 25 18 0 | … | … | … | … | … | … | 25 15 0 | … | Shoemaker. |
| 644 | Jack, J., | … | 25 2 0 | 0 | … | … | … | … | … | 24 17 0 | … | Weaver. |
| 645 | M'Owat, W., | … | 21 17 0 | … | … | … | … | … | … | … | … | Innkeeper. |
| 646 | Meikle, J., | … | … | … | … | … | … | … | … | … | … | Kirkmuirhill. |
| 647 | Pillans, R., | … | … | … | … | … | … | … | … | … | … | Draper. |
| 648 | Selkirk, Misses, | … | … | … | … | … | … | … | … | … | … | Houses. |
| 649 | Somerville, J., | … | 25 0 0 | 25 0 0 | … | 24 10 0 | … | … | … | 25 0 0 | … | Westyard-houses. |
| 650 | Symington, W., | … | … | … | … | … | … | … | … | … | … | Ponfeigh. |
| 651 | Cathcart, A., | … | … | … | … | … | … | … | … | … | … | Abington. |
| 652 | Fleming, Capt., | 24 15 0 | … | … | … | … | 24 10 0 | … | … | … | … | Custom's-houses. |
| 653 | Graham, J., | … | 24 5 0 | … | … | … | … | … | … | … | … | Houses. |
| 654 | Inglis, Rev. R., | … | … | … | … | … | … | … | … | … | … | Houses. |
| 655 | Muir, R., | … | 24 9 0 | … | … | … | … | … | … | 24 15 0 | … | Kirkfieldbank. |
| 656 | Noble, J., | 24 13 0 | … | … | … | … | … | … | … | 24 7 0 | … | Skirling. |
| 657 | Pinkerton, J., | … | … | … | … | … | … | … | … | … | … | Hazelbank. |
| 658 | Prentice, A., | 24 10 0 | … | … | … | … | … | … | … | … | … | Sawyer. |
| 659 | Summers, J., | 24 10 0 | … | … | … | … | … | … | … | … | … | Saddler. |
| 660 | Wilson, G., | 24 17 0 | … | … | … | … | … | … | … | … | … | Wright. |

Valuation Roll—1858-9.

| No. | Name | Biggar £ s. d. | Carluke £ s. d. | Carnwath £ s. d. | Carstairs £ s. d. | Crawfordjohn £ s. d. | Douglas £ s. d. | Dunsyre £ s. d. | Lanark £ s. d. | Lesmahagow £ s. d. | Wiston £ s. d. | Properties or Occupations |
|---|---|---|---|---|---|---|---|---|---|---|---|---|
| 661 | Affleck, A., | | | | | | 24 3 0 | | | | | Houses. |
| 662 | Brown, H., | | | 23 10 0 | | | | | | | | Ironmonger. |
| 663 | Brown, J., sen., | | 22 0 0 | | | | | | | | | Pothall. |
| 664 | Burns, Mrs H., | | | | | | | | | | | Highcross. |
| 665 | Hepburn, J., | 23 10 0 | | | | | | | | 24 0 0 | | Carrier. |
| 666 | Izzett, M., | | | | | | | | | | | Innkeeper. |
| 667 | Russell, W., | 23 0 0 | | | | | | | | 24 0 0 | | Shoemaker. |
| 668 | Shearer, J., | | | | | | | | | 24 0 0 | | Netherhouse. |
| 669 | Simpson & Baird, | | | | | | | | | | | Coalburn. |
| 670 | Summers, J., | 24 0 0 | | 23 0 0 | | | | | | | | Surgeon. |
| 671 | Alexander, R., | | | | | | | | | | | Wright. |
| 672 | Douglas, J., | | 22 15 0 | | | | | | | | | Surgeon. |
| 673 | Hamilton, W., | | 23 15 0 | | | | 23 0 0 | | | 23 9 0 | | Nemphlar. |
| 674 | Hutchison, J., | | | | 23 0 0 | | | | | | | Innkeeper. |
| 675 | Meikle, Misses, | | | 23 10 0 | | | | | | 23 8 0 | | Abbeygreen. |
| 676 | Russell, J., | | | 23 10 0 | | | | | | | | Houses. |
| 677 | Somerville, J., | | | 23 5 0 | | | | | | | | Houses. |
| 678 | Steel, W., sen., | | | | | | | | | | | Weaver. |
| 679 | Waddell, J., | 23 17 0 | 22 17 0 | | | | | | | | | Houses. |
| 680 | Wilson, S., | | | | | 22 15 0 | | | | | | Toll Contractor. |
| 681 | Brown, C., | | 22 7 0 | 22 10 0 | | | | | | | | Merchant. |
| 682 | Prentice, A., | 22 17 0 | | | | | | | | | | Wright. |
| 683 | Rae, J., | | 22 10 6 | | | | | | | | | Shoemaker. |
| 684 | Rankine, G., | | | | | | | | | | | Shoemaker. |
| 685 | Renton, A., | | 22 10 0 | | | | | | | | | Merchant. |
| 686 | Scott, W., | | | | | | | | | | | Shoemaker. |
| 687 | Somerville, W., | | 22 1 0 | | | | | | | 22 0 0 | | Houses. |
| 688 | Somerville, J., | | | | | | | | 22 4 6 | | | So. St Leonards. |
| 689 | Wilson, J., | | 22 10 0 | | | | | | | | | Carrier. |
| 690 | Young, J., | | | 21 0 0 | | | | | | | | Merchant. |

| VALUATION ROLL.—1858-9. NAME. | Biggar. £ s. d. | Carluke. £ s. d. | Carnwath. £ s. d. | Carstairs. £ s. d. | Crawford-john. £ s. d. | Douglas. £ s. d. | Dunsyre. £ s. d. | Lanark. £ s. d. | Lesma-hagow. £ s. d. | Walston. £ s. d. | PROPERTIES OR OCCUPATIONS. |
|---|---|---|---|---|---|---|---|---|---|---|---|
| 691 Arnot, T., | | 21 0 0 | | | | 22 0 0 | | | 21 14 7 | | MASON. |
| 692 Black, M., | | | | | | | | | | | Braehead. |
| 693 Cadzow, W., | | | | | | | | 14 16 6 | 21 7 0 | | Miner. |
| 694 Fleming, J., | | | 22 0 0 | | | | | | | | Maddermains. |
| 695 Paterson, A., | | 22 0 0 | | | | | | | | | Merchant. |
| 696 Pinkerton, Mrs, | | | | | | | | | 21 10 0 | | Crossford. |
| 697 Rankine, D. R., | | | | | | | | | 20 0 0 | | Surgeon. |
| 698 Smith, J., | | | | | | | | | | | Weaver. |
| 699 Somerville, J., | 22 0 0 | 22 0 0 | | | | | | 21 0 0 | | | Craighead. |
| 700 Wyld, J., | | | | | | | | | | | Spencer's Park. |
| 701 Cassie, J., | | | 21 0 0 | | | | | | 21 0 0 | | STEEL'S CROSS. |
| 702 Dalziel, G., | | | | | | | | | | | Merchant. |
| 703 Dymock, T., | | | | | | | | | | | Yardhouses. |
| 704 Frame, W., | | | 21 0 0 | | | | | | | | Quarrier. |
| 705 Gardner, R., | | 21 0 0 | | | | | | | 21 0 6 | | Smith. |
| 706 M'Ghie, W., | | 21 0 0 | | | | | | | 21 0 6 | | Wellburn. |
| 707 Magee, J., | | | | | | | | | | | Bishopbrae. |
| 708 Prentice, J., | | | | | | | | | | | Houses. |
| 709 White, J., heirs of, | | | | 22 10 0 | | | | | | | Houses. |
| 710 Wyld, J., | 20 17 6 | | | | | | | | 20 0 0 | | Ward's Park. |
| 711 Brown, C., | 20 0 0 | | | | | | | | | | MERCHANT. |
| 712 Clark, A., | | | | | | | | | 21 10 0 | | Houses. |
| 713 Cranstoun, L., | | | | | | 20 5 0 | | | 20 10 0 | | Burnside. |
| 714 Lawson, A., | | | | | | | | | | 22 10 0 | Wellbank. |
| 715 Moore, T., | | | | | | | | | 20 0 0 | | Merchant. |
| 716 Peat, M., | | | | | | | | | | | Dillarburn. |
| 717 Steele, T., | | | | | | | | | | | Smith. |
| 718 Tweedie, J., | 20 0 0 | | | | | | | | | | Draper. |
| 719 Veitch, M., | | | | | | | | | | | Linnville. |
| 720 Walker, D., | | 20 0 0 | | | | | | | | | Spirit-dealer. |

| Valuation Roll.—1858-9. Name. | Biggar £ | s. | d. | Carluke £ | s. | d. | Carnwath £ | s. | d. | Carstairs £ | s. | d. | Douglas £ | s. | d. | Dunsyre £ | s. | d. | Lanark £ | s. | d. | Lesma-hagow £ | s. | d. | Walston £ | s. | d. | Wiston £ | s. | d. | Properties or Occupations. |
|---|---|---|---|---|---|---|---|---|---|---|---|---|---|---|---|---|---|---|---|---|---|---|---|---|---|---|---|---|---|---|---|
| 721 Brown, Mrs J., | | | | | | | | | | | | | 19 | 19 | 0 | | | | | | | 20 | | 0 | | | | | | | MERCHANT. |
| 722 Caledonian Rail Co. | | | | 20 | | 0 | | | | | | | | | | | | | | | | | | | | | | | | | Houses. |
| 723 Dyce & M'Kinnell, | | | | | | | | | | | | | | | | | | | | | | | | | | | | | | | Wood Merchants. |
| 724 Forrest, W., | | | | | | | | | | | | | | | | | | | | | | | | | | | | | | | Nemphlar. |
| 725 Hamilton, D., | | | | | | | 20 | 0 | 0 | | | | 20 | | 0 | | | | 20 | | 0 | | | | | | | | | | Brachead. |
| 726 M'Grouther, A., | | | | | | | 20 | 0 | 0 | | | | | | | | | | | | | | | | | | | | | | Tile-work. |
| 727 Nimmo, Mrs, | | | | | | | | | | | | | | | | | | | | | | | | | | | | | | | Greenwell. |
| 728 Ovens, T., | 20 | | 0 | | | | | | | | | | | | | | | | | | | | | | | | | | | | House and Land. |
| 729 Pairman, R., | 20 | | 0 | | | | | | | | | | | | | | | | | | | | | | | | | | | | Surgeon. |
| 730 Paterson, W., | | | | 20 | | 0 | 20 | | 0 | | | | | | | | | | | | | | | | | | | | | | Merchant. |
| 731 Pinkerton, W., | | | | | | | 19 | 15 | 0 | | | | | | | | | | | | | | | | | | | | | | FLESHER. |
| 732 Prentice, A., sen., | | | | | | | | | | | | | | | | | | | | | | | | | | | | | | | Merchant. |
| 733 Rankine, A., | | | | 20 | 0 | 0 | | | | | | | | | | | | | | | | | | | | | | | | | House. |
| 734 Scoular, R., | | | | 19 | 12 | 0 | | | | | | | | | | | | | | | | 19 | 8 | 0 | | | | | | | Merchant. |
| 735 Somerville, J., | | | | 20 | 0 | 0 | | | | | | | | | | | | | | | | 19 | 5 | 0 | | | | | | | Craighead. |
| 736 Springall, M., | | | | 20 | 0 | 0 | | | | | | | | | | | | | | | | | | | | | | | | | Spirit-dealer. |
| 737 Thomson, G., | | | | | | | | | | | | | | | | | | | | | | | | | | | | | | | Wright. |
| 738 Watson, D., | 20 | | 0 | | | | | | | | | | | | | | | | | | | 20 | | 0 | | | | | | | Newton. |
| 739 Watson, A. W., | | | | | | | | | | | | | | | | | | | | | | | | | | | | | | | Sunnyside. |
| 740 Wiseman, J., | | | | | | | | | | 19 | 5 | 0 | | | | | | | | | | | | | | | | | | | Watchmaker. |
| 741 Brownlie, J., | 19 | 5 | | 19 | | 0 | | | | | | | | | | | | | | | | | | | | | | | | | SMITH. |
| 742 Cree, Mrs, late, | | | | | | | | | | | | | | | | | | | | | | | | | | | | | | | Nursery. |
| 743 Forrest, J., | | | | | | | | | | | | | 19 | 10 | 0 | | | | | | | | | | | | | | | | Carrier. |
| 744 Girdwood, Mrs, | | | | | | | 19 | 13 | 0 | | | | | | | | | | 19 | 8 | 0 | | | | | | | | | | Merchant. |
| 745 Haddow, Mrs A., | | | | | | | | | | | | | | | | | | | | | | | | | | | | | | | Houses. |
| 746 Lindsay, D., | | | | | | | | | | | | | | | | | | | | | | 19 | | 0 | | | | | | | Builder. |
| 747 Muir, T., | | | | | | | | | | | | | | | | | | | | | | | | | | | | | | | Mason. |
| 748 Park, W., | | | | | | | | | | | | | 19 | | 0 | | | | | | | | | | | | | | | | Postmaster. |
| 749 Robertson, J., | | | | 19 | | 0 | | | | | | | 19 | | 0 | | | | | | | | | | | | | | | | Houses. |
| 750 Sandilands, J., | | | | | | | | | | | | | 19 | | 6 | | | | | | | | | | | | | | | | Houses. |

| Valuation Roll—1858-9. Names of Farms. | Pstate. | Biggar. £ s. | Car-michael £ s. | Carn-wath. £ s. | Car-stairs. £ s. | Coulter. £ s. | Craw-ford. £ s. | Craw-ford-john. £ s. | Doug-las. £ s. | Dun-syre. £ s. | Lam-ington. £ s. | Lesma-hagow. £ s. | Libber-ton. £ s. | Names of Tenants. |
|---|---|---|---|---|---|---|---|---|---|---|---|---|---|---|
| 751 Baitlaws, etc., | 249 | | | | | | | | | | 670 15 | | | Denholm, Alex. |
| 752 Crookedstane, | 255 | | | | | | 557 3 | | 724 1 | | | | | Hunter, R., heirs. |
| 753 Gateside, | 241 | | | | | | 710 0 | | | | | | | Gillespie, J. |
| 754 Glenochar, | 253 | | | | | | | | | | | | | Hunter, R., heirs. |
| 755 Libberton Mains, | 244 | | | | | | 603 17 | | | | | | 705 13 | Brown, J. |
| 756 Normangill, | 255 | | | | | | 782 10 | | | | | | | Vassie, Richard. |
| 757 Nunnerie, etc., | 274 | | | | | | | | 659 0 | | | | | Wilson, John. |
| 758 Parkhall, etc., | 211 | | | | | | | | | | | | | Gillespie, T. |
| 759 Wandell Mill, | 241 | | | | | | | | | | 572 0 | | | Black, James. |
| 760 Weston and Todholes, | 244 | | | | | | | | | | | | | Whyte, W. |
| 761 Boghall, etc., | 294 | 470 0 | | | | | | | | 592 12 | | | | Brown, J. |
| 762 Byretown, | 263 | | | | | | | | | | | 527 16 | | Dykes, R. |
| 763 Callendean, | 244 | | | | | | | | | | | | | Hamilton, W. |
| 764 Castlemains, | 255 | | | | | 531 10 | | | | | | | | Tweedie, David. |
| 765 Coulterallers & Snaip, | 258 | | | | | | 420 10 | | | | | | | Watson, Andrew. |
| 766 Hartsyde, | 241 | | | 440 0 | | | | | | | | | | Lindsay, Eben. |
| 767 Lampits, East & West, | 244 | | | | | | | | | | 532 0 | | | French, James. |
| 768 Overburn, etc., | 249 | | | 500 0 | | | | | | | 481 0 | | | Gibson, W. |
| 769 Water-Meetings, etc., | 253 | | | | | | 550 0 | | | | | | | Wilson, William. |
| 770 Whelphill&Harecleugh | 243 | | | | | | 450 0 | | | | | | | Fletcher, Robert. |
| 771 Burnhead and Park, | 244 | | | 380 0 | 395 0 | | | | | | | | | French, W. |
| 772 Corbiehall, | 261 | | | | | | | | | | | | | Fleming, J. |
| 773 Draffan, etc., | 251 | | | | | | | | | | | | | Russell, A. |
| 774 Drumalbin, | 244 | 410 0 | | | | | | | | | | 385 0 | | Paterson, Wm. |
| 775 Dunsyre, | 241 | | | | | | | | | 421 10 | | | | Ray, Isabella. |
| 776 Glentaggart, | 241 | | | | | | | | 420 0 | | | | | Paterson, J. |
| 777 Kirkhope, | 252 | | | | | | 425 0 | 412 0 | | | | | | Milligan, J. |
| 778 Nethercleugh, etc., | 255 | | | | | | 421 4 | 395 0 | | | | | | Hogg, P. |
| 779 Netherton, | 242 | | | | | | | | | | | | | French, T. |
| 780 Stonehill, | 242 | | | | | | | | | | | | | Paterson, J. |

**VALUATION ROLL—1858-9.**

| No. | Names of Farms. | Estate. | Big-gar. | Car-luke. | Carn-wath. | Car-stairs. | Cov-ing-ton. | Coul-ter. | Craw-ford. | Craw-ford-john. | Dol-phin-ton. | Doug-lus. | Dun-syre. | Lan-ark. | Lib-ber-ton. | Petti-nain. | Sym-ing-ton. | Wal-ston. | Wis-ton. | Names of Tenants. |
|---|---|---|---|---|---|---|---|---|---|---|---|---|---|---|---|---|---|---|---|---|
| 781 | Boathaugh, etc., | 250 | | | | | | | | | | | | 364 | | | | | | Jack, Messrs. |
| 782 | Boreland, | 244 | | | | | | | | | | | 368 | | | | | 378 | | Hamilton, M. & T. |
| 783 | Dunsyre Mains, | 244 | | | | | | | | | | | 360 | | | | | | | Brown, A. |
| 784 | East-town, | 244 | | | | | | | | | | | | | | | | | | Brown, T. |
| 785 | Midlock, | 255 | | | | | | | 360 | | | | | | | | | | | Johnstone, Repr's. of |
| 786 | Muirhouse, | 244 | | | | | | 352 | | | | | | | | | | | | Purdie, T. & J. |
| 787 | Nesbit, | 259 | | | | | | | | | | | | | | | | | | Watson, J. |
| 788 | Strawfrank, | 261 | | | | 384 | | | | | | | | | | | | | | Alison, T. |
| 789 | Townhead, | 211 | | | | | | | | | | | | | 380 | | | | | Gibson, A. |
| 790 | Westraw Mains, | 247 | | | | | | | | | | | | | 370 | | | | | Hunter, W. |
| 791 | Birniehill, | 315 | | | | 321 | | | | | | | | | | 366 | | | | Brown, J. |
| 792 | Bonnington Mains, | 250 | | | | | | | | | | | | 310 | | | | | | Cunningham, J. |
| 793 | Calla, | 244 | | | 348 | | | | | | | | | | | | | | | Fleming, A. |
| 794 | Columbia and Hills, | 261 | | | | 320 | | | | | | | | | | | | | | Elder, J. |
| 795 | Elsrickle, | 308 | | | 299 | | | | | | | | | | | | | 360 | | Greenshields, D. |
| 796 | Glengeith, | 253 | | | | | | | | | | 337 | | | | | | | | Hunter, R. |
| 797 | Harelaw, | 245 | | | | 340 | | | | | | | | | | | | | | Alison, A. |
| 798 | Hazelside, | 241 | | | | | | | | | | | | | | | | | | Blaikie, J. |
| 799 | Libberton Mill, | 244 | | | | | | | | | | | | | 312 | | | | | Somerville, A. |
| 800 | Overtown, | 244 | | | | | | | | | | | 357 | | | | | | | Shaw, T. |
| 801 | Anniston, | 272 | | | | | | | | 300 | | | | | | | 309 | | | Craig, Mrs. |
| 802 | Blackhill, | 242 | | | | | | | | | | | | | | | | | | French, T. |
| 803 | Carnwath Mill, | 244 | | | | | | | | | | | | | | | | | | Smith, H. |
| 804 | Coulterlaugh, | 257 | | | | | | 300 | | | | | | | | | | | | Inch, J. |
| 805 | Glencaple, | 253 | | | | | | | 300 | | | | | | | | | | | French, J. |
| 806 | Hillend, | 304 | | | | | | | | | | | | | | | | | | Waddell, J. & W. |
| 807 | Hillhead, | 244 | | | | | | | | | | | | | | | | | 300 | Stoddart, A. |
| 808 | Howburn, | 283 | | | | | 290 | | | | | | | | | | | | | White, J. A. |
| 809 | Meadowflat, | 244 | | | | | 300 | | | | | | | | | | | | | Lindsay, J. |
| 810 | Townhead and Loch, | 262 | | | | | | | | | 301 | | | | | | | 318 | | Kay, J. & R. |

*l*

| No. | Names of Farms | Names of Tenants, Messrs. | Wis-ton £ | Wal-ston £ | Petti-nain £ | Les-maha-gow £ | Lan-ark £ | Lam-ing-ton £ | Dun-syre £ | Doug-las £ | Dol-phin-ton £ | Craw-ford-john £ | Craw-ford £ | Coul-ter £ | Car-stairs £ | Carn-wath £ | Car-mich-ael £ | Car-luke £ | Dig-gar £ | Estate |
|---|---|---|---|---|---|---|---|---|---|---|---|---|---|---|---|---|---|---|---|---|
| 811 | Abington, Nether, | Tweedie, T. | | | | | | | | | | 262 | | | | | | | | 255 |
| 812 | Bankhead, | Jack, T. | | | | | | | | | | | | | | 285 | | 285 | | 244 |
| 813 | Campshead, | Grieve, Michael. | | | | | | | | | | | 280 | | | | | | | 252 |
| 814 | Gilkerscleugh Mains, | Inch, T. | | | | | | | | | | 275 | | | | | | | | 255 |
| 815 | Hyndford, | Cunningham, A. | | | | | | | | | | | | | | | | | | 321 |
| 816 | Kileadzow, Hill of, | Alison, T. | | | | | 280 | | | | | | | | | | | 285 | | 244 |
| 817 | Roberton Mains, | Waugh, Esq., J. | | | | | | | | | 275 | | | | | | | | | 262 |
| 818 | Sornfallow, | Coubrough, D., heirs. | 280 | | | | | | | | | | | | | | | | | 242 |
| 819 | Stonehill, | Thorburn, R. | | | 275 | | | | | | | | | | | | 280 | | | 242 |
| 820 | Strathern-house, | Paterson, A. | | | | | | | | | | | | | | | | | | 265 |
| 821 | Bagshouse&Todhills, | Tarvit, R. | | | | | | | | | | | | | | | | | | 247 |
| 822 | Burnhouse, | Plenderleith, R. | 268 | | | | | | | | | | | | | | | | | 255 |
| 823 | Crawfordjohn, | Watson, Edward. | | | | | | | | | | 264 | | | | | | | | 251 |
| 824 | Draffan, South, | Pate, T. | | | | 270 | | | | | | | | | | | | | | 259 |
| 825 | Howcleugh, Upper, | Hogg, P. | | | | | | | | | | | 260 | | | | | | | 249 |
| 826 | Laughone, | Stoddart, T. | | | | 272 | | 261 | | | | | | | | | | | | 288 |
| 827 | Lesser Linn, | Carruthers, Mrs B. | | | | | | | | | | | | | | | | | | 249 |
| 828 | Littlegill, | Neilson, J. & J. | | | | | | 260 | | 266 | | | | | | | | | | 241 |
| 829 | Parish-holm, | Willison, John. | | | | | | | | | | 275 | | | | | | | | 252 |
| 830 | Whitecleugh, Upper, | Willison, J. | | | | 250 | | | | | | | | | | | | | | 251 |
| 831 | Auchrobert, | Brown, J. | | | | 250 | | | | | | | | | | | | | 260 | 242 |
| 832 | Barnhills, | Affleck, D. & W. | | | | | | | | | | | | | | | | | | 290 |
| 833 | Biggar Shiels, | King, W. | | | | | | | 255 | | | | | | | | | | | 245 |
| 834 | Cleghorn, | Callan, A. | | | | | 255 | | | | | | | | | | | | | 241 |
| 835 | East and West-hills, | Brown, jun, J. | | | | | | | | | | | | | | | | | | 244 |
| 836 | Eastyardhouse, | Wilson, J. | | | | | | | | | | | | | | 252 | | | | 247 |
| 837 | Midholm of Grange, | Johnstone, W. | | | 255 | | | | | | | | | | | | | | | 244 |
| 838 | Newbigging Mains, | Weir, W. & D. | | | | | | | | | | | | | | 255 | | | | 326 |
| 839 | Springfield, | Wilson, J. | | | | | | | | | | | | | | | | 255 | | 244 |
| 840 | Walston Place, | Stodart, J. | | 250 | | | | | | | | | | | | | | | | 244 |

VALUATION ROLL.—1858-9.

| No. | Names of Farms | Estate | Big. gar | Car. luke | Car. michael | Carn. wath | Car. stairs | Cov. ing. ton | Craw. ford | Craw. ford. john | Dun. syre | Lam. ing. ton | Lan. ark | Les. maha. gow | Lib. er. ton | Petti. nain | Sym. ing. ton | Wal. ston | Wis. ton | Names of Tenants |
|---|---|---|---|---|---|---|---|---|---|---|---|---|---|---|---|---|---|---|---|---|
| | | | £ | £ | £ | £ | £ | £ | £ | £ | £ | £ | £ | £ | £ | £ | £ | £ | £ | |
| 841 | Chesterhall, | 245 | | | | | | | | | | 240 | | | | | | | 240 | Stoddart, W. |
| 842 | Coldchapel, | 249 | | | | | | | | | | | | 246 | | | | | | Hadlow, J. |
| 843 | Cumberhead, North, | 297 | | | | | | | | | | | | 240 | | | | | | Sandilands, G. |
| 844 | Cumberhead, South, | 302 | | | | | | | | | | | | | | | | | | Sandilands, W. |
| 845 | Eastfield, | 247 | | | | | | | | | | | | | | 249 | | | | Lindsay, W. |
| 846 | Green, | 259 | | | | | | | | | | | | | | | | | | Gray, J. |
| 847 | Persielands, | 278 | 243 | | | 212 | | | | | | | | | | | | | | Hamilton, T. |
| 848 | Shortcleugh, | 256 | | | | | | | 240 | | | | | | | | | | | Paterson, Esq., A. |
| 849 | Walston, Wester, | 244 | | | | | | | | | | | | | | | | | | Brown, J. |
| 850 | Whiteshaw, | 269 | | | | | | | | | | | | | | | | 242 | | Gault, J. |
| 851 | Carmichael Policy, | 247 | | 250 | 239 | | | | | | | | | | | | | | | French, J. |
| 852 | Coblehaugh, | 250 | | | | | | | | | | | | | | | | | | Muirhead, J. |
| 853 | Covington Mains, | 244 | | | | | | 236 | | | | | 236 | | | | | | | Lindsay, Hugh. |
| 854 | Fallside, | 242 | | | | 240 | | | | | | | | | | | | | | Gillespie, T. |
| 855 | Haughs, etc., | 244 | | | | | | | | | | | | | | | | | | Ritchie, J. |
| 856 | Mains-Loanhead, | 249 | | | | | | | | | | | | | | | | | | Tweedie, J. |
| 857 | Newton of Wiston, | 249 | | | | | | | | | | 232 | | | | | | | 240 | Reid, J. |
| 858 | Tower of Cormiston, | 260 | | | | | | | | | | | | | | | | | 238 | Gibson, J. |
| 859 | Westhall, | 244 | | | | | | | | 232 | 230 | | | | | | | | | Brown, sen., J. |
| 860 | West-town, | 295 | | | | | | | | | | | | | 237 | | | | | Greenshields, A. |
| 861 | Abington, Over, | 255 | | | | | | | | 231 | | | | | | | | | | Inch, R. |
| 862 | Rent, | 254 | | | | | | | | | | | | 240 | | | | | | Dykes, A. |
| 863 | Boghouse, | 255 | | | | | | | | | | | | 220 | | | | | | French, J. |
| 864 | Cleghornmill, | 245 | | | | | | | | | | | 227 | | | | | | | Cassels, A., |
| 865 | Crimpcramp, | 259 | | | | | | | 225 | 230 | | | | | | | | | | Paterson, Esq., R. |
| 866 | Greenburn, | 242 | | | | | | | | | | | | | | | | | | Willison, J. |
| 867 | Midtown & Woodhead, | 254 | | | | | | | | | | | | 227 | | | | | | Wilson, J. |
| 868 | Nethertown, | 261 | | | | | 234 | | | | | | | | | | | | | Scott, W. |
| 869 | Rowhead and Biggar, | 000 | 230 | | | | | | | | | | | | | | | | | Brown, D. |
| 870 | Townfoot, | 296 | | | | | | | | | | | | | | | 230 | | | Gibson, L. |

VALUATION ROLL—1858-9.

| Names of Farms | Estate | Biggar | Carluke | Carmichael | Carnwath stairs | Covington | Coulter | Crawford | Crawfordjohn | Dolphinton | Douglas | Dunsyre | Lanark | Lesmahagow | Libberton | Symington | Wiston | Names of Tenants |
|---|---|---|---|---|---|---|---|---|---|---|---|---|---|---|---|---|---|---|
| 871 Broomerside, | 241 | | | | | | | | | | 221 | | | | | | | Greenshields, A. |
| 872 Debog, | 241 | | | | | | | | | | 220 | | | | | | | M'Kinlay, J. |
| 873 Fingland, | 254 | | | | | | | 220 | | | | | 215 | | | | | Rae, W. & W. |
| 874 Jerviswoodmill, | 293 | 220 | | 210 | | | | | | | | | | | | | | Stodart, D. |
| 875 Lindsaylands, | 000 | | | | | | | | | | | | | | | | | Cuthbertson, J. |
| 876 Mossplat, | 000 | | | | 220 | | | | | | 220 | | | | | | | Forrest, A. |
| 877 Poniel, | 241 | | | | 221 | | | | | | 225 | | | | | | | Newbigging, T., heirs |
| 878 Ryeflat, | 261 | | 204 | | | | | | | | | | | | | | | Aitken, J. |
| 879 West-town & Jancfield, | 241 | | | | | | | | | | | | | | | | | Inglis, J. |
| 880 Wolfclyde, | 272 | 210 | | | | | | | | | | | | | | | | Pairman, A. |
| 881 Browsbank, | 264 | 210 | | | | | | | | | | | | | | | | Smellie, H. |
| 882 Eastend, | 261 | | | | 214 | 211 | 214 | | 215 | | 212 | | | | | | | Black, R. |
| 883 Kennox, | 241 | | | | | | | | | | 212 | | | | | | | Wilson, J. |
| 884 Mountherrick, | 255 | | | | | | | | | | | | | | | | | French, Mrs. |
| 885 North Mains, | 244 | | | | | | | | | | | | | | | | | Forrest, J. |
| 886 Ponfeigh Place & Moor, | 247 | | | 210 | | | | | | | | | | | | | | Weir, C. |
| 887 Quothquhan, | 260 | | | | | | | | | | | | | | 215 | | | Ritchie, G. |
| 888 Shawhead, | 242 | | | 215 | | | | | 210 | | | | | | | | | French, J. |
| 889 Spittal, | 244 | | | 216 | | | | | | | | | | | | | | Cochrane, W. |
| 890 Thornhill and Nether, | 247 | | | | | | | | | | | | | | | | | Cadzow, R. |
| 891 Bogside, | 249 | | | 202 | | | | 205 | | | | | | | | | | Stewart, A. |
| 892 Broomhill, | 259 | | | 200 | | | | | | | | | | | | | | Cuthbertson, J. |
| 893 Clengh, | 275 | | | | | | | | | | | | | | | | | Ninmo, T. |
| 894 Elvanfoot, | 255 | | | 200 | | | | | | | | | | | | | | Anderson, T., heirs |
| 895 Fallhills & Muirfoot, | 245 | | 209 | | | | | | | | | | | | | | | Wallace, R. |
| 896 Law Farm, | 247 | | | | | | | | | | | | | | | | | Wallace, J. |
| 897 Meadowcoats, | 242 | | | | | | | | | | | | | | | | 200 | M'Kinlay, J. |
| 898 Nemphlar, West, | 244 | | | | | | | | | | | | 204 | | | | | Jack, J. |
| 899 Quothquhan, | 260 | | | | | | | | | | | | | | 210 | | | Sanderson, J. |
| 900 Westmillrig, | 245 | | | | | | | | | | | | | | | | 204 | Pratt, A. |

| No. | NAMES OF FARMS | Estate | Big-gar | Car-luke | Car-mich-ael | Carn-wath | Car-stairs | Cov-ing-ton | Craw-furd | Craw-furd-john | Dol-phin-ton | Doug-las | Dun-syre | Lan-ark | Let-mala-gow | Lib-ber-ton | Petti-nain | Sym-ing-ton | Wis-ton | NAMES OF TENANTS |
|---|---|---|---|---|---|---|---|---|---|---|---|---|---|---|---|---|---|---|---|---|
| | | £ | £ | £ | £ | £ | £ | £ | £ | £ | £ | £ | £ | £ | £ | £ | £ | £ | £ | |
| 901 | Caerwood, | 278 | 196 | | | | | | | | | | | | | | | | | Coubrough, A. |
| 902 | Caruwath, | 244 | | | | 190 | | | | | | | | | | | | | | Anderson, J. |
| 903 | Dykeford, etc., | 244 | | | | | | | | | | | 190 | | | | | | | Anderson, D. & W. |
| 904 | Eastertown, | 255 | | | | | | | | 199 | | | | | | | | | | French, Edward. |
| 905 | Eastwood, | 289 | | | | | | | | | | | | | | | | | | Allan, P. |
| 906 | Glespin, West, | 241 | | | | | | | | | | 198 | | | | | | | | Twedie, David. |
| 907 | Greenshields, | 276 | | | | | | | | | | | | | 190 | 190 | | | | M'Lean, W. |
| 908 | Westfield, | 248 | | | | | | | | | | | | | | | | 195 | | Waugh, J. |
| 909 | West Shields, | 263 | | | | | | | | | | | | | | | | | | Murdoch, A. |
| 910 | Westside, | 262 | | | | | | | | | 200 | | | | 199 | | | | | Black, H. |
| 911 | Auchtygemmel, | 251 | | | | | | | | | | | | | 185 | | | | 180 | Carruthers, T. |
| 912 | Bodinlee, | 242 | | | | | | | | | | | | | | | | | | Gillespie, T. |
| 913 | Clarkston, | 288 | | | | | | | | 184 | | | | | 180 | | | | | Prentice, J. |
| 914 | Craighead, | 255 | | | | | | | | 176 | | | | | | | | | | Hunter, H., heirs of. |
| 915 | Goat and Liscleugh, | 255 | | | | | | | | 187 | | | | | | | | | | Hunter, H., heirs of. |
| 916 | Greenfield, | 298 | | | | | | | | | | | | | | | | | | Dalgleish, J. |
| 917 | Kirkfield Mains, | 260 | | | | | | | | | | | | | 181 | | | | | Harvie, W. |
| 918 | Parkhouse, | 248 | | | | | | | | | | | | | | 183 | | | | Gibson, J. |
| 919 | Symington Mains, | 284 | | | | 185 | | | | | | | | | | | | 182 | | Stobo, Mrs J. |
| 920 | Woolfords, | 254 | | | | | | | | | | | | | | | | | | Somerville, J. |
| 921 | Auchenheath, | 251 | | | | | | 180 | | | | | | | 180 | | | | | Baxter, W. |
| 922 | Auchtygemmel, Nether, | 244 | | | | | | | | | | | | | 180 | | | | | Weir, F. |
| 923 | Covington Mill, | 332 | | | | | | | | 180 | | | | | | | | | | Lindsay, A. |
| 924 | Glentewing, | 293 | | | | | | | | | | | | | | | | | | Watson, W. |
| 925 | Jerviswood, | 242 | | | | | | | | | | | | 180 | | | | | | Cadzow, J. |
| 926 | Moat, | 247 | | | 180 | | | | | | | | | | | | | | | Gillespie, T. |
| 927 | Netherton, | 244 | | | | | | | | | | | | | | | | | | Lamb, J., heirs of. |
| 928 | Newsteading, | 265 | | | | | | | | | | | | 180 | | | | | | Irving, W. |
| 929 | North Faulds, | 277 | | | | | | | | | | | | 180 | | | | | 184 | Ritchie, G. |
| 930 | Shallowhead, | 277 | | | | | | | | | | | | | | | | | 176 | Plenderleith, Mrs. |

VALUATION ROLL—1858-9.

| VALUATION ROLL—1858-9. | NAMES OF FARMS | Estate | Dig-gar | Car-luke | Car-much-ael | Cara-wath | Car-stairs | Coul-ter | Craw-f.rd | Craw-ford-john | Dol-phin-ton | Doug-las | Dun-syre | Lan-ark | Les-maha-gow | Lib-ber-ton | Pet-ti-num | Sym-ing-ton | Wis-ton | NAMES OF TENANTS |
|---|---|---|---|---|---|---|---|---|---|---|---|---|---|---|---|---|---|---|---|---|
| 931 | Baitlaw, | 330 | | | | | | | | | | | | | | 175 | | | | Watson, A. |
| 932 | Hellstane, | 243 | | 175 | | | | | | | | | | | 175 | | | | | Gibson, J. & R. |
| 933 | Blackwoodyard, | 254 | | | | 175 | | | | | | | | | | | | | | M'Gowran, W. |
| 934 | Forthwest, | 314 | 174 | | | | | | | | | | | | | | | | | Anderson, J. |
| 935 | Langlees, | 335 | | | | | | | | | | | | | | | | | | Jackson, A. |
| 936 | Newtonfoot, | 241 | | | | | | | | | | 175 | | | | | | | | Gall, J. |
| 937 | Newtonhead, | 241 | | | | | | | | | | 175 | | | | | | | | Lawcock, A. |
| 938 | Uddington, | 241 | | | | | | | | | | 175 | | | | | | | | Gall, J. |
| 939 | Westraw, part of, | 247 | | | | | | | | | | | | | | | | | | Twaddle, J. |
| 940 | Wolfcrooks, | 241 | | | | | | | | | | | | | | | 175 | | | Kirkwood, J. |
| 941 | BROADFIELD, | 248 | | | | | | | | | | 173 | | | | | | | | Aitken, J. |
| 942 | Crossdyke, | 247 | | | | | | | | | | | | | | | | | | Core, A. |
| 943 | Haughhead, | 262 | | | | | | | | | 170 | | | | | | | | | Kay, sen., J. |
| 944 | Heathland, | 355 | | | | 170 | | | | | | | | | | | | | | Hamilton, T. |
| 945 | Hindshaw, South, | 249 | | 170 | | 170 | | | | | | | | | | | | | | Henderson, J. |
| 946 | Kirkgreen, | 282 | | | | | | | | | | | | | | | | | | Coltness Iron Co. |
| 947 | Mauldslie Moor, | 287 | | 170 | | 170 | | | | | | | | | | | | | | Scott, T. |
| 948 | Milton-Lockhart Mill, | 251 | | | | | 170 | | | | | | | | | | | | | Portous, R. |
| 949 | Newhouse, | 261 | | 171 | 171 | | | | | | | | | | | | | | | Dalziel, J. |
| 950 | Waterside, etc. | 265 | | | | | | | | | | | | | 172 | | | 172 | | Barr, J. & J. |
| 951 | BIGGAR SHIEL MAINS, | 290 | 160 | | | | | | | | | | | | | | | | | Brown, W. |
| 952 | Cormiston, | 369 | | | | | | | | 160 | | | | | | | | | | Williamson, A. |
| 953 | Crawfordjohn Mill, | 255 | | | | | | | | | | | | | | | | | | Galloway, J. |
| 954 | Eastfield, | 272 | | | | | | 168 | | 160 | | | | | | | | | | Gladstone, A. |
| 955 | Glendorch, | 253 | | | | | | | | | | | | | | | | | | Stewart, Patrick. |
| 956 | Hillridge, | 278 | | | | | | | | 166 | | | | | | | | | | M'Kenzie, M. |
| 957 | Kirkland, | 244 | 164 | | | | | | | | | | | | | | | | | Allan, J. |
| 958 | Netherhill & part Gles- | 242 | | | | | | | | | | | 141 | | | | | | | Haddow, P. |
| 959 | Windales,...........[pin | 360 | | | | | | | | | | | | | | | | | | Muirhead, A. |
| 960 | Wintermoor, | 264 | 160 | | | | | | | | | | | | | 160 | | 170 | | Lang, P. |

## VALUATION ROLL—1858-9.

| No. | Names of Farms. | Estate. | Big. gar. | Car. luke. | Carn. wath. | Car. stairs. | Cov. ing. ton. | Coul. ter. | Craw. ford. | Craw. ford. john. | Dol. phin. ton. | Doug. las. | Dun. syre. | Lan. ark. | Les. maha. gow. | Lib. ber. ton. | Petti. nain. | Sym. ing. ton. | Wis. ton. | Names of Tenants. |
|---|---|---|---|---|---|---|---|---|---|---|---|---|---|---|---|---|---|---|---|---|
| | | | £ | £ | £ | £ | £ | £ | £ | £ | £ | £ | £ | £ | £ | £ | £ | £ | £ | |
| 961 | Blackhill, | 279 | | | | | | | | | | | | | 155 | | | | | Stoddart, J., Heirs. |
| 962 | Candybank, | 264 | 157 | | | | | | | | | | | | | | | | | Brown, J. |
| 963 | Coulter Park, South, | 258 | | | | | | 156 | | | | | | | | | | | | Finlayson, T. |
| 964 | Greenfield, | 370 | | | 153 | | | | | | | | | | | | | | | Somerville, J. |
| 965 | Kirkton, | 255 | | | | | | | 154 | | | | | | | | | | | Hunter, G. |
| 966 | Middlehouse, | 366 | | 160 | | | | | | | | | | | | | | | | Cassells, G. |
| 967 | Numphlar, East, | 244 | | | 158 | | | | | | | | | | | | | | | Cadzow, W. |
| 968 | Newbigging Mill, | 244 | | | | | | | | | | | | 155 | | | | | | White, J., late, heirs. |
| 969 | Northholm of Grange, | 247 | | | | | 155 | | | | | | | | | | | | | Smith, J. |
| 970 | Sheriff-Flats, | 247 | | | 152 | | | | | | | | | | | | | | | Lindsay, Mrs. |
| 971 | Auchengray, | 320 | | | | | | | | | | 151 | | | 151 | | 161 | | | Meikle, R. |
| 972 | Birkwood Mains, | 265 | | | | | | | | | | | | | | | | | | Tudhope, G. |
| 973 | Broomfield & Rigside, | 241 | | | | | | | | | | | | | | | | | | Swan, J. |
| 974 | Greenhall, | 247 | | | | | | 152 | | | | | | | | | 150 | | | Taylor, R. |
| 975 | Hangingshaw, Nether, | 258 | | | | | | | | | | | | | | | | | | Watson, P. |
| 976 | Kilcadzow, Holl of, | 214 | | 150 | | | | | | | 150 | | | | | | | | | Forrest, A. |
| 977 | Kirkhouse, | 262 | | | | | | | | | | | | | | 152 | | | | Brown, R. |
| 978 | Whitecastle, West, | 000 | | | | | | | | | | | | | | | | | | Gibson, Brothers. |
| 979 | Woodend, | 282 | | | 152 | | | | | | | | | | 152 | | | | | Brown, J. |
| 980 | Woodhead, | 393 | | | | | | | | 145 | | | | | | | | | | Tudhope, R. |
| 981 | Birkcleugh, | 256 | | | 145 | | | | | | | | | | | | | | | Lammie, J. |
| 982 | Buchtknowe, | 273 | | | | | | | | | | | | | | 145 | | | | Todd, A. |
| 983 | Burnfoot, | 260 | | | | 145 | | | | | | | | | | | | | | Ritchie, D. |
| 984 | Cockridge, | 261 | | | | | | | | | | | | | | | | | | Scott, A. |
| 985 | Corramore, | 334 | | | | | | | | | | | | | | | | | | Brownlie, A. |
| 986 | Garrellwood, | 251 | | | | | | | | | | | | | 150 | | | | | Stoddart, T. |
| 987 | Mosscastle, | 255 | | | | | | | | 150 | | | | | 150 | | | | | Coke, W. |
| 988 | Mountain and Law, | 273 | | | 150 | | | | | | | | | | | | | | | Smith, J. |
| 989 | Northloanhead, | 281 | | | 153 | | | | | | | | | | | | | | | Howieson, J. |
| 990 | Sandylandsgate, | 244 | | 150 | | | | | | | | | | | | | | | | Hamilton, W. |

## Valuation Roll—1858-9.

| Estate | Names of Farms | Big. gar. | Car. luke. | Car. mich. ael. | Carn. wath. | Car. stairs. | Cov. ing. ton. | Coul. ter. | Craw. ford. | Craw. ford. john. | Doug. las. | Lam. ing. ton. | Lan. ark. | Les. maha. gow. | Lib. ber. ton. | Petti. nain. | Sym. ing. ton. | Wis. ton. | Names of Tenants. |
|---|---|---|---|---|---|---|---|---|---|---|---|---|---|---|---|---|---|---|---|
| 991 | Andershaw, | 241 | | | | | | | | | 142 | | | | | | | | Willison, J. |
| 992 | Auchenglen, part of, | 244 | | | | | | | | | | | 144 | 140 | | | | | Shirlaw, G. |
| 993 | Birkenhead, | 300 | | | | | | | | | | | | | 143 | | | | Meikle, J. |
| 994 | Cormiston House, | 331 | 145 | | | | | | | | | | | | | | | | Cleghorn, T. |
| 995 | Gillbank, | 246 | | | | | | | | | | | | | | | | | Brown, J. & J. |
| 996 | Glentewing, Easter, | 255 | | | 145 | | | | | 140 | | | | | | | | | Coke, J. |
| 997 | Halltown-Nemphlar, | 244 | | | | | | | | | | | | | | | | | Elder, J. |
| 998 | Muirhall, | 285 | | | | | | | | | | | | | | | | | Steel, T. |
| 999 | Polmonkshead, | 361 | | | | | | | | | 142 | | 147 | | | | | | Symington, Mrs, heirs |
| 1000 | Townhead, | 254 | | | | | | | | | | | | | | | | | Anderson, M. |
| 1001 | Baronald, | 345 | | | | | | | | | | | | 145 | | 136 | | | Smith, J. |
| 1002 | Cloburn, | 247 | | | | | | | | | | | 135 | | | | | | Paterson, Mrs J. |
| 1003 | Craigmethan, | 242 | | | | | | | | | | | | 135 | | | | | Wilkie, J. |
| 1004 | Eastsidewood, | 282 | | | 135 | | | | | | | | | | | | | | Todd, J., late, heirs. |
| 1005 | Hardgatehead, | 292 | | | 142 | | | | | | | | | | | | | | Sibbald, S. |
| 1006 | Moat, | 371 | | | | | | 136 | | | | | | 136 | | | | | Barr, Messrs. |
| 1007 | Pettinain-bank, | 247 | | | | | | | | | | | | | | 141 | | | Irvine, J., heirs of. |
| 1008 | Sandylands, | 242 | | | | | | | | | | | | | | | | | Forrest, J. |
| 1009 | Symington Mill, | 296 | | 140 | | | | | | | | | | | | | | | Thorburn, D. |
| 1010 | Unthank, | 258 | | | | 135 | | 136 | | | | | | | | | 140 | | Bertram, J. |
| 1011 | Boghall, | 244 | | | | | | | | | | | | | | | | | Somerville, J. |
| 1012 | Brownridge, | 249 | 135 | | | | | | | | | | | | | | | | Black, D. |
| 1013 | Carluke, | 286 | 132 | | | | | | | | | | | | | | | | Cassells, A. |
| 1014 | Dillars, | 288 | | | | | | | | | | | | | | | | | Neilson, D. |
| 1015 | Lambcatoh & Skylaw, | 273 | | | | 135 | | | | | | | | 135 | | | | | Baird, A. |
| 1016 | Middleholm & Bent, | 267 | | | | | | | | | | | | 131 | 134 | | | | Hamilton, A. |
| 1017 | Quothquhan, | 260 | | | | | | | | | | | | | | | | | Gray, J. |
| 1018 | Southfield, South, | 251 | | | | | | | | | | | | 135 | | | | | Pollock, W. |
| 1019 | Westerhills, | 247 | | | | | | | | | | | | | | | | | Clarkson, D. |
| 1020 | Westerhouse, | 341 | 133 | | | | | | | | | | | | | 133 | | | Wright, J. & J. |

VALUATION ROLL—1858-9.

| No. | Names of Farms | Estate | Big-gar £ | Car-luc. £ | Carn-wath £ | Car-stairs £ | Cov-ing-ton £ | Cou-ter £ | Craw-ford £ | Craw-ford-john £ | Dol-phin-ton £ | Doug-las £ | Lam-ing-ton £ | Lan-ark £ | Les-maha-gow £ | Lib-ber-ton £ | Petti-nain £ | Sym-ing-ton £ | Win-ton £ | Names of Tenants |
|---|---|---|---|---|---|---|---|---|---|---|---|---|---|---|---|---|---|---|---|---|
| 1021 | BOGHILL & RIGHEAD, | 398 | | | | | | | | | | | | | 126 | | | | | TUDHOPE, J. |
| 1022 | Boreland, | 251 | | | | | | | | | | | | | 130 | | | | | M'Ghie, J. & T. |
| 1023 | Brownhill, | 244 | | | | | | | | | | | | | | 130 | | | | Weir, R. |
| 1024 | Brownriggs, | 247 | | | | | | | | | | | | | | | 130 | | | Greenshields, J. |
| 1025 | Castlehill, | 244 | | | | | | | | | | | | | | | | 130 | | Robb, J. |
| 1026 | Eastfield, | 272 | | | | | | | | | | | | | 140 | | | | | Linton, J. |
| 1027 | Fence, | 242 | | | | | | | | | | | | 130 | | | | | | Hamilton, J. |
| 1028 | Gillhouse & pt. of Stob- | 381 | | | | | | | | | | | | | | | | | 132 | Greenshields, A. |
| 1029 | Muirhead, ..... [wood, | 242 | | | | | | | | | | | | | 135 | | | | | Aitken, W. |
| 1030 | Southfield, North, | 251 | | | | | | | | | | | | | 130 | | | | | Stewart, A. |
| 1031 | COALBURN, | 266 | | | | | | | | | | | | 130 | | | | | | Watson, T. |
| 1032 | Eastforth, | 275 | | | 130 | | | | | | | | | | | | | | | M'Culloch, G. |
| 1033 | Fullwood, | 244 | | 130 | | | | | | | | | | | | | | | | Wilson, Mrs. |
| 1034 | Glendowran, | 389 | | | 130 | | | | | | | | | | | | | | | Williamson, J. |
| 1035 | Greenhill, | 242 | | | | | | | | | | | | | | | | | 131 | Sadleir, J. |
| 1036 | Mossbank, | 255 | | | | | | | | 131 | | | | | | | | | | Law, J. |
| 1037 | Newtown, | 254 | | | | | | | | | 130 | | | | | | | | | Gillespie, J. |
| 1038 | Townfoot, | 262 | | | | | | | 130 | | | | | | | | | | | Thomson, T. & J. |
| 1039 | Turf-foot, | 340 | | | | | | | | 130 | | | | | | | | | | Watson, J. |
| 1040 | Underbank, | 251 | | | | | | | | | | | | | 126 | | | | | Scott, G. |
| 1041 | AUCHTOOL, | 251 | | | | | | | | | | | | | 125 | | | | | Duncan. J. |
| 1042 | Blackwoodyard, | 254 | | 125 | | | | | | | | | | | | | | | | M'Gowran, T. |
| 1043 | Candymill, | 244 | | | | | | | | | | | | | 125 | | | | | Smith, J. |
| 1044 | Hillend, | 251 | | | | | 131 | | | | | | | | | | | | | Tennant, J. |
| 1045 | Muirhouse, | 247 | | | | | | | | | | | | | 130 | | | | | Thomson, M., heirs. |
| 1046 | Muirsland, | 251 | | 130 | | | | | | | | | | | | | | | | Weir, J. |
| 1047 | Raes, | 246 | | | | | | | | | | | | | 130 | | | | | Cassels, J. |
| 1048 | Scorryholm, | 424 | | | | | | | | | | | | | 130 | | | | | Anderson, W. |
| 1049 | Shortcleugh, North, | 253 | | | | | | | 130 | | | | | | | | | | | Gibson, T. |
| 1050 | Stoneyburn, | 255 | | | | | | | 131 | | | | | | | | | | | Cranstoun, A. |

**VALUATION ROLL—1858-9.**

| No. | Names of Farms | Estate | Big. gar | Car. luke | Car. mich. ael | Carn. wath | Car. stairs | Cov. ing. ton | Coul. ter | Craw. ford | Dol. phin. ton | Doug. las | Dun. syre | Lan. ark | Les. mahagow | Lib. ber. ton | Petti. nain | Wal. ston | Win. ton | Names of Tenants |
|---|---|---|---|---|---|---|---|---|---|---|---|---|---|---|---|---|---|---|---|---|
| 1051 | Holm—Thankerton, | 247 | | | | | | 123 | | | | | | | | | | | | Fisher, J., Heirs. |
| 1052 | Loanhead, | 309 | | | | | | | | | | | | | | | | | | Brown, A. |
| 1053 | Maryfield, | 269 | | 125 | | 125 | | | | | | | | | 125 | | | | | Coltness Iron Co. |
| 1054 | Nethanfoot, | 242 | | | | | | | | | 118 | | | | | | | | | Mitchell, W. |
| 1055 | Newmill, | 262 | | | 122 | | | | | | | | | | | | | | | Black, J. |
| 1056 | Newside, | 247 | | 125 | | | | | | | | | | | | | | | | Core, J. |
| 1057 | Orchard, | 271 | | | | | | | | | | | | | 122 | | | | | Bell & Shirlaw. |
| 1058 | Priorhill, High, | 372 | | | | | | | | | | | | 124 | 120 | | | | | Barr, S. |
| 1059 | Whitecastle, East, | 330 | | | | | | | | | | | | 120 | | 126 | | | | Ritchie, J. |
| 1060 | Wiston Mill, | 245 | | | | 120 | | | | | | | | | | | | | 126 | Clarkson, J. |
| 1061 | BLACKCASTLE, | 339 | | | | | | | | | | | | | | | | | | LINDSAY, J. |
| 1062 | Charleston, | 250 | | | | | | | | | | | | | 120 | | | | | Gray, J. |
| 1063 | Colliclaw, | 245 | | | | | | | | | | | | | | | | | | Aitken, T. |
| 1064 | Dykehead, | 254 | | | | | | | | | | | | | | | | | | Barr, J. |
| 1065 | Eastertown, West, | 242 | | | 120 | | | | | | | | | | | | | | | Dougall, A. |
| 1066 | Howgate & Redmyre, | 247 | | | | | | | | | | | | 120 | | | | | | Tarvet, J. |
| 1067 | Huntlyhill, | 354 | | | | | | | | | | | | | | | | | 121 | Broomfield, A. |
| 1068 | Longwell, | 242 | | | | | | | | | | | | | | | | | | Haddow, R. |
| 1069 | Shodsmill, | 244 | | 120 | | | 122 | | | | | | | | | | | | | Barrie, J. |
| 1070 | Waygateshawhead, | 291 | | 118 | | | | | | | | | | | | | | | | Ferrie, J. |
| 1071 | BRACKENHILL, | 384 | | | | | | | | | | | | | | | | | | BARR, T. |
| 1072 | Carfin & Clydebank, | 301 | | | | | | | | | | | | 120 | 115 | | | | 120 | Smellie, W. |
| 1073 | Galla, Little, | 373 | | | 120 | | | | | | | | | | | | | | 120 | Fraser, R. |
| 1074 | Gill, | 356 | | | | 110 | | | | | | | | | | | | | | Letham, J. |
| 1075 | Hardington Mains, | 277 | | | | | | | | | | | | | | | | | 120 | Muir, W. |
| 1076 | Harleyholm, | 247 | | | | | | | | | | | | | | | | | | Paterson, W. |
| 1077 | Hinshelwood, Mid, | 000 | | | | | | | | | | | 120 | | | | | | | Liddell, J. |
| 1078 | Honeypath, | 000 | | | | | | | | | | | | | 115 | | | | | Macdonald, J. |
| 1079 | Kirkmuirhill, | 254 | | | | | | | | | | | | | | | | | | Hutchison, W. |
| 1080 | Nemphlar, East, | 244 | | | | | | | | | | | | 118 | | | | | | Scott, W. |

**VALUATION ROLL—1858-9.**

| No. | Names of Farms. | Estate | Biggar | Car-luke | Car-michael | Carn-wath | Coving-ton | Conl-tur | Craw-ford | Dol-phin-ton | Doug-las | Drum-syre | Lan-ark | Les-maha-gow | Lib-ber-ton | Pettl-nain | Sym-ing-ton | Wal-ston | Wis-ton | Names of Tenants. |
|---|---|---|---|---|---|---|---|---|---|---|---|---|---|---|---|---|---|---|---|---|
| | | £ | £ | £ | £ | £ | £ | £ | £ | £ | £ | £ | £ | £ | £ | £ | £ | £ | |
| 1081 | Biggar Common, | 278 | | | | | | | | | | | | | | | | | | Prentice, J. |
| 1082 | Bowhouse, | 247 | 114 | | | | | | | | | | | | | | | | | Muir, W. |
| 1083 | Coulter Mill, | 258 | | | 116 | | | | | | | | | | | | | | | Dick, J. |
| 1084 | Hangingshaw, Upper, | 258 | | | | | | 115 | | | | | | | | | | | | Bertram, J. |
| 1085 | Kypeside, Nether, | 254 | | | | | | 114 | | | | | | | | | | | | Semple, R. |
| 1086 | Millhill of Dykehead, | 247 | | | | | | | | | | | | | | 116 | | | | Ballantyne, W. |
| 1087 | Pool Farm, | 292 | | | | 115 | | | | | | | | | | | | | | Carmichael, W. |
| 1088 | Scrogtonhead, | 241 | | | | | | | | | | | | 115 | | | | | | Watson, R. |
| 1089 | Symington Lodge, | 296 | | | | | | | | | | | | | | | 110 | | | Renton, W. |
| 1090 | Wellburn, | 251 | | | | | | | | | | | | 111 | | | | | | M‘Ghee, W. |
| 1091 | Akinlophead, | 266 | | | | | | | | | | | | 110 | | | | | | Neilson, T. |
| 1092 | Auchintoroch, | 251 | | | | | | | | | | | | 110 | | | | | | Scott, J. |
| 1093 | Bank, | 262 | | | | | | | | 110 | | | | | | | | | | Bertram, R. |
| 1094 | Boat—Thankerton, | 247 | | | | | 106 | | | | | | | | | | | | | Tarvet, J. |
| 1095 | Easterhills, | 247 | | | | | | | | | 110 | | | | | | | | | Gibson, W., heirs of. |
| 1096 | Gladstanes, East, | 276 | | | | | | | | | 103 | | | | | | | | | Brown, Mrs. |
| 1097 | Hawkaland, | 297 | | | | | | | | | | | | | | 111 | | | | Burton, T. |
| 1098 | Lairs, | 254 | | | | | | | | | | | | 110 | | | | | | Tudhope, J. |
| 1099 | Langhouse, | 241 | | | | | | | | | | | | | 110 | | | | | Paterson, Esq., A. |
| 1100 | Stane, | 404 | 105 | | | | | | | | | | | | | | | | | Jackson, P. |
| 1101 | Crookboat, | 242 | | | 100 | | | | | | | | | | | | | | | Lamb, J. |
| 1102 | Dumbrexhill, | 302 | | | | | | | | | | | | 105 | | | | | | Pate, A. |
| 1103 | Eastfield, | 285 | | | | | | | | | | | | | | | | | 105 | Gibson, J. |
| 1104 | Edmonstone Mill, | 264 | 105 | | | | | | | | | | | | | | | | | Gibson, T. |
| 1105 | Garngour, South, | 395 | | | | | | | | | | | | 103 | | | | | | Peat, R. |
| 1106 | Hallhill, North, | 251 | | | | | | | | | | | | 105 | | | | | | Cadzow, W. |
| 1107 | Lammerlaw, | 350 | | | | | | | | | | | | 104 | | | | | | Watson, J. |
| 1108 | Stobilee & Windsor, | 245 | | | | | | | | | | | | | | | | 105 | | Barrie, A. |
| 1109 | Store Farm, East, | 247 | | | | | 100 | | | | | | | | | | | | | Bell, J. |
| 1110 | Warrenhill, Nether, | 247 | | | | | 102 | | | | | | | | | | | | | Twaddle, J. |

| Valuation Roll—1858-9. Names of Farms. | Estate | Big. gar. £ | Car. luke. £ | Car. michael. £ | Carm. wath. £ | Car. stairs. £ | Cov. ington. £ | Coul. ter. £ | Craw. ford. £ | Craw. ford john. £ | Dol. phin. ton. £ | Dun. syre. £ | Lan. ark. £ | Les. malina. gow. £ | Lib. ber. ton. £ | Pet.-ti. nain. £ | Wal. ston. £ | Wis. ton. £ | Names of Tenants. |
|---|---|---|---|---|---|---|---|---|---|---|---|---|---|---|---|---|---|---|---|
| 1111 Auchenheath, Woods | 251 | | | | | | | | | | | | | 100 | | | | | Bannatyne, J. |
| 1112 Balgray, Nether,—[of, | 255 | | | | | | | | | 100 | | | | 105 | | | | | Black, J. |
| 1113 Birkhill, | 297 | | | | 100 | | | | | | | | | 100 | | | | | Stobbs, W. |
| 1114 Ellanbank, | 000 | | | | | | | | | | | | | | 100 | | | | Donald, G. |
| 1115 Gladstane, West, | 276 | | | | | | | | | | | | | | 100 | | | | Aitken, J. |
| 1116 Hangingshaw, Nether | 258 | | | 105 | | | | 98 | | | | | | | | | | | Watson, P. |
| 1117 Highfield, | 257 | | 100 | | | | | 100 | | | | | | | | | | | Robb, J. |
| 1118 Moreshot, | 309 | | | | | | | | 100 | | | | | | | | | | Hamilton, W. |
| 1119 Skellyhill, | 266 | | | | | | | | | | | | | | | | | | Pate, A. |
| 1120 Woodlands, | 242 | | | | | | | | | | | | | 100 | | | | | Swan, A. |
| 1121 Bank, | 262 | | | | | | | | | | 110 | | | 100 | | | | | Bertram, R. |
| 1122 Burnbrae, | 251 | | | | | | | | | | | | | | | | | | Torrence, Mrs. |
| 1123 Bushelhead, | 299 | | 100 | | | | | | | | | | | 100 | | | | | Carruthers, T. |
| 1124 Killylees, | 254 | | | | | | | | | | | | | | | | | 100 | Torrence, W. |
| 1125 Langhill, | 245 | | | | | | | | 100 | | | | | 105 | | | | | Clarkson, J. |
| 1126 Little Clyde, | 243 | | | | | | | | | | | | | | | | | | Thomson, A. |
| 1127 Nemphlar, West, | 419 | | | | | | | | | | | | 100 | | | | | | Donaldson, A. |
| 1128 Tanhill, | 384 | | | | | 94 | | | | | | | 100 | | | | | | Hamilton, J. |
| 1129 Threepwood, | 242 | | | | | | | | 98 | | | | 100 | | | | | | Templeton, D. |
| 1130 Whitecleugh, Nether, | 256 | | | | | | | | | 100 | | | | 100 | | | | | Hislop, J. |
| 1131 Cowford, | 261 | | | | 96 | | | | | | | | | | | | | | Barr, W. |
| 1132 Girdwoodend, | 405 | | | | 95 | | | | | | | | | | | | | | M‘Morran, J. |
| 1133 Haywood, Upper, | 273 | | | | | | | | 98 | | | | | | | | | | Robb, J. |
| 1134 Law, | 247 | | 92 | | | | 96 | | | | | | | | | | | | Hamilton, W. |
| 1135 Marchlands,—[ton, | 277 | | | | 96 | | | | | | | | | | | | | 92 | Reid, J. |
| 1136 Mill-lands—Thanker- | 247 | | | | 95 | | | | | | | | | | | | | | Purdie, A. |
| 1137 Shortcleugh, South, | 253 | | | | | | | | | | | | | | | | | | Paterson, Esq., A. |
| 1138 Stabilee, | 245 | | | | | 96 | | | | | | | | | | | | | Barrie, A. |
| 1139 Store Farm, West, | 247 | | | | | 96 | | | | | | | | | | | | | Bell, J. |
| 1140 Undershieldhill, | 246 | | 92 | | | | 101 | | | | | | | | | | | | Cassells, J. |

| VALUATION ROLL—1858-9. NAMES OF FARMS. | Estate. | Big-gar. £ | Car-luke. £ | Car-mich-ael. £ | Carn-wath. £ | Car-stairs. £ | Cov-ing-ton. £ | Craw-ford. £ | Craw-ford-john. £ | Dol-phin-ton. £ | Doug-las. £ | Lam-ing-ton. £ | Lan-ark. £ | Les-maha-gow. £ | Petti-nain. £ | Sym-ing-ton. £ | Wal-ston. £ | Wis-ton. £ | NAMES OF TENANTS. |
|---|---|---|---|---|---|---|---|---|---|---|---|---|---|---|---|---|---|---|---|
| 1141 Ampherlaw, | 329 | | | | 90 | | | | | | | | | | | | | | Watson, J. |
| 1142 Bellstane, | 243 | | 90 | | | | | | | | | | | | | | | | Forrest, W. |
| 1143 Carmichael Mill, | 247 | | 91 | 91 | | | | | | | | | | | | | | | Paterson, J. |
| 1144 Castlehill, | 269 | 90 | | | | | | | | | | | | | | | | | Jack, J. |
| 1145 Green, | 264 | 90 | | | | | | | | | | | | | | | | | Crossan, J. |
| 1146 Lochanbank, | 254 | | | | | | | | | | | | | 90 | | | | | Brownlie, M. |
| 1147 Muirburn, | 266 | 90 | | | | | | | | | | | | 90 | | | | | Wilson, G. |
| 1148 Strawlaw, | 290 | | | | | | | | | | | | | 90 | | | | | Hislop, J. |
| 1149 Tower, | 242 | | | | | | | | | | | | | | | | | | Gall, J. |
| 1150 Westcrofthill, | 292 | | | | 90 | | | | | | | | | | | | | | Elder, J. |
| 1151 Cleugh, | 280 | | 87 | | | | | | | | | | | | | | | | Cunningham, D. |
| 1152 Crawfordwell, | 246 | 90 | | | | | | | | | 90 | | | | | | | | Davidson, A. |
| 1153 Greenwood, | 264 | | | | | | | | | | | | | | | | | | Crossan, J. |
| 1154 Hinshelwood, | 283 | | | | | | | | | | | | | | | | 91 | | Thorburn, J. |
| 1155 Kypeswaterhead, | 433 | | | | | | | | | | | | | 85 | | | | | Meikle, W. |
| 1156 Moreshot, Wester, | 418 | | | | 85 | | | | | | | | | | | | | | Wilson, W. |
| 1157 Netherton, | 358 | | | | | | | | | | 90 | | | 87 | | | | | Todd, J. |
| 1158 Tofts, West, | 241 | | 86 | | | | | | | | | | | | | | | | Macdougall, Mrs. |
| 1159 Westquarter, | 244 | | 90 | | | | | | | | | | | | | | | | Somerville, R. |
| 1160 Yett, West, | 244 | | | | | | | | | | | | | | | | | | Barrie, J. |
| 1161 Bogside, | 251 | | | | 85 | | | | | | | | | 85 | | | | | Brown, T. |
| 1162 Cleughmill, | 244 | | | | 85 | | | | | | | | | | | | | | Struthers, J. |
| 1163 Crookland, | 273 | | | | 85 | | | | | | | | | | | | | | Ballantyne, T., heirs. |
| 1164 Greenbank, | 244 | | 85 | | | | | | | | | | | | | | | | Wilson, T. |
| 1165 Johnshill, | 266 | | | | 85 | | | | | | | | | | | | | | Cassie, J. |
| 1166 Linnville, | 270 | | | | | | | | | | | | | | | | | | Dalglish, A. |
| 1167 Roothead, | 320 | | | | | | | | | | | | | | | | | | Hamilton, W. |
| 1168 Silvermains, | 261 | | | | 89 | | | | | | | | | 84 | | | | | Boyd, W. |
| 1169 Westmains, | 285 | | | | 86 | | | | | | | | | 84 | | | | | Smith, D. |
| 1170 Whitecleugh & Abbey, | 261 | | | | 85 | | | | | | | | | | | | | | Barr, W. |

## VALUATION ROLL—1858-9.

| No. | Names of Farms. | Estate. | Big-gar. | Car-luke. | Car-mich-ael. | Carp-wath. | Car-stairs. | Cov-ing-ton. | Comb-ter. | Craw-ford-john. | Dol-phin-ton. | Doug-las. | Dun-syre. | Lan-ark. | Lea-maha-gow. | Lib-ber-ton. | Petti-nain. | Sym-ing-ton. | Wis-ton. | Names of Tenants. |
|---|---|---|---|---|---|---|---|---|---|---|---|---|---|---|---|---|---|---|---|---|
| 1171 | Auchengray, Mid,.. | 320 | | | | 82 | | | | | | | | | | | | | | Ballantyne, G. |
| 1172 | Bottom, North,..... | 280 | | | | | | | | | | 80 | | | | | | | | Willison, J. |
| 1173 | Coulter Park, North, | 258 | 101 | | | | | | 82 | | | | | | | | | | | Bertram, A. |
| 1174 | East-tofts,........ | 211 | | | | | | | | | | 60 | | | | | | | | Pate, T. |
| 1175 | Hillend,.......... | 362 | | | | | 88 | | | | | | | | | | | | | Blakely, G. |
| 1176 | Newphlar, West,... | 244 | | | | 76 | | | | | | | | | | | | | | Jack, W. C. |
| 1177 | Sidewood, East,... | 292 | | | | | | | | | | | | 83 | | | | | | Todd, J. |
| 1178 | Sheilds,.......... | 242 | | | 85 | | | | | | | | | | | | | | | Brown, J. |
| 1179 | Sheafyknowes,..... | 261 | | | 87 | | | | | | | | | | | | | | | Robb, T. & J. |
| 1180 | Townhead, Ponfeigh, | 247 | | | | | | | | | | | | | | | | | | Weir & Adamson. |
| 1181 | Birks,............ | 265 | | 81 | | | | | | | | | | | | | | | | Hamilton, W. |
| 1182 | Boghall,.......... | 362 | 62 | | | | | 81 | | | | | | | | | | | | Brown, J. |
| 1183 | Corniston House,.. | 331 | | | | 81 | | | | | | | | | | 80 | | | | Williamson, A. |
| 1184 | Haywood, Lower,... | 273 | | | | 81 | | | | | | | | | | | | | | Nimmo, T. |
| 1185 | Monksfoot,........ | 241 | | | | | | | | | | 80 | | | | | | | | M'Quat, W. |
| 1186 | Spadgill,......... | 324 | | | 81 | | | | | | | | | | | | | | | Aitken, A. |
| 1187 | Strathbogie,...... | 264 | 81 | | | | | | | | | | | | | | | | | Gibson, J. |
| 1188 | Townfoot,......... | 247 | | | | | | | | | | | | | | | | | | Affleck, M., heirs of. |
| 1189 | Townhead,......... | 264 | 81 | | | | | | | | | | | | | | | | | Tweedie, J. |
| 1190 | Warrenhill, Upper, | 247 | | | | | | | | | | | | | | | | | | Bryce, A. |
| 1191 | Clecklands,....... | 254 | | | | | | | | 80 | | | | | 70 | | | | | Cooper, J. |
| 1192 | Craigheadmill,.... | 289 | | | | | | | | | | | | | 72 | | | | | Thomson, H. |
| 1193 | Glespin, East,.... | 211 | | | | | | | | | | 78 | | | | | | | | Ray, J. |
| 1194 | Hillside,......... | 266 | | | | | | | | | | | | | 78 | | | | | M'Grigor, J. |
| 1195 | Holmhead,......... | 435 | | | | | | | | 80 | | | | | | | | | | Watson, R. |
| 1196 | Middlemains,...... | 290 | | | | | | | | | | | | | | | 78 | | | Brown, J. |
| 1197 | Pettinain Crofts,. | 247 | 65 | | | | | | | | | | | | | | | | | Gibson, J. |
| 1198 | Scrogton,......... | 241 | | | | | | | | | | | | | | | | | | Greenshields, J. |
| 1199 | Stobwood & Hillhead, | 280 | | | | 76 | | | | | | 80 | | | | | | | | Prentice, J. |
| 1200 | Westmill,......... | 262 | | | | | | | | | 80 | 80 | | | | | | | | Core, D. |

| VALUATION ROLL—1858-9. | NAMES OF FARMS. | Estate. | Rig-gar. | Car-luke. | Car-michael. | Carn-wath. | Car-stairs. | Cov-ington. | Coul-ter. | Craw-ford. | Craw-ford-john. | Dol-phin-ton. | Doug-las. | Dun-syre. | Les-maha-gow. | Lib-ber-ton. | Petti-nain. | Sym-ing-ton. | Wis-ton. | NAMES OF TENANTS. |
|---|---|---|---|---|---|---|---|---|---|---|---|---|---|---|---|---|---|---|---|---|
| | | | £ | £ | £ | £ | £ | £ | £ | £ | £ | £ | £ | £ | £ | £ | £ | £ | £ | |
| 1201 | Brackenridge, West | 254 | | | | | | | | | | | | | 70 | | | | | Gillies, M. |
| 1202 | Burnhead | 244 | | 79 | | | | | | | | | | | | | | | | Jack, J. |
| 1203 | Cauder-water | 251 | | | | | | | | | | | | | 75 | | | | | Hamilton, R. |
| 1204 | Forth | 275 | | | | 76 | | | | | | | | | | | | | | Scott, J. |
| 1205 | Goathouse-knowes | 263 | | | | | | | | | | | | | | | | | | Watt, A. |
| 1206 | Lockhart Mill | 214 | | 56 | | | | | | | | | | | | | | | | Murray, J. |
| 1207 | Muirdykehead | 246 | | | | | | | | | | | | | 75 | | | | | Bain, G. |
| 1208 | Sadlerhead & Todhills | 266 | | | | | | | | | | | | | 68 | | | | | Scott, T. |
| 1209 | Townfoot | 242 | | | | | | | | | | | | | | | | | 79 | Lindsey, J. |
| 1210 | Woodyett | 279 | | | | | | | | | | | | | 75 | | | | | Shaw, J |
| 1211 | Arthurshiels, pt. of | 244 | | | | | | | | | | | | | | | | | | Hodge, W. |
| 1212 | Blair-reckoning | 266 | | | 75 | | | | | | | | | | 78 | | | | | Cook, J. |
| 1213 | Boghead | 256 | | | | | | | | | 75 | | | | 69 | | | | | Anderson, J. |
| 1214 | Dyke | 242 | | | | | | | | | | | | | 70 | | | | | Dickson, W. |
| 1215 | Holmhead | 212 | | | | | | | | | | | | | | | | | | Smith, W. |
| 1216 | Lupus | 265 | | | | | | | | | | | | | | | | | | Scott, W. |
| 1217 | Rowantreehill | 330 | | | 70 | 70 | | | | | | | | | | | | | | Prentice, J. |
| 1218 | Tapenhall | 441 | | 70 | | | | | | | | | | | | | | | | Ramsay, A., Repr's. |
| 1219 | Watchknowe | 242 | | | 70 | | | | | | | | | | | | | | | Weir, J. |
| 1220 | Wiston Place | 245 | | | | | | | | | | | | | | | | | 70 | Wilson, J. |
| 1221 | Affleck, Nether | 288 | | | | | | | | | | | | | 75 | | | | | Carruthers, B. |
| 1222 | Gatesile | 316 | | | | | | | | | | | | | 75 | | | | | Brown, J. |
| 1223 | Hoodsmill | 289 | | | | | | | 69 | | | | | | | | | | | Brownlie, J. |
| 1224 | Meadowhead | 262 | | | | | | | | | | 70 | | | | | | | | Mackenzie, G. |
| 1225 | Mountstuart | 241 | | | | | | | | | | | 70 | | | | | | | Lawson, G. |
| 1226 | Pennyflatts | 248 | | | | | | | | | | | | | 67 | | | | | Watson, D. |
| 1227 | Sheriffcleugh | 242 | | | | | | | | | | | | | 71 | | | | | Forsyth, R. |
| 1228 | Southwood | 255 | | | | | | | | 70 | 70 | | | | | | | | | Hamilton, J. |
| 1229 | Westmains | 290 | | | | | | 70 | | | | | | | | | | | | Noble, W. |
| 1230 | Watertown | 000 | 70 | | | | 70 | | | | | | | | | | | | | Walkinshaw, W. |

| Valuation Roll—1858-9. Names of Farms. | Estate. | Names of Tenants. | Wiston. | Symington. | Pettinain. | Libberton. | Lesmahagow. | Lanark. | Lamington. | Douglas. | Crawfordjohn. | Crawford. | Coulter. | Covington. | Carstairs. | Carnwath. | Carmichael. | Carluke. | Biggar. |
|---|---|---|---|---|---|---|---|---|---|---|---|---|---|---|---|---|---|---|---|
| | | | £ | £ | £ | £ | £ | £ | £ | £ | £ | £ | £ | £ | £ | £ | £ | £ | £ |
| 1231 Arthurshiel, part of, | 244 | Hodge, J. | | | | 69 | | | | | | | | | | | | | |
| 1232 Brownriggs, | 261 | Stewart, J. | | | | | | | | | | | | | | | | | |
| 1233 Catcraig, | 276 | Cassels, J., | | | | | | | | | | | | | | | | 65 | |
| 1234 Clannochdyke, | 251 | Lockhart, R. | | | | | | | | | | | | | | | | | |
| 1235 Cleugbbar, | 300 | Young, W. | | | | | 66 | | | | | | | | | | | | |
| 1236 Garrigour, North, | 415 | French, T. | | | | | 65 | | | | | | | | | | | | |
| 1237 Hareshaw, etc., | 286 | Marshall, T. | | | | | 65 | | | | | | | | | | | | |
| 1238 Hill, | 300 | Harrison, W. | | | | | | | | | | | | | | | 60 | | |
| 1239 Hinshelwood, | 416 | Shaw, W. | | | | | 67 | | | | | | | | | | | | |
| 1240 Newhouse, | 298 | Gilchrist, S. | | | | | | | | | | | | | | | | | |
| 1241 Auchenbeg, | 267 | Cooper, G. | | | | | 67 | | | | | | | | | | | | |
| 1242 Bogside,......[ton, | 243 | Barr, W. | | | | | 66 | | | | | | | | | | | 63 | |
| 1243 Brownshot & Langar-, | 427 | Forrest, J. | | | | | | | | | | | | | | | | | |
| 1244 Brackenridge, South, | 254 | Fallow, T. | | | | | 64 | | | | | | | | | | | | |
| 1245 Hillhouse, | 242 | Souter, J. | | | | | 64 | | | | | | | | | | | | |
| 1246 Howford, | 247 | Muir, R. | | | | | | | | | | | | | | | 53 | | |
| 1247 Lagsbeil, | 257 | Sinclair, J. | | | | | | | | | | | 63 | | | | | | |
| 1248 Waterhead, | 368 | Greenshields, W. | | | | | | | | | | | | | | | | | |
| 1249 Wellbrae, | 244 | Lindsay, H. | | | | | 65 | | | | | | | 64 | | | | | |
| 1250 Westshields, | 244 | Brown, J. | | | | | | | | | | | | | | 65 | | | |
| 1251 Birthwood, | 410 | Brown, J. | | | | | 63 | | | | | | | | | | | | |
| 1252 Birkwood, | 289 | M'Kirdy, Esq., J. G. | | | | | | | | | | | | | | | 60 | | |
| 1253 Burnhouse, | 242 | Prentice, T. | | | | | 60 | | | | | | | | | | 61 | | |
| 1254 Devonhill, | 247 | Greenshields, J. | | | | | | | | | | | | | | | | | |
| 1255 Eastertown, East, | 242 | Dougall, A. | | | | | | | | | | | | | | | | 51 | |
| 1256 Hungerhill & Chapel, | 340 | Hunter, R. | | | | | | | | | 60 | | | | | | | | |
| 1257 Leamside, | 324 | Aitken, D. | | | | | | | | | | | | | | 62 | | | |
| 1258 Lettershaws, | 332 | Watson, R. | | | | | | | | | | | | | | | 62 | | |
| 1259 Whinbush, | 276 | Frame, A. | | | | | | | | | | | | | | | | | |
| 1260 Windysheilds, | 261 | Miller, M. | | | | 62 | | | | | | | | | 62 | | | | |

| Estate | Names of Farms | Blg. gar. | Car-luke. | Car-mich-ael. | Carn-wath. | Car-stairs. | Coul-ter. | Craw-ford. | Craw-ford-john. | Dol-phin-ton. | Doug-las. | Dun-syre. | Lam-ing-ton. | Lan-ark. | Les-maha-gow. | Lib-ber-ton. | Sym-ing-ton. | Wal-ston. | Names of Tenants. |
|---|---|---|---|---|---|---|---|---|---|---|---|---|---|---|---|---|---|---|---|
| | | £ | £ | £ | £ | £ | £ | £ | £ | £ | £ | £ | £ | £ | £ | £ | £ | £ | |
| 1261 | LADESHEAD, | | | | | | | | | | | | | | 60 | | | | Dykes, J. |
| 1262 | Langknowe, | 249 | | | | | | | | | | | 60 | | | | | | Gibson, W. |
| 1263 | Mashockmill, | 376 | 60 | | | | | | | | | | | | | | | | Shirlaw, J. |
| 1264 | Mayfield, | 266 | | 60 | | | | | | | | | | | | | | | Dickson, A. |
| 1265 | Millmuir, | 242 | 60 | | | | | | | | | | | | | | | | Froud, H. |
| 1266 | Moss-side, | 243 | | | | | | | | | | | | | | 60 | | | Legat, J., heirs of. |
| 1267 | Muirlee, | 276 | | | | | | | | | | | | | | | | 60 | Prentice, J., do. |
| 1268 | Walston Mill, | 244 | 60 | | | | | | | | | | | | | | | | Turner, A. |
| 1269 | Wellhead, | 245 | | | | | | | | | | | | 60 | | | | | Wilson, P. |
| 1270 | Westerhouse, Hill of, | 311 | 60 | | | | | | | | | | | | | 60 | | | Hamilton, J. |
| 1271 | MIDHILL, | 276 | | | | | | | | | 60 | | | | | | | | Walker, J. |
| 1272 | Midtown, | 241 | 56 | | | | | | | | | | | | | | | | Gall, A. |
| 1273 | Muirdykehead, | 246 | | | | | | | | | | | | 57 | 58 | | | | Brown, G. |
| 1274 | Nemphlar, West, | 244 | | | | | | | | | | | | | | | | | Jack, J. |
| 1275 | Netherburn, | 409 | | | | | | | | | | | | | | | | | Todd, T. |
| 1276 | Oldtown, | 420 | | | 60 | | | | | | 60 | | | | 60 | | | | Aitken, W. |
| 1277 | Rawhills, | 242 | | | | | | | | | | | | | 60 | | | | Weir, R. |
| 1278 | Syde, | 242 | | | | | | | | | | | | | | | | | Sandilands, W. |
| 1279 | Tofts, East, | 241 | | | 57 | | | | | | | | | | | | | | Pate, T. |
| 1280 | Woodlands, | 265 | 59 | | | | | | | | | | | | 59 | | | | M'Morran, J. |
| 1281 | CROFTFOOT, | 244 | | | | | | | | | | | | | | 57 | | | Black, W., Heirs [of. |
| 1282 | Huntfield, | 330 | | | | | | | | | | | | | | | | | Smith, J. |
| 1283 | Janefield, | 328 | | 53 | | | | | | | | | | | | | | | Core, W. |
| 1284 | Prett's Mill, | 242 | | | | | | | | | | | | | | | | | Clarkson, R. |
| 1285 | Redshaw, | 242 | 56 | 56 | | | | | | | | | | | 55 | | | | Millwain, Rev. J. |
| 1286 | Shaws, | 247 | | | | | | | | | | | | | | | | | Smith, J. |
| 1287 | Tanhill, | 421 | | | 55 | | | | | | | | | | | | | | Shields, W. |
| 1288 | Viewfield, | 389 | 56 | | | | | | | | | | | | | | | | French, W. |
| 1289 | Whiteside, | 000 | | | | | | | | | | | | | 54 | | | | Mackie, A. |
| 1290 | Woodside, | 241 | | | | | | | | | 57 | | | | | | | | Swan, J., sen. |

n

## VALUATION ROLL—1858-9.

| No. | Names of Farms | Names of Tenants | Estate | Wiston £ | Symington £ | Liberton £ | Lesmahagow £ | Lanark £ | Lamington £ | Dunsyre £ | Douglas £ | Dolphinton £ | Crawford £ | Coulter £ | Covington £ | Carstairs £ | Carnwath £ | Carmichael £ | Carluke £ | Biggar £ |
|---|---|---|---|---|---|---|---|---|---|---|---|---|---|---|---|---|---|---|---|---|
| 1291 | Auchenbeg, | Inch, W. | 266 | | | | | | | | | | | | | | | | | |
| 1292 | Blackwoodside, | Barr, A. | 254 | | | | 55 | | | | | | | | | | | | | |
| 1293 | Blinklie, | Swan, J. | 242 | | | | 55 | | | | | | | | | | | 58 | | |
| 1294 | Brackeuridge, East, | Dent, J. | 254 | | | | | | | | | | | | | | | | | |
| 1295 | Coranill, | Allan, R. | 251 | | | | 54 | | | | | | | | | | | | 55 | |
| 1296 | Gladdenhill, | Stewart, J. | 488 | | | | 55 | | | | | | | | | | | | | |
| 1297 | Midtown, | Somerville, T. | 483 | | | | 55 | | | | | | | | | | | | | |
| 1298 | Millhouse, | Affleck, W. | 242 | | | | 50 | | | | | | | | | | | | | |
| 1299 | Northflatcrofts, | Aitken, Mrs. | 000 | | | | | | | | | | | | | | | | 53 | |
| 1300 | Woodlands, | Dykes, J. | 421 | | | | | | | | | | | | | | | | | |
| 1301 | Acrediand — Lam-[ington, | Watson, W. | 249 | | | | 60 | | | | | | | | | | | | | |
| 1302 | Birkenhead, | Elder, J. & W. | 244 | | | | | | | | | | | | | | | | | |
| 1303 | Blair, | Wilkie, Mrs. | 242 | | | | 52 | | 59 | | | | | | | | | | 53 | |
| 1304 | Castlemains, | Scott, Esq., T. R. | 211 | | | | 54 | | | | | | | | | | | | | |
| 1305 | Croftanrigh, | Crawford, W. | 303 | | | | | | | | 50 | | | | | | 50 | | | |
| 1306 | Forth, | Wilson, W. | 275 | | | | 56 | | | | 52 | | | | | | | | | |
| 1307 | Lowrie's-muir, | Bunten, T. | 251 | | | | | | | | | 55 | | | | | | | | |
| 1308 | Springhill, | Ballantyne, T. | 241 | | | | | | | | | 55 | | | 55 | | | | 50 | |
| 1309 | Thankerton Mill, | Galloway, W., heirs. | 247 | | | | | | | | 50 | | | | | | | | | |
| 1310 | Westend, | Barr, W. | 265 | | | | | | | | | | | | | | | | | |
| 1311 | Carmichael Bank, | Paterson, J | 247 | | | | 56 | | | | | | | | | | | | | |
| 1312 | Coalgill, | Scott, Esq., T. R. | 241 | | | | | 50 | | | | | | | | | | | 50 | |
| 1313 | Gair, | Forrest, R. | 243 | | | | | | | | | | | | | | | | 53 | |
| 1314 | Gill, | Thomson, A. | 246 | | | | | | | | | | | | | | | | | |
| 1315 | Halfmerkland, | Barr, R. | 402 | | | | | | | | | | | | | | | | | |
| 1316 | Longhill, | Smith, A. | 245 | | | | | | | | | | | | | | | | 50 | |
| 1317 | Northfield, | Reid, J. | 331 | | | | | | | | | | | | | | | | 50 | |
| 1318 | Shawfield, | Hamilton, W. | 333 | | | | | | | | | | | | | | | | | |
| 1319 | Springhill, | Anderson, T. | 364 | | | | | | | | | | | | | | | | | |
| 1320 | Woodside, | Fairie, J. | 251 | | | | 50 | | | | 50 | | | | | | | | | |

| Property | Parish | Proprietor | No. |
|---|---|---|---|
| Abbeygreen | Lesmahagow | Brown, W. | 442 |
| do. | do. | Frame, R., M.D. | 423 |
| do. | do. | Meikle, Misses | 675 |
| do. | do. | Scott, Mrs. | 537 |
| Aupherlaw | Carnwath | Somerville, S., M.D. | 329 |
| Auchengrey | do. | Robertson, G. | 320 |
| Auchenheath | Lesmahagow | Hamilton, Duke of | 251 |
| AUCHLOCHAN | Lesmahagow | Brown, J.T. | 266 |
| Auchmedan | do. | Douglas, J. | 413 |
| Auchren | do. | Meikle, R. | 397 |
| AUCHTYFARDLE | do. | Mossman, H. | 289 |
| Aulton | do. | Hamilton, W., late | 356 |
| Bankend | do. | Leighton, W., late | 318 |
| Bankhead | do. | Hastie, A., late | 317 |
| Bankhouses | do. | M'Gowran, W. | 566 |
| BARONALD | Lanark | Robertson, G. | 345 |
| Beanshields | Carluke | Selkirk, J. | 489 |
| Bellfield | Lesmahagow | Davidson, T. | 393 |
| do. | Crawford | Menzies, J. | 437 |
| do. | Lanark | Scott, J. | 445 |
| do. | Lesmahagow | Wilson, J. | 400 |
| Belstane, etc. | Carluke, etc. | Douglas, A. Lord, late | 243 |
| Bere Holm | Lesmahagow | Brown, Rev. A. | 451 |
| do. Mill | do. | Reid, A. | 618 |
| BIGGAR PARK | Biggar | Gillespie, A. | 294 |
| do. | do. | Gillespie, Mrs | 394 |
| BIGGAR SHIELS | do. | Stainton, E., late | 290 |
| Birkenhead | Lesmahagow | Thomson, J. | 300 |
| Birkfield | do. | Cultness Iron Co. | 268 |
| Birkhill | Lanark | Frame, J. | 503 |

| Property | Parish | Proprietor | No. |
|---|---|---|---|
| BIRKWOOD | LESMAHAGOW | M'KIRDY, J. G. | 265 |
| Birnichill | Carstairs | Hamilton, J. G. | 315 |
| BRITHWOOD | Coulter | Paterson, R. | 325 |
| do. | Lesmahagow | Todd, J. | 410 |
| Blackcastle | Carnwath | White, J. | 339 |
| do. | Walston | White, W. | 449 |
| BLACKWOOD | LESMAHAGOW | VERE HOPE, W. E. | 254 |
| Boghill and Righead | do. | Pagan, J., M.D. | 398 |
| BONNINGTON | Lanark | Ross, Sir W. E. | 250 |
| Boreland | Carluke | Jack, G. | 636 |
| do. | Lesmahagow | Lamb, J. | 426 |
| Brackenhill | Carluke | Hamilton, W. | 334 |
| BRADS | Carnwath | Douglass, Miss | 273 |
| Brae | Lesmahagow | Steel, T. | 508 |
| Braehead | Carnwath | Brown, Miss C. | 572 |
| do. | Douglas | Black, M. | 692 |
| do. | do. | Hamilton, D. | 725 |
| BRAIDWOOD | Carluke | Stevenson, N. | 299 |
| do. | do. | Shaw, J. | 578 |
| Brooklands | Lanark | Field, J. | 583 |
| Brownlie | Carluke | Harvie, J. | 333 |
| do. | do. | Stewart, A. | 347 |
| Browshot | Carnwath | Logan, Mrs A. | 427 |
| do. | do. | Simpson, J. | 439 |
| Burghlands | Biggar | Craig, W. C. | 412 |
| Burnbank | Carluke | Orr, Captain | 639 |
| Burnfoot | Carnwath | Hamilton, T. | 454 |
| do. | Lesmahagow | Cadzow, J. | 562 |
| CAERWOOD | BIGGAR | MITCHELL, W. G. | 278 |
| CAMBUS WALLACE | do. | Paul, J. | 382 |

| Property | Parish | Proprietor | No. |
|---|---|---|---|
| Capehall | Lesmahagow | Donald, R. | 601 |
| Carfin | Lanark | Anderson, S. | 301 |
| Carstairs | Carstairs | Monteith, R. | 261 |
| Castlebank | Lanark | Dyce, J. N. | 401 |
| Castlehill | Carluke | Shotts Iron Co. | 269 |
| do. | do. | Neelson, J. | 506 |
| Castleyett | Lanark | Thomson, Rev. V. | 470 |
| Catcraigs | Carluke | Orr, E. M. Captain | 376 |
| Clarty | Carnwath | Kirkland, Sir J. | 306 |
| Cleghorn | Carstairs | Lockhart, A. E. | 245 |
| Clydegrove | Lesmahagow | Tennant, J. | 447 |
| Coldstream | Carluke | Gray, J. | 475 |
| do. | do. | Somerville, W. | 519 |
| Corehouse | Lesmahagow | Cranstoun, Miss | 263 |
| Cormacour | Douglas | Paterson, A. | 280 |
| Cormiston | Libberton | Somerville, R. | 328 |
| Cormiston-Towers | do. | Wrightson, T. | 369 |
| Cornhill | do. | Collyer, W. D. | 331 |
| Corramore | Lesmahagow | Handyside, W. | 316 |
| Coulter-Maynes | Coulter | Logan, R. | 334 |
| Coulter-Allers | Coulter | Sim, Adam. | 257 |
| Culterhall | do. | Bailley, J. W. | 258 |
| Craigenburn | Carnwath | White, J. | 379 |
| Craighead | Carluke | Haggart, J. C. | 314 |
| Craigichouse | Carnwath | Cadzow, W. | 432 |
| Craignethan | Lesmahagow | Carmichael, T. | 492 |
| Crawford, etc. | Crawfordjohn | Montague, Lady, late | 242 |
| Crofton-Hill | Lanark | Colebrooke, Sir T. E. | 255 |
| Crossburn | Douglas | Vassie, J. | 467 |
| | | Howieson, Mrs Dr | 443 |

| Property | Parish | Proprietor | No. |
|---|---|---|---|
| Crossford | Lesmahagow | Henderson, J. | 455 |
| do. | do. | Laug, T. | 385 |
| Cumberhead, North | do. | Marshall, J. | 297 |
| do. South | do. | Birrell, Lieut.-Col. | 302 |
| Dalerig | Biggar | Gladstone, J. | 494 |
| Darnfillan | Lesmahagow | Semple, T. | 446 |
| Dolphinton | Dolphinton | Mackenzie, J. O. | 262 |
| Douglas Estates | Douglas, etc. | Hope, Countess of | 241 |
| Drums | Carluke | Lightbody, J. | 565 |
| Eastend | Carmichael | Carmichael, M. T. | 248 |
| Easterseat | Carluke | Hamilton, Mrs J. | 474 |
| do. | do. | Hamilton, J. | 486 |
| Eastfield | Biggar | Turnbull, M. | 550 |
| Eastquarter | Carluke | Walker, J. late | 429 |
| East-Shields | Carnwath | Logan, J. | 322 |
| East-tofts | Biggar | Forrest, J. | 414 |
| Edmonstone | do. | Brows, L. | 264 |
| Ellanbank | Lesmahagow | Ferguson, J. | 353 |
| Ellarshaw | Crawford | Ewart, R., late | 274 |
| Fairholm (Kirkton) | Carluke | Hamilton, J. | 296 |
| Falla | Carnwath | Ramsay, Mrs C. | 336 |
| do. | Walston | Rowatt, J., late | 308 |
| Fauldhouse | Lesmahagow | Smith, J. | 346 |
| Fallburn | Biggar | Bell, J. | 561 |
| Gallagreen | Carluke | Fraser, R. | 522 |
| Gallahill | Lanark | Marr, Rev. J. L., late | 496 |
| Garngour | Lesmahagow | French, T. | 415 |
| Gill | do. | Hamilton, G. | 357 |
| Gillfoot | Carluke | Gilchrist, J. | 312 |
| Gillhouse | Carnwath | Elder, J. | 381 |

| Property | Parish | Proprietor | No. |
|---|---|---|---|
| Gills | Carluke | Forrest, W. | 363 |
| Girdwoodend | Carnwath | Newbigging, W. | 405 |
| Gladdenhill | Carluke | Miller, J. | 488 |
| Glendowran | Crawfordjohn | Thomson, J., Capt. | 389 |
| Glentewan | do. | Dickson, W. J. | 332 |
| Gowanhill | Carstairs | Somerville, W. | 359 |
| Gowanside | Carluke | Ross, J. | 459 |
| Greenfield | Carnwath | Somerville, T., late | 309 |
| do. | do. | Wyndham, J., late | 370 |
| Greenhill | Lesmahagow | Semple, J. | 438 |
| Greenridge | do. | Semple, W. | 388 |
| Greenshields | Carnwath | Carmichael, W. | 493 |
| Hallcraig | Carluke | Robertson, Misses | 327 |
| Hardington | Wiston | Macqueen, R. | 277 |
| Harperfield | Lesmahagow | Gordon, Col. W. | 313 |
| Hartree (? Peebles) | Coulter | Dickson, D. | 272 |
| Hawksland | Lesmahagow | Burton, T. | 543 |
| Hazelbank | do. | Waugh, Dr | 539 |
| Heathland | Carnwath | Goldie, W. | 355 |
| Heathlands | Lesmahagow | Tudhope, J. | 460 |
| Heaviside | Biggar | Murray, J., late | 319 |
| Highcross | Lesmahagow | Burns, J. | 582 |
| Hill-end | Biggar | Edmonstone, Capt. | 362 |
| do. | | Howieson, Dr, late | 304 |
| Hillhead | Carluke | Allan, A. | 411 |
| Hinshelwood | Carnwath | Kidd, Professor | 416 |
| do. | do. | Stewart, G. | 560 |
| Holmfoot | Lanark | Howieson, Lieut.-Col | 403 |
| Holmhead | Crawfordjohn | Lorimer, G., late | 435 |
| Hopetoun Estate | Crawford | Hopetoun, Earl of | 253 |

| Property | Parish | Proprietor | No. |
|---|---|---|---|
| Howburn(Garvald foot) | Walston | Woddrop, W. H. A. | 283 |
| Huntfield | Libberton | Stark, J., M.D. | 330 |
| Huntlyhill | Lanark | Gillespie, W. | 354 |
| Hyndford | do. | Howieson, A. | 321 |
| Jerviswood | Lanark | Baillie, G. | 293 |
| Kerse | Lesmahagow | Greenshields J. | 295 |
| Kersewell | Carnwath | Bertram, W. | 259 |
| Kilcadzow | Carluke | Forrest, J. | 512 |
| Kilnhills | Lesmahagow | Brown, T. | 471 |
| Kings Inn | Carnwath | Carmichael, T. | 391 |
| Kirkbank | Lesmahagow | Thomson, J. | 338 |
| Kirkfield | do. | Stein, J. | 298 |
| Kypeswaterhead | do. | Hamilton, Capt. N. | 433 |
| Ladeshead | do. | Dykes, A. | 421 |
| Lamington | Lamington, etc. | Cochrane, A. B. | 249 |
| Lanmerlaw | Walston | Wyld, A. | 350 |
| Langlee | Biggar | Murray, Lord, late | 335 |
| Lawhead | Carnwath | Souter, D. R. | 281 |
| Leamside | do. | Murray, J. W. | 324 |
| Lee and Carnwath | Lanark, etc. | Lockhart, SirN.M'D | 244 |
| Lee Law | Lesmahagow | Blackwood, T. J. | 351 |
| Letham | do. | Semple, W. | 408 |
| Lindsaylands West | Biggar | Brown, Mrs | 311 |
| do. | do. | Cuthbertson, M. | 392 |
| Little Galla | Wiston | Haddow, A. C. | 373 |
| Logan | Lanark | Todd, J. | 378 |
| do. | Lesmahagow | Todd, W. | 579 |
| Loganbank | do. | Hamilton, W. | 424 |
| Loaningdale | Biggar | Lorraine, W. S. | 276 |
| Mansefield | Lanark | Irving, W. | 468 |

| Property | Parish | Proprietor | No. |
|---|---|---|---|
| MACLDSLIE | Carluke | Hozier, J. | 287 |
| Mavisbank | do. | Hamilton, J. | 515 |
| Middlehouse | do. | Lean, J. | 366 |
| Midgarnyour | Lesmahagow | Tudhope, J. | 480 |
| Midhinshelwood | Carnwath | Liddell, P. | 406 |
| Midtoftcombs | do. | Watson, W. | 399 |
| Midtown | Biggar | Gall, H. | 483 |
| MILTON-LOCKHART | CARLUKE | Lockhart, L., D.D. | 246 |
| Moat | Lesmahagow | Barr, Messrs | 371 |
| Moatyett | do. | M'Ghie, T. | 456 |
| Mossplatt | Carstairs | Buchanan, R. C. | 284 |
| MOUSEBANK | Lanark | Stodart, H. | 478 |
| Nellfield | Carluke | Reid, J. | 387 |
| Nemphlar | Lanark | Lockhart, — | 396 |
| do. West | do. | Lockhart, W. | 386 |
| Netherburn | do. | Wilson, J. L. | 419 |
| Netherfauld | Lesmahagow | Symington, W. | 409 |
| Netherton | do. | Brocket, A., late | 541 |
| NEWHOLM | do. | Newbigging, J. | 358 |
| Newick | DOLPHINTON | Lockhart, M. | 303 |
| New Mains | Lesmahagow | Jackson, Mrs. | 365 |
| do. | Carnwath | Logan, Miss | 307 |
| do. | do. | Logan, Rev. J. | 342 |
| NEWTON | Carstairs | Grossart, W. | 453 |
| do. | CRAWFORD | Irving, G. V. | 256 |
| do. | Lesmahagow | Shaw, W. | 559 |
| OGGS CASTLE | Libberton | Grierson, J. | 374 |
| Oldtown | Carnwath | Wilson, W. | 420 |
| ORCHARD | CARLUKE | Brown, J. | 271 |
| ORCHARDVILLE | Lanark | Stewart, R. | 538 |

| Property | Parish | Proprietor | No. |
|---|---|---|---|
| PATIHEAD HOUSE | Lesmahagow | Wharrie, J. | 429 |
| Peasehill | Lanark | Shand, W. A. | 577 |
| Ponfeigh | Lesmahagow | Symington, W. | 650 |
| Polmonkshead | Douglas | Douglas, J. C. | 361 |
| Pool | Carnwath | Tennant, J. | 292 |
| Priorhill | Lesmahagow | Dickson, J. R. | 372 |
| Riddoch Brae | do. | Steel, W. | 509 |
| Rosehill | do. | Young, J. | 530 |
| Rowantreehill | Carnwath | Whyte, A. C. | 380 |
| Scorryholm | Lesmahagow | Hamilton, T. | 383 |
| SHIELDHILL | Libberton | Chancellor, J. G. | 260 |
| Skellyhill | Lesmahagow | Steel, J. | 368 |
| Smylum Park | Lanark | Carmichael, Miss | 352 |
| Snar | Crawfordjohn | Johnstone, P. & J. | 305 |
| SPITTAL | Biggar | Murray, W., late | 344 |
| Springbank | Lesmahagow | Hamilton, A. | 393 |
| Springfield | Carluke | Pearson, A. | 326 |
| SPRINGHILL | Douglas | Gillespie, R., late | 364 |
| Stane | Biggar | M'Laggan, D., M.D. | 404 |
| STANMORE | Lanark | Lithgow, R. | 375 |
| do. | do. | Lithgow, W. | 476 |
| St John's Kirk | Covington | Waugh, John | 349 |
| STOCKBRIGGS | Lesmahagow | Alston, J. W. | 267 |
| Stockwell | Carluke | Gilchrist, R. | 452 |
| STOXEBYRES | Lesmahagow | Monteith, Douglas | 279 |
| Stonehill | do. | M'Glue, R. | 343 |
| STRANCLEUGH | Crawfordjohn | Williamson, W. | 390 |
| SUNNYSIDE | Lanark | Leishman, — | 275 |
| do. | Carnwath | Gillespie, A., late | 275 |
| SYMINGTON LODGE | Symington | M'Pherson, N. | 296 |

| PROPERTY | PARISH | PROPRIETOR | No. | | No. | PROPRIETOR | PARISH | PROPERTY | No. |
|---|---|---|---|---|---|---|---|---|---|
| Tanhill | Carluke | Allan, J., *late* | 431 | | 431 | Allan, A. | Carluke | Hillhead | 441 |
| do. | Lesmahagow | Hamilton, —, *late* | 402 | | 402 | Allan, J. *late* | do. | Tanhill | 431 |
| TEATH | do. | Steel, D. | 377 | | 377 | ALSTON, J. W. | LESMAHAGOW | Stockbriggs | 267 |
| Throughburn | Carnwath | Mitchell, G., Rev. | 436 | | 436 | Anderson, S. | Lanark | Carfin | 301 |
| Tintoside | Symington | Waugh, S. | 520 | | 520 | ANSTRUTHER, SirW.C. | CARMICHAEL,etc | Westraw, etc. | 247 |
| TOFT-COMBS | Biggar | Gibson, T. | 285 | | 285 | BAILLEY, G. | Lanark | JERVISWOOD | 293 |
| Townhead | Douglas | Rae, T. | 617 | | 617 | BAILLEY, J. W. | COULTER | CULTER-ALLERS | 258 |
| TROLOSS | Crawford | Wilson, Brothers | 310 | | 310 | Barr, Messrs. | Lesmahagow | Moat | 371 |
| Tupenhill | Carluke | LORD BELHAVEN | 441 | | 441 | BELHAVEN, Lord | Carluke | Tupenhill | 441 |
| Turf-foot | do. | Wilson, Miss J. | 340 | | 340 | BELL, A. | do. | Westerhouse | 341 |
| Verebills | Lesmahagow | Inglis, J | 288 | | 288 | Bell, J. | Biggar | Fullburn | 561 |
| Watersido | do. | Donald, W. | 521 | | 521 | BERTRAM, W. | CARNWATH | Kersevell | 259 |
| WAYGATESHAW | CARLUKE | STEEL, S., *late* | 291 | | 291 | Birrell, Lieut.-Col. | Lesmahagow | Cumberhead, South | 302 |
| Wellbank | Walston | Lawson, A. | 714 | | 714 | BUCCLEUGH, Duke of | Crawfordjohn | Whitecleugh, Upper | 252 |
| WESTBANK | Carstairs | MATHER, J., *late* | 323 | | 323 | Buchanan, R. C. | Carstairs | Mossplat | 284 |
| WESTERHOUSE | Carluke | BELL, A. | 341 | | 341 | Burns, G. | Lesmahagow | High Cross | 582 |
| Westmoreshot | Carnwath | Somerville, W. | 418 | | 418 | Burton, T. | do. | Hawksland | 543 |
| WESTRAW, etc. | CARMICHAEL,etc | Anstruther, SirW.C. | 247 | | 247 | BLACKWOOD, J. T | do. | LEE LAW | 351 |
| Westsidewood | Carnwath | Wilson, J. | 282 | | 282 | Brocket, A. | do. | Netherfauld | 541 |
| WEST-TOWN | Pettinain | SMITH, lI., *late* | 237 | | 237 | Brown, A., Rov. | do. | Bereholm | 451 |
| Westyard-houses | Carnwath | Elder, J., *late* | 642 | | 642 | Brown, J. T. | do. | AUCHLOCHAN | 266 |
| do. | do. | Somerville, J. | 649 | | 649 | BROWN, J. | Carluke | ORCHARD | 271 |
| Whitecleugh, Upper | Crawfordjohn | Buccleugh, Duke of | 252 | | 252 | BROWN, L. | BIGGAR | EDMONSTONE | 264 |
| Whiteside | Lesmahagow | Sinclair, J., *late* | 490 | | 490 | Brown, Miss C. | Carnwath | Braehead | 572 |
| do. | do. | Thomson, M. | 440 | | 440 | Brown, Mrs | Biggar | Lindsaylands | 311 |
| Whiteside-hill | do. | Tudhope, J. | 510 | | 510 | Brown, T. | Lesmahagow | Kilnhills | 471 |
| Wishaw | Carluke | Leggatt, J | 516 | | 516 | Brown, W. | Do. | Abbeygreen | 442 |
| Wilsontown | Carnwath | Dixon, W. | 464 | | 464 | Brown, W. | Carluke | Springfield | 326 |
| Wyndales | Symington | Somerville, W. | 360 | | 360 | Cadzow, J. | Lesmahagow | Burnfoot | 562 |
| Yardhouses | Carnwath | Dymock, T. | 703 | | 703 | Cadzow, W. | Carluke | Craighead | 432 |

| PROPRIETOR. | PARISH. | PROPERTY. | No. |
|---|---|---|---|
| Carmichael, Miss | Lanark | Smylum Park | 352 |
| Carmichael, T. | Carnwath | King's Inn | 391 |
| CARMICHAEL, M. T. | CARMICHAEL | EASTEND | 248 |
| Carmichael, T. | Carnwath | Craigie House | 492 |
| Carmichael, W. | do. | Greenshields | 493 |
| CHANCELLOR, J. G. | LIBBERTON | SHIELDHILL | 260 |
| COCHRANE, A. B. | LAMINGTON | LAMINGTON | 249 |
| COLEBROOKE, Sir T. E. | CRAWFORD | CRAWFORDJOHN | 255 |
| COLLYER, W. D. | Libberton | CORMISTON-TOWERS | 331 |
| Coltness Iron Co. | Lesmahagow | Birkfield | 268 |
| Craig, W. C. | Biggar | Burghlands | 412 |
| CRANSTOUNE, Miss E. | LESMAHAGOW | Corehouse | 263 |
| CUTHBERTSON, M. | Biggar | Lindsaylands, West | 392 |
| Davidson, T. | Lesmahagow | Bellfield | 393 |
| DICKSON, D. | Symington | Hartree (Peebles) | 272 |
| Dickson, J. R. | Lesmahagow | Priorhill | 372 |
| Dickson, W. J. | Crawfordjohn | Glentewan | 332 |
| Dixon, W. | Carnwath | Wilsontown | 464 |
| Donald, W. | Lesmahagow | Waterside | 521 |
| Donald, R. | do. | Capehall | 601 |
| DOUGLAS, Lord, late | Crawford, etc. | Harecleugh, etc. | 243 |
| Douglas, J. C. | Douglas | Polmonkshead | 361 |
| Douglas, Miss | Carnwath | Haywood | 273 |
| DOUGLAS, MENTEITH. | LESMAHAGOW | STONEBYRES | 279 |
| Douglas, J. | do. | Auchmedan | 413 |
| DYCE, J. N. | Lanark | CASTLEBANK | 401 |
| Dykes, A. | Lesmahagow | Ladeshead | 421 |
| Dymock, T. | Carnwath | Yardhouses | 703 |
| Elmonstone, Capt. | Biggar | Hillend | 362 |
| Elder, J. | Carnwath | Gillhouse | 381 |

| PROPRIETOR. | PARISH. | PROPERTY. | No. |
|---|---|---|---|
| Elder, J. | Carnwath | Westyardhouses | 642 |
| Ewart, R., late | Crawford | NUNNERIE | 274 |
| FERGUSON, J. | Lesmahagow | ELLANBANK | 353 |
| FIELD, J. | Lanark | BROOKLANDS | 563 |
| Forrest, A. | Carluke | Yeildshields | 422 |
| Forrest, J. | Biggar | EAST-TOFTS | 414 |
| Forrest, J. | Carluke | Kilcadzow | 512 |
| Forrest, W. | do. | Gills | 363 |
| Frame, J. | Lanark | Birkhill | 508 |
| Frame, R., M.D. | Lesmahagow | Abbeygreen | 423 |
| Fraser, T. | Carluke | Gallagreen | 522 |
| French, T. | Lesmahagow | Garngour | 415 |
| Gall, H. | do. | Midtown | 483 |
| GIBSON, T. | Biggar, etc. | Toftcombs | 285 |
| Gilchrist, R. | Carluke | Stockwell | 452 |
| GILCHRIST, J. | do. | GILLFOOT | 312 |
| GILLESPIE, A. | Biggar | BIGGAR PARK | 294 |
| Gillespie, A., late | Carnwath | Cleugh | 275 |
| Gillespie, Mrs | Biggar | BIGGAR PARK | 394 |
| GILLESPIE, R., late | Douglas | SPRINGHILL | 364 |
| Gillespie, W. | Lanark | Huntlyhill | 354 |
| Gladstone, G. | Biggar | Dalerig | 494 |
| Goldie, W. | Carnwath | Heathland | 355 |
| Gordon, Col. W. | Lesmahagow | Harperfield | 313 |
| Gray, J. | Carluke | Coldstream | 475 |
| GREENSHIELDS, J. | Lesnahagow | KERSE | 295 |
| GRIERSON, J. | Libberton | OGGS CASTLE | 374 |
| Grossart, W. | Carstairs | Newmains | 453 |
| Haddow, A. C. | Wiston | Little Galla | 373 |
| Haggart, J. C. | Carnwath | Craigenburn | 314 |

| Proprietor. | Parish. | Property. | No. |
|---|---|---|---|
| Hamilton, Duke of.. | Lesmahagow | Auchenheath | 251 |
| Hamilton, Capt. | do. | Kypeswaterhead | 433 |
| Hamilton, D. | Douglas | Brachead | 725 |
| Hamilton, G. | Lesmahagow | Auldton | 356 |
| Hamilton, J. C. | Carstairs | Birniehill | 315 |
| Hamilton, A. | Lesmahagow | Springbank | 395 |
| Hamilton, G. | do. | Gill | 357 |
| Hamilton, J. | Carluke | (Fairholm) Kirkton | 286 |
| Hamilton, J. | do. | Mavisbank | 515 |
| Hamilton, J., late | Lesmahagow | Tanhill | 402 |
| Hamilton, Mrs J. | Carluke | Easterseat | 474 |
| Hamilton, J. | do. | do. | 486 |
| Hamilton, T. | Lesmahagow | Scorryholm | 383 |
| Hamilton, T. | Carnwath | Burnfoot | 454 |
| Hamilton, W. | Carluke | Brackenhill | 384 |
| Hamilton, W. | Lesmahagow | Loganbank | 424 |
| Handyside, W. | Coulter | Cornhill | 316 |
| Harvie, W. | Carluke | Brownlie | 333 |
| Hastie, A., late | Lesmahagow | Bankhead | 317 |
| Henderson, J. | do. | Crossford | 455 |
| Home, Countess of | Douglas, etc. | Douglas Castle | 241 |
| Hopetoun, Earl of | Crawford | Leadhills | 253 |
| Howieson, A. | Lanark | Hyndford | 321 |
| Howieson, Dr, late | Wiston | Hillend | 304 |
| Howieson, Lieut.-Col. | Lanark | Holmfoot | 403 |
| Howieson, Mrs | Douglas | Crossburn | 443 |
| Hozier, J. | Carluke | Mauldslie | 287 |
| Hunter, H., late | Crawfordjohn | Craighead | 000 |
| Inglis, J. | Lesmahagow | Verehills | 288 |
| Irving, George Vere | Crawford | Newton | 256 |

| Proprietor. | Parish. | Property. | No. |
|---|---|---|---|
| Irving, W. | Lanark | Mansfield | 468 |
| Jack, G. | Carluke | Boreland | 636 |
| Jackson, Mrs | Lesmahagow | Newick | 365 |
| Johnston, P. and J. | Crawfordjohn | Snar | 305 |
| Kidd, Professor | Carnwath | Hinshelwood | 416 |
| Kirkland, Sir J. | do. | Clarty | 306 |
| Lamb, J. | Lesmahagow | Boreland | 426 |
| Lang, T. | do. | Crossford | 385 |
| Lawson, A. | Walston | Wellbank | 714 |
| Lean, J. | Carluke | Middlehouse | 366 |
| Leggat, J. | do. | Wishaw | 516 |
| Leighton, W., late | Lesmahagow | Bankend | 318 |
| Leishman, J. | Lanark | Sunnyside | 275 |
| Liddell, P. | Carnwath | Mid-Hinshelwood | 406 |
| Lightbody, J. | Carluke | Drums | 565 |
| Lithgow, R. | Lanark | Stanmore | 375 |
| Lithgow, W. | do. | do. | 476 |
| Lockhart, A. E. | Carstairs | Cleghorn | 245 |
| Lockhart, L., D.D. | Carluke | Milton-Lockhart | 246 |
| Lockhart, Sir N. M'D. | Lanark | Lee and Carnwath | 244 |
| Lockhart, W. | do. | Nemphlar | 386 |
| Lockhart, W. | do. | do. | 396 |
| Lockhart, M. | Dolphinton | Newholm | 244 |
| Logan, Miss | Carnwath | New Mains | 307 |
| Logan, J. | do. | Fastshields | 322 |
| Logan, Mrs A. | do. | Browshot | 427 |
| Logan, R. | Lesmahagow | Corramore | 334 |
| Lorimer, J. | Crawfordjohn | Holmhead | 435 |
| Lorraine, W. S. | Biggar | Loaningdale | 276 |
| M'Ghie, R. | Lesmahagow | Stonehill | 313 |

| Proprietor | Parish | Property | No. | Proprietor | Parish | Property | No. |
|---|---|---|---|---|---|---|---|
| M'Ghie, T. | Lesmahagow | Moatvett | 456 | Paterson, R. | Coulter | Birthwood | 325 |
| M'Gowran, W. | do. | Bentknowes | 566 | Paul, J. | Biggar | Cambus-Wallace | 382 |
| M'Kenzie, J. O. | Dolphinton | Dolphinton | 262 | Rae, J. | Douglas | Townhead | 617 |
| M'Kirdy, John G. | Lesmahagow | Birkwood | 265 | Ramsay, Mrs C. | Carnwath | Falla | 336 |
| M'Laggan, D., M.D. | Biggar | Stane | 401 | Reid, A. | Lesmahagow | Bereholm-mill | 618 |
| M'Pherson, N. | Symington | Symington Lodge | 296 | Reid, J. | Carluke | Nellfield | 357 |
| M'Queen, R. | Wiston | Hardington | 277 | Robertson, G. | Carnwath | Auchengray | 320 |
| Marr, Rev. J. L., late | Lanark | Gallahill | 496 | Robertson, G. | Lanark | Baronald | 345 |
| Marshall, J. | Lesmahagow | Cumberhead, South | 297 | Robertson, Misses | Carluke | Hallcraig | 327 |
| Mather, J., late | Carstairs | Westbank | 323 | Ross, Sir W. C. | Lanark | Boxnington | 250 |
| Meikle, R. | Douglas | Bogside | 505 | Ross, J. | Carluke | Gowanside | 459 |
| Meikle, Misses | Lesmahagow | Abbeygreen | 675 | Rowatt, J., late | Walston | Falla | 308 |
| Meikle, R. | do. | Auchren | 397 | Scott, J. | Lanark | Bellfield | 445 |
| Menzies, J. | Crawford | Bellfield | 437 | Scott, Mrs | Lesmahagow | Abbeygreen | 537 |
| Miller, J. | Carluke | Gladdenhill | 433 | Selkirk, J. | Carluke | Heanshields | 489 |
| Mitchell, Rev. G. | Carnwath | Throughburn | 436 | Semple, A. | Lesmahagow | Greenhill | 438 |
| Mitchell, W. G. | Biggar | Caenwood | 278 | Semple, T. | do. | Daryfillan | 446 |
| Montague, Lady | Lesmahagow | Craignethan | 242 | Semple, W. | do. | Greenridge | 388 |
| Monteith, R. | Carstairs | Carstairs | 261 | Semple, W. | do. | Letham | 408 |
| Mossman, H. | Lesmahagow | Auchfardie | 289 | Shand, W. A. | Lanark | Peasehill | 577 |
| Murray, J. | Biggar | Heaviside | 319 | Shaw, J. | Carluke | Braidwood | 578 |
| Murray, Lord, late | do. | Lauqlee | 335 | Shaw, J. | Lesmahagow | Newton | 559 |
| Murray, J. W. | Carnwath | Leamside | 324 | Shotts Iron Co. | Carluke | Castlehill | 269 |
| Murray, W., late | Biggar | Spittal | 314 | Sim, Adam | Coulter | Coulter-Maynes | 257 |
| Neilson, J. | Carluke | Castlehill | 506 | Simpson, J. | Carnwath | Browshot | 439 |
| Newbigging, J. | Carnwath | Girlwoodend | 405 | Sinclair, J., late | Lesmahagow | Whiteside | 490 |
| Newbigging, W. | Lesmahagow | Netherton | 358 | Smith, H., late | Pettinain | West-town | 337 |
| Orr, Capt. | Carluke | Catcraig | 376 | Smith, J. | Lesmahagow | Fauldhouse | 346 |
| Pagan, J., M.D. | Lesmahagow | Boghill | 398 | Somerville, J. | Carnwath | Westyardhouses | 649 |
| Paterson, A. | Douglas | Cormacoup | 280 | Somerville, T. | do. | Greenfield | 309 |

| Proprietor. | Parish. | Property. | No. |
|---|---|---|---|
| Somerville, S., M.D. | Carnwath | Ampherlaw | 329 |
| Somerville, W. | Symington | Wyndales | 360 |
| Somerville, W. | Carnwath | Westmoreshot | 418 |
| Somerville, W. | Carstairs | Gowanhill | 359 |
| Somerville, R. | Libberton | Cormiston | 328 |
| Souter, D. R. | Carnwath | Lawhead | 281 |
| Stainton, J., *late* | Biggar | Biggarshiels | 290 |
| Stark, J., M.D. | Libberton | Huntfield | 330 |
| Steel, D. | Lesmahagow | Teaths | 377 |
| Steel, J. | do. | Skellyhill | 368 |
| Steel, S. | Carluke | Waygateshaw | 291 |
| Steel, T. | Lesmahagow | Brae | 508 |
| Steel, W. | do. | Riddoch Brae | 509 |
| Stein, J. | do. | Kirkfield | 298 |
| Stevenson, N. | Carluke | Braidwood | 299 |
| Stewart, A. | do. | Brownlie | 347 |
| Stewart, B. | Lanark | Orchardville | 538 |
| Stewart, G. | Carnwath | Hinshelwood | 569 |
| Stewart, L. | do. | Brownrig | 000 |
| Stodart, H. | Lanark | Mousebank | 478 |
| Symington, W. | Lesmahagow | Netherburn | 409 |
| Symington, W. | do. | Ponfeigh | 650 |
| Tennent, J. | Carnwath | Pool | 292 |
| Tennent, J. | Lesmahagow | Clydegrove | 447 |
| Thomson, J. | do. | Birkenhead | 300 |
| Thomson, J. | Crawfordjohn | Glendowran | 389 |
| Thomson, J. | Lesmahagow | Kirkbank | 338 |
| Thomson, M. | do. | Whiteside | 440 |
| Thomson, V., Rev. | do. | Castleyett | 470 |
| Todd, W. | Lanark | Logan | 378 |
| Todd, J. | Lesmahagow | Logan | 579 |
| Todd, J. | do. | Birthwood | 410 |
| Tudhope, J. | do. | Heathlands | 460 |
| Tudhope, J. | do. | Midgarngour | 480 |
| Tudhope, J. | do. | Whitesidehill | 510 |
| Turnbull, M. | Biggar | Eastfield | 550 |
| Vasse, J. | Lanark | Croftonhill | 467 |
| Vere Hope, W. E. | Lesmahagow | Blackwood | 254 |
| Walker & Co. | Lanark | New Lanark | 270 |
| Walker, J., *late*. | Carluke | Eastquarter | 429 |
| Watson, W. | Biggar | Midtoftcombs | 399 |
| Waugh, J. | Covington | St John's Kirk | 349 |
| Waugh, Dr. | Lesmahagow | Hazelbank | 539 |
| Waugh, S. | Symington | Tintoside | 520 |
| Wharrie, J. | Lesmahagow | Pathhead | 429 |
| White, A. C. | Carnwath | Rowantreehill | 380 |
| Whyte, W. | do. | Blackcastle | 339 |
| Whyte, J. | Coulter | Coultermill | 379 |
| Whyte, W. | Walston | Blackcastle | 449 |
| Wilson, Bros. | Crawford | Tholoss | 310 |
| Wilson, J. | Lesmahagow | Bellfield | 400 |
| Wilson, J. L. | Lanark | Nemphlar-West | 419 |
| Wilson, R. | Walston | Howgate | 000 |
| Wilson, W. | Carnwath | Oldtown | 420 |
| Wodrop, W. H. A. | Walston | Howburn | 283 |
| Wrightson, F. | Libberton | Cormistone | 369 |
| Wyld, A. | Walston | Lammerlaw | 350 |
| Wyndham, J., *late* | Carnwath | Greenfield | 370 |
| Williamson, W. B. | Crawfordjohn | Strancleugh | 300 |
| Young, J. | Lesmahagow | Rosehill | 530 |

| Farm, &c. | Parish | Tenant | No. | Farm, &c. | Parish | Tenant | No. |
|---|---|---|---|---|---|---|---|
| Abington, Nether | Crawfordjohn | Tweedie, Messrs | 811 | Barnhills | Lesmahagow | Affleck, D. & W. | 832 |
| do. Over | do. | Inch, R. | 861 | Baronald | Lanark | Smith, J. | 1001 |
| Acred-land | Lamington | Watson, W. | 1300 | Bellstane | Carluke | Forrest, W. | 1142 |
| Affleck | Lesmahagow | Carruthers, R. | 1221 | do. | do. | Gibson, J. & R. | 932 |
| Akinlophead | do. | Neilson, T. | 1091 | Bent | Lesmahagow | Dykes, A. | 862 |
| Ampherlaw | Carnwath | Watson, J. | 1141 | Biggar Common | Biggar | Prentice, J. | 1081 |
| Andershaw | Douglas | Willison, J. | 991 | do. Mains | do. | Brown, W. | 951 |
| Annieston | Symington | Craig, Mrs | 801 | do. Shiels | do. | King, W. | 833 |
| Anston | Dunsyre | Shaw, T. | 800 | Birkclench | Crawfordjohn | Lannie, J. | 981 |
| Arthurshields | Libberton | Hodge, J. | 1231 | Birkenhead | Lesmahagow | Elder, J. & W. | 1302 |
| do. | do. | Hodge, W. | 1211 | do. | do. | Meikle, J. | 493 |
| do. | do. | Smith, J. | 1118 | Birkhill | do. | Stobbs, W. | 1113 |
| Auchenbog | Lesmahagow | Cooper, G. | 1241 | Birks | Carluke | Hamilton, W. | 1181 |
| do. | do. | Inch, W. | 1291 | Birkwood | Lesmahagow | M'Kirdy, J. G. | 1252 |
| Auchenglen | Lanark | Meikle, R. | 971 | do. Mains | do. | Tudhope, G. | 972 |
| do. | do. | Shirlaw, G. | 992 | Birniehill | Carstairs | Brown, J. | 791 |
| Auchengray, Mid | Carnwath | Ballantyne, G. | 1171 | Birthwood | Lesmahagow | Brown, J. | 1203 |
| Auchenheath | Lesmahagow | Baxter, W. | 921 | Blackcastle | Carnwath | Lindsay, J. | 1061 |
| do. Woods | do. | Rannatyne, J. | 1111 | Blackhill | Crawfordjohn | French, T. | 802 |
| Auchrobert | do. | Brown, J. | 831 | do. | Lesmahagow | Stodart, J., late | 961 |
| Auchintorroch | do. | Scott, J. | 1092 | Blackwoodside | do. | Barr, A. | 1292 |
| Auchtool | do. | Duncan, J. | 1041 | Blackwoodyards | do. | M'Gowran, W. | 933 |
| Auchtygremmel | do. | Carruthers, J. | 911 | Blair | do. | M'Gowran, T. | 1042 |
| do. Nether | do. | Weir, F. | 922 | do. | do. | Wilkie, Mrs | 1303 |
| Bagsmoor and Todhills | Walston | Tarvit, R. | 821 | Blair-reckoning | do. | Cook, J. | 1212 |
| Baitlaw, etc. | Libberton | Watson, A. | 931 | Blinklie | Carmichael | Swan, J. | 1293 |
| Baitlaws, etc. | Lamington | DENHOLM, ALEX. | 751 | Boat—Thankerton | Covington | Tarvet, J. | 1094 |
| Balgray, Nether | Crawford | Black, J. | 1112 | Boathaugh, etc. | Lanark | Jack, Messrs | 751 |
| Bauk | Dolphinton | Bertram, R. | 1093 | Boghall | Biggar | Brows, J. | 701 |
| Bankhead | Carnwath | Jack, T. | 812 | do. | Libberton | Brown, J. | 1142 |

| Farm, &c. | Parish | Tenant | No. |
|---|---|---|---|
| Boghall | Carnwath | Somerville, J. | 1011 |
| Bodinlee | Wiston | GILLESPIE, T. | 912 |
| Boghead | Crawford | Anderson, J. | 1213 |
| Boghill and Righead | Lesmahagow | Tudhope, J. | 1021 |
| Boghouse | Crawfordjohn | French, J. | 863 |
| Bogside | Carluke | Barr, W. | 1142 |
| do. | do. | Stewart, A. | 891 |
| do. | Lesmahagow | Brown, T. | 1161 |
| Bonnington Mains | Lanark | CUNNINGHAM, J. | 792 |
| Boreland | Lesmahagow | M'Ghee, H. T. | 1022 |
| do. | Libberton | Ritchie, J. | 1190 |
| do. | Walston | Hamilton, M. & T. | 782 |
| Bottom, North | Douglas | WILLISON, J. | 1172 |
| Bowhouse | Carmichael | Muir, W. | 1082 |
| Brackenhill | Carluke | Barr, T. | 1071 |
| Brackenridge, E. | Lesmahagow | Dent, J. | 1294 |
| do. S. | do. | Fallow, T. | 1244 |
| do. W. | do. | Gillies, M. | 1201 |
| Broadfield | Symington | Aitken, J. | 941 |
| Broomerside | Douglas | Greenshields, A. | 871 |
| Broomfield and Rigside | Biggar | Swann, J. | 973 |
| Brownbank | Carnwath | Smellie, H. | 881 |
| Brownhill | do. | Cuthbertson, J. | 892 |
| do. | Carluke | Weir, R. | 1023 |
| Brownridge | Carluke | Black, D. | 1012 |
| Brownriggs | Carstairs | Stewart, J. | 1232 |
| Browshot&Longgarton | Pettinain | Greenshields, J. | 1024 |
| Buchtknowe | Carnwath | Forrest, J. | 1243 |
| Burnbrae | do. | Todd, A. | 982 |
| do. | Dolphinton | Bertram, R. | 1122 |
| Burnfoot | Libberton | Ritchie, D. | 983 |
| Burnhead | Carluke | Jack, J. | 1202 |
| do. and Park | Carnwath | French, W. | 771 |
| Burnhouse | Carmichael | Prentice, T. | 1253 |
| do. | Wiston | Plenderleith, R. | 822 |
| Bushelhead | Carluke | Carruthers, T. | 1123 |
| Byretown | Lesmahagow | DYKES, R. | 762 |
| Caerwood | Biggar | Coubrough, A. | 901 |
| Calla | Carnwath | Fleming, A. | 793 |
| Callendean | do. | Hamilton, W. | 763 |
| Campshead | Crawford | Grieve, M. | 813 |
| Cauder-water | Lesmahagow | Hamilton, R. | 1203 |
| Candy-bank | Biggar | Brown, J. | 962 |
| Candy-mill | Carluke | Smith, J. | 1043 |
| Carfin and Clydebank | Lanark | Snellie, W. | 1072 |
| Carluke | Carluke | Cassells, A. | 1013 |
| Carmichael Bank | Carmichael | Paterson, J. | 1247 |
| do. Mill | do. | Paterson, J. | 1143 |
| do. Policy | do. | French, J. | 851 |
| Carnwath | Carnwath | Anderson, J. | 902 |
| do. Mill | do. | SMITH, H. | 803 |
| Castlehill | Carluke | Jack, J. | 1144 |
| do. | Lanark | Robb, J. | 1025 |
| Castlemains | Douglas | Scott, T. R. | 1305 |
| do. | Crawford | Tweedie, D. | 764 |
| Catcraig | Carluke | Cassells, J. | 1233 |
| Charleston | Lanark | Gray, J. | 1062 |
| Chesterhall | Wiston | Stoddart, W. | 841 |
| Clarkston | Lesmahagow | Prentice, J. | 913 |
| Clecklands | do. | Cooper, J. | 1191 |

| Farm, &c. | Parish | Tenant | No. |
|---|---|---|---|
| Cleghorn | Lanark | Callan, A. | 834 |
| do. Mill | do. | Cassels, A. | 864 |
| Clennochdyke | Lesmahagow | Lockhart, A. | 1234 |
| Cleugh | Carnwath | Nimmo, T. | 893 |
| do. | Douglas | Cunningham, D. | 1151 |
| Cleughbar | Lesmahagow | Young, W. | 1235 |
| Cleughmill | Carnwath | Struthers, J. | 1162 |
| Cloburn | Pettinain | Paterson, Mrs J. | 1002 |
| Coalburn | Lesmahagow | Watson, T. | 1031 |
| Coalgill | Douglas | Scott, T. R. | 1311 |
| Coblehaugh | Lanark | Muirhead, J. | 852 |
| Cocklaw | Walston | Ritchie, G. | 1151 |
| Cockridge | Carstairs | Scott, A. | 984 |
| Coldchapel | Lamington | Hadlow, J. | 842 |
| Collielaw | Lanark | Aitken, T. | 1063 |
| Columbia and Hills | Carstairs | Elder, J. | 794 |
| Corbiehall | do. | Fleming, J. | 772 |
| Cormiston | Libberton | Williamson, A. | 952 |
| do. House | do. | Williamson, J. | 1183 |
| do. | do. | Clegborn, T. | 994 |
| Corramill | Lesmahagow | Allan, R. | 1295 |
| Corramore | do. | Brownlie, A. | 985 |
| Coulter-Allers & Snaip | Coulter | Watson, A. | 765 |
| do. Haugh | do. | Inch, J. | 804 |
| do. Mill | do. | Dick, J. | 1083 |
| do. Park, N. | do. | Bertram, A. | 1173 |
| do. do. S. | do. | Finlayson, T., late | 963 |
| Covington Mains | Covington | Lindsay, H. | 853 |
| do. Mill | do. | Lindsay, A. | 923 |
| Crawford | Carstairs | Barr, W. | 1131 |

| Farm, &c. | Parish | Tenant | No. |
|---|---|---|---|
| Crawfordjohn | Crawfordjohn | Watson, E. | 823 |
| do. Mill | do. | Galloway, J. | 953 |
| Crawfordwell | Carluke | Davidson, A. | 1152 |
| Craighead | Crawfordjohn | Hunter, H., late | 914 |
| do. Mill | Lesmahagow | Thomson, H. | 1192 |
| Craignethan | do. | Smith, J. | 1003 |
| Crimp-cramp | Crawford | Paterson, R. | 865 |
| Croftanrigh | Dolphinton | Crawford, W. | 1306 |
| Croftfoot | Carluke | Black, W. | 1281 |
| Crookboat | Carmichael | Lamb, J. | 1101 |
| Crookedstane | Crawford | Hunter, R., late | 752 |
| Crookland | Carmichael | Kallantyne, — | 1101 |
| Crossdyke | do. | Core, A. | 942 |
| Cumberhead, North | Lesmahagow | Sandilands, G. | 843 |
| do. South | do. | Sandilands, W. | 844 |
| Debog | Douglas | M'Kinlay, J. | 872 |
| Devonhill | Carmichael | Greenshields, J. | 1254 |
| Dillars | Lesmahagow | Neilson, D. | 1014 |
| Draffan, etc. | do. | Russell, A. | 773 |
| do. South | do. | Pate, T. | 824 |
| Drumalbin | Carmichael | Paterson, W. | 774 |
| Dumbrexhill | Lesmahagow | Pate, A. | 1102 |
| Dunsyre | Dunsyre | £42 10s. Ray, M. | error? |
| do. Mains | do. | Brown, A. | 783 |
| Dyke | Carmichael | Dickson, W. | 1214 |
| Dykefoot | Dunsyre | Anderson, D. & W. | 903 |
| Dykehead | Douglas | Thorburn, R. | 1063 |
| do. | Lesmahagow | Barr, J. | 1064 |
| Eastend | Carstairs | Black, R. | 882 |
| Easterhills | Pettinain | Gibson, W., late | 1095 |

| FARM, &c. | PARISH | TENANT | No. |
|---|---|---|---|
| Eastertown | Crawfordjohn | French, F. | 904 |
| do. East | Lesmahagow | Dougall, A. | 1255 |
| do. West | do. | Dougall, J. | 1065 |
| Eastfield | Coulter | Gladstone, A. | 954 |
| do. | Pettinain | Lindsay, W. | 845 |
| do. | Symington | Linton, J. | 1026 |
| do. | Wiston | Gibson, J. | 1103 |
| Eastforth | Carnwath | M'Culloch, G. | 1032 |
| East and Westhills | Dunsyre | Brown, jr., J. | 835 |
| Eastsidewood | Carnwath | Todd, J., late | 1004 |
| East-tofts | Coulter | Bertram, A. | 1174 |
| East-town | Dunsyre | Brown, T. | 784 |
| Eastwood | Lesmahagow | Allan, A. | 905 |
| Eastyardhouses | Carnwath | Wilson, J. | 836 |
| Edmonstone Mill | Biggar | Gibson, S. | 1104 |
| Elmbank | Libberton | Donald, G. | 1114 |
| Ellsrickle | Walston | Greenshields, D. | 795 |
| Elvanfoot | Crawford | Anderson, T., late | 894 |
| Fallhills and Moorfoot | Carstairs | Wallace, R. | 895 |
| Fallside | Wiston | Gillespie, T. | 854 |
| Fence | Lesmahagow | Hamilton, J. | 1027 |
| Fingland | Crawford | Rae, W. & A. | 873 |
| Forth | Carnwath | Scott, J. | 1204 |
| do. East | do. | Wilson, W. | 1306 |
| do. West | do. | Anderson, J. | 934 |
| Fullwood | Lanark | Wilson, Mrs | 1033 |
| Gair | Carluke | Forrest, R. | 1313 |
| Galla-little | Wiston | Fraser, R. | 1073 |
| Garngour, N. | Lesmahagow | French, S. | 1236 |
| do. S. | do. | Peat, R. | 1105 |

| No. | TENANT | PARISH | FARM, &c. |
|---|---|---|---|
| 986 | Stoddart, T. | Lesmahagow | Garrellwood |
| 1222 | Brown, J. | Coulter | Gateside |
| 753 | GILLESPIE, J. | Douglas | do. |
| 1074 | Letham, J. | Lesmahagow | Gill |
| 1314 | Thomson, A | Carluke | do. |
| 995 | Brown, J. & I. | do. | Gillbank |
| 814 | Inch, T. | Crawfordjohn | Gilkerscleugh Mains |
| 1028 | Greenshields, A. | Carnwath | Gillhouse and Stobwood |
| 1132 | M'Morran, J. | Carnwath | Girdwoodend |
| 1296 | Stewart, J. | Carluke | Gladdenhill |
| 1096 | Brown, Mrs J. | Libberton | Gladstanes, East |
| 1115 | Aitken, J. | do. | do. West |
| 803 | French, J. | Crawford | Glencaplo |
| 955 | Stewart, P. | Crawfordjohn | Glendorch |
| 1034 | Williamson, J. | Crawford | Glendowran |
| 796 | HUNTER, R., late | do. | Glengeith |
| 754 | do. | do. | Glenochar |
| 776 | PATERSON, J., late | Douglas | Glentaggart |
| 924 | Watson, W. | Crawfordjohn | Glentewing |
| 996 | Coke, J. | do. | do. Easter |
| 1193 | Ray, J. | Douglas | Glespin, East |
| 946 | TWEEDIE, Wm. | do. | do. West |
| 915 | Hunter, H., late | Crawfordjohn | Goat and Liscleugh |
| 1215 | Watt, A. | Lesmahagow | Goathousecknowes |
| 1145 | Crossan, J. | Biggar | Green |
| 846 | Gray, J. | Carnwath | do. |
| 1164 | Wilson, J. F. | Carluke | Greenbank |
| 866 | WILLISON, J. | Crawfordjohn | Greenburn |
| 916 | DALGLEISH, J. | do. | Greenfield |
| 964 | Somerville, J. | Carnwath | do. |

| Farm, &c. | Parish | Tenant | No. |
|---|---|---|---|
| Greenhall | Pettinain | Taylor, R. | 994 |
| Greenhill | Wiston | Sadleir, J. | 1035 |
| Greenshields | Libberton | M'Lean, W. | 907 |
| Greenwood | Biggar | Crossan, J. | 1153 |
| Halfmerkland | Lesmahagow | Barr, R. | 1116 |
| Hallhill, North | do. | Calzow, W. | 1106 |
| Halltown—Neuphlar | Lanark | Elder, J. | 997 |
| Hangingshaw, Mid | Coulter | Aitken, J. | 1116 |
| do. Nether | do. | Bertram, J. | 975 |
| do. Upper | do. | Watson, P. | 1081 |
| Hardgatehead | Carnwath | Sibbald, J. | 1005 |
| Hardington Mains | Wiston | Muir, W., late | 1075 |
| Harelaw | Carstairs | Alison, A. | 797 |
| Harley Holm | Carnichael | Paterson, W. | 1076 |
| Hareshaw, etc. | Carluke | Marshall, T. | 1237 |
| Hartside | Lamington | Lindsay, E. | 766 |
| Haughs, etc. | Carnwath | Ritchie, J. | 855 |
| Haugh-head | Dolphinton | Ray, sen., J. | 943 |
| Hawksland | Lesmahagow | Burton, T. | 1097 |
| Haywood, Lower | Carnwath | Nimmo, T | 1184 |
| do. Upper | do. | Robb, J. | 1133 |
| Hazelside | Douglas | Black, J. | 798 |
| Heathland | Carnwath | Hamilton, T. | 944 |
| Highfield | Coulter | Robb, J. | 1117 |
| Hill | Lesmahagow | Harrison, W. | 1258 |
| Hillend | Biggar | Blakey, G. | 1175 |
| do. | Wiston | Waddell, J. & W. | 806 |
| Hillhead | Covington | Stoddart, A. | 807 |
| Hillhouse | Lesmahagow | Souter, J. | 1245 |
| Hillrigs | Biggar | M'Kenzie, W. | 956 |

| Farm, &c. | Parish | Tenant | No. |
|---|---|---|---|
| Hillside | Lesmahagow | M'Grigor, J. | 1194 |
| Hindshaw, South | Carluke | Henderson, T. | 945 |
| Hinshelwood Mid | Carnwath | Liddell, J. | 1077 |
| do. | do. | Shaw, W. | 1139 |
| do. | Walston | Thorburn, J. | 1154 |
| Holm-Thankerton | Covington | Fisher, J., late | 1051 |
| Holmhead | Crawfordjohn | Watson, R. | 1195 |
| do. | Lesmahagow | Smith, W. | 1215 |
| Honeypath | Dunsyre | Macdonald, J. | 1078 |
| Hoodsmill | Lesmahagow | Brownlie, J. | 1223 |
| Howburn | Walston | White, J. A. | 808 |
| Howcleugh, Upper | Crawford | Hogg, P. | 825 |
| Howford | Carmichael | Muir, R. | 1246 |
| do. | do. | Tarvet, J. | 1066 |
| Howgate and Redmyre | Carluke | Hunter, R. | 1256 |
| Hangerhill and Chapel | Libberton | Smith, J. | 1282 |
| Huntfield | Lanark | Broomfield, A. | 1067 |
| Huntlyhill | do. | Cunningham, A. | 815 |
| Hyndford | Carnwath | Core, W. | 1283 |
| Janefield | Lanark | Calzow, J. | 925 |
| Jerviswood | do. | Stoddart, D. | 874 |
| do. Mains | Lesmahagow | Cassie, J. | 1165 |
| Johnshill | Douglas | Wilson, J. | 883 |
| Kennox | Carluke | Alison, T. | 816 |
| Kilcadzow, Hill of | do. | Forrest, A. | 976 |
| do. Hole of | Lesmahagow | Torrance, W. | 1124 |
| Kellylees | Carluke | Marshall, A. | 1296 |
| Kingshill | Lesmahagow | Harvie, W. | 917 |
| Kirkfield-Mains | Carnwath | Coltness Irou Co. | 946 |
| Kirkgreen | Crawford | Milligan, J. | 777 |
| Kirkhope | | | |

| FARM, &c. | PARISH | TENANT | No. |
|---|---|---|---|
| Kirkhouse | Dolphinton | Brown, R. | 977 |
| Kirklands | Dunsyre | Allan, J. | 957 |
| Kirkmuirhill | Lesmahagow | Hutchison, W. | 1079 |
| Kirkton | Crawford | Hunter, R. | 965 |
| Kypeside, Nether | Lesmahagow | Semple, R. | 1085 |
| Kypeswaterhead | do. | Meikle, W. | 1155 |
| Ladeshead | do. | Dykes, J. | 1261 |
| Lagshiel | Coulter | Sinclair, J. | 1247 |
| Lairs | Lesmahagow | Tudhope, J. | 1098 |
| Lambcatch & Skylaw | Carnwath | Baird, A. | 1015 |
| Lammerlaw | Walston | Watson, J. | 1107 |
| Lampits, East & West | Carnwath | French, J. | 767 |
| Langhill | Wiston | Clarkson, J. | 1125 |
| Langhorne | Lamington | Stoddart, T. | 826 |
| Langhouse | Douglas | Paterson, A. | 1099 |
| Langknowes | do. | Gibson, W. | 1262 |
| Langlees | Biggar | Jackson, A. | 935 |
| Law | Carluke | Hamilton, W. | 1134 |
| do. Farm | do. | Wallace, J. | 896 |
| Leamside | Carnwath | Aitken, D. | 1257 |
| Lesser Linn | Lesmahagow | Carruthers, Mrs B. | 827 |
| Lettershaws | Crawfordjohn | Watson, R. | 1258 |
| Libberton-Mains | Libberton | Brown, J. | 755 |
| do. Mill | do. | Somerville, A. | 799 |
| Lindsaylands, West | Biggar | Cuthbertson, J. | 875 |
| Linnville | Lesmahagow | Dalgleish, A. | 1166 |
| Little Clyde | Crawford | Thomson, A. | 1126 |
| Littlegill | Lamington | Neilson, J. & J. | 828 |
| Loanhead | Carnwath | Brown, A. | 1052 |
| Lochanbank | Lesmahagow | Brownlie, M. | 1146 |

| FARM, &c. | PARISH | TENANT | No. |
|---|---|---|---|
| Lockhart-Mill | Lanark | Murray, J. | 1206 |
| Longhill | do. | Smith, A. | 1316 |
| Longwell | Wiston | Haddow, R. | 1068 |
| Lowrie's-moor | Lesmahagow | Bunten, T. | 1307 |
| Lupus | do. | Scott, W. | 1216 |
| Mains, Loanhead | Lamington | Tweedie, J. | 856 |
| Marchlands | Wiston | Plenderleith, J. | 1135 |
| Maryfield | Carluke | Coltness Iron Co. | 1053 |
| Mashockmill | do. | Shirlaw, J. | 1263 |
| Mayfield | Lesmahagow | Dickson, A. | 1264 |
| Mauldslie-Mains | Carluke | Scott, J. | 947 |
| Meadowcoats | Wiston | M'Kinlay, J. | 897 |
| Meadowflatt | Covington | Lindsay, J., *late.* | 809 |
| Meadowhead | Dolphinton | M'Kenzie, M. | 1224 |
| Midhill | Libberton | Walker, J. | 1016 |
| Middleholm and Eent | Lesmahagow | Hamilton, A. | 000 |
| Middlehouse | Carluke | Cassells, G. | 966 |
| Middle-Mains | do. | Brown, J. | 1196 |
| Midholm of Grange | Pettinain | Johnston, W. | 837 |
| Midlock | Crawford | Johnston, —, *late.* | 785 |
| Midmuir | Douglas | Gall, A. | 1258 |
| do. and Woodlands | Lesmahagow | Somerville, J. | 1297 |
| Millhill and Dykehead | do. | Wilson, J. | 807 |
| Millhouse | Pettuain | Ballantyne, W. | 1086 |
| Mill-lands, Thankerton | Lesmahagow | Affleck, W. | 1293 |
| Millmuir | Covington | Purdie, A. | 1136 |
| Milton-Lockhart Mill | Carmichael | Froude, H. | 1265 |
| Moat | Lesmahagow | Porteous, R. | 998 |
| do. | do. | Burr, Messrs | 1006 |
| | Wiston | Gillespie, J. | 926 |

| FARM, &c. | PARISH | TENANT | No. |
| --- | --- | --- | --- |
| Monksfoot | Douglas | M'Quat, W. | 1155 |
| Moreshot, Wester | Carnwath | Robb, J. | 1118 |
| Mosshank | Crawfordjohn | Law, J. | 1036 |
| Mosscastle | do. | Coke, W. | 987 |
| Mossplat | Carstairs | Forrest, A. | 876 |
| Moss-side | Carluke | Leggat, J., late | 1256 |
| Mountainblaw | Carnwath | Smith, J. | 988 |
| Mounthcrrick | Crawfordjohn | French, Mrs | 884 |
| Mountstewart | Douglas | Lawson, G. | 1225 |
| Muirburn | Lesmahagow | Wilson, G. | 1147 |
| Muirdykehead | Carluke | Pain, G. | 1207 |
| do. | do. | Brown, G. | 1273 |
| Muirhall | Carnwath | Steel, J. | 998 |
| Muirhead | Wiston | Aitken, W. | 1029 |
| Muirhouse | Covington | Thomson, M., late | 1045 |
| do. | Libberton | Purdie, J. & J. | 786 |
| Muirlee | do. | Prentice, J., late | 1267 |
| Muirsland | Lesmahagow | Weir, G. | 1046 |
| Nemphlar | Lanark | Calzow, W. | 967 |
| do. | do. | Donaldson, A. | 1137 |
| do. | do. | Jack, J. | 898 |
| do. | do. | Jack, W. C. | 1176 |
| do. | do. | Scott, W. | 1080 |
| Nesbit | Coulter | Watson, J. | 787 |
| Nethanfoot | Lesmahagow | Mitchell, W. | 1054 |
| Netherburn | do. | Todd, T. | 1275 |
| Nethercleuch, etc. | Crawford | Hogg, P. | 778 |
| Netherhill and Glespin | Crawfordjohn | Haddow, P. | 958 |
| Netherton | do. | French, T. | 779 |
| do. | Carmichael | Lamb, G., late | 927 |

| FARM, &c. | PARISH | TENANT | No. |
| --- | --- | --- | --- |
| Netherton | Lesmahagow | Todd, J. | 1157 |
| Nethertown | Carstairs | Scott, W. | 868 |
| Newbigging Mains | Carnwath | Weir, W. & D. | 838 |
| do. Mill | do. | White, J., late | 968 |
| Newhouse | Carstairs | Dalziel, J. | 949 |
| do. | Lesmahagow | Gilchrist, J. | 1240 |
| Newmill | Dolphinton | Black, J. | 1055 |
| Newside | Carmichael | Core, J. | 1056 |
| Newsteading | Lanark | Irving, W. | 928 |
| Newtonfoot | Douglas | Gall, J. | 936 |
| Newtonhead | do. | Lawcock, A. | 937 |
| Newtown | Crawford | Gillespie, J. | 1037 |
| do. of Wiston | Wiston | Reid, J. | 857 |
| Normangill | Crawford | Vassie, R. | 756 |
| Northfaulds | Lanark | Ritchie, G. | 929 |
| Northfield | Carluke | Reid, J. | 1317 |
| Northflat-crofts | Carmichael | Aitken, Mrs | 1299 |
| Northholm of Grange | Pettinain | Smith, J. | 969 |
| North-Loanhead | Carnwath | Howieson, J. | 989 |
| North Mains | Covington | Forrest, J. | 885 |
| Nunnerie | Crawford | Wilsox, J. | 757 |
| Oldtown | Carnwath | Aitken, W. | 1276 |
| Orchard | Carluke | Bell & Shirlaw | 1057 |
| Overburn | Lamington | Gilson, W. | 768 |
| Parish-holm | Douglas | Willison, J. | 829 |
| Parkhall | do. | Gillespie, T. | 758 |
| Parkhouse | Libberton | Gibson, J. | 718 |
| Pennyflatts | Covington | Watson, D. | 1226 |
| Persielands | Biggar | Hamilton, T. | 847 |
| Pettinain-bank | Pettinain | Irvine, J., late | 1007 |

| Farm, &c. | Parish | Tenant | No. | Farm, &c. | Parish | Tenant | No. |
|---|---|---|---|---|---|---|---|
| Pettinain Crofts | Pettinain | Gibson, J. | 1196 | Sheatfyknowes | Carstairs | Robb, T. & J. | 1179 |
| Polmoukshead | Douglas | Symington, Mrs. | 999 | Sherificleugh | Crawfordjohn | Forsyth, R. | 1227 |
| Poneil | do. | Newbigging, T., late | 877 | Sheriffflat | Covington | Lindsay, Mrs | 970 |
| Ponfeigh Place | Carmichael | Weir, C. | 1087 | Shodsmill | Carstairs | Barrie, J. | 1069 |
| Pool Farm | Carnwath | Carmichael, W. | 1087 | Shortcleugh, West | Crawford | Paterson, A. | 849 |
| Prior Hill, High | Lesmahagow | Burt, S. | 1058 | do. North | do. | Gibson, T., late | 1049 |
| Prett's Mill | Carmichael | Clarkson, R. | 1284 | do. South | do. | Paterson, A. | 1137 |
| Quothquhan | Libberton | Gray, J. | 899 | Shiels | Carmichael | Brown, J. | 1178 |
| do. | do. | Ritchie, G. | 887 | Skellyhill | Lesmahagow | Pate, A. | 1119 |
| do. | do. | Sanderson, J. | 899 | Sidewood, East | Carnwath | Todd, J. | 1177 |
| do. Mill | do. | M'Morran, — | 1176 | Silvermains | Carstairs | Boyd, W. | 1168 |
| Raehills | Lesmahagow | Weir, R. | 1277 | Sornfallow | Wiston | Coubrough, D., late | 818 |
| Raes | Carluke | Cassells, J. | 1047 | Southfield, North | Lesmahagow | Stewart, A. | 1030 |
| Redshaw | Lesmahagow | Millwain, Rev.J.,late | 1285 | do. South | do. | Pollock, W. | 1018 |
| Roberton Mains | Dolphinton | Watch, J. | 817 | Southwood | Crawford | Hamilton, J. | 1228 |
| Rodger Hill | Lesmahagow | Meikle, J. | 976 | Spadgill | Carnwath | Aitken, A. | 1186 |
| Roothead | Carnwath | Hamilton, W. | 1167 | Spittal | do. | Cochrane, W. | 889 |
| Rowantreehill | do. | Prentice, J. | 1217 | Springfield | Carluke | Wilson, J. | 839 |
| Rowhead and Biggar | Biggar | Brown, D. | 869 | Springhill | Douglas | Ballantyne, J. | 1308 |
| Ryefhat | Carstairs | Aitken, J. | 878 | do. | do. | Anderson, J. | 1319 |
| Sadlerhead & Todhills | Lesmahagow | Scott, T. | 1208 | Stabilee | Carstairs | Barrie, A. | 1138 |
| Sandilands | Carmichael | Forrest, J. | 1008 | Stane | Biggar | Jackson, P. | 1100 |
| do. Gate | Carluke | Hamilton, W. | 990 | Stobilee and Windsor | Lanark | Barrie, A. | 1108 |
| Scorryholm | Lesmahagow | Anderson, W. | 1048 | Stobwood and Hillhead | Carnwath | Prentice, J. | 1199 |
| Scrogtonhead | Douglas | Greensheilds, J. | 1198 | Stonehill | Crawfordjohn | Paterson, J., late | 780 |
| Scrogton | do. | Watson, R. | 1088 | do. | Carmichael | Thorburn, R. | 819 |
| Shallowhead | Wiston | Plenderleith, M. | 930 | Stoneyburn | Crawford | Cranstoun, A. | 1050 |
| Shawfield | Carluke | Hamilton, W. | 1318 | Store Farm, East | Covington | Bell, J. | 1109 |
| Shawhead | Crawfordjohn | French, J. | 888 | do. West | do. | Bell, P. | 1139 |
| Shaws | Carluke | Smith, J. | 1286 | Strathlogie | Biggar | Gibson, J. | 1187 |

| Farm, &c. | Parish. | Tenant. | No. |
|---|---|---|---|
| Strathern House | Carluke | Paterson, A. | 820 |
| Strawfrank | Carstairs | Alison, T. | 788 |
| Strawlaw | Biggar | Hislop, J. | 1148 |
| Syde | Lesmahagow | Sandilands, W. | 1278 |
| Symington Lodge | Symington | Renton, W. | 1089 |
| do. Mains | do. | Stobo, J., late | 919 |
| do. Mill | do. | Thorburn, D. | 1009 |
| Tanhill | Carluke | Hamilton, J. | 1128 |
| do. | Lesmahagow | Shields, W. | 1297 |
| Tupenhill | Carluke | Ramage, A., late | 1218 |
| Thankerton Mill | Covington | Galloway, W., late | 1369 |
| Thornhill, Nether | Carmichael | Cadzow, R. | 890 |
| Tofts, East | Douglas | Pate, T. | 1279 |
| do. West | do. | M'Dougall, Mrs. | 1158 |
| Townfoot of Ponfeigh | Carmichael | Affleck, M., late | 1188 |
| do. | Dolphinton | Thomson, T. & J. | 1038 |
| do. | Symington | Gibson, L. | 870 |
| do. | Wiston | Lindsay, J. | 1209 |
| Townhead | Biggar | Tweedie, J. | 1189 |
| do. | Lesmahagow | Anderson, M. | 1000 |
| do. | Libberton | Gibson, A. | 789 |
| do. of Loch | Dunsyre | Kay, J. & R. | 810 |
| do. of Ponfeigh | Carmichael | Weir & Adamson | 1180 |
| Tower | Lesmahagow | Gall, J. | 1149 |
| do. of Cormiston | Libberton | Gibson, J. | 858 |
| Threepwood | Lesmahagow | Templeton, D. | 1129 |
| Turf-foot | Carluke | Watson, J. | 1039 |
| Uddington | Douglas | Gall, J. | 938 |
| Underbank | Lesmahagow | Scott, G. | 1040 |
| Undershielhill | Carluke | Cassells, J. | 1140 |

| Farm, &c. | Parish. | Tenant. | No. |
|---|---|---|---|
| Unthank | Coulter | Bertram, J. | 1010 |
| Viewfield | Carnwath | French, W. | 1288 |
| Walston Mill | Walston | Turner, A. | 1268 |
| do. Place | do. | Stodart, J. | 840 |
| do. Wester | do. | Brown, J. | 849 |
| Wandell Mill | Lamington | Black, J. | 759 |
| Warrenhill, Nether | Covington | Black, J. | 1110 |
| do. Upper | do. | Twaddle, J. | 1190 |
| Watchknowe | Carmichael | Bryce, A. | 1219 |
| Waterhead | Lesmahagow | Weir, J. | 1248 |
| Watermeeting | Crawford | Greenshields, W. | 769 |
| Waterside | Carluke | Wilson, W. | 950 |
| Watertown | Carstairs | Barr, J. & J. | 1230 |
| Waygateshawhead | Carluke | Walkinshaw, W. | 1070 |
| Wellbrae | Covington | Ferrie, J. | 1249 |
| Wellburn | Lesmahagow | Lindsay, H. | 1090 |
| Wellhead | Lanark | M'Ghie, W. | 1200 |
| Westcrofthill | Carnwath | Wilson, P. | 1150 |
| Westend | Carluke | Elder, J. | 1310 |
| Westhill | Dunsyre | Barr, W. | 859 |
| Westerhills | Pettinain | Brown, sen, J. | 1019 |
| Westerhouse | Carluke | Clarkson, D. | 1020 |
| do. Mill of | do. | Wright, J. & J. | 1270 |
| Westfield | Dolphinton | Hamilton, J. | 910 |
| West Mains | Biggar | Black, H. | 1229 |
| Westmill | Carnwath | Noble, W. | 1169 |
| Westmillrig | Dolphinton | Smith, D. | 1200 |
| Westquarter | Wiston | Core, D. | 900 |
| Westshiels | Carluke | Pratt, A. | 1159 |
| | Carnwath | Somerville, R. | 1040 |
| | Carnwath | Brown, J. | 1250 |

| No. | FARM, &c. | PARISH | TENANT |
|---|---|---|---|
| 832 | Barnhills | Lesmahagow | Affleck, D. & W. |
| 1188 | Townfoot, Ponfeigh | Carmichael | do. M., late |
| 1298 | Millhouse | Lesmahagow | do. W. |
| 1186 | Spadgill | Carnwath | Aitken, A. |
| 1257 | Leauside | do. | do. D. |
| 941 | Broadfield | Symington | do. J. |
| 1115 | Gladstanes, West | Libberton | do. J. |
| 1106 | Hangingshaw, Mid | do. | do. J. |
| 870 | Ryeflat | Carstairs | do. J. |
| 1299 | Northflatcrofts | Carmichael | do. Mrs |
| 1063 | Collielaw | Lanark | do. T. |
| 1276 | Oldton | Carnwath | do. W. |
| 1029 | Moirhead | Wiston | do. W. |
| 797 | Harelaw | Carstairs | Alison, A. |
| 816 | Kilcadzow, Hill of | Carluke | do. T. |
| 778 | Strawfrank | Carstairs | do. T. |
| 957 | Kirklands | Dunsyre | Allan, J. |
| 905 | Eastwood | Lesmahagow | do. P. |
| 1295 | Coramill | do. | do. R. |
| 903 | Dykefoot | Dunsyre | Anderson, D. & W. |
| 902 | Carnwath Mill | Carnwath | do. J. |
| 1033 | Forth, West | do. | do. J. |
| 1213 | Boghead | Crawfordjohn | do. J. |
| 1000 | Townhead | Lesmahagow | do. M. |
| 894 | Elvanfoot | Crawford | do. T., late |
| 1319 | Springhill | Douglas | do. T. |
| 1048 | Scorrybolm | Lesmahagow | do. W. |
| 1207 | Muirdykehead | Carluke | Bain, G. |
| 1015 | Lambcatch & Skylaw | Carnwath | Baird, A. |
| 1171 | Auchengray, Mid. | do. | Ballantyne, G. |

| FARM, &c. | PARISH | TENANT | No. |
|---|---|---|---|
| Weetshiels | Lesmahagow | Murdoch, A. | 909 |
| Westside | Symington | Waugh, J. | 908 |
| Westown | Lesmahagow | Greenshields, A. | 860 |
| West-town & Todholes | Dunsyre | Whyte, W. | 760 |
| do. & Janefield | Douglas | Inglis, J. | 879 |
| Westraw Mains | Pettinain | Hunter, W. | 790 |
| do. part of | do. | Twaddle, J. | 939 |
| Whelphill & Harcleuch | Crawford | Fletcher, R. | 770 |
| Whinbush | Libberton | Frame, A. | 1259 |
| Whitecastle, East | do. | Ritchie, J. | 1059 |
| do. West | do. | Gibson Brothers. | 978 |
| Whitecleugh, Nether | Crawfordjohn | Hislop, J. | 1130 |
| do. Upper | do. | Willison, J. | 830 |
| do. & Abbey | do. | Barr, W. | 1170 |
| Whiteshaw | Carstairs | Gault, J. | 850 |
| Whiteside | Carluke | Mackie, A. | 1289 |
| Windales | Lesmahagow | Muirhead, A. | 959 |
| Windysheils | Symington | Miller, M. | 1260 |
| Wintermoor | Carstairs | Lang, P. | 960 |
| Wiston Mill | Biggar | Clarkson, J. | 1060 |
| do. Place | Wiston | Wilson, J. | 1220 |
| Wolfclyde | do. | Pairman, A. | 880 |
| Wolfcrooks | Coulter | Kirkwood, J. | 940 |
| Woodend | Douglas | Brown, J. | 979 |
| Woodhead | Carnwath | Tudhope, R. | 980 |
| Woodlands | Lesmahagow | Carmichael, — | 1120 |
| Woodside | Carmichael | Farie, J. | 1320 |
| Woodyett | Lesmahagow | Shaw, J. | 1210 |
| Woolfords | do. | Somerville, J. | 920 |
| Yett, West | Carnwath | Barrie, J. | 1160 |

| No. | Farm, &c. | Parish | Tenant |
|---|---|---|---|
| 1012 | Brownridge | Carluke | Black, D. |
| 1055 | Newmill | Dolphinton | do. J. |
| 798 | Hazelside | Douglas | do. J. |
| 759 | Wandel Mill | Lamington | do. J. |
| 882 | Eastend | Carstairs | do. R. |
| 1281 | Croftfoot | Carluke | do. W. |
| 1175 | Hillend | Biggar | Blakely, G |
| 1168 | Silvermines | Carstairs | Boyd, W. |
| 1052 | Loanhead | Carnwath | Brown, A. |
| 783 | Dunsyre Mains | Dunsyre | do. A. |
| 869 | Rowhead and Biggar | Biggar | do. D. |
| 1273 | Muirdykehead | Carluke | do. G. |
| 761 | Boghall | Biggar | do. J. |
| 1182 | do. | do. | do. J. |
| 962 | Candybank | do. | do. J. |
| 995 | Gillbank | Carluke | do. J. |
| 1196 | Middlemains | do. | do. J. |
| 1178 | Shiels | Carmichael | do. J. |
| 1250 | Westshiels | Carnwath | do. J. |
| 979 | Woodend | do. | do. J. |
| 791 | Birniehill | Carstairs | do. J. |
| 1222 | Gateside | Coulter | do. J. |
| 835 | East and Westdill | Dunsyre | do. J. |
| 859 | Westmill | do. | do. J. |
| 831 | Auchrobert | Lesmahagow | do. J. |
| 1253 | Birthwood | do. | do. J. |
| 755 | Libberton Mains | Libberton | do. J. |
| 849 | Walston, Wester | Walston | do. J. |
| 1096 | Gladstanes, East | Libberton | do. Mrs |
| 997 | Kirkhouse | Dolphinton | do. R. |

| Tenant | Parish | Farm, &c. | No. |
|---|---|---|---|
| Ballantyne, T. | Carnwath | Crookland | 1163 |
| do. T. | Douglas | Springhill | 1308 |
| do. W. | Pettinain | Millhill and Dykehead | 1086 |
| Bannatyne, J. | Lesmahagow | Auchinheath, woods of | 111 |
| Barr, A. | do. | Blackwoodside | 1292 |
| do. J. & J. | Carluke | Waterside | 950 |
| do. J. | Lesmahagow | Dykehead | 1064 |
| do. Messrs | do. | Moat | 1006 |
| do. R. | do. | Halfmerkland | 1315 |
| do. S. | do. | Priorhill, High | 1058 |
| do. T. | Carluke | Brackenhill | 1071 |
| do. W. | do. | Bogside | 1242 |
| do. W. | do. | Westend | 1131 |
| do. W. | Carstairs | Cowford | 1310 |
| Barrie, A. | Lanark | Whitecleugh & Abbey | 1170 |
| do. J. | Carluke | Stobilee and Windsor | 1108 |
| do. S. | Carstairs | Yett, West | 1060 |
| Bell, J. | Covington | Shodsmill | 1069 |
| do. J. | do. | Store Farm, East | 1109 |
| Bell & Shirlaw | Carluke | do. West | 1139 |
| Bertram, A. | Coulter | Orchard | 1057 |
| do. A. | do. | Coulter Park | 1173 |
| do. J. | do. | East-tofts | 1174 |
| do. J. | do. | Hangingshaw, Upper | 1084 |
| do. J. | Dolphinton | Unthank | 1010 |
| do. R. | do. | Bank | 1693 |
| do. R. | Dolphinton | Burnbrae | 1112 |
| Baxter, W. | Lesmahagow | Auchinleath | 921 |
| Black, H. | Dolphinton | Westfield | 910 |
| do. J. | Crawfordjohn | Balgray, Nether | 1112 |

| Tenant | Parish | Farm, &c. | No. | Tenant | Parish | Farm, &c. | No. |
|---|---|---|---|---|---|---|---|
| Brown, T. | Lesmahagow | Bogside | 1161 | Cleghorn, T. | Libberton | Cormiston House | 994 |
| do. T. | Dunsyre | East-town | 784 | Cochrane, W. | Carnwath | Spittal | 889 |
| do. W. | Biggar | Biggar Mains | 951 | Coke, J. | Crawfordjohn | Glentewing, Easter | 996 |
| Brownlie, A. | Lesmahagow | Corramore | 985 | do. W. | do. | Mosscastle | 987 |
| do. J. | do. | Hoodsmill | 1223 | Coltness Iron Co. | Carnwath | Kirkgreen | 946 |
| Brownfield, A. | Lanark | Huntlyhill | 1067 | Cook, J. | Carluke | Mayfield | 1053 |
| Bryce, A. | Covington | Warrenhill, Upper | 1190 | Cooper, G. | Lesmahagow | Blair-reckoning | 1212 |
| Bunten, T. | Lesmahagow | Lowrie's moor | 1207 | do. J. | do. | Auchenbeg | 1241 |
| Burton, T. | do. | Hawksland | 1097 | Core, A. | do. | Clecklands | 1191 |
| Cadzow, J. | Lanark | Jerviswood | 925 | do. D. | Carmichael | Crossdyke | 942 |
| do. R. | Carmichael | Thornhill, Nether | 890 | do. J. | Dolphinton | Westmill | 1201 |
| do. W. | Lesmahagow | Hallhill, North | 1106 | do. W. | Carmichael | Newside | 1056 |
| do. W. | Lanark | Nemphlar, East | 967 | Coulbrough, A. | Carnwath | Janefield | 1283 |
| Callan, A. | do. | Cleghorn | 934 | do. D. | Biggar | Caerwood | 901 |
| Carmichael, W. | Carnwath | Pool farm | 1087 | Craig, Mrs | Wiston | Sornfallow | 818 |
| Carruthers, B. | Lesmahagow | Affleck | 1221 | Cranstoun, A. | Symington | Annieston | 801 |
| do. Mrs B. | do. | Lesser Linn | 827 | Crawford, W. | Crawford | Stoneyburn | 1050 |
| do. T. | do. | Auchtygemmel | 911 | Crossan, J. | Dolphinton | Croftaurigh | 1305 |
| do. T. | Carluke | Bushelheed | 1123 | do. J. | Biggar | Green | 1145 |
| Cassells, A. | Lanark | Cleghorn Mill | 864 | Cunningham, A. | do. | Greenwood | 1153 |
| do. A. | Carluke | Carluke | 1013 | do. D. | Lanark | Hyndford | 815 |
| do. G. | do. | Middlehouse | 966 | do. P. | Douglas | Cleugh | 1151 |
| do. J. | do. | Catcraig | 1223 | Cuthbertson, J. | Lanark | Bonnington Mains | 792 |
| do. J. | do. | Raes | 1047 | Dalgleish, A. | Carnwath | Brownhill | 892 |
| do. J. | do. | Undershieldhill | 1140 | do. J. | Biggar | Lindsaylands, West | 875 |
| Cassie, J. | Lesmahagow | John's-hill | 1165 | Dalziel, J. | Lesmahagow | Linnville | 1166 |
| Clarkson, D. | Pettinain | Westerhills | 1019 | Davidson, A. | Crawfordjohn | Greenfield | 916 |
| do. J. | Wiston | Wistonhill | 1060 | do. A. | Carstairs | Newhouse | 949 |
| do. J. | do. | Longhill | 1125 | do. J. | Carluke | Crawfordwell | 1152 |
| do. R. | Carmichael | Prett's Mill | 1284 | Denholm, A. | Lamington | Baitlaws | 751 |

| Tenant | Parish | Farm, &c. | No. | Tenant | Parish | Farm, &c. | No. |
|---|---|---|---|---|---|---|---|
| Dent, G. | Lamington | Breckenridge | 1294 | Forrest, J. | Carmichael | Sandilands | 1008 |
| Dick, J. | Coulter | Coulter Mill | 1083 | do. R. | Carluke | Gair | 1313 |
| Dickson, A. | Lesmahagow | Mayfield | 1264 | do. W. | do. | Bellstane | 1142 |
| do. W. | Carmichael | Dyke | 1214 | Forsyth, R. | Crawfordjohn | Sheriffcleugh | 1227 |
| Donald, G. | Libberton | Ellanbank | 1114 | French, E. | do. | Eastertown | 904 |
| Donaldson, A. | Lanark | Nemphlar, West | 1127 | do. J. | do. | Boghouse | 863 |
| Dougall, A. | Lesmahagow | Eastertown, East | 1255 | do. J. | Carmichael | Carmichael Policy | 851 |
| do. A. | do. | Eastertown, West | 1065 | do. J. | Crawford | Glencaple | 805 |
| Duncan, J. | do. | Auchtool | 1041 | do. J. | Carnwath | Lampits, East & West | 767 |
| Dykes, J. | do. | Ladeshead | 1261 | do. J. | Crawfordjohn | Netherton | 779 |
| do. R. | do. | Byretown | 762 | do. Mrs | do. | Shawhead | 888 |
| do. W. | do. | Bent | 862 | do. T. | do. | Mountherrick | 384 |
| Elder, J. | Carstairs | Columbia and Hills | 794 | do. T. | do. | Blackhill | 802 |
| do. J. | Carnwath | Westcrofthill | 1150 | do. W. | Lesmahagow | Greenyards, West | 1236 |
| do. J. & W. | Lanark | Halltown-Nemphlar | 997 | do. W. | Carnwath | Burnhead and Park | 771 |
| Fallow, T. | Lesmahagow | Birkenhead | 1302 | Froude, H. | do. | Viewfield | 1288 |
| Farie, J. | do. | Breckenridge | 1244 | Gall, A. | Carmichael | Millmuir | 1265 |
| Ferrie, J. | do. | Woodside | 1320 | do. J. | Douglas | Midtown | 1228 |
| Finlayson, T., late | Carluke | Waygatcshawhead | 1070 | do. J. | do. | Newtonfoot | 936 |
| Fisher, J., late | Coulter | Coulter Park, South | 963 | do. J. | do. | Uddington | 938 |
| Fleming, J. | Covington | Holm, Thankerton | 1051 | Galloway, J. | Lesmahagow | Tower | 1149 |
| do. J. | Carstairs | Corbieball | 772 | do. W., late | Crawfordjohn | Crawfordjohn Mill | 953 |
| Fletcher, R. | Carnwath | Calla | 793 | Gault, J. | Covington | Thankerton Mill | 1309 |
| Frame, A. | Crawford | Whelphill | 770 | Gibson, A. | Carluke | Whiteshaw | 850 |
| Fraser, R. | Libberton | Whinbush | 1259 | do. J. | Libberton | Townhead | 789 |
| Forrest, A. | Wiston | Galla, Little | 1236 | do. J. | Biggar | Strathlogie | 1187 |
| do. A. | Carluke | Kilcadzow, Hole of | 976 | do. J. | Libberton | Tower of Cormiston | 858 |
| do. J. | Carstairs | Mossplat | 876 | do. J. | Wiston | Eastfield | 1103 |
| do. J. | Carnwath | Browshot & Longarton | 1213 | do. J. | Biggar | Edmonstone Mill | 1104 |
| do. J. | Covington | Northmains | 885 | do. J. | Lilberton | Parkhouse | 918 |

| Tenant | Parish | Farm, &c. | No. |
|---|---|---|---|
| Gibson, J. | Pettinain | Crofts | 1197 |
| do. J. & R. | Carluke | Belstane | 932 |
| do. L. | Symington | Townfoot | 870 |
| do. T, *late* | Crawford | Shortcleugh, North | 1049 |
| do. W. | Pettinain | Easterhills | 1095 |
| do. W. | Lamington | Langknowe | 1262 |
| do. W. | do. | Overburn | 768 |
| do. Brothers | Libberton | Whitecastle, West | 978 |
| Gilchrist, J. | Lesmahagow | Newhouse | 1240 |
| Gillespie, J. | Crawford | Newton | 1037 |
| do. J. | Douglas | Gateside | 753 |
| do. T. | Wiston | Bodinlee | 912 |
| do. T. | do. | Fallside | 854 |
| do. T. | do. | Moat | 926 |
| do. T. | Douglas | Parkhead | 758 |
| Gillies, M. | Lesmahagow | Breckenridge, West | 1201 |
| Gladstone, A. | Coulter | Eastfield | 954 |
| Gray, J. | Lanark | Charleston | 1062 |
| do. J. | Libberton | Quothquhan | 1017 |
| do. J. | Carnwath | Green | 846 |
| Greenshields, A. | Lesmahagow | West-town | 861 |
| do. A. | Douglas | Broomerside | 871 |
| do. A. | Carnwath | Gillhouse & Stobwood | 1028 |
| do. D. | Walston | Elsrickle | 795 |
| do. J. | Pettinain | Brownrigg | 1024 |
| do. J. | Carmichael | Devonhill | 1254 |
| do. J. | Douglas | Scrogton | 1198 |
| do. W. | Lesmahagow | Waterhead | 1248 |
| Grieve, M. | Crawford | Campshead | 813 |
| Haddow, J. | Lamington | Coldchapel | 842 |

| No. | Farm, &c. | Parish | Tenant |
|---|---|---|---|
| 958 | Netherhill and Glespin | Crawfordjohn | Haddow, P. |
| 1068 | Longwell | Wiston | do. R. |
| 1181 | Birks | Carluke | Hamilton, W. |
| 1016 | Middleholm and Bent | Lesmahagow | do. A. |
| 1228 | Southwood | Crawford | do. J. |
| 1128 | Tanhill | Lesmahagow | do. J. |
| 1270 | Westerhouse, Hill of | Carluke | do. J. |
| 1027 | Fence | Lesmahagow | do. J. |
| 782 | Boreland | Walston | do. M. & T. |
| 1203 | Caulerwater | Lesmahagow | do. R. |
| 944 | Heathland | Carnwath | do. T. |
| 847 | Persielands | Biggar | do. T. |
| 1134 | Law | Carluke | do. W. |
| 763 | Callandean | Carnwath | do. W. |
| 1167 | Roothead | | do. W. |
| 990 | Sandilandsgate | Carluke | do. W. |
| 1318 | Shawfield | do. | do. W. |
| 1238 | Hill | Lesmahagow | Harrison, W. |
| 917 | Kirkfield Mains | do. | Harvie, W. |
| 945 | Hindshaw, South | Carluke | Henderson, T. |
| 1148 | Strawlaw | | Hislop, J. |
| 978 | Whitecleugh, Nether | Crawfordjohn | do. J. |
| 1231 | Arthurshiel | Libberton | Hodge, J. |
| 1211 | Arthurshiels, part of | do. | do. W. |
| 825 | Howcleugh, Upper | Crawford | Hogg, P. |
| 778 | do. Nether | do. | do. P. |
| 989 | Northloanhead | Carnwath | Howieson, J. |
| 965 | Kirkton | Crawford | Hunter, G. |
| 915 | Goat and Liscleugh | Crawfordjohn | do. H. |
| 914 | Craighead | do. | do. H, *late*. |

| TENANT | PARISH | FARM, &c. | No. |
| --- | --- | --- | --- |
| Hunter, R., *late* | Crawford | Glenochar | 754 |
| do. R., " | do. | Glengeith | 796 |
| do. W. | Carluke | Hungerhill and Chapel | 1296 |
| do. W. | Pettinain | Westraw, Mains of ... | 790 |
| Hutcheson, G. | Lesmahagow | Rodgerhill | 973 |
| do. W. | do. | Kirkmuirhill | 1079 |
| Inch, J. | Coulter | Coultorhaugh | 804 |
| do. R. | Crawfordjohn | Abington, Over | 861 |
| do. T. | do. | Gilkerscleugh Mains | 814 |
| do. W. | Lesmahagow | Auchenheg | 1291 |
| Inglis, W. | Douglas | Westown and Janefield | 879 |
| Irving, W. | Lanark | Newsteading | 928 |
| Irvine, —, *late* | Pettinain | Pettinain Bauk | 1007 |
| Jack, J. | Carnwath | Bankhead | 812 |
| do. J. | Carluke | Burnhead | 1302 |
| do. J. | do. | Castlehill | 1144 |
| do. W. C. | Lanark | Nemphlar, West | 890 |
| do. Messrs | do. | do. | 1176 |
| Jackson, A. | do. | Boathaugh | 781 |
| do. C. | Biggar | Langlees | 965 |
| Johnstone, W. | do. | Stane | 1100 |
| do. —, *late* | Pettinain | Midholm of Grange | 837 |
| Kay, J. & R. | Crawford | Midlock | 785 |
| do. sen., J. | Dolphinton | Townfoot and Loch | 810 |
| Kirwood, — | do. | Haughhead | 943 |
| King, W. | Douglas | Wolfcrooks | 940 |
| Lamb, J. | Biggar | Biggarshiels | 833 |
| do. J., *late* | Carmichael | Crookboat | 910 |
| Lammie, J. | do. | Netherton | 927 |
|  | Crawfordjohn | Birkcleugh | 981 |

| No. | FARM, &c. | PARISH | TENANT |
| --- | --- | --- | --- |
| 960 | Wintermoor | Biggar | Lang, P. |
| 1036 | Mosshank | Crawfordjohn | Law, J. |
| 937 | Newtonhead | Douglas | Lawcock, A. |
| 1225 | Mount Stewart | do. | Lawson, G. |
| 1266 | Moss-side | Carluke | Leggat, J., *late* |
| 1074 | Gill | Lesmahagow | Letham, J. |
| 1077 | Hinshelwood | Carnwath | Liddell, J. |
| 925 | Covington Mill | Covington | Lindsay, A. |
| 766 | Hartsyde | Lamington | do. E. |
| 853 | Covington Mains | Covington | do. H. |
| 1249 | Wellbrae | do. | do. H. |
| 1209 | Townfoot | Wiston | do. J. |
| 1061 | Blackcastle | Carnwath | do. J. |
| 809 | Meadowflat | Covington | do. Mrs |
| 970 | Sheriff flats | do. | do. W. |
| 840 | Eastfield | Pettinain | Linton, J. |
| 1206 | do. | Symington | Lockhart, R. |
| 1234 | Clannochdyke | Lesmahagow | Mackie, A. |
| 1289 | Whiteside | do. | Marshall, A. |
| 000 | Kingshill | Carnwath | do. T. |
| 1237 | Hareshaw | Carluke | Meikle, J. |
| 993 | Birkenhead | Lesmahagow | do. R. |
| 971 | Auchengrey | Carnwath | do. W. |
| 1155 | Kypeswaterhead | Lesmahagow | Milligan, J. |
| 777 | Kirkhope | Crawford | Miller, M. |
| 1260 | Windyshiels | Carstairs | Milwain, T., Rev. |
| 1285 | Redshair | Lesmahagow | Mitchell, W. |
| 654 | Nethanfoot | do. | Muir, R. |
| 1246 | Howford | Carmichael | do. W. |
| 1082 | Bowhouse | do. | |

| TENANT | PARISH | FARM, &c. | No. | TENANT | PARISH | FARM, &c. | No. |
|---|---|---|---|---|---|---|---|
| Muir, W., late | Wiston | Hardington Mains | 1075 | Pate, A. | Lesmahagow | Skellyhill | 1119 |
| Muirhead, A. | Symington | Wyndales | 959 | do. T. | do. | Draffan, South | 824 |
| do. J. | Lanark | Coblehaugh | 852 | do. T. | do. | Dumbrex-hill | 1102 |
| Murdoch, A. | Lesmahagow | Westshiels | 909 | do. T. | Douglas | Tofts, East | 1279 |
| Murray, J. | Douglas | Lockhart Mill | 1206 | Paterson, A. | Crawford | Shortcleugh, South | 1137 |
| M'Culloch, G. | Carnwath | Eastforth | 1032 | do. R. | do. | Upper Howcleugh | 843 |
| M'Donald, J. | Dunsyre | Stoneypath | 1078 | do. A. | Carluke | Strathearn House | 820 |
| M'Dougall, Mrs. | Douglas | Tofts, West | 1158 | do. A. | Douglas | Langhouse | 1099 |
| M'Ghie, J. & T. | Lesmahagow | Boreland | 1022 | do. J. | do. | Glentaggart | 776 |
| do. W. | do. | Wellburn | 1090 | do. J. | Crawfordjohn | Stonehill | 780 |
| M'Gowran, J. | do. | Blackwoodyard | 1042 | do. J. | Carmichael | Carmichael Bank | 1311 |
| do. W. | do. | do. | 933 | do. Mrs J. | do. | do. Mill | 1143 |
| M'Grigor, J. | do. | Hillside | 1194 | do. J. | Pettinain | Cloburn | 1002 |
| M'Kenzie, G. | Dolphinton | Muirhead | 1224 | do. R. | Crawford | Crimp-cramp | 865 |
| do. M. | Biggar | Hillrigs | 956 | do. W. | Carmichael | Harleyholm | 1076 |
| M'Kinlay, J. | Wiston | Meadowcoats | 897 | do. W. | do. | Drumalbyn | 774 |
| do. | Douglas | Debog | 872 | Peat, R. | Lesmahagow | Garngour, South | 1105 |
| M'Kirdy, J. G. | Lesmahagow | Birkwood | 1252 | Plenderleith, M. | Wiston | Shilliehead | 930 |
| M'Lean, W. | Libberton | Greenshields | 907 | do. R. | do. | Burnhouse | 822 |
| M'Morran, J. | Carnwath | Girdwoodend | 1132 | Pollock, W. | Lesmahagow | Southfield, South | 1018 |
| do. —. | Libberton | Quothquhan Mill | 1176 | Porteous, R. | do. | Milton-Lockhart Mill | 948 |
| M'Quat, W. | Douglas | Monksfoot | 1185 | Pratt, A. | Wiston | Wiston Millrig | 900 |
| Neilson, D. | Lesmahagow | Dillars | 1014 | Prentice, J. | Carnwath | Rowantree-hill | 1217 |
| do. J. & J. | Lamington | Littlegill | 828 | do. J. | do. | Stobwood & Hillhead | 1199 |
| do. T. | do. | Akinlophead | 1091 | do. J., late | Biggar. | Biggar-common | 1081 |
| Newbigging, T., late | Douglas | Poniel | 877 | do. P. | Libberton | Muirlee | 1267 |
| Nimmo, T. | Carnwath | Haywood, Lower | 1184 | do. T. | Lesmahagow | Clarkston | 913 |
| do. T. | do. | Cleugh | 893 | Purdie, A. | Carmichael | Burnhouse | 1253 |
| Noble, W. | Biggar. | Westmains | 1229 | do. T. & J. | Covington | Mill-lands of Thank'ton | 1136 |
| Pairman, A. | Coulter | Wolfclyde | 880 | do. | Libberton | Muirhouse | 786 |

| Tenant | Parish | Farm, &c. | No. |
|---|---|---|---|
| Rae, W. & W. | Crawford | Fingland | 873 |
| Ramsay, A., *late* | Carluke | Tupenhill | 1218 |
| Ray, J. | Dunsyre | Dunsyre | 775 |
| Reid, J. | Wiston | Newton of Wiston | 857 |
| do. J. | do. | Marchlands | 1135 |
| do. J. | Carluke | Northfield | 1317 |
| Renton, W. | Symington | Symington Lodge | 1089 |
| Ritchie, D. | Libberton | Burnfoot | 983 |
| do. G. | Walston | Cocklaw | 1151 |
| do. G. | Lanark | Northfaulds | 929 |
| do. G. | Libberton | Quothquhan | 887 |
| do. J. | do. | Boreland | 1190 |
| do. J. | Carnwath | Haughs | 855 |
| do. J. | Libberton | Whitecastle, East | 1059 |
| Robb, J. | Lanark | Castlehill | 1025 |
| do. J. | Carnwath | Moreshot | 1118 |
| do. J. | do. | Haywood, Upper | 1133 |
| do. J. | Coulter | Highfield | 1117 |
| do. T. & J. | Carstairs | Sheafyknowes | 1175 |
| Russell, A. | Lesmahagow | Draffan, etc. | 773 |
| Sadleir, J. | Wiston | Greenhill | 1035 |
| Sanderson, J. | Libberton | Quothquhan | 899 |
| Sandilands, G. | Lesmahagow | Cumberhead, North | 843 |
| do. W. | do. | do. South | 844 |
| do. W. | do. | Syle | 1278 |
| Scott, A. | Carstairs | Cockridge | 984 |
| do. G. | Lesmahagow | Underbank | 1040 |
| do. J. | Carluke | Mauldslie Mains | 947 |
| do. J. | Lesmahagow | Auchenheath | 1092 |
| do. J. | Carnwath | Forth | 1204 |

| Tenant | Parish | Farm, &c. | No. |
|---|---|---|---|
| Scott, T. | Lesmahagow | Sadlerhead & Tolhills | 1208 |
| do. T. R. | Douglas | Coalgill | 1312 |
| do. T. R. | do. | Castlemains | 1304 |
| do. W. | Carstairs | Netherton | 868 |
| do. W. | Lanark | Nemphlar | 1080 |
| do. W. | Lesmahagow | Lupus | 1216 |
| Semple, R. | do. | Kypeside, Nether | 1085 |
| Shaw, J. | do. | Woodyett | 1210 |
| do. T. | Dunsyre | Anston | 900 |
| do. W. | Carnwath | Hinshelwood | 1239 |
| Shields, W. | Carluke | Tanhill | 1287 |
| Shirlaw, G. | Lanark | Auchengien, part of | 992 |
| do. J. | Carluke | Mauldslie Mains | 947 |
| Sibbald, J. | Carnwath | Hardgatehead | 1005 |
| Sinclair, J. | Coulter | Legshiel | 1247 |
| Smellie, H. | Biggar | Brownbank | 881 |
| do. W. | Lanark | Carfin and Clydebank | 1072 |
| Smith, A. | do. | Langhill | 1316 |
| do. D. | Carnwath | Westmains | 1161 |
| do. H. | do. | Carnwath Mill | 803 |
| do. J. | Libberton | Arthurshiels | 1181 |
| do. J. | Pettinain | Northolm of Grange | 969 |
| do. J. | Lanark | Baronald | 1001 |
| do. J. | Carluke | Candymill | 1043 |
| do. J. | do. | Shaws | 1286 |
| do. J. | Lesmahagow | Craignethan | 1003 |
| do. J. | Libberton | Huntfield | 1282 |
| do. J. | Carnwath | Mountainlaw | 988 |
| do. J. | Lesmahagow | Holmhead | 1215 |
| Somnerville, A. | Libberton | Libberton Mill | 799 |

| Tenant | Parish | Farm, &c. | No. |
|---|---|---|---|
| Somerville, J. | Carstairs | Boghall | 1011 |
| do. J. | Carnwath | Greenfield | 964 |
| do. J. | do. | Sidewood, West | 1177 |
| do. R. | Carluke | Westquarter | 1159 |
| do. T. | Lesmahagow | Midtown | 1297 |
| Souter, J. | do. | Hillhouse | 1245 |
| Steel, T. | Carnwath | Muirhead | 998 |
| Stewart, A. | Carluke | Bogside | 891 |
| do. A. | Lesmahagow | Southfield, North | 1030 |
| do. J. | Carstairs | Browriggs | 1232 |
| do. J. | Carluke | Gladdenhill | 1296 |
| do. P. | Crawfordjohn | Glendorch | 955 |
| Stobbs, W. | Lesmahagow | Birkhill | 1113 |
| Stobo, J., Mrs | Symington | Symington Mains | 919 |
| Stodart, A. | Covington | Hillhead | 807 |
| do. D. | Lanark | Jerviswood Mains | 874 |
| do. J. | Walston | Walston Place | 840 |
| do. J. | Lamington | Langhouse | 826 |
| do. J., late | Lesmahagow | Blackhill | 961 |
| do. T. | do. | Garrellwood | 986 |
| do. W. | Wiston | Chesterhall | 841 |
| Struthers, J. | Carnwath | Cleughmill | 1162 |
| Swan, J. | Carmichael | Woodlands | 1120 |
| do. J. | do. | Blinklie | 1293 |
| do. J. | Douglas | Broomfield & Rigside | 973 |
| Symington, M. | do. | Polmonkshead | 999 |
| Tarvet, J. | Carmichael | Howgate & Redmyre | 1066 |
| do. J. | Covington | Boat, Thankerton | 1094 |
| do. R. | Walston | Bagsmoor & Todhills | 821 |
| Taylor, R. | Pettinain | Greenhall | 974 |

| Tenant | Parish | Farm, &c. | No. |
|---|---|---|---|
| Tennant, J. | Lesmahagow | Hillend | 1044 |
| Templeton, D. | do. | Threepwood | 1129 |
| Thomson, A. | Carluke | Gill | 1314 |
| do. A. | Crawford | Little Clyde | 1126 |
| do. H. | Lesmahagow | Craigheadmill | 1192 |
| do. M., late | Covington | Muirhouse | 1045 |
| do. T. & J. | Dolphinton | Townfoot | 1038 |
| Thorburn, D. | Symington | Symington Mill | 1009 |
| do. J. | Walston | Hinshelwood | 1154 |
| do. R. | Carmichael | Stonehill | 819 |
| do. R. | Douglas | Dykehead | 1163 |
| Todd, A. | Carnwath | Buchtknowe | 982 |
| do. J. | Lesmahagow | Netherton | 1157 |
| do. J. | Carnwath | Sidewood, East | 1177 |
| do. J. | Lesmahagow | Netherburn | 1275 |
| do. J., late | Carnwath | Eastsidewood | 1004 |
| Torrens, W. | Lesmahagow | Kellylees | 1124 |
| Tudhope, G. | do. | Birkwood Mains | 972 |
| do. J. | do. | Boghill and Righead | 1021 |
| do. J. | do. | Lairs | 1098 |
| do. R. | do. | Woodhead | 980 |
| Turner, A. | Walston | Walston Mill | 1286 |
| Twaddle, J. | Covington | Warronhill, Nether | 1110 |
| do. J. | Pettinain | Westraw, part of | 939 |
| Tweedie, D. | Crawford | Castlemains | 764 |
| do. J. | Biggar | Townhead | 1189 |
| do. J. | Lamington | Mains of Loanhead | 856 |
| do. Messrs | Crawfordjohn | Abington, Nether | 891 |
| do. W. | Douglas | Glespin, West | 906 |
| Vassie, R. | Crawford | Normangill | 756 |

| Tenant. | Parish. | Farm, &c. | No. |
|---|---|---|---|
| Waddell, J. & W. | Wiston | Hillend | 806 |
| Walkinshaw, W. | Carstairs | Watertown | 1230 |
| Walker, J. | Libberton | Midhall | 1016 |
| Wallace, J. | Carluke | Law Farm | 000 |
| do. R. | Carstairs | Fallhills and Moorfoot | 895 |
| Watson, A. | Libberton | Baitlaw | 931 |
| do. D. | Coulter | Coulter and Snaip | 765 |
| do. E. | Covington | Pennyflats | 1226 |
| do. J. | Crawfordjohn | Crawfordjohn | 823 |
| do. J. | Carluke | Turf-foot | 1039 |
| do. J. | Carnwath | Ampherlaw | 1141 |
| do. J. | Walston | Lammerlaw | 1107 |
| do. R. | Coulter | Nesbit | 787 |
| do. R. | Crawfordjohn | Holmhead | 1195 |
| do. R. | Douglas | Scrogtonhead | 1081 |
| do. T. | Crawfordjohn | Lettershaws | 1258 |
| do. W. | Lesmahagow | Coalburn | 1031 |
| do. W. | Lamington | Acredland | 1301 |
| Watt, A. | Crawfordjohn | Glentewan | 924 |
| Waugh, J. | Lesmahagow | Easthouse Knowes | 1205 |
| do. S. | Dolphinton | Roberton Mains | 817 |
| Weir, C. | Symington | Westside | 908 |
| do. F. | Carmichael | Ponfeigh Place & Moor | 886 |
| do. J. | Lesmahagow | Auchtygemmel, Nether | 922 |
| do. J. | Carmichael | Watchknowe | 1219 |
| do. R. | Lesmahagow | Muirshead | 1046 |
| do. R. | do. | Rawhills | 1277 |
| do. W. & D. | Carnwath | Brownhill | 1203 |
| | do. | Newbigging Mains | 838 |
| Weir & Adamson | Carmichael | Watchknowe | 1219 |

| No. | Farm, &c. | Parish. | Tenant. |
|---|---|---|---|
| 968 | Newbigging Mill | Carnwath | White, J., *late* |
| 808 | Howburn | Walston | do. J. A. |
| 760 | Weston and Todhills | Dunsyre | Whyte, W. |
| 1303 | Blair | Lesmahagow | Wilkie, Mrs |
| 952 | Cormiston | Libberton | Williamson, A. |
| 1183 | do. | do. | do. A. |
| 1304 | Glendowran | Crawfordjohn | do. J. |
| 529 | Parish-holm | Douglas | Willison, J. |
| 991 | Andershaw | do. | do. J. |
| 1172 | Bottom, North | do. | do. J. |
| 866 | Greenburn | Crawfordjohn | do. J. |
| 830 | Upper Whitecleugh | do. | do. J. |
| 757 | Nunnerie | Crawford | Wilson, — |
| 1147 | Muirburn | Lesmahagow | do. G. |
| 839 | Springfield | Carluke | do. J. |
| 883 | Kennox | Douglas | do. J. |
| 867 | Midtown & Woodhead | Lesmahagow | do. J. |
| 836 | Eastyardhouse | Carnwath | do. J. |
| 1060 | Wiston Place | Wiston | do. Mrs |
| 1033 | Fullwood | Lanark | do. J. |
| 1200 | Wellhead | do. | do. P. |
| 1164 | Greenbank | Carluke | do. T. |
| 769 | Watermeetings | Crawford | do. W. |
| 1306 | Forth | Carnwath | Wright, J. & J |
| 1020 | Westerhouse | Carluke | |
| 1235 | Cleughbar | Lesmahagow | Young, W. |

Above list might have been more complete had the "led" farms been distinguished from those held or occupied by the tenant.

| FARM. | PARISH. | RENT, 1858-9. | TENANT. | RENT, 1863-4. | TENANT. |
|---|---|---|---|---|---|
| Campshead | Crawford | £280 0 0 | Grieve, M. | £530 0 0 | Vassie, R. |
| Castlemains | do. | 420 10 2 | Tweedie, D. | 506 3 0 | Tweedie, D. |
| Chester Hall, | Wiston | 330 0 0 | Stodart, W. | 550 0 0 | Muirhead, R. |
| Crookedstane | Crawford | 537 3 9 | Hunter, R. | 1112 11 0 | Boreland, — |
| Elvanfoot | do. | 205 0 0 | Anderson, T. | 350 0 0 | Tweedie, D. |
| Howcleugh | do. | 694 8 4 | Paterson, R. | 780 0 0 | Paterson, J. |
| Kirkton | do. | 154 0 0 | Hunter, G. | 190 0 0 | Hunter, G. |
| Midlock | do. | 360 0 0 | Johnstone, — | 490 13 0 | Johnston, — |
| Normangill | do. | 601 17 4 | Vassie, R. | 875 18 0 | Vassie, R. |
| Shortcleugh, South | do. | 338 0 0 | Paterson, A. | 418 0 0 | Paterson, A. |
| Stoneyburn | do. | 131 0 0 | Cranston, A. | 175 0 0 | Tweedie, D. |
| Abington, Nether | Crawfordjohn | 291 12 4 | Tweedie, M. | 461 13 0 | Morton, T. |
| do. Over | do. | 232 1 10 | Inch, R. | 291 5 0 | Hunter, H. |
| Craighead | do. | 184 7 4 | Hunter, — | 233 8 0 | Hunter, — |
| Crawfordjohn Mill | do. | 160 0 0 | Galloway, J. | 170 0 0 | Gibb, W., & Sons |
| Eastertown | do. | 198 16 0 | French, E. | 210 18 0 | French, E. |
| Gilkerscleugh Mains | do. | 275 5 6 | Inch, T. | 351 14 0 | Inch, T. |
| Holmhead | do. | 80 0 0 | Watson, R. | 110 0 0 | Watson, R. |
| Sheriffcleugh | do. | 70 0 0 | Forsythe, R. | 180 0 0 | Renton, —. |
| Whitecleugh, Nether | do. | 100 0 0 | Hislop, J. | 120 0 0 | Paterson, J. |
| Bottom | Douglas | 80 0 0 | Willison, J. | 115 0 0 | Willison, J. |
| Broomerside | do. | 220 18 8 | Greenshields, A. | 330 0 0 | Greenshields, A. |
| Hazelside | do. | 329 18 0 | Black, J. | 500 0 0 | Black, J. |
| Kennox | do. | 212 0 0 | Wilson, J. | 340 0 0 | Wilson, J. |
| Newtonhead | do. | 174 10 0 | Lawcock, R. | 326 0 0 | Tudhope, R. |
| Ponell | do. | 220 0 0 | Newbigging, J | 468 0 0 | Hamilton, T. |
| Culter-Allers | Coulter | 531 10 0 | Watson, A. | 630 0 0 | Watson, A., & Sons, |
| Quothquhan | Libberton | 214 17 0 | Sanderson, J. | 300 0 0 | Aiken, J. |
| Symington Mains | Symington | 182 0 0 | Stobie, M. | 285 0 0 | Cleghorn, T. |
| Windales | do. | 170 0 0 | Muirhead, R. | 300 0 0 | Forrest, A. |

| No. | Estate | Parish | Factor | Address. |
|---|---|---|---|---|
| 247 | Anstruther | Carmichael, etc. | Denholm, Robert, Esq. | Carmichael House. |
| 320 | Auchingray | Carnwath | Sutor, D. R., Esq. | 10 Gt. Stuart St., Edinburgh. |
| 266 | Auchlochan | Lesmahagow | Gibb, John, Esq., Banker | Lesmahagow. |
| 294 | Biggar Park | Biggar | Gillespie, J., Esq., W.S. | 81a George Street, Edinburgh. |
| 290 | Biggar Shiels | do. | Tawse, J. W., Esq., W.S. | 49 Queen Street, do. |
| 265 | Birkwood | Lesmahagow | Gibb, John, Esq., Banker | Lesmahagow. |
| 254 | Blackwood | do. | Smith, Andrew, Esq., Banker | do. |
| 250 | Bonnington | Lanark | Gray, John, Esq., Writer | Lanark. |
| 299 | Brailwood | Carluke | Tower, Clark, & Roberton, Writers | Glasgow. |
| 252 | Buccleuch | Crawford and Crawfordjohn | Maxwell, W., Esq. | Dubton, Thornhill. |
| 278 | Caerwood | Biggar | Murray, T., Esq. | Heaviside, Biggar. |
| 261 | Carstairs | Carstairs | M'Kenzie, J. O., Esq., W.S. | 9 Hill Street, Edinburgh. |
| 255 | Colebrooke | Crawford and Crawfordjohn | do. | do. |
| 302 | Cumberhead, South | Lesmahagow | Douglas, Archibald S., Esq. | 22 Young Street, do. |
| 241 | Douglas Estates, the (242–243) | Douglas, Lesmahagow, etc. | Scott, Thomas Rennie, Esq. | Castlemains, Douglas. |
| 248 | Eastend | Carmichael, Covington, etc. | Morrison & Marr, Writers | Lanark. |
| 277 | Hardington | Lanark and Wiston | Veitch, J., Esq. | Sanquhar. |
| 251 | Hamilton, Duke of | Lesmahagow | Grahame, Robert, Esq. | Hamilton Palace. |
| 273 | Haywood | Carnwath | Todrick, T., Esq., Banker | Haddington. |
| 304 | Hillend | Wiston | Watkins J. H., Esq. | 77 West Nile Street, Glasgow. |
| 253 | Hopetoun | Crawford and Crawfordjohn | Hare, S. B., Esq. | Philipston House, Linlithgow. |
| 293 | Jerviswood | Lanark | Stodart, D., Esq., Banker | Lanark. |
| 259 | Kersewell | Carnwath, Culter, etc. | M'Kenzie, J. O., Esq., W.S. | 9 Hill Street, Edinburgh. |
| 249 | Lamingtoune | Lamingtoune, etc. | M'Conochie & Duncan, W.S. | 10 do. |
| 324 | Leamside | Carnwath | M'Allan & Chancelor, W.S. | 19 Young Street, do. |
| 244 | Lee and Carnwath | Lanark, Carnwath, etc. | Bell & M'Lean, W.S. | 7 Hill Street, do. |
| 276 | Loanindale | Biggar and Libberton | Gillespie, John, Esq., W.S. | 81a George Street, do. |
| 246 | Milton-Lockhart | Carluke | Stodart, D., Esq., Banker | Lanark. |
| 292 | Pool | Carnwath | Hunter, Blair, & Cowan, W.S. | 7 York Place, Edinburgh. |
| 279 | Stonebyres | Lesmahagow | Walker & Melville, W.S. | do. |

| MAGNATES OF THE UPPER WARD OF LANARKSHIRE. | Deputy-Lieuts. | Police. | Income Tax. | Assessed Taxes. | Prison Board. | Public Buildings. | Estate. |
|---|---|---|---|---|---|---|---|
| Belhaven, Lord, Lord-Lieutenant of the County, Wishaw House, | ... | ... | ... | ... | ... | ... | 441 |
| Colebrooke, Sir T. E., M.P. for the County, of Abington House,... | do. | ... | ... | ... | ... | ... | 255 |
| Cochrane, A. B., M.P. (for Honiton), of Lamingtoune House, ... | do. | ... | ... | ... | ... | ... | 249 |
| Adams, Provost, of Lanark,... | ... | ... | ... | ... | do. | do. | 000 |
| Alston, J. W., Esq., of Stockbriggs, | ... | ... | do. | ... | ... | do. | 267 |
| Anderson, S., of Carfin,... | ... | ... | do. | ... | ... | do. | 301 |
| Anstruther, Sir W. C., of Westraw, | do. | ... | ... | ... | ... | do. | 247 |
| Brown, J., Esq., of Orchard, | ... | ... | ... | ... | ... | do. | 271 |
| Brown, J. T., Esq., of Auchlochan, | ... | ... | do. | ... | ... | ... | 266 |
| Carmichael, M. T., Esq., of Eastend, | ... | ... | do. | do. | ... | do. | 248 |
| Chancellor, J. G., Esq., of Shieldhill, | do. | ... | ... | ... | ... | ... | 260 |
| Dickson, D., Esq., of Hartree,... | ... | do. | do. | do. | do. | do. | 272 |
| Gilchrist, J., Esq., yr. of Gillfoot, | ... | do. | ... | do. | ... | ... | 312 |
| Greenshields, J., Esq., of Kerse,... | ... | do. | do. | do. | ... | ... | 295 |
| Hozier, J., Esq., of Mauldslie, | do. | ... | ... | ... | ... | ... | 287 |
| Irving, George Vere, Esq., of Newton, | ... | ... | ... | do. | ... | do. | 256 |
| Lockhart, A. E., Esq., of Cleghorn,... | do. | ... | ... | ... | ... | ... | 245 |
| M'Lean, Hector, W.S., 7 Hill Street, Edinburgh, | do. | ... | ... | ... | ... | ... | 0?? |
| Monteith, R., Esq., of Carstairs, | do. | ... | ... | ... | do. | ... | 261 |
| Mossman, H., Esq., of Auchtyfardle, | do. | ... | ... | ... | ... | do. | 289 |
| Scott, T. R., Esq., of Castlemains, | ... | do. | ... | ... | ... | do. | 241 |
| Sim, Adam, Esq., of Coulter-Maynes, | ... | ... | ... | do. | ... | do. | 257 |
| Somerville, T., Esq., of Greenfield, | ... | ... | ... | do. | ... | do. | 308 |
| Stein, J., Esq., of Kirkfield, | ... | ... | do. | do. | ... | ... | 298 |
| Vere, W. E. H., Esq., of Blackwood, | ... | ... | do. | do. | ... | ... | 254 |
| Wilson, J., Esq., of Westsidewood,... | do. | ... | ... | do. | ... | do. | 312 |

Sir Archibald Alison, Bart., Sheriff-Depute of Lanarkshire.
J. Neil Dyce, of Castlebank, Sheriff-Substitute do.
T. M. Shirley, Sheriff-Clerk-Depute do.
George Mackay, Hamilton, Chief Constable do.

Thomas Dykes, Hamilton, Clerk of Lieutenancy.
John Dykes, Hamilton, Clerk of Supply.
W. Morrison, Lanark, Clerk of Police.
F. Macgillivray, Superintendent of Police, Upper Ward.

| No. | Name of Estate. | Mansion. £ s. d. | Domain. £ s. d. | Wood. £ s. d. | Game. £ s. d. | Home Farm. £ s. d. | Grass Parks. £ s. d. | Minerals. £ s. d. |
|---|---|---|---|---|---|---|---|---|
| 236 | Auchlochan | 70 0 0 | 105 0 0 | 55 0 0 | | 38 0 0 | 7 0 0 | 800 0 0 |
| 2-9 | Auchtyfardle | | 100 0 0 | | | 16 7 0 | 140 0 0 | |
| 265 | Birkwood | | 299 10 0 | | | 110 5 0 | | 108 12 6 |
| 278 | Caerwood | 40 0 0 | 493 16 0 | 40 0 0 | | | 220 0 0 | |
| 261 | Carstairs | 180 0 0 | | 79 12 6 | | 490 0 0 | | |
| 263 | Corehouse | 150 0 0 | 50 0 0 | 50 0 0 | 10 0 0 | 105 0 0 | 727 0 0 | |
| 257 | Coulter-Maynes | 80 0 0 | 120 0 0 | | | | | |
| 258 | Coulter-Allers | 40 0 0 | 520 0 0 | 12 10 0 | | 150 0 0 | | |
| 248 | Eastend | | | 3 0 0 | | | 76 0 0 | |
| 264 | Edmonstone | 50 0 0 | | | | 228 0 0 | | |
| 277 | Hardington | 70 0 0 | 195 0 0 | 5 10 0 | | | | |
| 295 | Kerse | 75 5 0 | | | | | 265 8 6 | |
| 259 | Kersewell | 35 2 0 | 80 0 0 | | | | | |
| 276 | Loningdale | 130 0 0 | 20 0 0 | | | 200 0 0 | | |
| 287 | Mauldslie | | 282 0 0 | 69 12 0 | 90 0 0 | | | 322 10 0 |
| 246 | Milton-Lockhart | 60 0 0 | 109 11 2 | 20 0 0 | | 200 0 0 | 125 0 0 | |
| 256 | Newton | 36 0 0 | | 12 0 0 | | 673 0 0 | | 425 17 0 |
| 271 | Orchard | 66 0 0 | | 16 0 0 | | 150 0 0 | | |
| 260 | Shieldhill | 80 0 0 | 300 0 0 | 20 0 0 | | | | 90 8 0 |
| 267 | Stockbriggs | | | 70 0 0 | 56 0 0 | 22 0 0 | 410 5 0 | |
| 279 | Stonebyres | 70 0 0 | | 200 0 0 | | | 101 0 0 | 4901 16 0 |
| 254 | Blackwood | | 150 0 0 | 34 0 0 | | 950 0 0 | | |
| 250 | Bonnington | | 100 0 0 | 104 15 0 | | | | |
| 245 | Cleghorn | 55 0 0 | | 88 8 0 | | | 95 15 0 | |
| 255 | Crawford | 56 0 0 | 72 15 0 | 31 10 0 | 52 0 0 | | 720 0 0 | 299 11 0 |
| 262 | Dolphinton | | 280 0 0 | 545 0 0 | | | | 1650 5 0 |
| 253 | Douglas Castle | 25 0 0 | | | 67 0 0 | | | 751 0 0 |
| 241 | Hopetoun | 90 0 0 | 27 10 0 | 15 10 0 | | | 199 5 0 | 250 0 0 |
| 249 | Lamington | 240 0 0 | 224 0 0 | 159 0 0 | | | | |
| 244 | Lee | | | | | | | |

| No. | Name of Estate | Mansion £ s. d. | Policy £ s. d. | Wood £ s. d. | Game £ s. d. | Home Farm £ s. d. | Grass Parks £ s. d. | Minerals £ s. d. |
|---|---|---|---|---|---|---|---|---|
| 247 | Anstruther | 20 0 0 | | 55 0 0 | 90 0 0 | | 150 5 0 | 315 0 0 |
| 312 | Bankend | | | 3 0 0 | | | 130 1 0 | |
| 314 | Bantaskine | | | 50 0 0 | | | | |
| 289 | Biggar Shiels | | | 26 10 0 | | | | |
| 300 | Birkenhead | | | | 5 0 0 | | | 16 0 0 |
| 252 | Buccleuch, Duke of | | | | | | | |
| 306 | Clarty | 70 0 0 | | 5 0 0 | | 112 0 0 | 340 10 0 | |
| 316 | Cornhill | | | | | | | |
| 297 | Cumberhead, North | | | | 20 0 0 | | | |
| 302 | do. South | | | | 2 | | | |
| 315 | Dalserf | | | | | | | |
| 284 | Drumpeller | | | | | | | 300 0 0 |
| 248 | Douglas, Lord, late | | | | | | | |
| 274 | Ellarshaw | | | | | | | |
| 286 | Fairholm | | | 17 5 0 | | | 18 10 0 | |
| 283 | Garvaldfoot | | | 13 11 3 | | | | 6166 14 8 |
| 251 | Hamilton, Duke of | | 206 0 0 | 80 0 0 | | | | |
| 272 | Harperfield | | | 13 0 0 | | | | 124 1 0 |
| 273 | Hartree | | | | | | | |
| 313 | Haywood | | | 10 0 0 | | | | |
| 293 | Jerviswood | | | 10 0 0 | | | | |
| 242 | Lawhead | 60 0 0 | 22 0 0 | 60 0 0 | | | 485 12 0 | 412 0 0 |
| 281 | Montague, Lady, late | | | | | | 29 5 0 | |
| 303 | Newholm | | | | | | 444 18 0 | |
| 307 | Newmains | | | 22 10 0 | | | | 170 0 0 |
| 292 | Pool | 75 0 0 | 80 0 0 | 15 0 0 | | | | |
| 275 | Sunnyside | 10 0 0 | | 25 0 0 | | | | |
| 296 | Symington Lodge | | | 10 0 0 | | | | |
| 288 | Verelhills | | | | | | | |
| 282 | Westsidewood | | | | | | | |

| No. | Name of Estate. | House. £ s. d. | Grounds. £ s. d. | Wood. £ s. d. | Game. £ s. d. | Farm. £ s. d. | Parks. £ s. d. | Minerals. £ s. d. |
|---|---|---|---|---|---|---|---|---|
| 329 | Ampherlaw | 11 0 0 | 14 0 0 | 2 10 0 | | 190 0 0 | | |
| 356 | Auldton | | | 2 10 0 | | | | |
| 318 | Bankhead | 50 0 0 | | 5 10 0 | | | | 150 0 0 |
| 345 | Baronald | 52 0 0 | | | | | | |
| 294 | Biggar Park | | | | | | 18 0 0 | |
| 299 | Braidwood | 30 0 0 | 70 0 0 | 44 0 0 | | 150 0 0 | 229 10 0 | |
| 333 | Brownlie—"Harvie" | | | | | 130 0 0 | | |
| 347 | do. —"Stewart" | | | | | | | |
| 331 | Cormiston-Towers | | | | | 80 0 0 | | |
| 334 | Corramore | | | | | 100 0 0 | | |
| 353 | Ellanbank | 40 0 0 | | 3 2 6 | | | | |
| 308 | Elsrickle | | | | | | | |
| 346 | Faulldhouse | 40 0 0 | 17 10 0 | | | | 120 0 0 | |
| 332 | Glentewan | | | | | | 106 10 0 | |
| 337 | Hallcraig | 30 0 0 | | | | | | |
| 355 | Heathland | | | | | | | |
| 330 | Huntfield | 35 0 0 | | 3 0 0 | | | | |
| 345 | Huntlyhill | | | 25 0 0 | | | | |
| 298 | Kirkfield | | | 2 0 0 | | | | |
| 335 | Langlees | | | | | | | |
| 324 | Leamside | | | | | | | |
| 342 | Newmains | 38 0 0 | | 4 11 3 | | 90 0 0 | 444 18 0 | 52 0 0 |
| 374 | Ogg's Castle | 80 0 0 | | 25 0 0 | | | | |
| 352 | Saylum Park | | 10 0 0 | 20 0 0 | | | | |
| 326 | Springfield | 40 0 0 | | | | | | |
| 364 | Springhill | 50 0 0 | | | | 60 0 0 | | |
| 375 | Stanmore | 32 0 0 | 61 17 0 | | | | | |
| 343 | Trows | 15 0 0 | | | | | | |
| 340 | Turf-foot | 30 0 0 | | | | | | 88 4 10 |
| 291 | Waygateshaw | | | | | 430 10 0 | | 222 14 6 |

| No. | Name of Estate | House (£ s. d.) | Grounds (£ s. d.) | Wood (£ s. d.) | Game (£ s. d.) | Farm (£ s. d.) | Parks (£ s. d.) | Minerals (£ s. d.) |
|---|---|---|---|---|---|---|---|---|
| 437 | Bellfield | | | | | 70 0 0 | | |
| 325 | Birthwood | | | | | 289 0 0 | | |
| 339 | Blackcastle | | | | | 100 0 0 | | |
| 382 | Cambus-Wallace | | | | | 70 0 0 | | |
| 401 | Castlebank | 65 0 0 | 55 0 0 | 2 10 0 | | | 25 10 0 | 45 0 0 |
| 280 | Cormacoup | | | | | 472 0 0 | | |
| 328 | Cormiston | | | | | | | |
| 379 | Coulterhall | 20 0 0 | | | | 149 0 0 | | 15 0 0 |
| 322 | Eastshiels | | | | | 210 0 0 | | |
| 336 | Falla | | | | | 240 0 0 | | |
| 357 | Gill | | | 8 10 0 | | | | 140 0 0 |
| 312 | Gillfoot | | | | | 77 0 0 | | |
| 359 | Gowanhill | | | | | 175 0 0 | | |
| 319 | Heavisiide | | | | | 300 0 0 | | |
| 338 | Killbank | | | | | 140 0 0 | | |
| 311 | Lindsaylauds | | | | | 110 0 0 | | |
| 378 | Logan | | | | | 140 0 0 | | |
| 386 | Nemphlar | | | | | 120 0 0 | | |
| 365 | Newick | | | | | 150 0 0 | | |
| 349 | St John's Kirk | | | | | 200 0 0 | | |
| 368 | Skellyhill | | | | | 90 0 0 | | |
| 305 | Snar | | | 1 0 0 | 35 0 0 | 360 0 0 | | |
| 344 | Spittal | | | | | 200 0 0 | | |
| 390 | Strancleugh | | | | | 125 0 0 | | |
| 377 | Teaths | | | | | 140 0 0 | | |
| 285 | Toftcombs | | | | | 120 0 0 | | |
| 310 | Troloss | | | 4 0 0 | 35 0 0 | 365 0 0 | | |
| 323 | Westbank | | | | | 210 0 0 | | |
| 341 | Westerhouse | | | | | | | |
| 337 | West-town | | | | | 260 0 0 | | |

| Name of Property | Occupied £ s. d. | Let £ s. d. | Parish |
|---|---|---|---|
| Auchmedan | 95 0 0 | 32 2 0 | Lesmahagow |
| Auchren | 90 0 0 | | do. |
| Auldton | 192 10 0 | | do. |
| Bankhouses | 27 0 0 | 7 10 0 | do. |
| Beanshiels | 54 0 0 | 5 7 0 | Carluke |
| Bellfield | 75 0 0 | | Lanark |
| Biggar Park | 115 0 0 | 2 18 3 | Biggar |
| Birkhill | 45 0 0 | 5 0 0 | Lanark |
| do. | 163 2 0 | 51 15 0 | Lesmahagow |
| Blackcastle | 28 0 0 | 51 0 0 | Walston |
| Boghill and Righead | 33 0 0 | 131 0 0 | Lesmahagow |
| Bogside | | 16 12 4 | Douglas |
| Boreland | 26 0 0 | | Carluke |
| Brackenhill | | 119 10 0 | do. |
| Brae | 50 0 0 | | Lesmahagow |
| Brooklands | 32 0 0 | | Lanark |
| Brownhill | | 135 0 0 | Libberton |
| Burnfoot | 46 0 0 | 25 4 0 | Carnwath |
| Capehall | 30 0 0 | | Lesmahagow |
| Castleyett | 2 0 0 | 66 7 0 | Lanark |
| Cateraig | 62 0 0 | 146 12 0 | Carluke |
| Clydegrove | 7 0 9 | 13 4 0 | Lesmahagow |
| Clydevale | | 38 0 0 | do. |
| Cormiston | 90 0 0 | 160 0 0 | Libberton |
| Corramore | 45 0 0 | 150 0 0 | Lesmahagow |
| Coldstream, East | | | Carluke |
| do. South | | 47 0 0 | do. |
| do. West | 82 0 0 | 60 10 0 | do. |
| Craighead | 20 0 0 | | do. |
| do. | | | do. |

| No. | Name of Property | Occupied £ s. d. | Let £ s. d. | Parish | No. |
|---|---|---|---|---|---|
| 413 | Craighead | 52 0 0 | 45 0 0 | Lesmahagow | 517 |
| 397 | Craigiehall | 68 7 6 | | Carnwath | 492 |
| 356 | Croftonhill | | | Lanark | 467 |
| 366 | Crossburn | | 78 0 0 | Douglas | 413 |
| 489 | Crossford | 90 0 0 | 37 0 0 | Lesmahagow | 385 |
| 445 | do. | 30 0 0 | | do. | 607 |
| 394 | Darnfillan | 75 0 0 | 3 7 6 | do. | 446 |
| 503 | Drums | 35 0 0 | | Carluke | 565 |
| 338 | Easterseat | 60 0 0 | | do. | 486 |
| 449 | Eastfield | | 38 6 0 | Biggar | 550 |
| 398 | Eastquarter | | 30 0 0 | Carluke | 429 |
| 505 | Fastside | 100 0 0 | 30 0 0 | do. | 609 |
| 636 | Ellanbank | | 81 10 0 | Lesmahagow | 353 |
| 384 | Elsrickle | | 28 0 0 | Walston | 620 |
| 508 | Gallagreen | 35 0 0 | 8 0 0 | Carluke | 522 |
| 583 | Galla, Little | 6 0 0 | 130 0 0 | Wiston | 373 |
| 374 | Garngour, North | 7 10 0 | 82 0 0 | Lesmahagow | 415 |
| 454 | Gillhouse | | 140 0 0 | Carnwath | 381 |
| 601 | Girdwoodend | 8 0 0 | 96 2 4 | do. | 405 |
| 470 | Gladdenhill | | 55 0 0 | Carluke | 488 |
| 417 | Glendowran | 181 0 0 | | Crawfordjohn | 389 |
| 447 | Gowanhill | 175 0 0 | 16 0 0 | Carnwath | 359 |
| 517 | Gowanside | 71 0 0 | | Carluke | 459 |
| 369 | Graystone | 30 0 0 | | Lesmahagow | 602 |
| 334 | Greenfield | | 153 0 0 | Carnwath | 370 |
| 514 | Greenhill | 80 0 0 | | Lesmahagow | 438 |
| 516 | Greenridge | 130 0 0 | | do. | 388 |
| 475 | Greenshiels | | 50 0 0 | Carnwath | 493 |
| 432 | Hawksland | 40 0 0 | | Lesmahagow | 512 |
| 736 | Hazelbank | 40 0 0 | | do. | 539 |

| Name of Property | Occupied £ s. d. | Let £ s. d. | Parish | No. |
|---|---|---|---|---|
| Hillend | | 170 0 0 | Biggar | 362 |
| Hillhead | 87 0 0 | 11 0 0 | Carluke | 411 |
| Hinshelwood | | 34 5 0 | Carnwath | 569 |
| do. | | 96 0 0 | do. | 416 |
| Holmfoot | 70 0 0 | 34 0 0 | Lanark | 403 |
| Holmhead | | 80 0 0 | Crawfordjohn | 435 |
| Kilbank | 140 0 0 | 84 0 0 | Lesmahagow | 338 |
| Kypeswaterhead | 10 0 0 | 82 0 0 | do. | 433 |
| Ladeshaw | 70 0 0 | 22 0 0 | do. | 421 |
| Letham | | 113 0 0 | do. | 408 |
| Linnsville | 2 15 0 | 103 0 0 | do. | 413 |
| Loganbank | | 100 0 0 | Lanark | 424 |
| Mansefield | 66 15 0 | 16 0 0 | Carluke | 468 |
| Mavisbank | 32 0 0 | 160 0 0 | do. | 515 |
| Middlehouse | | 160 0 0 | Lesmahagow | 366 |
| Midgarngour | | 60 10 0 | do. | 480 |
| Midbinshelwood | 119 0 0 | 34 15 0 | Carnwath | 406 |
| Midtown | 16 0 0 | 55 0 0 | Carluke | 468 |
| do. | | | Lesmahagow | 483 |
| Moatyett | 55 0 0 | 41 10 0 | do. | 456 |
| Mousebank | 21 0 0 | | Lanark | 478 |
| Nemphlar | 120 0 0 | 101 0 0 | do. | 396 |
| Nemphlar, West | | 38 0 0 | do. | 419 |
| Netherfauldhouse | | 186 0 0 | Lesmahagow | 608 |
| Netherton | | 48 0 0 | do. | 358 |
| Notherwell | | 16 0 0 | Biggar | 511 |
| Newick | 150 0 0 | | Lesmahagow | 365 |
| Nowmains | 70 0 0 | 60 0 0 | Carstairs | 453 |
| Oldtown | 36 0 0 | 69 0 0 | Carnwath | 420 |
| Orchard | 2 10 0 | | Lesmahagow | 451 |

| Name of Property | Occupied £ s. d. | Let £ s. d. | Parish | No. |
|---|---|---|---|---|
| Orchardville | 37 0 0 | 4 10 0 | Lanark | 538 |
| Path-head | 27 10 0 | | Lesmahagow | 629 |
| Polmonkshead | | 154 0 0 | Douglas | 361 |
| Priorhill | 2 0 0 | 121 0 0 | Lesmahagow | 372 |
| Riddochbrae | 50 0 0 | 8 0 0 | do. | 509 |
| Rosehill | | 43 0 0 | do. | 530 |
| Scorryholm | 90 0 0 | 130 0 0 | do. | 383 |
| Skellyhill | 13 0 0 | 66 0 0 | do. | 368 |
| Springbank | | 106 0 0 | do. | 395 |
| Stane | | 115 0 0 | Biggar | 404 |
| Stanmore | 111 17 0 | 21 4 0 | Lanark | 375 |
| Stobwood | | | Carnwath | 380 |
| Stockwell | 62 0 0 | 10 0 0 | Carluke | 452 |
| Strancleugh | 125 0 0 | | Crawfordjohn | 390 |
| Tanhill | 56 0 0 | 29 0 0 | Carluke | 431 |
| do. | | 100 0 0 | Lesmahagow | 402 |
| Teaths | 140 0 0 | | do. | 377 |
| Throughburn | | | Carnwath | 436 |
| Tintoside | 45 0 0 | 80 0 0 | Symington | 520 |
| Trows | 32 0 0 | | Lesmahagow | 343 |
| Tupenhill | | 172 0 0 | Carluke | 441 |
| Waterside | 44 0 0 | 74 0 0 | Lesmahagow | 521 |
| Westermoreshot | | 108 18 0 | Carnwath | 418 |
| West-town | 260 0 0 | | Pettinain | 337 |
| Whitecastle | | | Libberton | 328 |
| Whiteside | | 297 10 0 | Lesmahagow | 440 |
| Whitesidehill | | 80 0 0 | do. | 510 |
| Wyndales | 5 0 0 | 50 0 0 | Symington | 360 |
| Yieldshields | 62 0 0 | | Carluke | 422 |
| Yett | 50 0 0 | 170 0 0 | do. | 512 |

| PROPRIETORS. VALUATION ROLL, 1858-9. | Big-gar. | Car-luke. | Car-michael. | Carn-wath. | Car-stairs. | Cov-ing-ton. | Coul-ter. | Craw-ford. | Craw-ford-john. | Dol-phin-ton. | Doug-las. | Dun-syre. | Lamp-ing-ton. | Lan-ark. | Les-mahagow. | Lib-ber-ton. | Petti-nain. | Sym-ing-ton. | Wal-ston. | Wis-ton. | Total. |
|---|---|---|---|---|---|---|---|---|---|---|---|---|---|---|---|---|---|---|---|---|---|
| Above £3000 | | | 1 | 1 | | | | 2 | 1 | | 1 | 1 | 1 | | 2 | 1 | 1 | | | | 8 |
| £2000 and under 3000 | | 1 | 1 | | | | | | 1 | 1 | | | | 1 | 2 | 1 | | | | | 8 |
| 1500 | | 2 | | | | 2 | 2 | | | | | | | 1 | 1 | | | | | | 8 |
| 1250 | 1 | 1 | | | | | | | | | | | | 1 | 1 | | | | 1 | 1 | 7 |
| 1000 | 1 | | | 3 | | | | | 1 | | | | 1 | 1 | 1 | | | | 1 | | 7 |
| 900 | 1 | 2 | | 1 | | | | 2 | | 1 | 1 | | | | 2 | | | 1 | | 1 | 21 |
| 800 | 1 | 1 | | | | | | 1 | 1 | | | | | 3 | 1 | 1 | | | 1 | 1 | 8 |
| 700 | | 2 | 1 | | 2 | | 2 | | 2 | | | | | 2 | 3 | 2 | | | | 1 | 9 |
| 600 | 1 | 1 | | 6 | | | | 2 | 1 | | 2 | | | 1 | 3 | 1 | | 1 | | 1 | 6 |
| 500 | | 2 | | 2 | | | 1 | | 1 | | | | | 2 | 1 | 1 | 1 | 1 | | 1 | 7 |
| 400 | 1 | | | 3 | 1 | 1 | | | | | | | | 2 | 5 | 1 | | 1 | | 1 | 11 |
| 300 | 6 | 1 | 3 | 2 | | | | | 2 | | 1 | | | 3 | 5 | 1 | | | | | 20 |
| 250 | 4 | 7 | | 1 | 1 | 1 | 1 | 4 | | | 3 | | | 1 | 21 | 1 | | | | 1 | 13 |
| 200 | 4 | 11 | | 3 | | | | 1 | 1 | 1 | 2 | | | 6 | 8 | 1 | | 1 | | | 18 |
| 175 | 7 | 13 | 1 | 1 | 1 | 1 | 1 | | 1 | 5 | 1 | 1 | | 3 | 10 | 1 | | 1 | | 1 | 11 |
| 150 | 4 | 17 | | 6 | | | | | 4 | 1 | 9 | 1 | | 2 | 8 | | | 1 | 2 | | 15 |
| 125 | 15 | 37 | 1 | 16 | 4 | 3 | 2 | 2 | 8 | 2 | 8 | 2 | 3 | 5 | 10 | 1 | | 2 | 1 | 4 | 21 |
| 100 | 19 | 11 | | 4 | 6 | 6 | 1 | 1 | 10 | 5 | 11 | 1 | | 9 | 11 | 1 | | 3 | 3 | 6 | 30 |
| 80 | 4 | 17 | 1 | 6 | 9 | | 2 | 2 | 1 | 1 | 20 | | | 21 | 23 | | 1 | 5 | 3 | 1 | 28 |
| 65 | 9 | 20 | | 18 | 7 | 3 | | 3 | | | 3 | | | 20 | 31 | 9 | 1 | 1 | | | 29 |
| 50 | 20 | 86 | | 27 | 2 | 6 | 2 | 3 | 10 | 2 | | | 3 | 24 | 3 | 1 | | | | 4 | 36 |
| 40 | 12 | 58 | | 46 | | | | 3 | 1 | 5 | | | | 20 | 20 | 9 | | 2 | 2 | 6 | 38 |
| 30 | 21 | 12 | | 12 | 2 | | | 3 | 1 | 1 | 3 | 1 | 1 | 7 | 35 | 1 | 1 | 3 | 3 | 1 | 78 |
| 20 | | | | | | | | | | | | | | | 108 | | | | | | 124 |
| 16 | | | | | | | | | | | | | | | 53 | 9 | | 5 | | | 28 |
| 12 | | | | | | | | | | | | | | | 8 | 1 | | 1 | 3 | | 77 |
| 8 | | | | | | | | | | | | | | | | | | | | | 117 |
| 4 | | | | | | | | | | | | | | | | | | | 3 | | 328 |
| 2 | | | | | | | | | | | | | | | | | | | | 6 | 257 |
| Under | | | | | | | | | | | | | | | | | | | | 1 | 53 |

| Tenants. Valuation Roll, 1858-9. | Biggar | Car-luke | Car-michael | Carn-wath | Car-stairs | Cov-ing-ton | Coul-ter | Craw-ford | Craw-ford-john | Dol-phin-ton | Doug-las | Dun-syre | Lam-ing-ton | Lan-ark | Les-maha-gow | Lib-ber-ton | Petti-nain | Syming-ton | Wal-ston | Wil-ton | Total |
|---|---|---|---|---|---|---|---|---|---|---|---|---|---|---|---|---|---|---|---|---|---|
| £750 and under £800 | | | | | | | | | | | | | | | | | | | | | 1 |
| 700 „ 750 | | | | | | | | | | | | | | | | 1 | | | | | 3 |
| 650 „ 700 | | | | | | | | | | | 1 | | | | | | | | | | 3 |
| 600 „ 650 | | | | | | | | | | | | | | | | | | | | | |
| 550 „ 600 | | | | | | | | 2 | | | | | | | | 2 | | | | | 4 |
| 500 „ 550 | 1 | | | | | | | | | | 1 | | | 1 | | 1 | | 1 | | 1 | 4 |
| 450 „ 500 | | | 1 | 1 | | 1 | 1 | 1 | 1 | 1 | 1 | | | 1 | 1 | 3 | 1 | | | 2 | 3 |
| 400 „ 450 | | 4 | | 1 | 2 | 1 | | 3 | 1 | 1 | 5 | | 1 | 2 | 4 | 3 | 2 | 1 | 1 | 5 | 8 |
| 350 „ 400 | | 2 | 1 | 1 | 3 | 2 | 1 | 1 | 1 | 1 | 4 | | 1 | 4 | 5 | 3 | 1 | 1 | 1 | 3 | |
| 300 „ 350 | 1 | 1 | 3 | 1 | | 1 | | 1 | 1 | 3 | 2 | | 1 | 3 | 8 | 2 | 1 | 2 | 1 | 3 | 10 |
| 250 „ 300 | | 6 | 1 | 1 | 4 | 1 | 3 | 1 | 2 | 1 | 2 | 1 | 2 | 1 | 6 | 5 | 2 | 2 | 1 | 5 | 16 |
| 200 „ 250 | 4 | 9 | 6 | 4 | 1 | 1 | 1 | 2 | 2 | 3 | 6 | 1 | 2 | 6 | 19 | 2 | 3 | 2 | 2 | 2 | 33 |
| 175 „ 200 | | 3 | 5 | 6 | 2 | 1 | 3 | 1 | 1 | 2 | 9 | 1 | 2 | 5 | 23 | 1 | 2 | 1 | 3 | 1 | 60 |
| 150 „ 175 | 5 | 10 | 10 | 3 | 3 | 2 | 1 | 2 | 2 | 1 | 6 | 3 | 2 | 7 | 15 | 5 | 1 | 2 | 8 | 4 | 36 |
| 125 „ 150 | 4 | 18 | 6 | 8 | 5 | 5 | 2 | 3 | 5 | 3 | 3 | | 1 | 8 | 40 | 2 | 2 | 1 | 1 | 5 | 47 |
| 100 „ 125 | 7 | 12 | 10 | 8 | 4 | 2 | 2 | 1 | 1 | 7 | 6 | 1 | 3 | 13 | 16 | 1 | 3 | 4 | 3 | 8 | 70 |
| 75 „ 100 | 8 | 11 | 6 | 17 | 3 | 3 | 4 | 2 | 5 | 8 | 3 | 1 | 2 | 6 | 10 | 1 | 3 | 1 | 2 | 12 | 75 |
| 50 „ 75 | 12 | 15 | 5 | 9 | 2 | 1 | 3 | 4 | 4 | 22 | | 1 | 7 | 8 | 5 | 4 | 5 | 1 | 75 | |
| 40 „ 50 | 20 | 16 | 2 | 5 | 7 | 3 | 1 | 3 | 4 | 48 | | 6 | 12 | 6 | 2 | 4 | 114 | | | | |
| 35 „ 40 | 24 | 41 | 3 | 10 | 15 | 5 | 8 | 2 | 10 | 22 | 9 | 15 | 28 | 62 | 69 | | | | | | |
| 30 „ 35 | 75 | 52 | 6 | 14 | | | 10 | | | 48 | 22 | 43 | 226 | 39 | | | | | | | |
| Under 4 | 75 | 198 | 51 | 51 | 15 | 5 | 8 | 8 | 10 | 7 | 48 | 1 | 3 | 43 | 226 | 4 | 1 | 5 | 3 | 12 | 721 |
| | 446l. | 1748l. | 25l. | 599l. | 190l. | 19l. | 69l. | 23l. | 153l. | 17l. | 549l. | 36l. | 36l. | 164l. | 1522l. | 39l. | 39l. | 94l. | 24l. | 54l. | 5810l. |
| „ 2 | 13l. | 15l. | | 36l. | 4l. | | | | 4l. | | 5l. | | | 17l. | 23l. | | | | 15s. | 15s. | 121l. |
| Empty | 32l. | 78l. | 10s. | 54l. | 4l. | | 20l. | 3l. | 7l. | | 6l. | | | 13l. | 127l. | | | | 2l. | 2l. | 349l. |

| Nomenclature of Proprietors. | Estate. | Biggar | Carluke | Carmichael | Carnwath | Carstairs | Covington | Coulter | Crawford | Crawfordjohn | Dolphinton | Douglas | Dunsyre | Lamington | Lanark | Lesmahagow | Libberton | Pettinain | Symington | Walston | Wiston |
|---|---|---|---|---|---|---|---|---|---|---|---|---|---|---|---|---|---|---|---|---|---|
| Alston, J. W. | 267 | | | a | | | a | | | | | | | | | a | | | | | |
| Anstruther, Sir W. C. .......293, | 247 | | b | | | | | a | | | | | | | | | | a | | | |
| Baillie, — | 258 | a | | b | b | | | c | | | | | | | b | | | | | | |
| Bertram, W. .......271, 264 | 259 | | c | b | b | | c | | | | | | | | c | a | a | | b | | |
| Brown, — | 266 | | a | | c | | | | c | | | | | | | | | | | | b |
| Carmichael, —? | 248 | | | | | | | | | | | | | | | | | | | | |
| Chancellor, J. G. | 260 | | | a | | | | | | | | | | | | | | | | | |
| Cochrane, A. B. | 249 | | | | | | | | a | | | | | a | | a | | | c | | |
| Colebrooke, Sir T. E. | 255 | | b | a | b | c | | c | a | a | | | | | | c | | | | | ac |
| Cranstoun, Miss F. | 263 | | bc | | | bc | | | | c | | | | | aac | a | | | | | |
| Dickson, —? | 272 | | | | | | | | b | a | | a | | | | | | | | | |
| Douglas, —? | 241 | c | a | | | | | | b | c | | c | | | | a | a | | | | |
| Hamilton, —? | 251 | | a | | a | | | | a | c | | a | a | a | c | b | b | | | a | a |
| Hopetoun, —? | 253 | | | | | | | | | c | | | | b | | | | | | | |
| Irving, G. V. ?? | 256 | | b | | | | | | | | | | | | | b | | | | | |
| Lockhart, —?? | 244 | | | | | | | | | | | | | | | | | | | | |
| Lorraine, W. S. | 276 | | | | | a | | | | | c | | | | a | b | | | | | |
| Mackenzie, J. O. | 262 | | | | | | | | | | a | | | | | b | | | | | |
| Mackirdy, J. G. | 265 | b | | | | | | | | | | | | | | | | | | | |
| Mitchell, W. S. | 278 | | | | | | | | | | | | | | | | c | | c | | |
| Monteith, —.......279, | 261 | | | | | | | | | | | | | | | | | | | | |
| Mossman, H. | 289 | | | | 2 | c | | | | | | | | | | 2 | | | | | |
| Ross, Sir W. C. | 250 | | | | | b | | a | | | | | | | | a | | | | | |
| Sim, Adam | 257 | | | | | | | | | | | | | | | c | | | | | |
| Somerville, —??? | 309 | | | | b | | | | | | | | | | | | | | | | |
| Souter, D. R. | 281 | | | | | | | | | | | | | | | | | | | | |
| Steel, —?? | 291 | | | | | | | | | | | | | | | | | | | | |
| Vere Hope, W. E. | 254 | | b | | | | | | | | | | | | | 2 | | | | | |
| Wilson, —??? | 282 | | | | | | | | | | | | | | | a | | | | | |
| Woddrop, W. H. A. | 283 | | c | | | | | | c | | | | | | | | | | | b | |

* a—i.e., larger; b, less; c, lesser—on Valuation Roll.

| Nomenclature of Proprietors. | Estate. | Biggar. | Carluke. | Carmichael. | Carnwath. | Carstairs. | Covington. | Coulter. | Crawford. | Crawfordjohn. | Dolphinton. | Douglas. | Dunsyre. | Lamington. | Lanark. | Lesmahagow. | Libberton. | Pettinain. | Symington. | Walston. | Wiston. |
|---|---|---|---|---|---|---|---|---|---|---|---|---|---|---|---|---|---|---|---|---|---|
| Buccleuch, Duke of | 252 | | | | | | | | b | c | | | | | | | | | | | |
| Birrell, Lieut.-Colonel | 302 | | | | | c | | | | | | | | | | c | | | | | |
| Buchanan, R. C. | 284 | | c | | c | | | | | | | | | | | | c | | | | |
| Collyer, W. D. | 331 | | | | | | | c | | | | | | | | | | | | | |
| Ewart, R. | 274 | | | | c | | | | | | | | | | | | | | | | c |
| Ferguson, J. | 353 | | | | b | | | | | | | | | | | | | | b | | |
| Forrest, ? ? | 363 | | 3 | | | | | | | | | | | | | | | | | | |
| Gibson, T. | 285 | | c | | | | | | | | | c | | c | 2 | | | | | | |
| Gilchrist, J. | 312 | * c | c | | | | | | | | | | | | | c | | | | | |
| Gillespie, ? ? ? ? | 275 | b 2 | b | | | | | | | | | | | | | c | | | | | |
| Gordon, Lieut.-Colonel | 313 | | | | | | | | | | | | | | | | | | | | |
| Greenshields, J. | 295 | | | | | | | | | | | | | | | c | | | | | |
| Handyside, W. | 316 | | | | | | | | | | | | | | | c | | | | | |
| Howieson, ? | 304 | | | | | | | | | | | | | | | c | | | | | |
| Hozier, J. | 287 | | | | | | | | | | | | | | | | | | | | |
| Inglis, J. | 288 | | | | | | | | | | | | | | | b | | | | | |
| Johnstone, P. & J. | 305 | | | | | | | | c | | | | | | | c | | | | | c |
| MacGhie, R. | 343 | b | | | | | | c | | c | | | | | | | | | | | |
| Macpherson, N. | 290 | | | | | | | | | | | | | | c | | | | | | |
| Macqueen, R. | 277 | | | | | | | | | | | b | | | | | | | | | b |
| Marshall, J. | 297 | | | | | | | | | | | | | | c | | | | | | |
| Paterson, —, | 280 | | | | | | | | | | | | | | | | | | | | |
| Robertson, ? ? | 320 | | c | | c | | | | c | | | | | | | c | | | c | | |
| Stainton, E. | 290 | | | | | | | | | | | | | | | | | | | | |
| Stark, J. | 330 | | c | | | | | | | | | | | | | b | | | | | |
| Stein, J. | 298 | | | | | | | | | | | | | | | | | | | | |
| Stevenson, N. | 299 | | | | | | | | | | | | | | | | c | | | | |
| Tennant, J. | 292 | | | | | | | | | | | | | | | b | | | | b | |
| Thomson, J., ? | 300 | | | | b | | | | | | | | | | | b c | | | | | |
| Whyte, —. 380, 379, | 329 | | | | 2 | | | c | | | | | | | | | | | | | |

*a—i.e., larger; b, lesser; c, lesser—on Valuation Roll.*

| Nomenclature of Tenants | Estate | Biggar | Carluke | Carmichael | Carnwath | Carstairs | Covington | Coulter | Crawford | Crawfordjohn | Dolphinton | Douglas | Dunsyre | Lamington | Lanark | Lesmahagow | Libberton | Pettinain | Symington | Walston | Wiston |
|---|---|---|---|---|---|---|---|---|---|---|---|---|---|---|---|---|---|---|---|---|---|
| Alison, —. | 797, 788 | | | | | | | | | | | c | | a | | | | | | | |
| Black, J. | 798, 759 | b | | | | c c | | | | | | | c c | | | | a | | | | |
| Brown, —.??? | 753 | | | | | c | | | | | | | c | | | | | | | | |
| Brownlie, A. | 985 | | | | | | | | | | | | | a | | c | | | | | |
| Denholm, A. | 751 | | | | | c c | | | | | | | | | | a | | | | | |
| Dykes, R. | 762 | | | | | c | | | | | | | | | | | | | | | |
| Elder, J. | 794 | | | | | | | | | | | | | | c | | | | | | |
| Fleming, — | 792, 772 | | | | | c | | | | c | | | | | | | c | | | | |
| Fletcher, R.?? | 770 | | | | | | | | b | | | | | b | c | | | | | | |
| French, —.?? | 767 | | | | | | | | | | | | | | | | | | | | |
| Gibson, — | 789, 768 | | | | | | | | | | | | | | c | | | | | | |
| Gillespie, — | 758, 753 | | | | | | | | | | | | | | | | | | | | |
| Greenshields, D. | 794 | | | | | | | | | | | | | a | | | | | | | |
| Hamilton, — | 784, 763 | | | | | | | | b | | | a a | | | | | | | | | |
| Hogg, P. | 778 | | | | a c | | | | a a c | | | | | | | | | c | | c | |
| Hunter, R.??? | 752 | | | | b | | | | c | c | | | | | | | | | | | |
| Jack, M. | 781 | | | b | | | | | b | | | | | | | | | | | | |
| Johnstone, — | 795 | | | | | | | | | | | | | | c | | c | | | | |
| Lindsay, E. | 766 | | | | | | | | b | | | | | | | c | | | | | |
| Milligan, J. | 777 | | | | | | | | | | | | | | | | | | | | |
| Paterson, —.?? | 774 | | | | | | | | | | | | | | | | | | | | |
| Purdie, T. & J. | 786 | | | | | | | | b | | | | | | | | c | | | | |
| Russell, A. | 773 | | | | | | | | a | | | | | | | | | | | | |
| Shaw, T. | 800 | | | | | | | a b | | | | | | | | | | | | | |
| Somerville, A. | 799 | | | | | | | | | | | | | | | | | | | | |
| Tweedie, D. | 764 | | | | | | | | | | | | | | | | | | | | |
| Vassie, R. | 756 | | | | | | | | | | | | | | | | | | | | |
| Watson, —. | 787, 765 | | | | | | | | b | | | | c | | | | | | | | |
| Whyte, W. | 760 | | | | | | | | | | | | | | | | | | | | |
| Wilson, — | 769, 757 | | | | | | | | a a | | | | a | | | | | | | | |

| PARISH | Presby-tery | PATRON. | Pop. 1861. | Sit-tings | MINISTER, 1857. | Died | MINISTER, 1864. | Ord. | PAROCHIAL TEACHERS. |
|---|---|---|---|---|---|---|---|---|---|
| Biggar | Biggar | Hawarden, Viscountess | 2049 | ... | Christison, John, M.A. | ...... | Christison, John, M.A., | 1823 | Morrison, James |
| Carluke | Lanark | Lockhart of Lee | 6283 | 1000 | Wylie, John, D.D. | ...... | Wylie, John, D.D., | 1818 | Fraser, John |
| Carmichael | do. | Anstruther, Sir W. C. | 805 | 450 | Lamb, W., D.D. | 1863 | Vary, J., (Pettinain) | 1835 | Braidwood, Thos. |
| Carnwath | do. | Lockhart of Lee | 3561 | 1021 | M'Lean, A. H. | ...... | M'Lean, A. H., | 1834 | Mason, Alexander |
| Carstairs | do. | Struthers of Craigcoll | 1066 | 400 | Struthers, W., M.A | ...... | Struthers, W., M.A., | 1844 | Murray, John |
| Coulter | Biggar | Cochrane or Dickson | 472 | 325 | Riach, J. G., M.A | ...... | Anderson, J., M.A., | 1846 | MacGowan, A. |
| Covington | do. | Austruther or Lockhart | 548 | ? | Watson, Thomas | 1862 | Watson, Thomas, | 1821 | Hunter, A., M.A. |
| Crawford | Lanark | Crown | 670 | 320 | Anderson, T., 1820 | ...... | Morrison, W., A. & S., | 1863 | Lang, William |
| do. Leadhills | do. | Hopetoun, Earl of | 1000 | ? | Smith, Stewart | ...... | Smith, Stewart, | 1847 | Hastie, P. |
| Crawfordjohn | do. | Colebrooke, Sir T. E. | 1111 | 209 | Goldie, W. | 1862 | Paton, J. A. H, | 1862 | Robb, William |
| Dolphinton | Biggar | Home, Countess of | 305 | 140 | Aiton, John, D.D. | 1863 | Stevenson, R. J., | 1863 | Smith, John |
| Douglas | Lanark | do. do. | 2611 | ? | Stewart, A., LL.D | 1862 | Smith, W., | 1858 | Scott, James |
| Dunsyre | Biggar | Crown...... [Cochrane | 312 | 245 | Renton, G. C., | ...... | Waugh, R., A. & S. | 1844 | Porteous, M. |
| Lamington | do. | Home, Countess of, or | 300 | ? | Hope, Charles | 1862 | Miller, Thomas, | 1862 | Paton, S. |
| Lanark | Lanark | Crown | 8243 | 2000 | M'Glashan, A. / MacReady, A. | ...... | M'Glashan, A., / MacReady, A., | 1842 / 1853 | Gray, John / Dunlop, A. M. |
| do. St Leonards | do. | Heads of Families | ... | ... | M'Naughton,A.,D.D | ...... | M'Naughton,A.,D.D., | 1818 | } Campbell, Dun. |
| Lesmahagow | do. | Hamilton, Duke of | 7746 | 1330 | Burns, Thomas | ...... | Burns, Thomas, | 1839 | |
| do. 2d charge | do. | do. | | | | | | | |
| Libberton | Biggar | Lockhart of Lee | 800 | 450 | Craik, A., D.D. | 1857 | Lawrie, John, M.A., | 1857 | Black, W. |
| Pettinain | Lanark | Anstruther, Sir W. C. | 428 | 240 | Vary, J. (Carmichael) | ...... | Bell, John, | 1842 | Birrell, A. G. |
| Symington | Biggar | Lockhart of Lee | 536 | 300 | Forbes, John | ...... | Forbes, John, | 1840 | Bell, John |
| Walston | do. | do. [Home | 407 | ? | Wilson, John. | 1858 | Hogan, John, | 1850 | Murray, Jos. [J. |
| Wiston&Roberton | Lanark | Crown or Countess of | 830 | 370 | Smith, David | ...... | Smith, David, | 1846 | Core, W., & Black, |

Free Church—Abington and Crawfordjohn

do. Carluke, White, J., ..........1845
do. Coulter, Proudfoot, J., ......1827
do. Carnwarth, Walker, J., ......1842
do. Douglas, Gordon, C., ........1861
do. Lanark, Stark, T., ...........1841
do. Lesmahagow, Laing, J., M.A., 1856

U.P. Church—Biggar, Nor., Smith,D.,D.D.,1823
do. So., Dunlop,J., M.A.,1847
do. Braehead (Carnwath), Banks, A., 1848
do. Carluke, Nelson, A., ..........1837
do. Carnwath, Barrie, J., ..........1835
do. Crossford (Lesmahagow),Weir,J.,1850
do. Douglas, Jamieson, J., ..........1820

U.P. Church—Lanark, M'Luckie, J., 1858
do. Lanark, Johnston, J., .....1836
do. Lesmahagow, Cordiner,J., 1847
do. Roberton, Scott, R. D.,...1845

Episcopalian—Dolphinton, Private Chapel
do. Lamington, Kershaw, E. D.
do. Lanark, Leyland, L., .....1848

| Farms. Stock, Crop, &c. Names in *Italics* imply "*led farms*;" those in CAPITALS, occupied, etc., by the Owners. | Hill Pasture. Acres. | Low Pasture. Acres. | In Grass. Acres. | In Meadow. Acres. | Cheviot Ewes. No. | Cheviot Rams. No. | Cheviot Hoggs. No. | Feeding Sheep. No. | Black-faced Ewes. No. | Black-faced Tups. No. | Black-faced Hogs. No. | Milch Cows. No. | Calves. No. | Queys. No. | Feeding Cattle. No. | Horses, work. No. | Horses, Saddle. No. | Oats. Acres. | Turnips. Acres. | Potatoes. Acres. | Shep-herds. No. |
|---|---|---|---|---|---|---|---|---|---|---|---|---|---|---|---|---|---|---|---|---|---|
| *Crawford* | | 16 | 100 | 20 | 1680 | 30 | 420 | | | | | 2 | | 1 | | 1 | | | | 1 | 4 |
| do. | | 8 | 4 | 25 | 1620 | 30 | 420 | | | | | 3 | | 4 | | 1 | | 10 | 3 | 1 | 3 |
| do. | | 11 | 2 | 10 | 1600 | 27 | 400 | | | | | 6 | 2 | 4 | | 2 | 1 | 5 | 1 | 1 | 3 |
| do. | | 35 | 7 | | 1460 | 25 | 340 | | | | | 6 | 2 | 15 | | 2 | | 5 | 2 | 1 | 7 |
| do. | | 8 | 2 | 20 | 1360 | 22 | 360 | 200 | | | | 4 | 5 | 9 | | 2 | 2 | 14 | 6 | 1 | 3 |
| do. | 2400 | | 7 | 6 | 1280 | 21 | 340 | | 1460 | 25 | 340 | 8 | 4 | 3 | | 3 | 1 | 6 | 2 | 1 | 4 |
| *Do.* | | | 2 | 4 | 1240 | 21 | 360 | | 620 | 11 | 120 | 6 | 2 | 2 | | 2 | | | | 1 | 3 |
| CRAWFORDJOHN | | | | 10 | 1080 | 18 | 320 | | | | | 2 | | | | 2 | | | | 1 | 2 |
| *Crawford* | | | | | 1000 | 18 | 360 | 300 | | | | 2 | 1 | 2 | | 5 | | | | 1 | 2 |
| do. | 2500 | | 15 | 12 | 950 | 16 | 260 | | | | 50 | 2 | | 5 | | 3 | | 30 | 12 | | 2 |
| *Craufordjohn* | 1200 | 190 | 40 | 8 | 850 | 14 | 200 | | | | | 40 | 10 | 20 | | | 1 | 5 | 4 | 3 | 1 |
| *Wiston* | 800 | 45 | 30 | | 800 | 13 | 170 | | | | | 18 | 6 | 10 | | | | | | 1 | 2 |
| *Crawfordjohn* | | 120 | | 8 | 720 | 10 | 140 | | 1440 | 25 | 400 | 38 | | 12 | | | | 30 | 13 | 1 | 1 |
| do. | | | 13 | 30 | 600 | 10 | 90 | | 1160 | 21 | 240 | 1 | 4 | 4 | | | | | 13 | 1 | 1 |
| do. | 500 | 15 | 14 | | 440 | 7 | 110 | | 980 | 18 | 180 | 20 | 1 | 8 | | 3 | 1 | | 2 | | 1 |
| *Crawford* | 600 | 15 | 2 | 100 | 400 | 6 | 90 | | 920 | 16 | 140 | 10 | 4 | 8 | | 2 | | | 3 | 2 | 1 |
| do. | | 16 | | | 400 | 6 | | | 680 | 12 | 140 | 21 | | 8 | | | | | | 1 | 1 |
| do. | | | | 60 | 360 | | | | 600 | 10 | 140 | 7 | 10 | 20 | | | | | | 1 | 1 |
| dn. | | | 30 | 70 | | | | | 600 | 10 | 120 | 3 | 2 | 4 | | 6 | | | | 1 | 3 |
| do. | 2000 | 60 | | 6 | | 15 | | | 410 | 8 | 120 | 2 | 1 | 1 | | 2 | | | | 1 | 3 |
| *Crawfordjohn* | 1500 | | | 15 | | | | | 460 | 9 | 120 | 1 | | 5 | | 4 | | | | | 2 |
| do. | 1000 | 8 | | 20 | | | | | 360 | 7 | 90 | 26 | 10 | 10 | | 4 | | 36 | 15 | 3 | 2 |
| do. | 1000 | 12 | 50 | 2 | | | | 90 | | | | 6 | 2 | 4 | | 2 | | 1 | | 1 | 1 |
| do. | 1000 | 30 | 60 | 18 | 350 | 6 | 90 | | | | | 1 | 1 | 1 | | | | 20 | 8 | 2 | 2 |
| do. | | 25 | 7 | 6 | 280 | 6 | 70 | | | | | 200 | 10 | 5 | | | | 24 | 9 | 3 | 1 |
| *Crawford* | | | 4 | 14 | | | | | | | | 20 | 8 | 16 | | 4 | | 1 | 5 | 2 | 1 |
| *Wiston* | | | | 16 | | | | | | | | 12 | 6 | 12 | | 4 | | 25 | 5 | 2 | 1 |
| *Crawford* | | | | 12 | | | | | | | | 15 | 3 | 4 | | 2 | | 22 | | 2 | 1 |
| *Symington* | | | | 3 | | | | | | | | | | | | | | | | | 1 |

| Farms, Crop, Stock, &c. | Servants (No.) | Wood (Acres) | Sheep, Feeding (No.) | Hoggs (No.) | Rams (No.) | Sheep (No.) | Horses, Saddle (No.) | Horses, Work (No.) | Swine (No.) | Cattle, Feeding (No.) | Queys (No.) | Calves (No.) | Cows (No.) | Potatoes (Acres) | Turnips (Acres) | Barley (Acres) | Oats (Acres) | In Grass (Acres) | In Meadow (Acres) | Low Pasture (Acres) | Hill Pasture (Acres) |
|---|---|---|---|---|---|---|---|---|---|---|---|---|---|---|---|---|---|---|---|---|---|
| Symington | 9 | | 100 | | | | 1 | 10 | 2 | 36 | 16 | 12 | 16 | 36 | 43 | 1 | 99 | 122 | | 96 | 190 |
| Carnwath | 8 | 8 | | 30 | | 180 | 5 | 6 | 5 | | 12 | 6 | 30 | 5 | 26 | | 60 | 10 | 2 | 82 | 70 |
| Wiston | 7 | | 120 | 140 | 10 | 600 | 1 | 6 | 8 | | 14 | 10 | 23 | 3 | 15 | | 38 | 18 | 9 | 58 | 400 |
| Crawfordjohn | 4 | 20 | | 140 | | 120 | 1 | 4 | 7 | | 20 | 10 | 26 | 3 | 8 | | 22 | 11 | 16 | 70 | |
| Carnwath | 5 | 16 | | | | | 1 | 3 | 7 | | 9 | 8 | 25 | 3 | | | 27 | | | 36 | 200 |
| Wiston | 8 | 13 | | | | | 1 | 7 | 10 | | 18 | 10 | 25 | 5 | 5 | 2 | 54 | 20 | 4 | 64 | |
| Symington | 7 | 4 | | 80 | 5 | 320 | 1 | 5 | | 2 | 27 | 18 | 25 | 6 | 24 | | 55 | 5 | 5 | 110 | 200 |
| Wiston | 8 | 10 | | 20 | 1 | 30 | | 5 | 6 | | 18 | 10 | 24 | 5 | 24 | 2 | 43 | 30 | 10 | 70 | |
| Carnwath | 8 | | | 40 | | 30 | 1 | 6 | 3 | | 23 | 12 | 28 | 8 | 20 | | 36 | 9 | 4 | 53 | 200 |
| Wiston | 8 | 10 | | | | 350B | | 6 | 7 | | 26 | 13 | 24 | 3 | 19 | | 41 | 10 | 6 | 85 | 650 |
| Carnwath | 5 | 5 | 40 | 120 | | | 1 | 6 | 7 | | 12 | 8 | 30 | 6 | 21 | 1 | 46 | 16 | | 36 | |
| Wiston | 6 | 23 | 240 | | 60 | 600 | 1 | | 4 | | 24 | 12 | 23 | 2 | 13 | 1 | 20 | 8 | 20 | 70 | 200 |
| Carnwath | 7 | | | | | | 1 | 4 | 4 | 24 | 16 | 6 | 24 | 4 | 16 | | 60 | 8 | | 40 | 600 |
| Dolphinton | 7 | 15 | | 120 | | 480 | 1 | 4 | 8 | 18 | 49 | 8 | 23 | 2 | 18 | 1 | 55 | 6 | 19 | | 850 |
| Carnwath | 6 | | 100 | 240 | | | | 5 | 3 | | 17 | 20 | 22 | 4 | 23 | | 30 | 13 | 36 | 68 | 32 |
| Wiston | 5 | | | | | 330 | 2 | 3 | 8 | | 22 | 12 | 22 | 2 | 7 | | 43 | 42 | 7 | 83 | 600 |
| Crawfordjohn | 9 | 80 | | 100 | | 200 | 1 | 3 | 6 | | 23 | 8 | 12 | 8 | 12 | 1 | 25 | 15 | 3 | | 140 |
| Carnwath | 8 | 3 | | | | | 1 | 10 | 12 | | 24 | 19 | 13 | 3 | 6 | | 100 | | 9 | 218 | |
| Wiston | 7 | 20 | | 10 | | 250 | 1 | 10 | 5 | | 14 | 15 | 18 | 5 | 37 | 2 | 90 | 6 | 10 | 40 | 100 |
| Dolphinton | 8 | 115 | | | | | 1 | 6 | 9 | | 32 | 12 | 24 | 9 | 36 | | 80 | | 6 | 60 | 154 |
| Carnwath | 9 | 100 | 100 | | 60 | | | 7 | 7 | 2 | 40 | 7 | 30 | 12 | 35 | | 80 | 10 | | | 800 |
| do. | 8 | 2 | | 20 | | 50 | 1 | 9 | 8 | 3 | 30 | 17 | 40 | | 30 | 1 | 70 | 6 | 2 | 27 | |
| do. | 5 | 5 | | | 2 | 200 | 1 | 7 | 7 | | 19 | 20 | 22 | 2 | 29 | | 67 | 20 | | 50 | |
| do. | 1 | 35 | | | | 150 | 1 | | 4 | | 19 | 15 | 25 | 20 | 10 | | 40 | | 10 | 55 | |
| do. | 5 | 1 | | 10 | | | 1 | 4 | 3 | | 12 | 13 | 30 | 3 | 8 | 2 | 40 | 35 | 2 | 50 | |
| do. | 4 | 2 | | | | | 1 | 7 | 8 | 2 | 19 | 12 | 20 | 8 | 10 | | 82 | 22 | 2 | 45 | 130 |
| Wiston | 7 | 2 | | 20 | | 50 | 1 | 3 | 6 | 3 | 12 | 5 | 30 | 3 | 22 | | 38 | 20 | 6 | | |
| do. | 4 | | | | | 200 | 1 | 2 | 14 | | 8 | 5 | 17 | | 11 | 1 | 36 | | 4 | 46 | |
| Symington | 7 | 2 | | 55 | | 150 | 1 | 3 | 7 | | 12 | 7 | 26 | | 12 | | 36 | 21 | 15 | 60 | 500 |
| do. | | 10 | 6 | | | | 1 | 6 | 4 | | 24 | 12 | | 4 | 16 | 2 | 40 | | | | |

**Notes:**
a—Pounds only given—space not allowing s. or d.
b—Poor for 1849, casual not included; for 1863, registered only.
c—Biggar, Carluke, and Lesmahagow have each two manses.

Total: 613 / 615

| STATISTICS | Biggar | Carluke | Carmichael | Carnwath | Carstairs | Covington | Crawford | Crawfordjohn | Coulter | Dolphinton | Douglas | Dunsyre | Lamington | Lanark | Lesmahagow | Libberton | Pettinain | Symington | Walston | Wiston |
|---|---|---|---|---|---|---|---|---|---|---|---|---|---|---|---|---|---|---|---|---|
| Parochial Stipend (a) | 290l | 312l | 225l | 274l | 256l | 209l | 272l | 272l | 217l | 158l | 307l | 157l | 121l | 333l | 629l | 226l | 162l | 164l | 158l | 204l |
| do. Manse | 29l | | 20l | | | 20l | 18l | | 26l | | 38l | 26l | 20l | | 36l | 22l | 20l | 20l | | 20l |
| do. Globe | 34l | | 30l | | | 40l | 17l | 36l | 34l | 50l | 43l | 13l | 23l | | 46l | 18l | 23l | 15l | 35l | 51l |
| do. Manse and glebe | | 67l | | 55l | 65l | | | | | | | | | 10l | | | | | | |
| Teinds—unexhausted | 193l | 535l | | 118l | 308l | | 585l | 147l | | | 73l | | | 601l | 993l | | | | | |
| Poor on Roll in 1849 (b) | 54 | 126 | 10 | 103 | 8 | 10 | 70 | 31 | 10 | 2 | 93 | 7 | 9 | 168 | 138 | 51 | 5 | 10 | 11 | 28 |
| do. Expenditure, 1849 | 276l | 765l | 70l | 695l | 73l | 101l | 391l | 174l | 91l | 19l | 634l | 64l | 72l | 986l | 708l | 155l | 50l | 91l | 64l | 139l |
| do. on Roll in 1863 | 63 | 132 | 20 | 85 | 8 | 7 | 48 | 27 | 9 | 2 | 74 | 7 | 5 | 209 | 193 | 21 | 6 | 9 | 10 | 17 |
| do. Expenditure, 1863 | 429l | 1254l | 170l | 815l | 91l | 111l | 503l | 306l | 119l | 18l | 585l | 56l | 55l | 1166l | 1530l | 217l | 55l | 60l | 107l | 193l |
| School Stipend—Old | 34l | 34l | 34l | 34l | 34l | 28l | 34l | 33l | 34l | 26l | 34l | 31l | 34l | | 34l | 30l | 32l | 34l | 31l | 31l |
| do. —New | 50l | 70l | 34l | 60l | 60l | 50l | 50l | 50l | 45l | 35l | 53l | 45l | 53l | | 53l | 53l | 35l | 60l | 45l | 53l |
| Schoolmaster's House | 12l | 23l | 23l | 8l | 10l | 6l | 10l | 10l | 6l | 6l | 10l | 6l | 13l | | 10l | 6l | 4l | 8l | 5l | 22l |
| Schools—Parochial | 1 | 1 | 1 | 1 | 1 | 1 | | 1 | 1 | 1 | 1 | 1 | 1 | 1 | 1 | 1 | 1 | 1 | 1 | 2 |
| do. —District | 2 | 1 | 1 | 5 | 1 | | 3 | 3 | 57 | | 5 | | | many | | | | | | |
| Scholars, 5 to 15 years, 1861 | 313 | 940 | 143 | 471 | 195 | 58 | 274 | 132 | 154 | 40 | 391 | 42 | 55 | 1089 | 1310 | 113 | 60 | 50 | 81 | 102 |
| Free Church Manse | | 14l | | 22l | | | | | | | 23l | | | | 36l | | | | | 10l |
| U.P. do. do. (c) | 26l | 30l | | 39l | | | | | | | 23l | | | | 36l | | | | | |
| Other do. do. | | 20l | | | | | | 2 | 1 | 1 | | | 1 | | 24l | | 2 | | | |
| Inns—with Posting, 1864 | 3 | 4 | 3 | 3 | 3 | 1 | 1 | 3 | | | 2 | | 2 | 5 | 10 | | | | | |
| do. —without Posting, 1864 | 2 | 5 | | 4 | 1 | | 2 | | | | 1 | | | 8 | 9 | | | 1 | 1 | 1 |
| Post-Offices | 1 | 1 | 1 | 1 | | 1 | | 1 | 1 | | 2 | | 1 | 1 | 4 | | 1 | 1 | | 1 |
| Police stationed | 2 | 2 | | 3 | | | 1 | | | | 3 | | | 5 | 6 | | | | | |
| Coal Works | | 8 | | 4 | | | | | | | 1 | | | 1 | 3 | 8 | 2 | | 4 | 10 |
| Ironstone Works | | 1 | | 2 | | | | | | | 1 | | | | 1 | | | | | |
| Limestone Works | 1 | 4 | 1 | 3 | | | | | | | | | | | 2 | | | | | |
| Mineral Works | | 2 | | 1 | | | | | | | | | | | | | | | | |
| Gas Works | 1 | 1 | | 1 | 1 | | 1 | 1 | | | 1 | | | 1 | | | | | | 1 |
| Tile Works | | | | 1 | | | | | | | | | | | | | | | | |
| Electors—Proprietors | 73 | 126 | 27 | 67 | 18 | 2 | 14 | 14 | 6 | 6 | 34 | 3 | 2 | 37 | 172 | 8 | 2 | 13 | 4 | 10 |
| do. —Tenants | 24 | 56 | | 63 | 24 | 15 | 21 | 30 | 14 | 12 | 23 | 12 | 11 | 36 | 165 | 24 | 16 | 9 | 10 | 23 |

## NOTES REGARDING THE PARISH OF CULTER AND THE VARIOUS FAMILIES THAT LIVED IN IT.

*(Being the Paper contributed by J. W. Baillie, Esq., of Culter-Allers, as referred to at page 285, Vol. I. of this Work.—A. M.)*

THE parish of Culter, as far as the titles in the Culter-Allers charter chest show, was at one time possessed partly by Menzies of Menzies and partly by the Earl of Linlithgow. The Menzies family seem to have been in possession of their half of the barony of Culter about the year 1300, but there are no titles in the chest that show they possessed the estate then, and none show that any other proprietor possessed Culter-Allers before them. The part possessed by the Earl of Linlithgow seems to have been in the hands of various persons, both as to property and superiority, before it came into his hands. The lands held of Menzies were Culter-Allers, Snipe, Badinsgill, Over Hangingshaw or Middle Hangingshaw, and Nether Hangingshaw, Gardiner's Land, Wolfclyde. Of those held of the Earl of Linlithgow, the lands of Unthank were held—1st, of Lord Seton; 2d, of Lord Douglas, before the Earl of Linlithgow got them; and we find him, when disponing the half of the barony of Culter, with the patronage of the parish kirk, to Sir W. Baillie of Lamington, in 1632, excepting from the disposition,—

1. Twa oxengate of land of the town and lands of Wolfclyde, feued to Thomas Muir. 2. Twa oxengate of land of the town and lands of Wolfclyde, feued to Andrew Jobson. 3. The lands of Isobel Hill, feued to William Bertram, portioner of Nisbet, and to Alexander Bertram, his second son, in fee. 4. A cotland, extending to ane oxengate of land, in the townhead of Culter, feued to John Brown. 5. The lands of Birthwood, feued to Wm. Lindsay; also the sax oxengate of land of the said town and lands of Coulter, feued to said Wm. Lindsay. 6. The Half Miln of Coulter, Half Miln lands, etc., and of the lands of Woodlands, and of twa oxgate of land of the town and lands of Coulter, and Smiddy, feued to Alexander Menzies of Coulter.

The lands of Culter-Mains hold of the Crown, and it is not known of whom the lands of Nisbet hold; and the Culter-Allers chest affords little information about either of these properties.

The family of Menzies of Culter-Allers seems to have been a younger branch of that of Menzies of Menzies, and to have possessed the lands of Culter-Allers without titles.

In Douglas' Baronage, under the title of Lockhart of Lee, it is mentioned that Isobel Lockhart, daughter of James Lockhart of Lee, who was retoured heir to his father on 6th Sept., 1548, and died in 1585, married A. Menzies of Culter-Allers; and in various other books

*t*

of antiquities mention is made of the older members of the family. He seems to have been father of A. Menzies, *primus.*

The oldest deed relating to the lands of Culter-Allers is an original charter, dated 26th July, 1605, granted by Adam Menzies of Boltoquhane, heritable proprietor of the lands and others therein mentioned, with consent of A. Menzies of Menzies and Dun. Menzies of Comrie, in favour of A. Menzies of Culter-Alloris, *primus*, and his heirs male and assignees whomsoever, of the lands of Culter-Allis, an equal half of the lands of Baldonisgill, the lands called Gardiner's Lands, these eight oxgates of land in the village of Culter then possessed by himself, these five oxgates of land in the village of Culter —formerly occupied by W. Richardson and John Hutchison, then by W. Richardson and himself, together with an equal half of the grain-mill of the said village of Culter, with half of the mill lands, and astricted multures, free multures, and dry multures thereof; to be holden of the said Adam Menzies of Boltoquhane for payment of the sum of fifty merks Scots. Infeftment followed on this charter, and sasine is recorded in the particular register at Hamilton, 27th August, 1605. Mr A. Menzies, *primus*, got a lease of the teinds of sixteen oxgate of lands of the town and lands of Culter, two oxgate called the Milne Lands of Culter, two oxgate of the lands of Woodlands, Culter-Allis, Gardiner's Lands, from the Master of Linlithgow, principal tacksman of the teinds in 1606; and purchased the feu-duties of Culter-Allers, Badinsgill, Gairdiner's Land, 13 oxgate of land in Culter, with the Half Milne and Milne Lands thereof, one oxgate in Culter occupied by M. Richardson, Wolfclyde, etc., during his own lifetime.

A. Menzies, *primus*, lived at Culter-Allers, and built or added to the house that stood there, as a mantelpiece was found lately, which had been used as a lintel of the stable, which contains the arms of the family and the letters A. M. and M. B. A. Menzies left the following children:—A. Menzies of Culter-Allers, 2d; J. Menzies, portioner of Wolfclyde, who married Margt. Brown, daughter of Gilbert Brown of Hartree and Jean Hay his wife; W. Menzies, to whom he left some feu and teind duties.

A. Menzies of Culter-Allers, 2d, obtained a precept of *clare constat* from J. Menzies of Enoch, the superior, son and heir of the late Adam Menzies of Boltoquhane, with consent of Sir A. Menzies of Menzies, and D. Menzies, his eldest son, for infefting him as heir to his father, the said A. Menzies, *primus*, in the lands of Culter-Alloris, half of the lands of Baldonisgill, the lands called Gairdneris Lands, thirteen oxgang of land in Culter, half of the mill and mill-lands of Culter. This deed is dated 26th April and 16th Oct., 1620. Infeftment followed in favour of Mr A. Menzies, 2d, and sasine is dated 16th, and recorded in the register of sasines at Lanark, 31st Jan., 1621.

Mr Menzies, 2d, entered into a contract of feu with Alexander, Earl of Linlithgow, whereby the Earl obliged himself to grant a feu disposition, in his favour, of the other half of the mill, mill-lands, and astricted multures of the mill of Culter, the lands of Woodlands, three oxgate of land in the town of Culter occupied by himself, one oxgate occupied by Alex. Jamieson and John Paton, four oxgate occupied by Wm. Paton, four oxgate occupied by James Black, and the Smiddy of Culter. The contract is dated 16th Feb., 1630, and a feu disposition followed, dated 2d Dec., 1630. The holding is of "the said noble Earl, and his heirs and successors, for the yearly payment of the sum of £17 Scots, at two terms in the year, Whitsunday and Martinmas, in winter, by equal portions."

The lands of Over Nether and Windy Hangingshaw were possessed by Adam Inglis of Langlands Hill, in the parish of Broughton, and county of Peebles; but there are no titles of the Hangingshaws in his person in the chest. Mr Inglis and his son, M. Inglis, borrowed from A. Wright, merchant-burgess of Edinburgh, the sum of £413 Scots on 15th and 16th Nov., 1631; and he wadsetted the said lands to the Rev. R. Somerville, minister at Culter, his brother-in-law, between the years 1631 and 1633; he also borrowed from Sir W. Baillie of Lamington the sum of 700 merks Scots, and from Mr A. Menzies of Culter-Allers, 2d, the sum of 613 merks 5s Scots, on 11th April, 1635. Mr Menzies, 2d, acquired right to these debts, by disposition and assignation from A. Wright. Disposition from J. Somerville, son and heir to R. Somerville, and assignation by Sir W. Baillie, afterwards led an apprisement of the property.

Mr Menzies, 2d, had frequent quarrels with his neighbour, Wm. Lindesay of Birthwood; and he accused Lindesay, 1st, of maiming and injuring his servant; 2d, of taking away more than his own share of the corn growing on the common ground at the Holygill-water-foot; 3d, stopping and impeding the highways on Culter-water; 4th, damming and dyking up the water-gates agreed on between them; 5th, stopping gates used for leading peats and fodder from the Back-side Common; 6th, demolishing a dyke above the Bridgend of Culter; 7th, hounding and chasing of Menzies, his family, his men, tenants and servants, off their own part of the White Common. To such an extent did the quarrel go, that neither of them communicated in Culter church, for which Mr Currie, the minister, was ordained to summon them before the Presbytery of Lanark on 20th April, 1637; and they having appeared on 25th May, confessed their not communicating, alleging malice and variance as the cause thereof. The Presbytery ordained them to confess their fault publicly, out of their own seats, and then quietly to deal with them. The Presbytery resolved, because they have both promised faithfully, under the pain of double penalty, at the next occasion to communicate.

Mr Menzies married Jane Baillie, daughter of Sir W. Baillie of Lamington. They lived at Culter-Allers. Mr Menzies, 2d, left the following children:—A. Menzies of Culter-Allers, 3d; J. Menzies, who acquired the lands of Over, Nether, and Middle Hangingshaw by disposition from his eldest brother on 1st Jan., 1650; W. Menzies; S. Menzies, who bought the lands of Unthank, 12th April, 1666; Miss — Menzies, married J. Bertram of Nisbet, 15th Sept., 1642.

A. Menzies of Culter-Allers, 3d, obtained a precept of *clare constat*
from J. Menzies of Enoch, the superior, for infefting him as heir to
his father in the lands of Culter-Allis, half of the lands of Baldonisgill, the lands of Gairdner's Land, thirteen oxgang of land in the
town of Culter, half of the mill and mill lands of Culter, seven oxgangs of land in the town of Culter—which belonged to D. Menzies,
nephew and heir to D. Menzies, portioner of Culter, the lands of
Snaip, four oxgangs, called the Cowlands Oxgang, the Brewland
house and garden, at the mill of Culter, the lands of Wyndynhill,
half of the lands of Windgillfutt, the other half of Baldonisgill. This
deed is dated 16th Nov., 1647; infeftment, etc., followed.

Mr Menzies, 3d, entered into a contract of alienation with James
Menzies of Enoch, the superior, whereby the said J. Menzies sold to
him the half of the lands and half mill of Culter; the contract is
dated 17th Nov., 1647, upon which a charter of resignation was obtained from the Crown on 23d July, 1649. Mr Menzies, 3d, entered
into a contract with Sir W. Baillie of Lamington, whereby Sir William
sold him, but under reversion on payment of the consideration money,
his half of the barony of Coulter, with the patronage of the kirk of
Coulter; this deed is dated 6th July, 1665. It is not known whether
the lands sold him were redeemed or not, but the Menzies family
seem never to have presented to the kirk of Coulter.

Mr Menzies, 3d, was a Commissioner of Supply by Act of Parliament, 23d April, 1685. Mr Menzies, 3d, built a waulk-mill and
dwelling-house on part of the ten-pound land of Culter belonging to
him; and John Brown of Culter-Mains, although he did not make the
least interruption thereto, yet, after the same was finished, and notwithstanding that Mr Menzies had served law-borrows against him, the said
John Brown, in manifest contempt thereof, and of the laws of the
realm, being accompanied with J. Vallange, tement there, J. Brown
there, W. Brown, miller there, Luke Vallange, son to the said J. Vallange, J. Patoun there, Mungo Inglis there, A. Inglis there, and divers
others, accomplices; all armed with swords, pistols, axes, and other
instruments, did, upon the —— day of July, 1681, come to the ground
of the said lands, and there most illegally, by violence and oppression,
did demolish the said dwelling-house, and rendered the same uninhabi-
table. Mr Menzies obtained criminal letters, with concurrence of the
Lord Advocate, against Mr Brown, dated 30th July, 1681.

Mr Menzies, 3d, married, first, Jeane Seton, daughter of the late
Sir John Seton of St Germans, and by contract of marriage, dated
5th May, 1648, he conveyed to her in liferent, during her lifetime,
and to the heirs male of the marriage, whom failing, to his heirs male
or of line whatsomever, the lands of Culteralloris, half of Baldonisgill,
Gairdner's Land, thirteen oxengate of land in Culter, mill of Culter,
seven oxengate of land in Culter, Snaip, the Cowland, the Brewland,
house and yard at the mill of Culter, Windynhill, Windgillfutt, the
other half of Baldonisgill. Mr Menzies, 3d, built part of the present
house of Culter, and planted most of the trees, most probably about

the time of his marriage. Mr Menzies, 3d, married, second, Isobel Sandilands, and, third, Mary Hepburn, daughter of — Hepburn, and widow of the late Geo. Livingtone of Saltcoats, Haddingtonshire. Mr Menzies, 3d, had, by his first marriage, A. Menzies, 4th, yr. of Culter-Allers; J. Menzies, advocate, Edinburgh.

The lands of Unthank were possessed by John Gifford, by charter from Alexander, Lord Seton, dated 27th July, 1338; from him they passed to Elizabeth Gifford, spouse of Hugh de Spensa, by charter from Lord Douglas, dated 10th April, 1381. They appear to have been in the family of Spens till 15th March, 1501, without titles, when they were acquired by George Trotter, sister's son, and one of the heirs of the late Edmond Spens of Unthank, and Elizabeth Spens, sister, and another of the heirs of the said Edmond Spens, and spouse to Philip ——, by letter of reversion by A. Spens, son of W. Spens of Unthank, for payment of 18 merks. James Hamilton of Finart acquired the lands of Unthank by charter from A. Spens on 14th April, 1528; and on 29th March, 1541, Alexander, Lord Livingston, the superior, granted the non-entry, ward duties, etc., of the lands of Unthank, then occupied by Wm. Bailzie of Bagbie since the death of the late Edmond Spens, Richard Bailzie, father to W. Bailzie, to Geo. Trotter, therein designed of Prentenan, and Elizabeth Hop Pringle, his spouse. Mr and Mrs Trotter got a charter of confirmation from Lord Livingston, the superior, of the lands of Unthank, on 29th March, 1541; and on 24th April, 1574, the lands of Unthank were sold by them to William Bailzie of Bagbie. Mention is made of this gentleman in Pitcairn's Criminal Trials, Vol. I., p. 127, as having been a juror on the trial of John Steill, *alias* Kempy Steill, Adam and Richard Bell, convicted by an assize, and hanged for common theft and reset of theft, of common murder and rape, and for intercommuning with English thieves and traitors, before James Preston, provost of Edinburgh, depute-justiciary, 30th Jan., 1524-5. And again, at p. 382—Convocation—invading James, Lord Somerville, 1555, Nov. 22. W. Baillie of Bagbie, Nicholas, his brother, Michael Shorte, his servant, and three others, were replegiated by James, Earl of Mortoune, to his regality of Dalkeith, to underly the law, on Jan. 17, next, for convocation of the lieges, to the number of six score persons, armed in warlike manner, and invading James, Lord Somerville, for his slaughter, committed on 1st Oct., last. W. Symontoune of that ilk became surety.

A. Bailzie of Bagbie succeeded his father in the lands of Unthank. This gentleman was appointed ruling elder to the Presbytery of Lanark for the parish of Roberton on 18th July, 1639. Mr A. Bailzie never made up any titles to Unthank; he executed, however, a disposition of it, containing a procuratory of resignation in favour of his son, Major Alex. Baillie of Bagbie, who, on 19th July, 1642, obtained a charter of resignation of the said lands from Sir W. Baillie of Lamington, the superior, who had acquired the half of the barony of Culter, and the patronage of the kirk of Culter, by disposition from the Earl of Linlithgow, on 27th May, 1632. Major Claud Baillie, brother to Major A. Baillie, obtained a precept of clare constat from Sir W. Baillie, for infefting him as heir to his brother in said lands, on 12th Nov., 1644. From him the lands of Unthank passed to Sam. Menzies, brother to A. Menzies of Culter-Allers, 3d, by disposition dated 12th April, 1666, and on 6th Sept., 1673, they were sold by S. Menzies to A. Menzies, younger of Culter-Allers, 4th.

The lands of Birthwood are previously mentioned as having been feued by the Earl of Linlithgow to W. Lindsay previous to the year 1632. Andw. Lindsay, his son, married Margt. Menzies, daughter of — Menzies, who succeeded him therein: they afterwards were acquired by A. Menzies, younger of Culter-Allers, 4th.

A. Menzies, younger of Culter-Allers, 4th, was appointed one of the Commissioners of Supply, and Lieutenant of the Upper Ward of Lanarkshire Militia, by Act of the first Parliament of the Prince of Orange, 14th March, 1689. A. Menzies, younger of Culter-Allers, 4th, resided chiefly at Birthwood, and farmed it along with the farm of Culter-Allers. He was a person of dissipated habits, and was drowned in 1689, while crossing the Clyde at the ford at Culter-Mains when intoxicated. The ford since called Sandy's Ford.

A. Menzies, 4th, yr. of Culter-Allers, married, first, Anne Blair, daughter of Sir Adam Blair of Carberrie, Knight, and by contract of marriage between them, dated 4th Nov., 1671, he, with consent of his father, conveyed the lands of Culter-Allers, Badronsgill, Woodlands, Snaip, Windyhill, half of Windgillfoot, Dambrae, alias Isobelhill, Unthank, part of the ten-pound land of Coulter (except the Maynes of Coulter, then possessed by A. Menzies, 3d), to himself, and the heirs male of the marriage, whom failing, to return to the heirs male of the said A. Menzies, 3d. There were no children of the marriage. A. Menzies, 4th, married, second, Mary Livington, second daughter of George Livington, Saltcoats, by whom he had two children:—A. Menzies of Culter-Allers, 5th; Margt. Menzies, who married, first, — Hamilton of Pencaitland; second, the Hon. — Carmichael of Skirling, son of the Earl of Hyndford. Mrs Menzies, while Miss Livington, and her mother, Mrs Mary Hepburn, are mentioned by Wodrow as fined for being present at a conventicle.

A. Menzies of Culter-Allers, 5th, advocate, obtained from his grandfather, on 12th May, 1691, a precept of clare constat, for infefting him as heir to his father in the lands of Birthwood and Stanegill, half of the lands of Windgillfoot, the lands of Dambrae, with the commonty of the six oxgate of land formerly possessed by A. Mitchell, also the commonty of the six oxgates of land formerly possessed by W. Brown, with the commonty of that oxgate of land formerly possessed by J. Brown, the lands of Unthank, the lands of Isobel-hill—commonly called the Dambrae, with proportional part of the White Common of Culter belonging to them, two oxengate of land of the town and lands of Wolfclyde—formerly belonging to A. Jobson, six oxengate of land in the town of Culter—formerly possessed by A. Mitchell. Alex.

Menzies, 5th, on 11th April, 1701, served heir in general to his grandfather, and was infeft in the half lands and half myln of Coulter; and on 24th Aug., 1702, he obtained a charter of confirmation, from the Crown, of the half of the lands, barony, and mill of Culter, comprehending the lands of Culter-Allers, the lands of Badingsgill, half of the lands of Windgillfoot, half of the lands of Nisbet, Snaip, half of the ten-pound land of Culter, and commonty called the White Common, the lands of Easter, Wester, and Nether Hangingshaw, the lands called Gardner's Land, the lands of Windhill, half of the mill of Culter and mill lands, the third part of the lands of Wolfclyde, the lands of Cassawend; and on 5th Oct., 1732, he obtained a precept of *clare constat* from Margaret, Lady Baillie of Lamington, for infefting him as heir to his grandfather in half of the mill of Culter, the lands of Woodlands, three oxgate of land in the town of Culter, that oxgate of land in the town of Culter lying contiguous to the Stanecroft, and those four oxgates of land in the town of Culter formerly occupied by J. Black. A. Menzies, 5th, seems to have possessed other lands in Culter, without titles, in particular the lands of Eastmains and Shaw, the lands of Gardner's Land, half of the mill and mill land of Culter, the third part of Wolfclyde, Dambrae *alias* Isobel-hill, another third part of Wolfclyde, and the third part of Wolfclyde.

A. Menzies, 5th, was appointed a Commissioner of Supply by Act of Parliament, 8th Sept., 1696, and again subsequently.

The family of Menzies, Culter-Allers, seems to have been at its zenith at the commencement of the incumbency of A. Menzies, 5th. He possessed the whole of the parish of Culter but Culter-Mains and the portion of Nisbet belonging to the Bertrams. A. Menzies, 5th, married Mary Menzies, daughter of Sir W. Menzies of Gladstaines, but had no family. A. Menzies became security for his wife's brother, T. Menzies, and in process of time got quit of almost all of the above property. By disposition dated 9th Feb., 1733, and recorded in the books of Council and Session, 9th March, 1736, he sold to William Dickson of Kilbucho, the lands and estate of Culter, including the lands of Easter, Wester, and Nether Hangingshaw and Unthank; the lands of Birthwood, and Standgill, and Windgillfoot; in 1736, when he died, he had only the lands of Culter-Allers, Badingsgill, Woodlands, half of the lands of Windgillfoot, Snaip, Windyhill, commonty called the White Common, and the manor place of Culter.

R. Menzies, Writer to the Signet, son of Dr J. Menzies, who was son of J. Menzies, advocate, 2d son of A. Menzies, 3d, served heir in special to A. Menzies, 5th, in the lands he possessed at his death. He also got the Mosshead Park, by disposition, from Wm. Dickson of Kilbucho. R. Menzies built a great part of the mansion house at Culter, and the stables, and altered the avenue, which previously ran across the front park, to its present place, and planted the trees in the present avenue. He also enclosed the house park with a stone and lime wall. Part of the present glebe of Culter, called Gardiner's Rig and Salmon Riggs, then belonged to Mr Menzies, and part of the park at Culter formed part of the glebe at Culter. The old school-house of Culter stood within the enclosure, and the school-green was behind it. A petition was presented by Mr Menzies, for an excambion, to the Presbytery of Biggar, which was granted, and the school-green and part of the glebe of Culter was given off to Mr Menzies in exchange for Gardiner's Rig and Salmon Rigs.

R. Menzies was of a litigious disposition, and at the time of his death, in 1769, he left his affairs in a state of bankruptcy, and his lands were sold to Mr Jas. Baillie, writer in Edinburgh. Mr Menzies married Margt. Thomson, daughter of the Rev. J. Thomson, minister of West Libberton, by whom he had no family.

Mr James Baillie above mentioned was a son of Mr George Baillie of Hardingtoun and Bagbie, and grandson of Mr Jas. Baillie, Writer to the Signet, who purchased these properties in 1721. J. Baillie's father was A. Baillie of Hillhouse, son of R. Baillie, brother of Major Claud Baillie, and son of a Baillie of Bagbie and Unthank before mentioned. In 1701, J. Baillie, W.S., sat as a juryman on the service of A. Menzies, 5th, and in the retour he is designed "of Wells." He is mentioned in the history of the family of Baillie of Lamingtoun as being "son of — Baillie of Hillhouse, who was brother-german to Mr William Baillie of Hardington."

The lands of Coulter-Allers, Badingsgill, Woodlands, Snaip, with the common called the White Common, the manor place of Culter, the superiority of the lands of Easter, Wester, and Nether Hanging-shaw, and tack of the lands of Windyhill and Paddock Pool, were purchased by J. Baillie for £7400 sterling, by decreet of sale dated 7th Aug., 1771. Mr Baillie obtained a charter of sale from the Crown and was infeft on the precept therein contained, and the sasine is recorded in the General Register, 30th March, 1772.

Wm. Dickson of Kilbucho disponed the lands he acquired from A. Menzies, 5th, to his son J. Dickson, on 11th Feb., 1760. He sat for some years as member of Parliament for the county of Peebles. W. Dickson built North Coulter House, the property of Mr Sim. J. Dickson having become embarrassed, granted a trust disposition in favour of trustees for his creditors of his whole estate on 11th June, 1768, which was ratified after his death by D. Dickson, his brother and heir, on 25th Nov., 1771. D. Dickson was at one time a writer in Edinburgh, he afterwards entered the church, and became minister of Kilbucho and afterwards of Newlands. General William Dickson, his eldest son, acquired the lands sold by A. Menzies, 5th, by disposition from his uncle's trustees on 11th Aug., 1775 ; and the Rev. D. Dickson and his son the General having become embarrassed, conveyed their property to trustees on 7th Sept., 1774, by which the trustees acquired right to the property purchased by Gen. Dickson. Gen. Dickson and his trustees sold the lands and estate of Coulter to J. Dickson, advocate, brother of the General, on 22d Nov., 1777, and J. Dickson bought the superiority of the said estate from Lady Ross Baillie of Lamington in the same year.

Mr Dickson sold to Mr J. Baillie of Coulter-Allers, the lands of Easter, Wester, and Nether Hangingshaw, part of Westfield, Templedale, and Unthank, with the multures of these and his other lands, by disposition dated 19th March, 1778, and renounced his right to redeem the superiority of Hangingshaw the same day.

Mr Dickson not having retained a crown-holding of sufficient extent to constitute the right of voting, Mr Baillie redisponed the lands of Unthank to Mr Dickson, and on 25th Dec., 1786, Mr Dickson executed a feu-charter in Mr Baillie's favour of the lands of Unthank, part of Westfield, the lands of Windyhill and Paddock Pool, piece of ground at Culter Bridge and Simpson's Park, for a feu-duty of ten shillings Scots.

Mr Dickson executed another feu-charter of the mill and mill lands of Culter, the lands of Westfield, Simerton and Gardiner's lands, with the multures of Birthwood, in favour of Mr Baillie, on 11th April, 1787, for a feu-duty of ten shillings Scots.

Mr Baillie executed a deed of entail of the above lands in favour of himself and heirs, whom failing, in favour of his grand-nephew, Mr Robert Granbery Baillie. Mr Baillie died in 1818; he was succeeded by R. G. Baillie, who died 13th October, 1863; succeeded by his son, J. W. Baillie.

Mr Dickson feued the lands of Culter Park to A. Lindsay, schoolmaster at South Leith, for a payment down of £980, and a feu-duty of twelve shillings Scots, on 6th Jan., 1787; and W. Lindsay, merchant in Leith, his son, sold them to Mr R. G. Baillie in Feb., 1820.

Mr Dickson sold the lands of Birthwood to Mr Jas. Denholm; from him they passed to his son, W. Denholm, and to his grandson, Hum. Denholm, and on his death they were purchased by R. Paterson, and are now in possession of his son, the present proprietor.

The lands of Coulter, with the superiority of Unthank, Culter Park, Mill and Mill Lands, Cornhill and Shaw, were purchased by Mr Sim from the representatives of the late J. Dickson, in 1836.

The lands of Wolfclyde, Causeyend, Eastfield or Manor Place of Culter, are still the property of D. Dickson of Hartree.

The lands of Cornhill were feued by J. Dickson to Geo. Gillespie of Biggar Park, from whom they passed to R. Bruce Campbell, brewer in Edinburgh, by purchase, and from whom they were purchased by W. Haudyside, the present proprietor.

It is supposed that the part of Nisbet, that belonged to Culter-Allers, must have been purchased from A. Menzies, 5th. The Bertrams of Nisbet seem to have possessed that estate from a remote period. The furthest back known to me is William Bertram, designed portioner of Nisbet. He seems to have been born previous to the year 1600. He married —, and had two sons, John his successor, and the Rev. A. Bertram, minister at Kilbucho. W. Bertram possessed part of the farm of Culter Park called the Dambrae, to which his son A. was to succeed at his death. He was succeeded by his son J. Bertram, who married — Menzies, daughter of A. Menzies of Culter-

Allers, 2d. Mrs Bertram died in 1642. J. Bertram was succeeded by his son A. Bertram, who married Grizel Muir (presumed to have been a daughter of Muir of Anniston). He erected the Nisbet burying-place in Culter church-yard in 1701. He possessed the lands of How-cleugh and Crimp Cramp in the parish of Crawford, in addition to those of Nisbet. He left—Wm., his heir, A. Bertram, W.S., Janet, married to Rev. J. Forrester, minister at Culter, and other daughters.

W. Bertram was appointed, by the Court of Session, factor on the estate of Hardington and Bagbie. He was appointed factor to the Duke of Douglas. He purchased the lands of Kerswell, in the parish of Carnwath, in —. He married Cecilia Kennedy, daughter of Gilbert Kennedy of Auchtifardle, and left—A. Bertram, his heir; Gilbert Bertram, merchant and banker in Edinburgh, who married Grizel Hay, daughter of John Hay of Haystone; Euphemia Bertram, married George Baillie of Hardington; Anne, married the Rev. John Brown of Culter-Mains; Cecilia, married Hugh Mossman, writer in Edinburgh; Jane, married Henry Ferguson.

Archd. Bertram, born —. In 1745 he and several neighbouring proprietors apprehended a number of the rebels in the parish of Lam-ington. The rebels were confined in church all night, and sent to Lanark next day. He married Miss M. Porterfield, daughter of J. Por-terfield of Fulwood, Ayrshire, and left—Wm., his heir; A. Bertram, for many years a physician in Hull, afterwards in Lanark; Jane, married A. Lockhart of Cleghorn and Wiston; and other issue.

Col. Wm. Bertram, born —, and married Jane Lockhart, daughter of Sir Wm. Lockhart, and left—Wm., his heir; Allan, commander in the navy; Cecilia, married to Jas. Macallan, W.S.; and other issue.

Major W. Bertram, H.E.I.C.S., born 1788; married Louise Le Pere, from Mauritius, died 1839, leaving W. Bertram,. the present pro-prietor of Nisbet, Howcleugh, Crimp Cramp, and Kerswell.

W. Bertram was born 23d April, 1826; was in the army; married Adelaide Bertram, widow of J. D. Collyer, and has issue.

The parish of Culter was a rectory. The names of the rectors, as shown by the *Origines Parochiales Scotiæ*, are:—

Sir Richard, parson of Cultyr—witness to deeds between 1208 and 1211, and in 1228-9—between 1208-1232; Mr Pieres Tylliol, parson of Culter, swore fealty to Edward I. in 1296; Thos. of Balkask, rector of Culter in 1388; Mr Geo. Schoviswood was rector in 1449-1450—Bishop of Brechin and Chancellor of Scotland from 1456 to 1460; W. Halkerstone, presented to the benefice between 1482-84.

The deeds in the Culter-Allers charter chest show the Hon. and Rev. Jas. Livingston, son of the Earl of Linlithgow, designed parson of Culter, in a deed dated 29th Mar., 1541; and the *Orig. Par. Scot.* mentions Arch. Livingston parson of Culter at the Reformation.

The Rev. R. Somerville, minister at Culter, let a lease of the teinds to Alexander, Earl of Linlithgow, on 17th Feb., 1607, for 19 years, at a rent of 300 merks Scots, or £16 13s 4d sterling, which was pro-rogate by the Commission on 10th Dec., 1617, for 36 years, at a

yearly rent of 520 merks Scots, or £28 17s 9¼d sterling. Mr
Somerville died about 1642. On 5th Sept., 1633, he was censured
and sharply reproved by the Presbytery of Lanark for leaving his
flock and going to a burial on the Sabbath-day.

The Rev. J. Currie succeeded Mr Somerville at Culter, and mention is made of him, as of Culter, on 20th April, 1637; and in 1643
he entered into a contract with his patron, Sir W. Baillie of Lamington, and his heritors, A. Menzies of Culter-Alloris, 2d, W. Bertram,
portioner of Nisbet, J. Bertram and (the Rev.) Mr A. Bertram (minister at Kilbucho), his sons, J. Menzies of Wolfclyde, T. Muir there,
A. Jobson there, and A. Mitchell, portioner in Culter, whereby they
agreed that the stipend to the minister of Coulter and his successors,
in all time coming, should be 650 merks Scots, or £36 2s 2¾d sterling,
and 20 merks yearly for communion elements, to be paid in terms of
the following locality:—

1. A. Menzies of Culter-Allers, for lands of Culter-
Allers, Badronsye, Woodlands, Snow, Windinghill, half
of Windingillfoot, the Four Shilling Land sometime per-
taining to the deceased S. Black, being one-fourth part
of the Sixteen Shilling Land of the town of Coulter,

|  | Merks Scots. |  |  |
|---|---|---|---|
| Gardiner's Land, Mill Lands, Seryan Acre, and Brewland, | 185 | 0 | 0 |
| 2. A. and J. Bertram, - - - - | 52 | 0 | 0 |
| 3. W. Bertram, for lands of Dambrae, - - - | 18 | 0 | 0 |
| 4. J. Menzies for the 20s Lands of Wolfclyde, - | 22 | 6 | 8 |
| 5. T. Muir for the Six Shilling Land of Wolfclyde, | 11 | 3 | 4 |
| 6. A. Jobson for the Ten Shilling Land of Wolfclyde, | 11 | 3 | 4 |
| 7. A. Mitchell, - - - - - - - | 20 | 0 | 0 |
| 8. Sir W. Baillie for Hangingshaw, - - - | 20 | 0 | 0 |
| 9. Sir W. Baillie, out of the teinds of the other lands in the parish not specially allocated, - - - | 310 | 0 | 0 |
|  | 650 | 0 | 0 |
| And for communion elements, - - - - | 20 | 0 | 0 |
|  | 670 | 0 | 0 |

During the incumbency of Mr Currie a process was brought against
Molly M'Watt in Nisbet for witchcraft, which terminated without
producing any remarkable result. During Mr Currie's incumbency, the brethren of the Presbytery, on 25th May, 1637, finding
the church of Coulter to want a bell, and the church-yard dyke not
built, was appointed with the consent of the parochiners the 15th day
of June for their pastor and heritors to condescend upon a taxation
for the buying of a bell, and building of the church-yard dyke. And
on 8th June Mr Currie reports that his parochiners of Coulter have
promised to have a bell for the church bought, the quire of the church
and the church-yard dyke built betwixt and Martinmas next. A letter
from the Rev. J. Forrester, minister at Culter, to R. Menzies, W.S.,

states, that Mr Currie was laid under sentence by the Presbytery in 1653, and that he does not act as minister afterwards.

The Rev. Anthony Murray was admitted minister at Culter 8th Aug., 1654. He was a Presbyterian, and is said to have been "an eminently, godly, learned, famous, faithful minister of the Lord Jesus Christ." He continued at Culter till 1663, when he was ejected for nonconformity. He was also a surgeon, and when ejected from his living, practised in that capacity, and it is believed acted as factor to the Earl of Wigtown. He bequeathed a sum of money to the kirk-session of Culter, the interest to educate poor children.

The Rev. Patrick Trent was admitted minister at Culter at the ejection of Mr Murray. He was an Episcopalian. The proceedings of the Presbytery of Lanark state that he was one of a Committee of Presbytery appointed to perambulate the parishes of Libberton and Quothquhan. Mr Trent seems to have left Culter in 1672; and in Lawson's History of the Scot. Epis. Church, a Mr Pat. Trent is mentioned at Linlithgow. As the Earl of Linlithgow was patron of Culter, and held a great part of the land there, it is probable that Mr Trent, minister at Linlithgow, was formerly at Culter.

The Rev. A. Murray returned to his charge at the departure of Mr Trent in Dec., 1672, but was again removed from it.

The Rev. John Menzies was minister at Culter from the second removal of Mr Murray till the Revolution of 1688, and was probably an Episcopalian. The Rev. A. Murray returned to his charge at the Revolution, and continued at Culter till his death in 1692.

The Rev. W. Russell was admitted minister at Culter in 1692, and continued till 11th May, 1693, when he was translated to Morham in Haddingtonshire. The heritors petitioned the Presbytery to moderate in a call to Mr Russell.

The Rev. T. Colthart was admitted minister at Culter on 27th Sept., 1694. Being unpopular in the parish, he resigned his living on 11th Sept., 1696. After Mr Colthart's resignation there seems to have been no fixed minister at Culter till 26th Jan., 1700, when the Rev. J. Forrester was appointed on a petition from the heritors. He was much respected in the parish. He kept the session records with his own hands, and with great accuracy. He died in the year 1750, and was the last of the ministers of Culter who lived in the present school-house, which was formerly the manse.

The Rev. J. Brown of Culter-Mains, minister at Symington, was appointed to Culter on the death of Mr Forrester. He was much respected, resided at Culter-Mains, and died in the year 1769.

The Rev. W. Lockhart succeeded Mr Brown as minister at Culter. At his appointment, the glebe of Culter ran straight up Eastmains Hill, and did not contain the statutory quantity of arable land. Mr Lockhart would not accept of the glebe as it then stood, and insisted on having the proper quantity of arable land. The exchange appears to have been effected about the year 1774, when there was added to the glebe, off the farm of Eastmains, 4 acres 3 roods 30 falls, at £1 1s per acre, worth annually £5 3s 8$\frac{2}{12}$ths, and 3 acres 3 roods 32 falls, at 7s per acre, worth annually £1 7s 4d. Mr Lockhart resided at Culter Mains for the few first years of his ministry, the old manse was let, and the present manse built for him about 1774.

Mr Lockhart was translated to Glasgow about the year 1784, and was succeeded by the Rev. W. Strachan. In his incumbency an augmentation was awarded, which exhausted the teinds of the parish, and which was converted into money, and which is the locality upon which the stipend is drawn at present.

---

## INCREASE IN VALUE OF FARMS ON CULTER-ALLERS ESTATE.

CULTER-ALLERS and Snaipe let in 1672, for 1777 merks Scots, or 93l. 11s. 10d. sterling; 1673, for 2000 merks, or 100l. 8s. 4d.; 1778, for 225l.; 1783, for 250l.; 1797, for 290l.; 1809, for 530l.; 1822, for 480l.; 1841, for 530l.; and 1860, for 680l.; terms 19 years; increase 586l. 8s. 2d. Terms, thirlage, "their haill corn except the seed," 1672; "his haill grindable corns, and to pay multure, with knaveship and bannock," 1673; their "haill grindable corn," 1673; "haill grindable corn," 1757; "whole grindable corn, and to pay every 13th boll of multure meal," 1778; "whole grindable victual," 1797; in 1809, 1822, 1841, 1860, no thirlage. Rent in kind; 1672, "to graze fourty hogs yearly;" 1673, "carriage of 50 loads of coals, and oatmeal 2 b. 2 p.;" 1797, "hens 6, chickens 6, sucking lambs 2;" do. 1809, 1822, "wedder, one 3-years' old, 2 sucking lambs;" do. 1841; do. 1860; with 6l. 14s. 1d. per ann. on every 100l. spent by the proprietor on improvements on the farm.

Mill and farm of Culter, 1691, no money-rent for the mill, but to give eight days' work a-year about the Manor house; for the farm to pay yearly "for the knaveship and bannock, six bolls of oatmeal, and for the mill-land six bolls, half-meal half-bear, charitied under deduction of half a boll thereof for the first year, to pay 4 capons, 20 hens, and carry six loads of coals yearly." In 1696, mill rent 24l. Scots, or 2l. sterling, with 2 bolls malt, 2 bear, 4 meal, "8 kain hens, 4 do. capons;" 1749, Scots 42l., or 3l. 10s. sterling. In 1778, rent 23l., with 16 bolls clad oatmeal; 1787, mill rent 11l. 10s.; 1816, mill rent, with land added 192l., and "21 good hens, 21 chickens, and the carriage of 21 load of coal."

Birthwood, half of, in 1717, rent 69l. 0s. 2d., "to pasture forty sheep;" thirlage, "their grindable corn, to pay the twenty-fourth corn." Culter-Park, 1749, Scots 33l. 6s. 8d., sterling 2l. 15s. 6d.; 1782, sterling 41l. 10s.; 1815, 124l.; 1823, 127l. 5s. 10d.; 1834, 120l.; 1842, 160l.; 1850, 160l.; 1861, 180l., with 6l. 14s. 1d. interest on outlay. Rent in kind, 1834, 12 good hens, 12 chickens, driving of 20 loads coals, and so continues—thirlage none.

Unthank rental, 1749, Scots 66*l.* 13*s.* 4*d.*; sterling 5*l.* 10*s.* 11*d.*; 1777, rent 35*l.*; 1796, 44*l.*; 1815, 115*l.*; 1834, 120*l.*; 1853, 134*l.* and 5*°/₂* on outlay; rental in kind, 1815, 6 good hens, 6 chickens, carriage of 6 loads coals, so continues; thirlage, "whole grindable corn (seed and horse corn excepted); in 1834, 1853, no thirlage. Middle-Hangingshaw rental, 1796, 33*l.*; 1815, 90*l.*; 1834, 90*l.*; 1841, 110*l.*, with 6*l.* 14*s.* 1*°/₂* on outlay; rent in kind, 6 hens, 6 chickens, and carriage of 6 loads of coals, and so continues; thirlage, all grindable victual, except 5 bolls of oats, seed, and horse corn; since 1834, free of thirlage. Upper Hangingshaw, rental 1815, 152*l.*; 1834, 115*l.*; 1841, 122*l.*; 1843, 111*l.*; rental in kind, 1815, 12 good hens, 12 chickens, and carriage of 12 loads of coals, and so continues; thirlage, none since 1815. Nether-Hangingshaw, rent in 1777, 53*l.*; 1796, 65*l.*; 1815, 75*l.*; 1834, 146*l.*; 1853, 155*l.*; add rent in kind, 1796, 6 hens, 6 chickens, and carriage of 6 loads of coal; 1834, 12 good hens, 12 chickens, and carriage of 20 loads of coals; thirlage, 1777, all grindable corns and victuals, seed corn only excepted; 1796, all grindable victual, except 10 bolls of oats, seed, and horse corn; 1815, all grindable victuals, except as in 1796; since then, free of thirlage. Coulter-Mains, rent, in 1766, 86*l.* 3*s.* 4*d.*

*Locality of the Stipend of Culter.*—1. Valued teinds of Culter-Allers. Snaipe, park and enclosures, as obtained Feb. 8, 1775, 35*l.* 5*s.* 9¼*d.* 2. Teinds, valued July 8, 1778, Unthank, 4*l.* 19*s.* 4½*d.*; Westfield, 4*l.* 5*s.* 9¾*d.*; Hangingshaw-Nether, 9*l.*; Westfield-Croft, 1*l.* 13*s.* 4*d.*; Gardiner's land, 2*l.*; Hangingshaw, Upper and Middle, 8*l.* 8*s.* 3½*d.*; Paddock's-pool and Windy-hill, 1*l.* 8*s.* 3¼*d.*; Temple-dale, 3*s.* 4*d.*; Simpson's Park, 1*s.* 8½*d.* 3. Valued teinds, July 8, 1778, Culter-Park, 6*l.* 11*s.* 7*d.* 4. Birthwood, valued Feb. 22, 1643, oats 1 b. 2 f. 1 p. 2¼ l.; bear 3 f. 3½ l., and money, 5*l.* 17*s.* 9¾*d.* 5. Teinds for Nesbit, March 5, 1760, 16*l.* 16*s.* 8*d.* 6. Coulter-Mains and Cornhill, July 8, 1778, 36*l.* 4*s.* 2¼*d.* 7. Coulter-Maynes, 4th March, 1767, 10*l.* 11*s.* 4*d.* money, meal 12 b. 3 f.—3½ l. 8. Eastfield, Causewayend, and Wolfclyde, July 8, 1778, valued teinds 16*l.* 19*s.* 11⁷*d.* 9. Teinds of lands in Kilbucho, annexed to Culter, 46*l.* 12*s.* 8*d.* Summation—oats, 1 b. 2 f. 1 p. 2⅔ l.; beans, — b. 3 f. — p. 3¼ l.; meal, 12 b. 3 f. — p. 3½ l.; money, 204*l.* 19*s.* 11⁷*d.*

## MEMORIALL ANENT THE RIGHT TO THE TEINDS OF THE LANDS DISPONED BY CULTER-ALLERS TO KILLBUCHO.

THERE being no laity titular, the teinds parsonage and vicearrage of the parish of Culter belonged to the minister, and Mr Robert Somervile, the then incumbent, set a tack of the teinds of the said haill parish parsonage and vicearrage to Alexander, Earl of Lithgow, his heirs, male, and successors for 19 years after expiry of the then current tack, and thereafter during the Earl's lifetime, and his heirs male, their lifetimes for the yearly payment to the minister of 300 merks; and this tack was—

10th December, 1617—By the commission, prorogate for two 19 years longer on account of the augmentation of the minister's stipend at that time to 520 merks.

2d December, 1630.—The said Alexander, Earl of Lithgow, dispones to Sir William Baillie of Lammingtoun the superiority of the half of the barrony of Culter, with the right of patronage of the kirk in which Sir William was regularly infeft; and the Earl assigned to him the above tack and decreet of prorogation.

26th December, 1632.—Sir William having the right of patronage thus really establisht in his person, and right to the teinds in virtue of the above assignation, he, by a translation subscrived by him, conveys and makes over to Alexander Menzies of Culter-Allors, the 2d, the above tack and decreet of prorogation, with the assignation thereof in his favours, so far as concern'd or might be extended to the lands then belonging to him within the said parish, for payment to him, his heirs and successors, during the spaces foresaid, or in their option to the minister of Culter, of 160 merks Scots money for their relief of the above stipend of 520 merks *protanto*, and relieving them of all future augmentations, and contains this speciall clause: " And after the expiring of the spaces rexiv'd above expremit of the sarnen tacks rexiv'd above mentionat, evev as I sall present a new minister, and that my heirs and successors after me sall present new ministers to the said kirk, parsonage, and viccarrage thereof, that I, my heirs and successors, sall move and cause the said ministers, parsons, and viccarrs of the said kirk of Culter, with my consent, and with consent of my heirs or successors, patrons of the said kirk from time to time, set new tacks of the said teinds, parsonage, and viccarrage of the above lands to the said Allex^r· Menzies, and his aforesaids, for pay^t of the said proportional part of the said tack, duty, and minister's stipend effeiring to the rait and quantity of the said teinds at the terms foresaids, and be equal portions (as said is), and that for such space or spaces as may stand by the laws of this realm, and to denude ourselves of the right of the said teinds, parsonage, and viccarrage, with all title, kindness, and possession we have or may pretend thereto, in the person of the said Allexander Menzies, and his foresaids, be all other lawfull rqt. tittle and security *et omni habile modo*, and y^e, I, my heirs and successors, patrons of the said kirk of Culter, sall consent to all tacks and right to be set by the ministers, parsons, and vicarrs of Culter from time to time at onie time heirafter, and sall never heirafter purchase onie tacks of the said teinds in my own person, or in the person or persons of my heirs and successors, or in the person or persons of onie others to my or their use and behoof, directly or indirectly; and in case I, my heirs or successors, sall dispone the right of the said patronage of the said kirk of Culter, that we sall take

the parties in whose favours alienation sall be made oblist, to cause
the ministers, parsons, and viccarrs of the said kirk of Culter, who
sall happen to be heirafter prescribit, ratify and set new tacks of the
said teinds to the said Allexander Menzies, in manner above mentionat, and that the sarnen pairties in whose favours alienation sall
be made, sall be oblist to consent thereto in manner above."

In this shape stands the teinds of the whole lands disponed to
Killbucho, except the lands of Birthwood, Standgill, and Windgillfoot, and Lindsay's six oxgangs, which are valued conform to a decreet
of valuation dated 22d February, 1643; and the teind is fully
exhausted by the minister's stipend, as appears from the decreet of
locality, 1650.   The lands of Unthank value, in stock and teind,
converting the victual at £6 5s the boll (£211 10s Scots), which by
said decreet of locality is burdened with £38 15s Scots of stipend.
The lands of Hangingshaws value, in stock and teind, £601 13s 4d,
which is burdened with 10 bolls victual, at 10 merk the boll, of stipend; and Mitchell's six oxgangs in Culter, reckoning them an eighth
part of the ten pound land of Culter, value, in stock and teind,
which is burdened with £12 10s Scots, or two bolls victual, payable
to the ministers, per said decreet of locality; and which several quotas
of stipend will fully exhaust the parsonage teinds, grazing being the
most considerable article of these farms.

----

### NOTES REGARDING THE PARISH OF DOUGLAS.

IN the summer season, when viewed from the surrounding heights,
the parish of Douglas presents a beautiful landscape of hill and dale,
wood and stream.   Douglas-water meanders through the whole
length of the parish, and receives in its course several tributaries and
streamlets which take their rise near from the adjoining hills; many of
them make their way to Douglas-water through deep and romantic
glens, on whose sides the geologist can trace, in regular order,
the records of our primeval earth.

From the accession of the first Archibald, Lord Douglas of Douglas,
to the present time, much has been done by that noble family to
improve the natural aspect of this parish, in so far as they have
planted large tracts of land upon sides of the hills that rise up from
the vale of Douglas-water, and have given an air of fertility to a district
formerly bleak and wild.   One of the principal features of the landscape is Douglas Castle, with its parks, lawns, lakes, woods, and
gardens, now one of the seats of the right honourable Lucy Elizabeth
Douglas of Douglas, Countess of Home, and formerly the residence
of the great and warlike house of Douglas, who occupy such a prominent part in the annals of our country.

The present castle was built by the Duke of Douglas in the year
1760, and is still unfinished.   It is situated upon an eminence near

the site of the old Castle Dangerous. Some years ago this was ascertained, when an embankment, stakes, etc., were found at the base, put in to prevent the water from encroaching upon the mound. This eminence is abrupt on almost all sides, and Douglas-water appears to have at one time swept round a considerable part of its base, the intervening space being occupied by a wall and moat.

Near the present building stands one of the towers of the former castle, which was burned upon the 11th of December, 1758; the fire, as is stated in the public journals of that time, commenced in a small room adjoining the Duchess' bed-room, and all her ladyship's jewels, etc., with the whole of the furniture in the upper part of the house, were then completely destroyed.

The castle is surrounded with many venerable ash and plane trees that must have stood the blast of centuries. One of them is still pointed out as the tree on which the "Englishmen were hanged." The Douglas family have expended large sums in improving and beautifying the grounds and scenery around Douglas Castle, and the garden is beautifully laid off; and has lately received certain improvements by the Earl of Home.

*Turnpike Roads.*—The Edinburgh and Ayr turnpike road, under the Corsethill Trust, runs through the whole length of the parish (11 miles), and is intersected at Douglas Mill by the Glasgow and Carlisle road, which runs along the east side of the parish for about five miles; so that in the good old times of the mail-coach, Douglas enjoyed advantages superior to most of its neighbours.

*Tolls.*—1st. Douglas Mill Toll, about two and a-half miles from Douglas, and five and a-half from Lesmahagow (now removed to Happendon Bridge, being two or three hundred yards to the north of its former site), on the Glasgow and Carlisle road; 2d. Check bar to said toll, at Parkhead, about a mile to the south of Douglas Mill; 3d. Weston Toll, on the Edinburgh and Ayr road, about two miles to the west of Douglas; 4th. Check bar to Moorfoot Toll, at Uddington, about two and three-quarter miles to the east of Douglas. The revenue from these bars, for the year 1860, is above £400.

*Parish Roads.*—The principal are:—1st. The road from the Carlisle road, near Parkhead, to the Wildshaw Limeworks, and thence to the neighbouring parish of Wiston and Roberton; 2d. The road from the Glasgow and Ayr road, at Jeanfield, to Earlsmill, the Glespin coal works, Andershaw, and the adjoining parish of Crawfordjohn; 3d. The road to Lanark from Happendon Bridge, running along the north side of Douglas-water to the adjoining parish of Lesmahagow; 4th. The road from Douglas village, by Brachead, the glebe, Springhill, and Kirktondyke, leading towards the parish of Crawfordjohn. The total length of parish roads is 21 miles, and the annual expense for keeping these in repair amounts to £117, raised by an assessment on 50 ploughgates at 42s, and 24 horses at 10s 6d.

Many of the stones employed in the building of the present castle were obtained from the lands of Cornacoup, a distance of four miles, and were conveyed upon a rude and simple machine called a Slipe, drawn by one horse. This carriage was about two yards square, and was formed by planks nailed across two pieces of wood, formed somewhat like the keel of a ship, for the purpose of gliding along the ground, and supplied the place of the more modern invention of wheels, and, often could only convey one stone at a time.

An old inhabitant, alive in 1820, was wont to relate that he recollected the time when all the coals were brought to the town from Burnhouse in sacks thrown across the horses' backs; that there were no regular roads at that time, and no carts.

*Bridges.*—The only bridges worthy of notice are—(1) the Happendon Bridge, on the Carlisle road, across Douglas-water, near to the grand entrance to Douglas Castle; (2) Jeanfield Bridge, on the Edinburgh and Ayr road, across Douglas-water, and about two and three-quarter miles to the west of the town of Douglas.

*Woods.*—The plantations in this parish are extensive, and cover 1600 acres, consisting principally of larch, spruce, and Scotch fir—the timber of which is found to be of superior quality, and was largely used in the formation of the Caledonian Railway, and there are some very fine old ash and plane trees scattered over the Douglas estate, evidently pointing out the sites of former steadings. When the principal war instrument was the bow and arrow, and the highest ornament on the table a wooden bowl, each man was bound to plant a certain number of ash and plane trees around his house, the former for the bows, and the latter for the household utensils.

In the hurricane of 7th February, 1856, 15,217 trees above twelve feet in length, and six inches in diameter at the small end, were overthrown, and many of these of strong dimensions were actually snapped through at the middle.

*Land.*—This being in a great measure a pastoral district, the arable portion is confined almost entirely to the vale of Douglas-water, and the soil being of a loose, sandy description, the crops are as early as in the lower parts of the county. As the hills are clothed to their summits with a thick, green verdure, the sheep farms in this parish are held in high repute by store farmers.

In 1774, the annual value of the lands in the parish was £2496 9s 11d, it is now £9004 17s 2d.

From documents still extant it is found that, 26th Dec., 1755, a gentleman sold 2 cows for £4 18s; 1st Nov., 1756, James Gillespie, tenant in Bodinglee, paid to a person in this parish for a "fatted ox and 2 cows £14;" 6th Sept., 1756, John Stevenson, Earlsmill, received for a gelding £13 13s; 14th May, 1756, paid to John M'Cadam of Craigengillan for 10 West Highland stots, £30 8s 4d. At the payment thereof, on 1st July, he gave £2 10s of discount. 10th April, 1756, paid James Gillespie for a bull, £4 11s; 12th Jan., 1756, paid for a fatted veal, 10s. In 1759, hens sold at 5d each, and capons 7d. Eggs are said to have sold at 1d a-dozen. In 1784, a purchase was made of 15 wedder sheep at 15s each, and 5 lambs at 5s each. Oats—29th June, 1757, paid James Gillespie for 4 bolls of corn, £4; 1st May, 1786, paid for 20 bolls of oats, £14 10s. Ale, porter, etc.—in 1756 porter was 3s a-dozen; ale, 1s 6d a-dozen; a hogshead of white port from London, £17 11s 3d. Wages, etc.—8th Jan., 1756, James Sleigh paid James Clunie for a pair of shoes, 4s; 19th Jan., 1726, George Draffan, Douglas, received, for going twice to Lanark, 48 miles, 1s; 7th April, 1757, John Forest, tailor, received, for two days' work, 1s; 10th June, 1756, William Davidson received his half-year's wages as barnman, £1 17s; 1756 paid Griffen, gunsmith in London, for a gun and mounting a barrel, £40 18s 6d.

It appears that 6d a-day was the wage of labourers and artizans, and how our forefathers could subsist upon such allowance, is quite a mystery, as the meal was seldom less than 14s or 15s a boll. James Greenshields, labourer at Scrogton, and great-grandfather to the present postmaster, brought up a family of nine children, and never had more than 6d a-day. The principal meal then was a potful of "greens" boiled, and mashed with a little butter and a sprinkling of oatmeal. The wife used to say, "She was never feared for the weans after the green-kail was bladed." Potatoes were then unknown as a staple article of sustenance. My great-grandmother kept all that she raised in a parcel under her drawers until the new-year, as a treat to her son who was then in Glasgow, and who used to pay her a visit at that time. Old men in Douglas, alive about the year 1820, recollected the time when there was not a hat or a black coat in the church except the minister's.

There are about 100 men employed on Lady Home's establishment here, consisting of wrights, woodmen, hedgers, labourers, etc., and the average wage allowed to them is two shillings and sixpence a-day, the wrights receiving higher wages.

*Minerals.*—The parish is rich in minerals, and the coal, ironstone, limestone, freestone, etc., crop out in all directions among the deep ravines. This, by geologists, is said to be the southernmost part of the great basin that commences below Glasgow, and the old red sandstone crops out a little beyond the southern boundary of this parish, and no coal is found through a large tract of country for miles beyond that. Other practical men suppose that it is a distinct basin by itself, as the seams of coal are different from those farther down the Clyde; but this may be accounted for by the strata being, as it were, the higher edge of the great basin.

At Rigside, the workable seams are nine in number, and vary from two to eight feet in thickness. These all dip northwards to the water of Douglas, and come to the surface on the high ground, at an angle of 45°—1 in 2, and 1 in 2½, but flatter as they come down to the river. Of these seams the Big-drum, Little-drum, and Kirk-road, on the whole, are the most valuable. The lowest of these is the Duke's-quarry, a seam of two feet in thickness, and said to be equal to the Newcastle coal; but from its being at the greatest depth,

and from the small demand for coal in this neighbourhood, it is unprofitable in the working.  The aggregate amount of these seams is
forty-one feet eleven inches.  In some parts of the parish there are
supposed to be twelve seams of coal, and some of great thickness,
ten and even fifteen feet.

Mr Swan is at present working a gas or cannel coal seam by a
ten fathom pit, which lies far above the nine seams of common coal.
It is sixteen inches thick, and works in large, square masses, covered
with white clay, from being so near the surface.  It is as good
almost as first-class gas making coal—only inferior to Boghead and
Lesmahagow in the quantity of ash.  Dr Penny gives the following
analysis:—

| | | |
|---|---:|---|
| Volatile matters, | 54·57 | per cent. |
| Fixed carbon, | 21·82 | ,, |
| Ash, | 21·16 | ,, |
| Sulphur, | 1·37 | ,, |
| Water, | 1·08 | ,, |
| | 100 | |

The Earl of Home is at present constructing a tramway from this
pit towards the Lesmahagow Railway, which will greatly increase the
demand for this very valuable coal.

A hundred years ago peat was used as fuel in Douglas, and was
obtained from a large commonty about a mile and a-half to the east
of Douglas, and to which all the feuars have, by their deeds, a legal
right, but this has been long since discontinued.

The ironstone has not been wrought, and little can be said as to
its value.  The limestone has long been wrought at Wildshaw, but
since the introduction of portable manures, for some years only to a
limited extent.  There are also various seams of fire-clay, and on the
north side of the parish there is one of immense thickness.  With
such a rich store of minerals, the manufacturers need never despair
—Douglas will be able to supply them for centuries.

*Fishing.*—As the streams are small, it is only at certain seasons,
and under particular circumstances, that the angler can expect to
meet with success.  Fly-fishing is good in the months of April and
May, or immediately after a spate.  As to the flies, I have tried all
that the fancy or ingenuity of man could contrive, and I find that
the most successful are the black and red heckle, the hare bug, and
Hollin's fancy—these will succeed where all others fail.  Trout and
pike are the only fish to be found in Douglas-water, and may be caught
on any blustering day between Happendon and Crookboat.

These streams are all much fished, but the supply makes its
appearance on each return of spring.  Any fisher, however unsuccess-
ful, will be repaid by a visit to the streams in the Upper Ward.  The
bracing air, the wild and picturesque landscape, the purling rivulet,
the heath-clad hills, the hoarse cry of the moorfowl, the wild note of
the curlew, the bleating lamb, and the bounding deer, are objects
well calculated to dissipate care for a season from the breast of the

toil-worn citizen, and elevate his mind, from engrossing pursuits, to the contemplation of the beauties of creation.

*Libraries.*—1. The library at Newmains, called the Douglas Castle Operatives' Library, consists of about 550 volumes, treating principally on science and history, moral and religious subjects. This library was instituted seven years ago by the overseers and workers in connection with Douglas Castle, and belongs exclusively to them. It was originally formed by subscription, since then augmented by a quarterly payment of 4½d from each member.

*Schools.*—Female Industrial School. This school was instituted ten years ago by the late Right Hon. Lady Douglas, and Mrs Howison of Crossburn, for the benefit of the poorer classes of the town, and is still carried on by the family, who pay the teacher a salary of £25 a-year, and furnish her with a house, together with coals, gas, and the sewing materials. The principal branches taught are—reading, writing, and sewing, and the wages are, for reading and sewing, 1d a-week, and with writing, 1½d. The school is well taught, and has been of great benefit to the town.

*Churches.*—The Free Church was built in 1845; the United Presbyterian Church in 1817; Established Church built in 1795.

*Manses, etc.*—Established. This manse is a handsome, commodious, and substantial erection; was built in 1827, and has all the necessary appurtenances of stable, byre, barn, etc., with suitable garden, enclosed with a high stone wall. The glebe contains about 40 Scotch acres, and the stipend consists of 144 bolls of meal, and 104 qrs. 6 bush. 3 pks. 2 qts. of barley, with £10 for communion elements. The manse and glebe were formerly situated within what are now the policies of Douglas Castle, and a large glebe given to the then incumbent, to compensate for his removal.

Free Church Manse—built in 1849. This is also a commodious house, and is situated on the rising ground to the east of the Edinburgh and Ayr road, close upon the west-end of the town.

United Presbyterian Manse—This manse was built by subscription in 1853. It is situated close upon the Free Church manse, and is one of the handsomest and most commodious in the locality, and commands a beautiful view of the upper part of the parish. It reflects the highest credit upon the worthy occupant, the Rev. Mr Jamieson, that the members of the Established Church, as well as his own, contributed towards the erection of this manse, and Lord James Douglas supplied all the home-wood gratuitously. Mr Jamieson was the first U. P. minister in this parish, and the Rev. John Jeffray, now in Newcastle, the first Free Church minister.

The Cameronian Church, which stood so long at Rigside, was taken down about fifteen years ago, and a new place of worship erected on the opposite side of Douglas-water.

*Paupers.*—There was no assessment for their relief until the year 1846. Previous to that time they were maintained by the church collections, and any deficiency was supplemented by a voluntary contribution from the heritors. There is now a regular assessment laid upon lands and heritages, the gross rental of which for the year from Whitsunday, 1858, to Whitsunday, 1859, was £10,990 9s 7½d, and the sum assessed on was £10,509, and the rate of assessment was 1s 4d per pound for the year. All the clergymen, and teachers, and tenants under £4 are exempted from this assessment. The number of regular paupers on the roll for half-year to Martinmas, 1858, was 83; and for half-year to Whitsunday, 1859, 82; and the sum expended upon these, and upon occasional paupers, and for management, etc., during the year to Whitsunday, 1859, was £638 6s 1d. The average allowance to each registered pauper for the year was £6 1s 6d. The affairs of the poor are judiciously managed; the funds, formerly deficient, being in a healthful state.

The principal trade in the town of Douglas is weaving, and as there is little employment for females except pirn-winding, it is presumed that this adds considerably to the poor rates.

Sir Walter Scott visited Douglas in 1830, preparatory to his publication of "Castle Dangerous," and had a long interview with Thos. Haddow, an old inhabitant of Douglas, and one well versant in the history of the house of Douglas. Thomas breakfasted with Sir Walter at Douglas Mill, and furnished him with all the information of which he was possessed relative to that subject.

The Highlanders passed through Douglas in their disastrous retreat from England, stripping the inhabitants of their shoes.

*Persecution.*—From the influence of the Marquis of Douglas, the Presbyterians maintained their own form of worship, there being a *curate* and a Presbyterian minister at the same time in Douglas.

*Baptism Stone.*—On Glentaggart farm, betwixt the house and Duncaton, on the road to Shawhead, there stands a boulder of about three feet in length, two and a-half in height, and one and a-half in thickness, surrounded by a number of smaller stones; this stone contains, on the top, two small compartments, which were used for baptizing during the Persecution times.          J. H.

---

[THE tack or lease of Bodinglee and Maidengill, in the parishes of Robertoun and Douglas, is given *in extenso;* the provisions being curious and instructive as to the increase in value of land; these sheep farms let in 1727 for £300 Scots—the equivalent of £25 sterling; and the farm of Bodinglee (912) alone is now rented at £180, that of Maidengill being incorporated with Parkhall (758); both farms are now held by a lineal descendant, name and surname alike, of the tacksman of 1727.—A. M.]

IT is agreed on and finally ended betwixt the parties following, viz., an high and mighty Archibald, Duke of Donglass, on the one part, and John Gillespie, in Hill-end of Robertoun, and Thomas

Gillespie, in Millriggs of Wistoun, on the other part, in manner following, that is, said noble Duke has lettin and settin as hereby (ffor the causes after speci) letts and setts to the said John and Thomas Gillespie joyntly, and their heirs and evers (secluding assignes and submen), all and haill the five merks land of Madeugill, presently possessed by Alex. Hutcheson, tenent therein, with the houses, biggings, yards, and haill pertinents thereto belonging, lying within, the paroch and regality of Douglas and Sheriffdom of Lanark, and that for the haill time and space of eleven years next following there entry thereto, whilk is hereby declared to be and begin to the arable land thereof att the term of Martimas, and twenty-seven years, and to the houses, yards, meadows, and grass all the term of Whitsunday first year after, and so forth to continue, &c.: whilk tack the said noble Duke and obleges him, his heirs and successors, to warrand att all hands as law will, ffor the whilks causes the said John and Thomas Gillespies binds and obleges them contlic and seallic, and their heirs and evers, to content and pay yearly, and ilk year during the space of the said tack, to the said noble Duke, his heirs and evers, or assignes, and to his Grace's ffactors, in his name, having power to receive the samen, till and haill the sum of three hundred pounds Scotts money, all two terms in the year, Whitsunday first to come, and so furth to continue, together with sixteen hens yearly, or five shillings Scots for each hen att the terms used and wont; and it is agreed upon betwixt the said parties that the said John and Thos. Gillespies shall bring yr. haill grindable victuall growing on the said lands to his Grace's milen, called Milnholm-miln, and pay the multures, and perform the other services used and wont att the samen miln; as also it is agreed upon betwixt the said parties that the said tenents are to be eased of and disburdened of all due service and lend shaw payable furth of the said lands during the space foresaid; it also is agreed upon that the said tenents are to disburden and relieve the said noble Duke, and his fords of the haill cesses publick burdens and officers' dues imposed or to be imposed upon, and payable furth of the samen lands during the space of this tack; and, in like manner, it is agreed upon betwixt the said parties that in case the said tenents shall suffer and permit two terms duly to run in the third term, the said, that then in that case this tack shall, *ipso facto*, become void and null, as if the samen had never been made, but prejudice always to the said noble Duke and his heirs, to saitt execution for payment of the tack duly that and shall be resting for the time; and likewise it is agreed on betwixt the parties that in respect the said Alex. Hutcheson in getts the bear cropt of the said lands free of rent the year of his removall therefrae, therefore it is agreed upon that the said John and Thomas Gillespies shall have the bear cropt thereof free of rent the year of their removall therefrae on that place of the lands where the bear fall happens to be; and lastly, the said John and Thomas Gillespies hereby obliges them contly and scally, and their foresaids, to leave

the haill houses as sett to them in a sufficient habitable condition
att the experation of their tack or there removall therefrae, and to
the performance of the haill premisses both parties obliges them and
their forsaids to others, and the party failrier to pay to the party
observer, or willing to observe, the sum of sixty pounds money
forsaid for ilk failrie att our performance, consenting to the registra-
tion hereof in the books of councill and session, or any other register
competent within the kingdom, to have the strength of an decreet
interponed yrto that all necessar execution six days pass hereon, as
effers, and their heirs. In witness whereof (written on stamp paper
be John Henderson, servitor to John Howison, clerk to the regality
of Douglas) both parties have subscreved these as follows: Edward,
noble Duke att Douglas, and with the twelfth day of August, 1727,
ninth day of January, 1728, and twenty-eight years, before these
witnesses, and John Howison and Thomas Gillespie.

DOUGLAS.

Bertram, *witness.*

Again, in 1794, " It is contracted, agreed, and ended betwixt the
Right Hon. Arch. Lord Douglas of Douglas on the one part, and John
Gillespie, tenant in Bodinglee on the other part." " The said Arch.
Lord Douglas hereby sets, etc., to the said John Gillespie and his heirs,
secluding assignees and sub-tenants, all and whole the lands and farm
of Bodinglee, as present possessed by himself, with houses, biggings,
yards, and pertinents, lying within the parish of Robertoun, barony
of Douglas, and shire of Lanark, and that for all the days, years, and
space of nineteen years." " Reserving always full power to the said
Arch. Lord Douglas, to search for, work, heap up, and carry away
coal, lime, and stone, clay for bricks, or any other metal or mineral
which may be found on the said lands, and to erect milns, build
houses, and other accommodation for manufactories, and workmen
that may be employed at the said works, and to take off ground for
kail-yards, and for maintaining cows and horses necessary for the said
manufactories, or workmen that may be employed at the said work in
carrying on the same, and also to alter roads or make new ones, to
enclose or plant any part of the ground set; the said John Gillespie
being always allowed such deduction out of his rent for the damage
done by said operation," etc.; " upon the other hand, the said John
Gillespie, etc., to pay the sum of sixty-four pounds sterling of annual
rent for above," etc. " To pay the Baron fee used and wont, and also,
if required, to keep one dog or hound for the said Arch. Lord Douglas;"
" there shall be a break at the end of every seven years of this tack,
for the master as well as the tenant, upon their giving notice of their
intention so to do."

[The prosperity of the cotton mills erected at New Lanark, and the
working of lime at Newton-Wiston and Wildshaw, Douglas, will
account for the provisions as to possible manufactories, lime, etc.,
being embodied in the lease of 1794.—A. M.]

## A FEW ROUGH NOTES ON THE PARISH OF DOUGLAS—1860.

THE ground, in general, is a light soil, unfit to bear wheat with profit to the cultivator, but it produces oats and barley of first-rate qualities. There are some fine meadows of natural hay, which are more valuable than the best arable land in the parish. The ground, at a distance from the river, is hilly, moorish, wild, and uncultivated; but it produces excellent and sound pasture for sheep. There are no herds of black cattle reared in the parish, as in the olden time.

The Kirkton of Douglas "was a burgh of barony before 1668. In 1685 the Marquis of Douglas got from the King and Parliament the right of holding a weekly market and two annual fairs at the town of Douglas, and of levying tolls and customs at these markets and fairs." Douglas is a market town—Friday is the market day. About sixty years ago the market was well attended; corn, meal, etc., were exposed for sale. Now there is no appearance of business—indeed, there is no business, although two or three individuals from the country are in the habit of visiting the town weekly, every Friday; the object which they have in view is to keep the "Market Friday" from becoming extinct. It is surmised that this is not the true motive, from the manner in which some of these individuals generally leave the town. The fairs in Popish times were all held in the churchyard. After the Revolution they continued to be held there till the middle of the last century. The shoemakers were the last to leave the churchyard, and that only twenty-five years ago.

There are some very old houses in Douglas. On the north side there is a "two-storey house" called "The Scribe Tree," from the rude figure of a tree cut on the south door. This house, in the olden time, was the head inn in the town. When smuggling was carried on to a great extent between the Isle of Man and Scotland, frequently bands of smugglers made the "Scribe Tree" their resting-place for the night. There was then an excise officer in Douglas, but he was no object of fear. In the morning, after the smugglers left, he followed them for a mile, at a respectful distance, calling upon them to surrender, and firing his pistols, charged with powder; and the smugglers would say to him—"That is enough; you have done your duty; good morning." The officer, invited by the smugglers to meet *some travellers* in the inn, accepted the invitation. The oldest houses are on the south side of the churchyard, some having arched chambers. They were built before the Reformation, and inhabited by those connected with St Bride's Church.

There is in Douglas a building, three stories in height, called "Red Hall." It belonged to the Flemings, who emigrated to Douglas after the settlement of Theobald the Fleming in Douglasdale. Wherever the Flemings had a settlement, they had a Red Hall.

*w*

The houses in Douglas, at the Reformation, consisted of one storey, except those at the Cross of two stories, and covered with "divots," and thatched with straw. A little before the Revolution, a few were covered with slates. The houses that have been built within the last forty years are better in many respects. The number of houses is decreasing; but those now built are superior in comfort and appearance, all being slated. The population of the town has greatly increased since the middle of the last century, the increase resulting from the extinction of small farms, and the "ousting" of the cottars from these small farms. The town has an antique appearance at the Cross. The streets are narrow, and of very irregular appearance. They were formed long before the introduction of carts. Few of the old houses are built on the same line. Lady Jane Douglas, sister of the Duke of Douglas, lodged, with her two sons, a few days at the "Scribe Tree Inn," after she was denied admittance into Douglas Castle, and repulsed from it by her brother.

*The village of Uddington.*—Nearly three miles north-east of Douglas is the ancient and rude-looking village of Uddington. The population of this village at the Revolution was but a little short of half the population of Douglas; now the number of its inhabitants is greatly reduced, cottage after cottage having been erased. The inhabitants, though poor, are more comfortable than many are in the same grade of life, each cottage having a patch of land, or "a plain," attached to it, the rent of which is trifling.

Cases of fever few; a case of typhus rare, and when it occurs has been *imported*. Cholera never visited the parish. The water, in town and parish, is particularly good. There are many aged persons in the parish. One female in the village is ninety-six, and there are a few males and females between eighty and ninety.

Pennant, who travelled through the wilds of Crawfordjohn to Douglas, when he reached the brow of the hill which commanded an extensive view of Douglasdale, was struck with the beauty of the scenery, like fairy vision, bursting upon his view.

The names of a number of places are of British or of Celtic origin. *Douglas—Dhuglas,* the dark-blue stream. This is descriptive. *Glentaggart,* near the south boundary of the parish. *Gleann-sagart—*the priest's glen. There was a chapel in Roman Catholic times at the place. *Airnsalloch,* a small stream from the south-east, which joins Douglas-water a mile south-west from the town. *Airneseileach—*the sloe and willow stream, descriptive. There are on its banks sloe and willow bushes in great abundance. The *Inch—Innis,* the island—a place at the four-mile stone from Douglas on the road to Muirkirk. In the olden time a few acres of land, bounded by *Monks-water* on the north and by Douglas-water on the south, formed an island, or inch, as it was pronounced by the Saxons. There is a house on the land called "The Inch," although there is now no island. *Auchandaff,* a farm on the south bound of the parish. *Auchandamh—*the ox field. The Celtic names of places are comparatively few. The Saxons early entered the parish. To many places they gave new names, and some of these were translated by them from the Celtic.

Auchensaugh is the only hill of note in the parish. There the Covenants were renewed in 1782. It commands a wide horizon. From it Ben-Lomond and Ben-Ledi, hills of the Gael, are visible in a clear day. Cormacoup Hill, west of Douglas; the old road from Ayr to Edinburgh ran along the side of it. Brown Hill, half-a-mile east of Douglas. Hawk-shaws, three miles west of Douglas.

The principal stream is Douglas-water. It rises near the foot of Cairntable, and runs through the parish in its length, dividing it nearly into two equal parts, and falls into the Clyde at "Crookboat." Its tributaries on its right bank are—Kennox-water, Andershaw lane or water, Airnsalloch, Parkhead-burn, and Craig-burn. On its left bank—Monks or Mucks water, Smuggler's-burn, Moura-burn, Bridelea-burn, and Poniel-water. In Douglas-water there is a considerable number of fish. The greater part are small. The water is much fished by young lads, who are expert fishers. Scarcely a fisher comes from a distance to Douglas-water for a day's sport. In all its tributaries there is fish in abundance, but of small size. In Douglas-water there are trout, perch, and pike. The perch made their escape from a pond in front of Douglas Castle, which after a heavy fall of rain burst, and they were carried into Douglas-water.

There is no natural wood of any extent in the parish, but patches, chiefly of birch, are still found in some of the hollows on the hills. There are many thousand acres of plantations, consisting of larch, spruce, pine, etc., among which are intermingled oak, ash, elm, etc. The spruce and larch are being cut fit for every domestic purpose. Douglas parish, in the olden time, was covered with wood. The peat mosses contain many trunks of trees, particularly of oak, and some of large dimensions. The oldest and largest trees are at Douglas Castle; they are ash trees. Thirty years ago, one was blown down. When sawn across near the root, 600 rings were counted, indicating the age of the tree. Near the centre many of the rings were obliterated. Two of these aged occupants of the vale still remain; one of them is called "the Hanging Tree." In the wars between Scotland and England, prisoners were hanged on that tree. A few years ago a high wind broke off the branch in which the hook was fixed to which the executioner made fast his rope. That part of the branch, with the hook as it was attached to it many centuries ago, is preserved at Douglas Castle.

Ash trees were to be found at every farm-house which was built in the olden time. The yew tree makes the best bow, the ash the next. Tenants were bound to plant ash trees for bows, as every male was bound to learn and practise archery. The law was strongest on this point, and the *laird* saw that the law was obeyed. In many places ash trees of a great age are standing, where for centuries there have been no houses. The best bows were made of the yew tree, and it was reserved for the use of the lords of the soil and their sons; seldom

was a bow of yew seen in the hands of a vassal.  The tenant was also
bound to plant the alder tree; and this tree is to be found to this day,
not only at old castles, but at old farm-houses.  It was planted for a
particular and useful purpose.  The wood of the alder was accounted,
in old times, preferable to every kind of wood for arrows.  The
plane tree was in great abundance at every farm-house.  It was
planted by the tenant for domestic use.  The wood of this tree
was in old times of great value in the hands of the turner, it being
well adapted for wooden bowls, platters, and other domestic utensils,
which were then in more universal use.

There are two lakes in the parish—one between the town and
Douglas Castle.  It covers fourteen acres of ground.  The other is
nearly a mile below the castle, and close to the right bank of Douglas-
water, and covers about thirty acres of land.  Both lakes are artificial.
They abound with trout and perch; there are also pike in both sheets
of water; some have been taken upwards of seven pounds in weight.
Both lakes are strictly preserved, and so is Douglas-water within the
castle grounds.  The whole of Douglas-water, excepting these
three miles, is open to every angler.  On these lakes there are
swans, Canadian geese, wild ducks, teal, etc.

There is also an artificial loch or reservoir in the western boundary
of the parish, commonly called "Glenbuck Loch," which covers a
great extent of ground.  The embankments were constructed by the
Catrine Cotton Mill Company, to procure a supply of water for their
machinery in summer drought, when the Water of Ayr is low.  If
both embankments were to give way at the same time, one part (the
greater part) would roll down the Ayr, and the other would rush
into the Douglas-water.  The Catrine Company are bound to pay all
the damages which the water might do should it burst the embankments.  There are trout and perch in the loch; sometimes perch are
taken in great numbers.  The line that divides the county of Lanark
from that of Ayrshire runs across the loch.

The turnpike road from Carlisle to Glasgow runs through the
parish from south to north, two miles east of Douglas.  It enters the
parish three miles east from Douglas, and leaves the parish about
four miles from the town, and enters the parish of Lesmahagow.
The road from Ayr to Edinburgh passes through Douglas.  It
enters the parish six miles west of the town, at the boundary line
between the county of Ayr and the county of Lanark.  It leaves the
parish about four miles from Douglas, where it enters the parish of
Carmichael.  There are few parish roads, and these few are in a most
disgraceful state, except one of two miles leading from the Ayr and
Edinburgh road at Janefield to the Glespin coalpits, and another of
one mile leading from the Carlisle road, at the southern boundary of
the parish, to the "Wildshaw Limeworks."

A survey was made for a railway from Muirkirk, to join the Caledonian four miles below Abington.  The line would have crossed the
parish three miles above Douglas.  An Act of Parliament was obtained

for a line from Motherwell to join the line from Muirkirk. The junction would have been a little below Cormacoup. The line would have passed within less than a mile of Douglas.

There are four stone bridges over Douglas-water—one at Janefield, a mile and a-half above the town; the second at Happendon, on the Glasgow and Carlisle road, two and a-half miles below Douglas. This bridge consists of two arches. The third is five miles below Douglas, has two arches, unites the parishes of Lesmahagow and Carmichael; and the fourth near the junction of Douglas-water with the Clyde, and unites the same parishes. There is a stone bridge over Monks or Mucks-water, in the parish, about fifty yards above its junction with Douglas-water. It is on the Muirkirk road, four miles above Douglas. There are also stone bridges over nearly the whole of the small streams that flow into Douglas-water. There are three wooden bridges over Douglas-water; they were constructed to bear the passage of loaded carts. The one is at "Table Stane;" the second at the town; the third at Douglas Castle, on the road leading to the garden. These have an elegant appearance.

There are three toll-bars in the parish—one a mile and a-half west of Douglas, on the Muirkirk road; another on the Glasgow and Carlisle road, at Douglas-mill, three miles from Douglas, with a check-bar a mile and a-half south of the bar; and the third is at Uddington, on the Edinburgh and Ayr road. There is also a toll-bar on the Douglas and Muirkirk road, on the *very line* that unites the counties of Ayr and Lanark. The toll-house is in Ayrshire.

The "Douglas Arms" is the head inn. In it man and horse will find excellent accommodation. It is patronised by the most respectable persons in the parish and neighbourhood, and by commercial travellers, etc. There are five public-houses in the village besides the Douglas Arms Inn, and these are supported chiefly by the working-classes. The patronage is cordially given, and by many to an extent which is ruinous to themselves and families.

Earls-mill is the only corn mill in the parish. It is three miles south of Douglas. The motive power is water, from Andershaw-burn. The machinery has many of the modern improvements. It can prepare the finest flour and make the best oatmeal.

There is a "Waulk Mill" and also a "Dye Work" on the Douglas-water, three miles above the town. There has been in that district a "waulk mill" and a dye work from time immemorial. Connected with the dye work there is a mill for carding wool, and it is only a few years since the carding of wool by machinery was introduced into the parish. In the olden time all the wool was carded at home by hand cards. In farm-houses, the men, in long winter nights, carded the wool, and the females span it, and with song, work, and the merry laugh, the night passed away.

In 1685, the Marquis of Douglas obtained from the King and Parliament the right of holding a weekly market and two annual fairs at Douglas, and of levying tolls and customs there.

There were five yearly fairs held in the town. The "March Fair," on the third Friday of March—new style—chiefly for hiring servants. "Whitsun-Friday," first Friday after the old term, for settling accounts, and hiring. "June Fair," second Wednesday—old style—for hiring servants for harvest, and general business. "October Fair," third Wednesday—old style—for hiring, and general business. "Martinmas Fair," first Friday after the old term, general business, and hiring. Of these fairs, four are *extinct*.

At all of the fairs there were shoemakers' stalls, coopers with every kind of wooden vessel, etc.; stalls of various kinds; and there were carts with pigs, whose squeaking is a variety in the hubbub. The public houses are much patronised. *The publican's prayer* here for a good fair is: "A fine day till the people are gathered, and after that, a doon-richt pour o' rain the haill day." There is much dancing at fairs. There are penny reels, from *early* in the afternoon to a late hour, in the Mason Lodge, which is rented for dancing on fair days. The dancing hall is well attended. The shouting (the hoo-hoohing) of the bumpkins, and the clatter of their iron-shod shoes, as they lumber through the reel, produce a noise which sets conversation at defiance. There is something exceeding grotesque in the ball-room evolutions of a lout when under the spell of whisky and the fiddle.

There is a daily arrival of letters from north, south, etc., and a daily morning delivery in town. There is a daily morning dispatch to Muirkirk, and an evening arrival at same place.

There are three churches in the parish, and all in the town. 1. Established Church. 2. The U.P. Church, built in 1817, settled ministry in 1820. Sittings 350, of these 100 are free sittings. There is a manse; stipend £100. The members belong to five parishes. 3. Free Church, built in 1845, a settled ministry, with a manse. 4. There is a small congregation of Baptists; there is no church; there is no settled ministry. 5. There is a large body of "non-hearers," of all ages, and all relationships—old and young, father and son, mother and daughter, etc.

There are five schools in the parish. In town—1. The Parish School. 2. A venture school. 3. The Countess of Home's industrial school for girls—school-room and house for teacher. 4. A school at Rigside, four miles below Douglas. School-room and dwelling-house, and £5 of salary, paid by the Earl of Home. 5. A school at Table Stane, three miles above Douglas—school-room and dwelling-house. A widow teaches a few girls to read, sew, and knit. £5 of salary paid by Earl of Home. The parish school-house, etc., and the two last-mentioned school-houses, were built by the Lord Douglas. They are excellent buildings, and suitable.

The people are industrious, but not provident, or saving for "a rainy day." When stagnation in weaving comes, they look to the House of Douglas for assistance, which is always given, and generally by furnishing them with out-door labour till they obtain a supply of work from their employers. This reliance on the House of Douglas militates against providence and self-reliance. Males and females dress respectably on Sabbath—all the church-going class do so. There are many places where the people have better church-going habits. With regard to morality, they can, all things considered, bear comparison with their neighbours.

Great changes have taken place respecting funerals since the end of last century. In olden times, when the funeral was from the country, the coffin was carried to the grave on the backs of two horses walking abreast, being, by a particular kind of harness, kept close to each other. The coffin was placed before the riders, who held it with one hand, and guided the horses with the other. The horses had black trappings, furnished by the session, called the "Horse Claiths." Now there is a hearse, which can be drawn by one or two horses. There was "service" in every case (entertainment in eating and drinking) given to the funeral attendants, according to the means of the bereaved family. Bread and cheese were first presented; ale followed, then whisky and rum, brandy and wine; sometimes there were two "rounds" of each of these. The poorest invariably gave oatcakes and cheese, ale, whisky, and short-bread. The poor were often seriously injured by the mode in which funerals were conducted, and it sometimes required years to discharge the debts which they had contracted, to be *foolishly* like their neighbours. Many partook too freely of the liquors, and some were so intoxicated that they could not follow the coffin to the grave.

At funerals in the country, before the "service" began, two men made their appearance, one carrying on a small barn "wecht" tobacco pipes for the company. This individual stuck a pipe in the button hole of the coat of every man, and the other man, following, hung on the pipe in the button hole a piece of tobacco about a foot and a-half in length. At every funeral in the country there was a great variety of biscuits, cakes, etc., which were carried round in barn riddles, and sometimes in barn "wechts." Every man took up unbroken a portion of each kind, kind after kind in great variety being presented in succession. The pieces taken up were conveyed to the pockets, which, in many cases, were crammed. The children were anxiously looking for the return of their fathers, to receive their share of the funeral dainties which they had brought from the house of mourning. Sometimes the question was asked, "When is father going to a funeral?" In the town, there is now no "service" at funerals, by agreement entered into forty years ago. In the country, wine and biscuits are presented, and this change in the mode of conducting funerals has been in all respects most beneficial.

The belief in witchcraft still lingers in the parish, particularly with the aged and those who live among the hills. The rowan tree is still used as a charm against witchcraft as regards cattle. There are some houses in which the cattle would not be deemed safe if it were awanting. Among the hills, if a hint be given of the disbelief in witchcraft, immediately the unbeliever is reminded of the witch of Endor. This is considered as *settling the point.*

In 1780, the usual breakfast was oatmeal porridge, or brose, with a little milk. The principal part of dinner was broth, or, as it was usually called, "kail," from colewort and barley, beaten in a mortar, constituting the greatest portion of the ingredients. The quantity of butcher meat in the preparation of this dish was small, frequently not a morsel, when the broth was called "muslin kail." For supper, there was in every farm-house *sowans,* which " in fragrant lunt set a' their gabs asteering." The bread was generally oat-cakes. In many farm-houses it was composed of pease and oats in proportion, according to taste. This bread was called "mashlam." There has been a great change for the better. In the past age there were no vegetables, except colewort or "green kail," rarely a few cabbages were to be seen. Now in every cottage garden there is a quantity of vegetables. Now not a pot is put on the fire (except by the very poorest) to make "muslin kail." The people are now better fed and clothed than their ancestors were.

Twenty years after the beginning of the present century butcher meat, fresh, could seldom be procured in Douglas. The consumption was so small that it was deemed prudent not to kill an ox or a cow till buyers were obtained for at least two-thirds of the animal. At the end of last century, it was not deemed safe to kill a sheep till there was a certainty of selling the four quarters of it. In 1780, tradition says before a sheep was killed for sale, that the public crier gave "intimation that a sheep was to be killed next day" if customers were found; that the minister had agreed to take the near hind leg, the baron bailie the far hind leg; that two families had joined to take the near fore leg, and if a buyer did not "cast up" for the far fore leg in three hours, that the sheep would be sent to the hill. At Martinmas, families that could afford to purchase a fat ox or fat cow "laid in" what was called "their mart." It was cut into pieces and salted. Poor families that could not individually purchase a "mart," united in purchasing an ox or a cow for their "mart." Now beef, mutton, etc., may be purchased *fresh* in Douglas every day, and may be called good. Lamb and veal, in their season, can also be obtained, but sheep and lambs are cheaper in the Glasgow markets than where they are reared.

In the middle of the last century tea was a luxury heard of by some, but enjoyed by few. About 1770 a few individuals, for some particular *occasion,* partook of it. It was for many years a beverage of the greatest rarity, and enjoyed only by the rich, as the price was high. It is not more than eighty years since it was *clandestinely* partaken of by many "gudewives" in town and country. The "tea equipage," the tea-pot, cups, etc., were placed in a cup-board, the door of which the "gudewife" held in her hand, ready to shut it on the appearance of any intruding on her enjoyment. It was then considered extravagant for the wife of a tradesman to drink tea.

Property in village, held in feu; all being vassals to the house of Douglas. All the land in the parish is held in vassalage, except the Douglas estate, which holds of the crown. There is, strictly speaking, only one "laird" in the parish, all the rest of the proprietors are but *gudemen*. The estate of Cormacoup is entailed, and the greatest part of the Douglas estate. Property has greatly increased in value since the beginning of the century. Houses and gardens in the town have increased one-third in value, and some *one-half*. It is the same with regard to land and rents.

In the sixteenth century the wages of the labouring man in the Upper Ward were 1½d per day, and the wages of an overseer were 2d. These were the wages paid at the "gold diggings on Glengonar" and Elvan-water, under the management of Bulmer, the German, who collected £100,100 of gold in these places. After the Union, wages rose. They reached in the beginning of the seventeenth century 4d per day for a labourer, and 6d for a mason. At the middle of said century they were 6d per day, and in 1790, 6d per day, with board. In the beginning of the present century wages were 1s 2d per day; of a mason, 1s 6d. Half-yearly wages of a female servant were 30s to 40s; half-yearly wages of male farm servant, £3 10s to £4. In 1771, wages of farm servants per annum, £5; of a maid servant, £2 10s. In 1791, wages of farm servants, £7 to £10; of a maid servant, £3 to £4. Labourers, in 1771, received 10d and 1s per day; in 1791 they received 1s 2d and 1s 4d. In 1859, wages of a labouring man, per day, 2s 3d to 2s 6d; of a mason, 4s 6d. Half-yearly wages of a woman servant, £4 to £6; of a farm servant, £12. The earnings of the handloom weavers are most fluctuating. Sometimes they are as low as 6s, and in a few weeks rise to 8s and 20s.

Retail prices of a few articles for 1751–61, extracted from a "merchant's" shop book. He was a general dealer, well entitled to the name of *Mungo A'Things*. His book points to the habits of the people in those days. Whisky and tobacco were then in great demand. These are the two articles that most frequently occur. 1751—Whisky, one pint (Scotch pint), 1s 8d; tobacco, 1 lb., 10d; gunpowder, 1 lb., 1s 2d; leadshot, 1 lb., 2d; 1 barrel herring, 6s; 1 doz. tobacco pipes, 3d. 1753—1 lb. sugar, 1s 2d; 1 stone of wool (24lbs.), 4s 6d. 1754—1 lb. soap, 8d; 1 lb. starch, 6d. 1755—100 herrings, 3d; ben leather (for shoe soles), per oz., 1¼d; ½ lb. black soap, 4d. 1756—Stone of beef, 24 oz. in lb., 4s 6d. 1758—Stone of whole pease, 1s 4d; 1 peck meal, 11d. 1759—A stone of wool, 4s 6d. 1760—A sheep skin, 4½d. 1761—A pint of tar (for sheep, Scotch pint), 5d; "a dram," 2d. There was whisky at 1s 8d Scotch pint. The consumption of whisky great. No tea in any family account. Very little sugar; only three families bought a few pounds. As little soap. This says little for *cleanly habits* in the Upper Ward. Much wool sold; all for home use. Ben leather in demand at the beginning of winter, for *shoe repairs*. Farmers, etc., *soled* their own shoes.  Gunpowder and shot in demand at certain seasons, for more than *crow-shooting*—for poaching.  Much of the wool bought was manufactured at home, for sale when made into cloth.  The merchant took yarn, cloth, etc., from the *gudewives* for tobacco, etc.  Often cloth, etc., was received and stood marked as part payment of account.  In that age servants, when meal was being *milled*, were sent to the mill to sift the meal, etc., frequently six, eight, or ten "drams" are marked as *sent to the servants at the mill*, and these are charged at 2d per "dram."

The right honourable the Countess of Home possesses the greatest part of the parish—not resident; A. Paterson, Esq., of Cormacoup, resident; — Douglas, Esq., of Monkshead; R. Gillespie, Esq., of Springhill; Mr R. Meikle, Bogside Cottage, resident, and a practising surgeon.  There are a few who pay a mere trifle of stipend, etc.  The Douglas estate pays nineteen shillings in the pound on parochial burdens; the other lands only one shilling in the pound.

Since the establishment of the rural police, the number of vagrants has greatly decreased.  A few are still skulking among the hills.  On entering the town they beg, but not openly, unless the officer be absent on his rounds.  Before the introduction of the rural police, the parish was a place of refuge for vagrants of every kind, when driven out of Ayrshire by the police in Muirkirk.

When there was no restraint on vagrants of any description, not a few were carried through the parish on hand-barrows.  The greater part of these were what they appeared to be, cripples, but some were impostors with the perfect use of their limbs.  To enjoy ease they betook themselves to the *barrow mode* of begging, and found it more profitable than that of seeking alms on foot.  The parish of Douglas had a full share of these vagrants.  Every barrow required at least two persons to convey it from house to house; and in the country, where the distance was great, a horse and cart was employed.  Conveying cripples from house to house was not only attended with toil, but with expense.  Since the rural police was established not a cripple in a barrow has appeared in Douglas.

Bracken-lea Spot, commonly called "the Spot," was a small independent farm, till added, a few years ago, to the farm of Parish-holm, when it was held as a "subset."  It is about half-a-mile below Parish-holm, and on the right bank of Douglas-water.  Bracken-lea Spot was distinguished by the peculiarity of its situation.  Being situated at the base of the range of hills south of it, the sun does not shine on it during the three months of winter.  The family, during that time, could not, from any part of the farm, see the sun.  His rays they beheld on the opposite range of hills.

In the beginning of this century almost every farmer lodged beggars.  There were a few *onsteads* distinguished by this kind of hospitality to the wandering poor.  The byre, the stable, barn, etc., were usually the sleeping-places for vagrants.  In some *onsteads* there was an outhouse in which there were the beggar's bed and blankets.

The old stagers were always welcome. No newspapers in that age reached the country. In the kitchen the beggars entertained the family by narrating the news of the district through which they had travelled. An old wanderer said, "The country folks are wild for news, and they get great abundance of them." On being asked what she did when she had no news, her ready answer was, "I mak a wheen, and they tak as well as the true anes, and sometimes far better. There are only two or three farm-houses where beggars *now* find shelter for a night. Frequently the blankets on the beggar's bed were stolen, and large pieces were cut off them.

There are no insane persons in or belonging to the parish. There are three fatuous persons. They reside in the town. One is upwards of 60, one 30, one 16; all are harmless; all unable to do anything for their support. There are four dumb persons in the parish; one, a girl, is a handloom weaver; three are males.

There are no remains of ancient songs or ballads connected with Douglasdale. If there were songs or ballads they have perished, as there is not a fragment of Douglasdale poetry. Douglasdale cannot produce a single stanza of old ballad poetry.

The parish is rich in minerals. There are many seams of coal on both sides of Douglas-water; at Douglas, at Craigie-hall, three miles above the town, there is a seam of coal nine feet in thickness, and of superior quality, but this seam has not been wrought since the end of last century. Every coalmaster has *satisfied* himself with taking the "*crop coal,*" which is obtained with little expense. Coal is also wrought at Cormacoup, four miles above Douglas; excellent coal could be got there by sinking deeper. Coal has long been wrought at Rigside, four miles below Douglas; the quality is inferior to that at Douglas and above it. There is Cannel coal at Rigside, which is used in some gas-works, as being cheaper than the Cannel coal at Auchenheath, Lesmahagow, but the gas is inferior, and impregnated with sulphur; there are also seams of excellent coal in the north-west part of the parish. At one time great quantities of coal were carted from Craigie-hall and Rigside to Crawford, Moffat, etc., etc., but since the opening of the Caledonian Railway that traffic has entirely ceased. All the minerals on the Douglas estate in the parish do not belong to the estate; all the minerals were "*reserved*" with the lands that were purchased from the Earl of Selkirk.

There is a great abundance of ironstone in the parish; there are also numerous and valuable seams of *black band* in many parts of the parish. There is excellent fire-brick clay in the north-west part of the parish in great abundance.

There is an unexhaustible supply of limestone; it abounds in every part of the parish where there is coal; it has been wrought four miles above Douglas; it has been wrought at Wildshaw, three miles south-east of Douglas, from time immemorial; the lime produced at Wildshaw is excellent; before the opening of the Caledonian Railway, it was carried to Moffat and the district around, for building and agriculture; it requires particular preparation for plastering.

On Poniel-water there is marble in great abundance, "*chimney pieces*" and "*tables*" have been manufactured from it; some of these may be seen in Douglas Castle. Traces of lead have been found in one or two places in the parish, but so slight as to afford no inducement to spend money in searching for it.

The deposits of sandstone are extensive; blocks of great magnitude may be obtained; it yields kindly to the chisel, and "*stands the weather.*" Some of Douglas freestone has stood the test of more than 700 years, and promises to stand as long again.

A whinstone formation, or "*trap dyke*," enters the parish southeast of Douglas, runs across it, and enters the parish of Muirkirk, west of Douglas; it can be traced in Ayrshire for a considerable distance. The metal, in a state of fusion, forced duly through a stratum of sandstone which has been made friable, where it is in juxtaposition to the trap, by the action of intense heat; the formation is about forty feet in breadth. A mile south of Douglas, it has been opened as a quarry, where stones for "*road metal*," "*drystone dykes*," and building houses are dug; houses built with this stone, by Moffat masons, in their "*best style*," have a fine appearance.

A few years ago the draining of sheep pasture among the hills commenced, but little was done till lately, when almost every tenant *set about the work* in good earnest, and the change produced on the quality of the herbage is great, and pays well.

Before the farmers began to drain the land, particularly the muirs, the streams, after a great fall of rain, rose slowly, and having arrived at their height, decreased in the same manner; the channels of the rivers then were sufficiently large to contain the water that flowed into them, and thus it passed away without overflowing the banks, except when the fall of rain or the melted snow had been unusually great; but now, from the numerous *drains* which have been made, the river rises to high flood in an incredibly short time, tears up the banks, and overflows the holms to a great extent; at particular seasons, the injury done to land and crops is very great, and, as drainage is increasing, the evil also is increasing. The channel of Douglas-water, must be one-half larger than it now is, or the holms on its banks must cease to be cultivated.

Three centuries ago a breed of grey horses was established in Clydesdale by the Hamilton family; it was on horses of this breed that the old regimental "corps of cavalry"—the Scots Greys—was first mounted, and it still retains its colour. At a later period a different race was introduced in the west, and chiefly in Clydesdale, which still remains; it is excellently adapted both for cart and carriage; their breed, in a highly improved state, is found on almost every farm; in the parish there are also horses, which, though not "*thorough bred*," have a considerable "*sprinkling of blood*," and on these the spruce farmers of Douglas are mounted.

The first person who ploughed with two horses, without a "*gadman*," was an English farmer from Northumberland, of the name of Frater, who took a lease of the farm of Wolfcrooks, in the north boundary of Douglas parish, about the middle of last century; the neighbours and others flocked to Wolfcrooks to see, as a wonderful sight, a man ploughing with two horses, without a man to guide them; at that time every plough was drawn by four horses. In the beginning of last century there was scarcely a fence of any kind in the parish; the oldest kind was the earthen, or "turf-dyke;" it was a very imperfect fence, and required to be repaired every year. *Dykes* of this kind for defending the arable fields, or for "march dykes," were repaired every year after the crops were sown; towards the end of the century "*dry stone dykes*" began to be built. Forty years ago there were few thorn hedges, and these few were in a wretched state from want of dressing. Within the last twelve years a considerable number of wire fences have been *raised*. When properly constructed, they present an insuperable barrier to sheep and cattle, but they afford no shelter from the cold blast, and in the landscape they have a cheerless appearance.

The prevailing names of the older families are—Inglis, Symington, Stevenson, Dickson, Willison, Wilson, M'Kinlay, Brown, Haddow, Johnstone, Crawford, Sloan. There have been millers of the name of Stevenson in Earls-mill since its erection in the sixteenth century. There is a farmer in Monkshead called Symington, whose ancestors have been tenants of the same farm for some hundreds of years. There are many in the parish of the name of Symington. The name of Dickson is borne by many in the parish, and all who bear this name boast of their descent from "Doughty Dickson," the faithful adherent of the great and good Sir James Douglas. The names which have been given abound in the parish. There is not an individual of the name of Douglas in the parish, except an old man who lately came from a neighbouring parish. The non-resident proprietor of Monkshead is Douglas. It is strange that in the seventeenth and eighteenth centuries the name of Douglas was borne but by a few. Now the name of Douglas, we may say, is extinct. The name of even that powerful family has ceased to be connected with the estate of Douglas—the family and the name gone.

The "trockit" and "black-faced" sheep, about the end of last century, constituted the greatest part of the flocks on every farm. The face and legs of the trockit sheep were blotched with black and white; they were inferior to the real black-faced sheep. The pure black-faced sheep were distinct from these, and in greater numbers. "His body is of a plump, barrel shape; his head is horned, and his face and legs are black as jet, without any mixture of white. His face is set off with a thick, prominent collar of wool surrounding his neck. His wool is superior, both in quantity and quality, to the trockit sheep." "It is uncertain whence the black-faced breed was originally derived, but there is a tradition of its having been *first* planted upon the King's farm in the forest of Ettrick. That farm used to contain 5000 sheep for the use of the King's household, and *probably* gave rise to that mode of sheep-farming which still subsists in the south of Scotland, namely, store-farming" The present system of sheep-farming does not appear to have taken place till about the end of the reign of James VI. Before that period the mountainous south country districts were kept under a stock of black cattle, and some small straggling flocks of sheep. "When the sheep farming came to be extended, the practice of muir burning, for the improvement of the sheep pasture, was introduced, and has continued." "A farm in the country of Ardgour, not far from Fort-William, was turned, in the year 1764, into sheep pasture. In the month of June, twenty-nine scores of ewes and wedders were brought from Douglas, in Clydesdale, and placed upon it. This was the *first stock of south country sheep* that was settled beyond the chain. Their price at Douglas, on an average, was 6s 6d each. Their driving from Douglas to Ardgour, in twelve days, cost 5d a-head, and only three of the whole flock were left upon the journey. As the farm was rented, the grass of each sheep stood only 6½d."

Forty years ago a few goats were kept on some farms; now there are none, this kind of stock being found unprofitable.

There are roe deer in the woods. It was considered, when the first of them was seen in the plantations, that they had escaped from the deer park at Hamilton. They are now in considerable numbers, and carefully protected. Foxes are in considerable numbers. They do not burrow in the ground, but make their abode under the dense brushwood and under rubbish from the branches of felled trees in the plantations around Douglas. The farmers complain of no depredations committed by them on lambs and poultry. The abundance of hares, rabbits, pheasants, etc., offer them a supply of food without exertion. When there were few plantations, and game scarce, the farmers sustained great loss of lambs and poultry. Beaters are sent into the wood, and scores of persons, with guns, are stationed so as to command the avenue which the fox must enter when he moves before the beaters, and a number of foxes are killed at every "fox-shooting." No fox-hounds have hunted in the parish within the memory of the oldest inhabitant.

There are otters in Douglas-water, and the havoc which they make of the fish in the water and its tributaries is great. Fishes partly devoured are frequently found, the remains of the otter's supper. The otter is a dainty fellow; it is only certain parts of the fish it will eat when he has "pick and wale" at command.

There were no rabbits in the parish in a wild state before 1830. They first made their appearance three miles below the town, and increased rapidly. In a few years they overspread the whole of the parish, and found also their way into the neighbouring ones. The farmers loudly complained of the depredations committed by them. In a severe winter they barked hundreds of trees and thorn hedges.

Every young plantation, when not protected, was entirely destroyed. The Earl of Home is endeavouring to extirpate them, but the extermination is slow, on account of the extent of cover.

There are squirrels in the woods, but at one time they were more numerous. From a cause unknown, they have decreased.

There is not a magpie in the parish. No sooner does one enter it than it is shot. Their destruction is for the preservation of game. There are jays in the plantations. Wood pigeons are in great numbers, and do damage. Jack-daws are numerous about Douglas Castle, and build in holes of the aged trees, etc.

Forty years ago there was a rookery at Douglas Castle, and the number of its inhabitants was great; but on account of the damage which they did, they were expelled. After forty years' banishment, they returned and took possession of their former habitation; and this happening to take place in the year in which the Earl of Home entered into possession of the Douglas estates, the people regarded their return as a *lucky omen*—that it was something that *boded luck* to both parties taking possession.

Game is abundant, and in great variety—pheasants, black-game, grouse, partridges, wild-ducks, snipes, hares, rabbits, etc. The game is preserved carefully, and at great expense, but the poacher manages to obtain game in season and out of season.

Corn-growing parishes suit poultry best. Douglas cannot be called a poultry-producing parish, although there be a poultry-house at every *onstead*, the inhabitants of which are only a few hens and a cock. There are no geese in the parish, except a few at Douglas Castle. At every farm-house a few ducks are to be seen. Cadgers, with donkeys and creels, perambulate the parish and collect eggs, chickens, etc., the gudewife receiving tea, tobacco, etc.

There are many hives of bees in the parish. It is well adapted to the keeping of bees. Pasturage affords greater and better supply of food for bees than land under cultivation. Where heather abounds, and is in flower, bees can collect more honey in six weeks than they could in many places during the season. Many in the town who keep bees take the hives into the muirs, and place them under the care of the shepherd when the heather is in bloom. Honey, superior to that which was gathered on the thyme-clad Hybla and Hymettus, and of which the ancients boasted, is obtained every year, in great abundance, from the heather bloom of Auchensaugh, Elvan's-hill, and Glespen-muir. The produce of honey in a *favourable year* is great; but the product from bees is very precarious.

Flax is not now grown in the parish. In the olden time great quantities were raised by the farmer for home consumption. Female servants in farm-houses, at the beginning of this century, had part of their wages paid in flax. It was usual for them to have a *forpet* of flax seed sown, and the produce, little or much, formed part of their wages. There is now no flax-mill in the parish. It may be stated that female servants in many places had fleeces of wool given

to them as part of wages. There is now no inducement to grow flax
and manufacture it at home. All the various fabrics which formerly
were made of flax can be obtained cheaper.

In the days of our forefathers every farmer sowed hemp seed.
The portion of ground set apart for the seed was called *the hemp-rig*,
as a ridge of land was usually what was required; but if the ridges
were small, two were considered necessary. The hemp was made
into various articles for home use. The principle article was ropes,
and used for various purposes. In the winter evenings the hemp
was manufactured. Now there is no "*hemp-rig.*"

Hazleside is about two miles west of Douglas. The house and
lands of Hazleside were given by good Sir James Douglas to his
trusty servant "Thomas Dickson." Dickson fell fighting with the
English at the chancel door of St Bride's Church on Palm Sunday.
There is scarcely a vestige of the old mansion of Hazleside remaining.
There are indications that it had been a building of magnitude
and strength. Some very old trees remain and continue to brave
the blasts of winter. They consist of plane and ash. The greater
is plane. Hazleside (the site of the house) is now included in
the south-west end of a large plantation that was formed about
the end of last century. The place that is now called Hazleside
is a farm-house of two stories. It is upon the site of what was the
old farm building belonging to Hazleside. The name of the "office
buildings" of Hazleside was the "Byers," and by some of the oldest
inhabitants of the vale it is still called the "Byers." Parts of the
old building were arched.

A company of Highlanders, on their retreat from England in
1745, visited Douglas on their way to the north. They halted two
days in Douglas. To the inhabitants they were most unwelcome
visitors. They made free with property of every kind which they
required or had a desire to possess. Shoes were an article which
they were very desirous to obtain. Some of them were barefooted,
and others had shoes in the *last stage of service*. Tradition says that
when an inhabitant was seen by them with a pair of good shoes, he
was saluted with *shange progues!* If the person showed no inclina-
tion for an exchange, by parting with his shoes, they were, without
ceremony, pulled off. The same party carried off from Douglas Castle
a sword, which, after the battle of Culloden, was recovered by the
Duke of Douglas, and is now in Bothwell Castle. From the
manner in which the Highlanders conducted themselves, they were
a heavy burden upon the town. They were got quit of in rather
a curious way. An individual in Douglas wrote a letter, as if it
had been written by an officer in His Majesty's army (who, with
a company of soldiers, was in pursuit of the enemy), and sent it to
Douglas. The substance of the letter was, that the people of Douglas should use all means to detain the Highlanders till the King's
troops should reach Douglas. The letter was dropped on the street.
In the morning it was picked up by a Highlander and taken to

Douglas Castle, which the Highland officers had taken possession of for their quarters. In an hour after the letter had reached the castle, the Highlanders were moving from Douglas under the maledictions of those who had suffered from them.

There are no Roman remains in the parish. No camps, Roman or British. Part of the head of a bronze spear was found in a rivulet near Cormacoup—supposed to be Roman.

On the top of Kirktondyke-hill (now covered with wood), there are the remains of a cairn called the "Captain's Cairn." The remains indicate a small cairn. Tradition is silent respecting it.

"Bryce's Cross" is three miles south of Douglas, on the summit of the Blackgate-hill. It consists of a very small cairn of stones, about three feet in height. Tradition says that a packman of the name of Bryce was murdered on the spot where the cairn has been raised. In Catholic countries a cross is erected where a murder has been committed. This was also the usage in Scotland in Catholic times. The cross is gone; but the little cairn marks the spot. It is on the old track over the hill from Glasgow to Douglas. The old road is along the edge of a black "flow-moss."

There were Covenanters belonging to the parish. Some of them suffered much in the persecuting times. One called Alexander Brown—some of his descendants live in town. Another of the name of Grey; there are also descendants of his living in Douglas. And James Gavin, a tailor, had his ears cut off by Claverhouse's dragoons, who found him in his hiding-place on Airne-Salloch-burn, a mile south of Douglas. Gavin was transported to Barbadoes. After the Revolution he returned to Douglas, and built a house of one storey in the High Street. On the lintel of the door the tailor's "goose," "cawboard," and "shears" are sculptured, and remain to this day. A number of cottars, believed to have embraced *Covenanting principles*, were ejected from the land of Cormacoup; but few were persecuted in the parish.

The meal basin of John Brown, the "godlie carrier," who was shot by Claverhouse at Priesthill, is in Douglas. The basin is of plane tree, and capacious. It will hold two pecks of meal—*old measure*. It gives indications of the ravages of time by the number of *worm holes* which it displays. It is preserved as a valued relic of a godly man who sealed his testimony with his blood.

A rolling pin was used in the preparation of oatcakes for a few Covenanters who came to a farm-house, weary and hungry, in their flight from "Bothwell Brig." The gudeman was friendly to the *Covenanting cause*, and with heart and hand encouraged those who supported it. The oatcakes which had been prepared for family use were soon exhausted. A maiden was instantly set to work to prepare more. Tradition says that for *three* hours the fugitives kept the maiden, who was not *slack* at work, busily engaged in preparing cakes for them. Tradition also says that for *two hours* they ate faster than she could prepare for them. The rolling pin, which was

*y*

of so much service on that disastrous day to the men of the covenant, is carefully preserved at Douglas.

On the right bank of Douglas-water, two miles below Douglas Castle, there is an oblong mount called Boncastle. The name by some is supposed to be derived from a fort of observation which was situated upon its summit. Eighty years ago, when the House of Douglas was desirous to get the town of Douglas transferred to Mill-holm, near the base of Boncastle, that mount was fixed on for the site of the parish church. The project failed, as what would have been given to the people as the value of their houses in Douglas, would not have raised houses for them at Millholm.

The burial place of suicides is on the boundary line between the parishes of Douglas and Crawfordjohn, and on the march between (of old) two "lairds' lands." The form of graves is distinctly seen, although no burial has taken place there within the memory of the oldest inhabitant. Long after it ceased to be a burial place, many felt "eerie" in passing it under cloud of night.

Auchensaugh is a hill south-east of Douglas, and nearly mid-way between Douglas and Crawfordjohn. On a level spot on the east side of the hill, the covenants were renewed in 1712. The form which was observed at Borland-hill, in the parish of Lesmahagow, when the covenants were renewed in 1689, was followed there except the confession of individual sins, which was omitted.

The meeting of Estates at Edinburgh granted leave to raise a regiment, chiefly of "west countrymen," to be under the command of the Earl of Angus. There were rumours of an invasion from Ireland, and also reports that Claverhouse was raising troops in the north. "A general meeting" of Covenanters was held on the 13th of May, 1689, at Douglas. At this meeting it was agreed to "embody the next day." On the 14th of May, 1689, "The Angus Regiment" (as it was called) was embodied in a holm called the Marquis's Holm, on the north bank of Douglas-water, and about an hundred yards south of the town. The regiment was to consist of twenty companies, forming two battalions. The necessary complement of men was readily obtained. Of those who enlisted, a considerable number belonged to Douglas and its neighbourhood. The command was given to James, Earl of Angus, eldest son of the Marquis of Douglas, and from him it was called "the Angus Regiment." Afterwards it was called "the Cameronian Regiment," some say in honour of Cameron, who fell at Ayr's Moss. Most probably it was called "the Cameronian Regiment" from the number of men who composed it being of like principles with Cameron. It is now the 26th Regiment of the line. Immediately after being enrolled it marched to Edinburgh, and took up a position before the Castle—which still held out for James—and was of service in the reduction of that stronghold. In three months after being enrolled at Douglas, it covered itself with glory at Dunkeld. The Cameronian Regiment distinguished itself at home and abroad, and its valour has suffered no diminution.

Between the town and the castle, and on the east side of the approach to the castle, is the "Gallow Knowe." It is a small eminence, a little swell of the ground. When the Barons of Douglas possessed the power of death and life over their vassals, not a few were hanged for little than "*just to please the Laird.*" Tradition has handed down the case of a customer weaver in Poniel district, who, having been accused of pilfering yarn given him by the gudewives of the district to make into cloth, was tried, and found guilty. The sentence passed upon him was, that next day he was to be hanged on the Gallow Knowe. When he was upon the ladder, and the rope was about his neck, the laird asked him if he could recommend an honest weaver to the district. The answer was—"As I am a dying man, I cannot, with a clear conscience, recommend any weaver as honest." "Take him down," was the order of the Baron; "it's better to keep the ill kent, than to tak the unkent." On the Gallow Knowe many brave Southerns came to an untimely end. The "Gallow Tree" and the "Hanging Tree" at the castle were in requisition for the work when the castle was taken by Scots or English.

James V. was on his way from the west to Douglasdale, alone. A little to the east of the place where Muirkirk now stands, he came upon a company of gypsies encamped, and preparing their noon-day meal. He was invited to join them in the repast, and readily accepted the invitation. He asked not, for conscience' sake, how the mutton had been procured. After a few rounds of something to drink stronger than the water of the neighbouring spring, he began, as was his practice, to use too much freedom with the younger females. This exasperated the gypsies. After much foul speech on both sides, the gypsies, to punish him, when they were about to move their camping-places for the night, strapped upon his back a heavy budget, and forced him to carry it to Cormacoup, where he revealed to the gudeman who he was, and sent a note to the Earl of Douglas to come to Cormacoup with some followers. On the arrival of the Earl he ordered the gypsies to be hanged on a tree. This was done; the tree remains, and is called the "hanging tree."

According to tradition, the village of Uddington had almost obtained the honour of being made a royal burgh by James V., "the King of Commons," and of royal burgh making celebrity. His majesty slept one night in Uddington, and the house in which he slept has been preserved. It is a very humble-looking structure, and is now used as a byre and barn. There is scarcely an opening to admit light, and the doorways are very low.

Tradition says that James V., travelling in disguise, slept one night at Kirktondyke—a farm-house of humble appearance about a mile south-east of Douglas; in the morning, after a homely breakfast, he sent one of the household to Douglas Castle with the message, the Marquis was to come to Kirktondyke, and speak to the "Guidman of Ballangeich;" the Marquis instantly obeyed the command; after a long conference they separated—the Marquis returned to the castle, and the King went on his way to Crawford Castle.

Near Cairntable there are vestiges of a fort; it is known that in the olden time the Douglasses had a stronghold "on the skirts of Cairntable." The castle appears to have been a strong place. Archibald, seventh Earl of Angus, when threatened by Henry of England for slaying Ralph Ivers, says—"Is my brother-in-law offended because I am a good Scottish man? Because I have revenged the defacing of the tombs of my ancestors at Melrose upon Ralph Ivers? They were better men than he, and I ought to have done no less! And will he take my life for that? Little knows King Henry the skirts of Cairntable. I can keep myself there from the English host!"

On the farm of Glentaggart (the priest's glen), there was a chapel; nothing is known respecting it, and not a vestige of the building remains; but the font, which is stone, has been preserved.

Near Andershaw there was a chapel, and burying-ground connected with it; the font stone, after being mutilated by the builder's hammer, was put into a "drystone dyke." Near the site of the chapel there is a well, called "the chapel well;" in purity and goodness it cannot be excelled; this spring is of extraordinary strength; it forms at once a stream remarkable for its volume of water.

At Parish-holm, west boundary of the parish, there was a chapel founded by James IV. "In 1531 James V. granted in Mortmain to Schir George Eirmair, the chaplain of said chapel, and to his successor there the four merk lands of Parroch-holm."

About four miles east of Douglas there is a farm-house called "the chapel;" at this place there was a chapel or small church—no part of it remains; it furnished too readily materials for house-building to be spared. The chapel here, and those that were at Andershaw and Glentaggart, were places of worship before St Bride's Church of Douglas and the chapel at Parish-holm were built; church accommodation was amply provided for the people by the Roman Catholics, and the priests were comfortably supported.

Douglas is a "burgh of barony;" has a baron bailie, and a baron court, and there is a jail connected with the baron court. The culprit can be imprisoned only for a short time without examination, but he can be remanded again and again. Lately an improvement was made upon the jail; there are now two cells, formerly there was only one; when there happened to be two criminals—one a male, and the other a female—only one of them could be incarcerated at the same time. According to an old Scottish Act, the window or opening of the baron jail *must* "be to the street;" the reason given was, that the prisoner might not be forgotten and starved to death, as by the window being to the street he could make his necessities known. Thirty years ago, when the prisoner had the sympathy of the good dames near the jail, they handed him tea-and-toast between the bars of the window; since then the space between the bars is greatly contracted; tea-and-toast cannot be introduced, but they can whisper him a word of comfort, and bid good night.

Of old, in Douglas, the baron bailie had great power, and exercised it in ecclesiastical matters. He apprehended and imprisoned parties who would not submit to the discipline of the church. He put out of the parish "incomers" who had not *"testificates,"* and who either could not, or would not, procure them.

There are four libraries in town—Established Church Library, U. P. Church Library (400 vols., free), Free Church Library, Parochial School Library; one at *New Mains,* for the workmen connected with the Douglas estate; at Rigside, one Sabbath School Library; at Table Stane, one Sabbath School Library.

There is a gas work in the parish, by a company, in £1 shares; price, to consumers, 7/6 the 1000 feet. The late Lord Douglas gave a donation of £200, to assist in erecting the work, that it might be a greater benefit to the town; the streets are *scantily* lighted from the donation; the work pays a high dividend.

After the Reformation two-thirds of St Bride's Church was appropriated to the service of the Protestant religion, and continued to be the parish church till 1781, when a new church was ordered on an eminence on the east side of the village. A part of the ruins was converted into the Baron jail and court house, after the Kirkton of Douglas had been made a burgh of Barony, sometime before 1668. The heaviest stroke fell upon St Bride's Church after it ceased to be a place of worship. Much of it was pulled down to raise the walls of the parish church. This wholesale delapidation was the work of a *Goth*—the factor to the Duke of Douglas. If the chancel had not contained sepulchral monuments belonging to the house of Douglas, the whole of the building would have been swept away. There is a tower with a bell at the west end of the chancel. There are some very old houses on the south of St Bride's Church. The lower storey of some of them is arched. These houses were connected with the church. St Bride's is in the middle of the churchyard. The old manse, glebe, and garden were situated within what now forms part of "the *policies*" of the castle. The ruins are carefully preserved. Many travellers (and the number is increasing) visit them, and express their admiration of these remains of antiquity.

The dress of the men in the middle of the last century was composed of a very coarse fabric. The cloth was of the natural colour of the wool, and called "hodden grey." Lairds thought themselves well dressed for church with a black *kelt* coat of their wives spinning and dying. The married women wore a *"close mutch."* Their Sunday gown was *"lindsey-woolsey."* The young women wore their hair tied round with a *"snood,"* and the plaid drawn over their heads supplied the want of a bonnet. What a contrast between the past and the present age in female dress! Sixty years ago few were clothed in black at funerals. With some the only part of the black clothing was the coat. The company presented garments of almost every colour. One part of the *dress* was grey, another part of it was blue, etc. The clothes at that time, without exception, were manufactured at home, and were in general of a coarse fabric. The artistic labour bestowed upon garments in that age did not indicate that the tailor had been guided by any *scientific* principles *in taking the measurement* of the wearer, and in the cutting of the cloth. The clothes were deemed a "*perfect fit*" if the person for whom they were made could *wriggle* himself into them. No matter how tight they were, or how loosely they hung about him; it was not a "*misfit*" unless they were so small as not to admit the body and its members. Tailors at the end of last century made the greater part of female apparel, at least the gown was made by them. Tailors sixty years ago and less went to the houses of their employers and "*made and mended*" clothes. It was a bustling time when the tailors were in the house. Home made clothing is now used only by the shepherds and the small farmers for "*every day's wear.*"

The principal employment is handloom weaving. Nearly all the weavers are in the town. The number of weavers is 230. A few years ago the number was 300. Before end of last century there were thirty "*customer* weavers" in Douglas; now there are only two, and these are sufficient to make into cloth all the home spun materials. Boys are put *early* to the loom, and *too soon* become their "*own masters.*" About twenty young women are handloom weavers. They earn their own bread, and also contribute to the support of the younger branches of the family, and in this *latter duty* they are more dutiful than their brothers.

The condition of the poor is greatly improved. In the olden time the weekly allowance doled out by the session was exceedingly scanty. Those who could walk received *tickets* or *badges* from the session giving them a *licence* to beg within the parish. Since the operation of the Poor Law Act the comfort of the poor is greatly increased by additional allowance and medical attendance. The poor in the parish of Douglas receive more from "*the board*" than the poor in the neighbouring parishes.

In the town there are grocers 10; bakers 2; weavers 230; watchmaker, etc., 1; drapers, etc., 5; banks two (Commercial and City of Glasgow); booksellers 2; shoemakers 3; tailors 6; butcher 1; surgeon 1; joiners 4; slaters 2; plasterer 1; plumber 1; dealers in crockery ware 3; carriers 2—one to Glasgow twice a-week, one to Edinburgh once a-week; coach 1; *dancing master* 1; *rural policeman*—his residence in Douglas—has a wide district—1; weavers' agents 3; lodging houses for vagrants and chapmen, etc., 4; smiths 2; a fiddler 1; saddler 1; chimney sweepers 3; mole catcher 1; post runner 1—every lawful day to Uddington and Rigside, etc.; innkeepers 6; a blind letter-carrier to New Mains, Castlemains, etc.

Every farmer had a plough made before he commenced the labour of the field. He provided wood, and engaged a carpenter to make the plough, and this was *always* accomplished by him in *one day*.

The farmer not only provided the wood, but also the necessary iron work. The plough was considered to be of good workmanship if it lasted, after a few repairs, in working order for a year. The carpenter received one shilling, with victuals, for a long day's work. Iron ploughs then were not dreamed of, ploughs which the farmer has found to be the best, notwithstanding the price paid for them.

At middle of last century there were no carts in the parish. Everything was carried on horseback—as grain to the mill, coals from the heugh or pit. This mode of transit may account for, in part, the narrow streets in towns which have any claim to antiquity. The vehicle which preceded the *cart* was the car. On it the corn was carried from the field to the barn-yard. In many respects the car is better adapted to a hilly country than the cart; where the car would be more suitable in the field than the cart.

A little before the end of last century the gudewife, when on horseback, was generally seated behind her husband, on a comfortable kind of saddle called a pillion. The riding-dress of the dame was in keeping with her plain every-day clothing, an ample "skirt" of home manufacture. If the day was fine, a black silk hood, drawn over a close "mutch," covered her head. If the day threatened rain, a grey woollen hood was the covering which she donned, and a home-spun cloak, of a fabric so close as to be almost waterproof. The gudeman's "braid blue bonnet"—his body covering half cloak, half coat in form, and his "gamushions," were in harmony with the appearance of his dame. There was nothing of vulgarity in the mode of locomotion. It was in this way that Queen Elizabeth went to Parliament, when she rode through the streets of London, seated on a pillion behind the Lord-Chancellor.

It was not till near the end of the last century that umbrellas made their appearance in the parish. The first person who used one attracted the attention of old and young. Many satirical remarks were made upon the bearer of it. Its usefulness, with that of the *plaid*, was frequently discussed, and the conclusion universally arrived at was, that it was a useless article, and that it was a silly vanity that caused the individual to carry it. The first time that one was brought to church, some of the *unco guid* cried out against the act as a profanation of the Sabbath, and that it was more like going to the play than to the house of prayer.

At the beginning of this century there was "tent preaching" in the parish at the celebration of the Lord's Supper, in July, by the Established Church, which set up "the tent" in the "kirk-yard." A number of the neighbouring churches were vacant on that day by the ministers being at Douglas; a number of both sexes from the parishes where the churches were vacant came to Douglas, and the gathering at the "*tent*" was great; many who came to Douglas did not come to worship, but to spend the day, as a holy-day, in recreation and sensual enjoyment, and not a few, on leaving the town, afforded evidence of the kind of potations in which they had indulged. The Lord's

Supper was administered by the Reformed Presbyterian Church in August, and on the Sabbath on which it was administered there was "tent preaching," and this continued to be the practice till lately. There being no public-house near Rigside, innkeepers came from Lanark and Douglas on the Sabbath morning with "tents" for the sale of porter, and ale, and spirits, etc.; the tents for *drinking in* were pitched within 200 yards of the tent for *preaching in*. Half-a-score, at least, of canvas-covered tents was considered not more than sufficient for furnishing refreshments for the people; these tents were full of company from morning to night; in the afternoon many were reeling about drunk, and two or three fights took place in the course of the day; when the assembly broke up, some were left on the field in a helpless state of drunkenness. The scenes described by Burns in his "Holy Fair" fall far short of those which were seen at Rigside. When servants made engagements for the summer half-year, this was one of the stipulations, viz., that they should have "Douglas' race fair day, and Rigside sacramental day to themselves." The abolition of tent preaching has been productive of good order and decency on "sacramental occasions." The want of tent preaching is regretted by some who had seen the tent in its palmy days, and who had visited it for the purpose of being amused.

Rigside is four miles north-east of Douglas, on the Ayr and Edinburgh road. The original name of the place was Newton, and it was designated by this name in the seventeenth and in the middle of the eighteenth century. The designation Rigside was derived from a house that bore that name in the district. It consists for the most part of colliers' houses. Lord James Douglas, the lord of the manor, caused new and comfortable cottages to be built in the room of those that were pulled down. The old habitations had been wretchedly constructed, and slovenly kept; and when pulled down, their appearance was miserable in the extreme.

Braidlea-burn is a small stream which has its source in the hills west, north-west of Douglas, and falls into the Douglas-water opposite the town. It runs into a deep ravine clothed with natural wood. In this ravine good Sir James Douglas, with his little band of trusty followers, secreted himself after leaving Hazleside on that Palm Sunday when he slew the English in the chancel of St Bride's Church, took possession of the Castle of Douglas, and razed it to the ground. It was in the ravine of Braidlea-burn that he waited for the signal of advance, to be given by his faithful servant, "Doughty Dickson," who went in disguise as a "thrasher," with arms beneath his cloak. The place in the ravine where the ambuscade rested was about 400 yards from the church, and in sight of it, as there were no buildings on the west side of the churchyard.

Tradition assigns the following reason why James V. so frequently visited Douglasdale:—That his Majesty, when he appeared in Douglasdale, was on his way to visit a "lady" of the name of Lindsay, who lived a few miles south-east of Uddington, where he slept one night. His connexion with the lady was in keeping with the character which history has given us of "the King of the Commons." The greater part of his time was spent in visiting the many mistresses which he had in various parts of the kingdom. His followers said it was to make himself minutely acquainted with the state of the country that he strolled through in disguise. Few believed that apology then, and fewer believe it now.

Smiling-gill is a small dell or hollow, about 400 yards west of Douglas, and nearly opposite to it. It is a pleasant and retired spot, and for open-air preaching a more suitable place could not be found. In this little dell the Reformed Presbyterians (or Cameronians as they were commonly designated) about the middle of the last century administered the sacrament of the Lord's Supper. There was a great assembly when that "ordinance" was to be "administered." Many came from a great distance in Scotland, and some even from Ireland, regardless of toil and expense. A number of ministers engaged in the work. The services were exceedingly protracted. Many inhabitants of Douglas, eighty years ago, went to the "Craigbraehead," a little eminence on the west side of the town, and adjoining to it, from which the place where the dell was situated (but not the dell itself) could be seen, and there heard, at three o'clock on Monday morning, the singing of psalms, that part of the service which should have been concluded on Sabbath evening, but which had been postponed on account of the length of the previous services, until three o'clock on Monday morning; after this there was a cessation or interval of seven hours before the commencement of the proper work on Monday. Many, during the hours of rest, never left the place of worship, but having wrapped themselves in their plaids, etc., lay down to sleep, at least to lie in a recumbent posture till the work of the day began. The fervour of the mountain preacher was not cooled by the protracted services of Sabbath, and the attention of the multitudes was unabated. The practice of their fathers, during many years of persecution, to worship in the open air, and to administer the sacraments in some secluded spot, had been adopted by them, and they found themselves more at home on the mountain side than in the comfortably seated meeting-house, where they could then worship God, none daring to make them afraid.

Janet Clelland lived in "Slidderie Brae," then a street in Douglas, with houses only on the south side; then unpaved with "steppingstanes." Here and there, after a fall of rain, the street was in a slippery state; hence the name of "Slidderie Brae." Capt. Paton, who was severely wounded in the skirmish at Ayr's Moss, and taken prisoner, was brought to Douglas on the evening of the day of the fight, with his wounds undressed. Janet Clelland, a "motherly and handy woman," dressed his wounds, and administered to his comforts as far as circumstances would permit. Honourable mention is made of her by Wodrow. The house in which she lived is still standing. Janet Clelland was "a mother in Israel," and her memory lives with

z

those who take an interest in the history of those who struggled, and bled, and died, on behalf of civil and religious liberty.

There are a number of mineral springs in the parish. There are three strong chalybeate springs near the town—one at Springhill, in a plantation behind the house; another in Mansefield; and a third at Brachead. The water of these springs is more strongly impenetrated with iron than the water of some celebrated chalybeate wells. The water, sprinkled on clothes lying on the washing-green, makes them red with the oxide of iron. When a little strong tea is poured into a tumbler half filled with the water, the mixture soon becomes black as ink—the gallic acid having combined with the iron in the water: and one equally strong is at Elvanshill-wood. There are also a few springs so strongly impenetrated with the carbonic of lime, that the spouts at kettles in daily use are soon closed up by it. There is one of this kind and strength at Wildshaw lime works. No medicinal use is made of these springs. For drinking they are not agreeable, except to an acquired taste. They cannot be used in the washing of clothes, and the chalybeate is ruinous to clothes when it is applied to them on the bleaching-green.

Robert Dick is the blind letter-carrier from the post-office, Douglas (but not officially connected with it), to Castlemains, the residence of Thomas Rennie Scott, Esq., Chamberlain to the Countess of Home. Robert Dick is a wonderful man, considering his age and total blindness. He was a soldier under the late Lord Archibald Douglas, when Colonel of the Forfarshire Militia. His eye-sight having failed him from amaurosis, he was discharged, and returned to Douglas, that he might earn a comfortable livelihood. Mr Scott employed him to carry his letter-bag daily to and from Castlemains to the post-office at Douglas. When a "runner" was appointed by the post-office, for daily and free delivery of letters, etc., between Douglas and Rigside—which included all the places visited by the blind carrier—Mr Scott did not accept of the free delivery, but retained his faithful bagman at full pay. For many years the old soldier has punctually performed his postal duties. In summer and in winter, in heat and cold, in rain and in sleet, in frost and in snow, he may be seen holding on the noiseless tenor of his way. So well is he acquainted with the track over which he daily moves, that he can tell at which part of it he is as correctly as if he was blessed with perfect vision. Not only does he find his way to Castlemains, etc., but he can move on with equal ease and certainty to Uddington, and deliver letters, papers, and small parcels with which he has been entrusted. No complaints have ever been made against the blind letter-carrier for any neglect of duty. A money letter *is safe*, and this is more than can be said of it if committed to the post-office, where it is at the mercy of dissipated and pilfering officials.

Traditionary statements, if not recorded, will soon be lost. Many curious things have already perished. In the olden time, at "rockings," the old and elderly of both sexes entertained and amused one another with traditionary tales and anecdotes of various kinds; while the younger branches were enjoying themselves with fun and frolic. Newspapers have given a fatal blow to tradition. The extinction of it is only a matter of time, and that time will soon come. Now the conversation is not about what was *said* and *done* in bygone ages, but about the news of the day. With what zest did our fathers, the patriarchs of the parish, with the " nappy ale " mantling in the "bicker," take up, for instance, the traditions respecting the Cove- nanters, and as they quaffed the generous "barley bree," became warmer and louder in their praises of the heroic sufferers in the " reeling time!" Now it is politics, or something as unprofitable. With regard to truth, there may have been more of it in *tradition* than there may be in the newspapers. **J. J.**

[The " Rough Notes on the Parish of Douglas " were contributed by a minister who had been upwards of forty years in charge of a chapel there, and who recently demitted his charge to spend the last years of a useful life among friends resident in the south-east of Scotland. His paper shows him to be an amiable man. **A. M.**]

[The remarks on seeking for gold at Leadhills should have been given in continuation of the paper by J. N. at page 48.—A. M.]

At Leadhills, the search for gold, as an article of commerce, had been abandoned, although small quantities continued to be obtained by desultory and unauthorised washings, and sold as objects of curiosity. In 1863, however, the search for gold was more gene- rally resumed by the miners at Leadhills during their leisure hours; and in a few months many thousand grains were procured, princi- pally from the head of Longcleugh burn, the scene of Bulmer's operations. The average quantity of gold obtained per day was about twelve grains. This, considering the inefficient means used, and the small and rude apparatus employed in washing, is a good proof that it still might be wrought to profit. At the head of Longcleugh burn, as well as at many other places, the debris is upwards of fifteen feet in depth, the whole of which has more or less gold in it, pro- ducing, on an average, five grains per cubic yard of earth. Between this debris and the rock there is a layer of clay, mixed with which are gravel and oxide of iron, varying from one to ten inches thick, which is very rich of gold, producing ten grains per cubic foot. The largest nugget obtained in 1863 weighed seventy-two grains, being much less than those formerly procured, viz., from one to thirty ounces.

The Lanarkshire gold field extends for about twenty-five miles in length by twelve miles in width, yet it is only on Crawford Moor, in the neighbourhood of Leadhills, along the banks of the Glengonar and Shortcleugh waters and their tributaries, viz., over about eight square miles, that gold has ever been found in any great quantities.

From this space of ground, according to the best information that can be procured, upwards of £500,000 worth of gold has been obtained.

The rocks in the district are of the inferior stratified series, under the granwacke group, consisting of gneiss, mica, and clay-slate, and are traversed in every direction by auriferous quartz and other veins. These veins, with the exception of the one mentioned as being found "powdered with small gold" at Longcleugh-head, have never been wrought for gold, although small specks of the precious metal have been discovered in several of them at the surface; and it is quite evident that from these quartz veins the gold has been washed and dispersed over the district. It is very possible that from some at least of these veins, if proper means were adopted for reducing the quartz, a profitable yield might be realised. Here also, as well as in other gold regions, these veins must have been much richer at the surface than below; otherwise, as large nuggets would have been obtained in working them as are found in the alluvial deposits, which has not been the case as yet. I have therefore reason to think that none of the quartz veins in this district will produce gold—much, if any, below the surface. Indeed, there is sufficient data to prove that the auriferous quartz veins become degraded, as they descend, into veins of lead; for in the immediate vicinity of Leadhills, where the veins are now rich in lead, gold in large quantities has been obtained from the alluvial deposits on the sides of the streams traversing the said veins. This fact can only be accounted for by the supposition that these deposits have been washed off from the surface of the veins, which now at a lower depth produce lead.

J. N.

The Leadhills district of the parish of Crawford has received fair attention, in the "History of the Mines at Leadhills," as given at pages 50 to 63, Vol. I. of this Work; in the quotations from Pennant's tour last century; in the graphic article from *Household Words* of 1852; and the excellent paper by J. N. on the present state and prospects of the mines, with the account of gold-finding there; and no one could better inform on the subject, as the works are under his direction; and large as the recent outlay has been, it has already resulted in employing nearly double the number of miners, and at wages twice what they are reported to have been in 1857. The church at Leadhills forms part of the building locally known as the Hall—the shooting quarters of the Earls of Hopetoun, and home of their representative in the village. The accommodation in the church is good, the attendance regular, and the minister an earnest labourer among a flock living within the square mile which forms the reclaimed land in this upland district. A movement has recently taken place which has resulted in securing money enough to endow the chapel, and render it in future a church—*quoad sacra*. The manse is one of the least comfortable in Scotland; small in size, low in site, and most uninviting in appearance; but its present occupant has a library of extent and value rare for the district. The bracing air of the southern Highlands of Scotland does much to maintain the health of the miners,—otherwise their houses are ill ventilated; but it is one of the institutions of the locality to have a doctor, and one more experienced or more worthy it might be hard to find anywhere than is the present medical attendant of the miners. Born in the village, on the field in the Peninsula, North America, the West Indies, and elsewhere, he came home again, and has long been the educated and the hospitable man of the village; and few visit it who have not heard of his well-earned good name.

Crowning a knoll near the lower end of the village, is the kirkyard, of considerable extent, well enclosed, and thickly overgrown with grass, rank and tall, compared with the sparse vegetation around. The headstones—upright and well lettered—are numerous, and remarkable in that the legend of the accidents which so frequently bring death to the miner, are cut into—written on these memorials of the dead. At page 41 of this volume the Scotch miner is taunted with his love of "heavy literature"—his preference for the theological works of Chalmers to those of Channing, and the scarcity of light reading on the shelves of the Leadhills Library. This is more smart than accurate, as the catalogue of books shows on its pages the novels of Scott, Galt, and others; with a choice selection of books on biography, travels, chemistry, etc. A. M.

---

## ADDENDA ET CORRIGENDA.

### Vol. I.

Page 6, line 14—For "608," read, "606."

Page 7, line 9—For "Their capital," read, "The important city of Goden, on the Firth of Forth."

Page 18, line 28—For "axe," read, "hammer."

Page 19, line 1—"A short distance outside the rampart." It has, since this was written, been ascertained that the well referred to is situated upwards of a mile from this camp. We may here state that the pre-parochial antiquities of the parish of Lesmahago have been, since these pages were written, investigated with the utmost care and diligence by J. B. Greenshields, Esq., yr. of Kerse, to whom, indeed, we were indebted for most of our information on the subject. As he has now concentrated the information he has obtained into his "Annals of Lesmahago," we refer our readers to that work for details.

Page 19, line 10—Delete, "or Fauldhouse."

Page 20, line 5—After "jet," insert, "or rather cannel coal."

Page 20, line 6—For "Two similar celts," read, "A similar celt."

Page 20, line 7—"Another at Rogerhill." This is the same weapon as that described in page 18, as in the possession of Hope Vere, Esq.

Page 20, line 27—"Eighteen others." There is every reason to believe that there were only two urns found in this locality.

Page 20, line 29—For "Leeland," read, "Lee land."

Page 26, line 21—"Stone font." See Vol. II., p. 56.

Page 31, line 27—"A still larger example." When this was written, we had only seen an engraving of this weapon. Since then, however, we have had an opportunity of inspecting the implement itself, and have now no hesitation in stating, that our idea of it was a wrong one—that it is correctly described in the catalogue of the Arch. Museum in Edinburgh, 1856-7, and that it is, looking to its size, a hammer, although of such an unusual shape, that without adverting to its dimensions it might easily be mistaken for a large flail stone.

Page 56, line 13—Delete "the younger."

Page 59, line 23—After "purchased," insert, "or leased."

Page 69, line 20—For "Alexander I.," read, "Alexander II."

Page 150, line 23—For "baillie," read, "taillie."

Page 161, line 11 from bottom of page—For "270, 336, 316, 409, 318, 413," read, "270, 336; 316, 409; 318, 413."

Page 166, line 5—For "pp.," read, "p. 272, No. 329."

Page 184, line 22—For "1699," read, "1669."

Page 189, line 33—For "92," read, "92*."

Page 191, line 33—For "1699," read, "1669."

Page 239, last line—For "We have already seen he was censured," read, "He was censured, as we afterwards have occasion to mention more particularly."

Page 242, line 2—For "1783," read, "1683."

Page 391, line 31—For "Plate XIV.," read, "Plate XV., Figs. 1 & 2."

Page 442, line 7—For "1740," read, "1704."

## VOL. II.

Page 41, line 30—For "Alexander," read, "Archibald."

Page 46, line 7—For "took," read, "book."

Page 60, line 8—Delete "largely increased the possessions of the family, by his marriage with one of the daughters and co-heiress of Sir John Crawford of Crawfordjohn, and." This statement has been continually made in the histories of the house of Douglas, but is evidently erroneous. See Vol. I., p. 122.

Page 93, line 7—For "James," read "William."

Page 113—For "John, Lord Somerville," read, "Somerville of Cambusnethan."

Page 137, line 7—For "second marquis," read, "third marquis."

Page 142, line 24—For "Sir William," read, "Sir James."

Page 205, line 7—This statement is inaccurate, as there was no allegation that the conveyance of the lands of Draffan was forged. This accusation is confined to the barony of Crawfordjohn, etc., and the lands of Draffan were resigned as an equivalent of the back rent of them and certain moveable property, that Sir James Hamilton of Fynart had appropriated to himself without legal authority.

Page 215, line 8—After "would," insert "not."

Page 235, line 7—In giving this date we followed Wodrow, but since these pages were in type, we have found the following document among the Lauderdale papers in the British Museum. (Add. MSS., 23,116, fol. 121:—

"Edin. 1 April, 1679.—The phannaticks in Clidsdale are still so bold to resist and to assault the King's forces by force of arms. I gave formerly account that a party of armed men, well mounted on horseback, had surprised two or thrie dragoons in their quarters in the paroch of Lesmahagoe in Clidsdale. And what is now to be informed is the second part of the same tune, which is as follows:— Upon Sunday last, early in the morning, Major White (whose company of foot lyes at Lanark) got notice of a field conventicle which was to be kept within the paroch of Lesmahagoe (which belongs to the Duke of Hamilton). This being a great distance for foot to march and to come in time to dissipate them, the major commanded out a party of twenty dragoons, commanded by Lieut. Dalzell and Ensigne Menzies; upon their march to the place, they observed several persons at a distance going to the conventicle, some of which they followed. All of them took the mosses, where they catcht three or four prisoners, and left six dragoons to guard them. The rest of the dragoons went on to the place where the conventicle was kept, and ordered the other six to follow. Before they came at the place they took other thrie prisoners on horse-back, well mounted and well armed, and thereafter they observed where the conventicle was, but at that distance could not perceive that ther ver armed men. Then they marched and put a hill betwixt them and the conventicle, thinking thereby to surprize them. Bot when they came over the hill they perceived thrie or four companies of foot drawn up in order, about a hundreth a piece, and a troop of horse about sixty. Ther were of the foot about a hundreth and twenty armed with muskets and firlocks, the rest were armed with swords, halberts, and pickforks, and such like. The troop of horse were vell mounted, all of them had holster pistols, and many of them had carebines. Several of them had periwiggs and stuff cloaks, and some of them blew when they perceived the dragoons advancing (who wer bot fourteen with ther officers). The Whiggs formally drew out a party of eighty foot and advanced, the rest designed to surround the dragoons; whereupon the officers of the dragoons required them, in the King's name, to dissipate; whereupon the commander of the Whiggs' horse answered disdainfully, Farts in the King's teeth and the counsells, and all that has sent you, for we appear year for the King of heaven; and immediately thereafter the commanded party of the Whiggs presented and fired, and at the same time the dragoons fired upon them, and immediately thereafter the Whiggs' horse and foot fell in pell mell upon the dragoons, and wounded Lieut. Dalzell mortally, one whereof in the groyn or lisk with a partisan or pitchfork, and took him and seven dragoons prisoners. The Ensigne and the other seven dragoons made their retreat and escaped. The first six dragoons that guarded the thric prisoners thought it fitt never to come up, bot went straight back to Lanark with ther prisoners. The scuflle fell out about eleven o'clock on Sunday. After this they read the covenant to the Lieut. lying upon the ground wounded, and therafter went to ther conventicle, wher ther was four sermons and lectures, and at seven o'clock at night they dismissed the Lieut. and the seven dragoons ther prisoners, bot kept their horse and armes; one of the commanders of the Whiggs' foot was knowne to be of the name of Cleland, whose father lives in the town of Douglas. The captain of the Whiggs' horse is supposed one Hamiltoune, second son to the deceased Sir Thomas Hamiltoune of Prestoune. The rest are not yet knowne. Major White, immediately upon notice of this, sent several parties to follow the Whiggs, and to try whether they wer dissipate or wer yet together in army, and at the same time dispatched hither Ensigne Menzies, who gave this account to the committee of council this day at ten o'clock, and ve expect further account from Major White and my Lord Ross to-morrow what has further followed upon this. The committee is to report this to the council the morrow, and no doubt the council will send to yr. Grace the Major's letter, with what further account they get of this affair upon Thursday next. Ther is five or six prisoners sent in by my Lord Airlie from Kerse and Teviotdale, who are great rogues but of mean quality. This proves to be no good effects of the meeting at Hamiltoune that I wrote of by the last, at which meeting the Earle of Pearth was, and this day it is reported here that he is gone or going to London."

This document is not only interesting as a confidential account of the occurrence, drawn up for the information of the Government at the time, or from its discrepancy with Wodrow, but from the evidence it gives us of a *secret* military organisation among the Covenanters, which fully accounts for their unexpected success at Drumclog, and throws a new light upon many of the after proceedings of the officers and troops employed by the Government.

Page 273, l. 25—For "Mr Robert Burns," read "Mr Robert Birnie."

Page 318, line 2—For "Reformation," read "Restoration."

Page 332, line 12—Delete from "He married" to the end of the paragraph, and insert "He married Margaret Baillie, heiress of Lamington, by whom he had a daughter, who married Robert Dundas of Anniston. Their daughter and heiress married Admiral Sir John Lockhart Ross, by whose grandson the property is now held." (*See Lamington and Carstairs.*)

Page 340, line 20—For "1639," read "1369."

Page 412, line 10—For "Lady Carmichael," read "Lady Margaret Carmichael."

Page 509, line 4—For "1433," read "1543."

G. V. I.

# INDEX TO VOL. I.

## By G. V. I.

## PERSONS.

2 a

## PLACES.

# INDEX TO VOL. II.

## By G. V. I.

---

## PERSONS.

## PLACES.

[An INDEX, distinct and full, should enhance the value of these Volumes. The labour of constructing such has been undertaken by A. M.; and for such errors as may exist he alone is responsible.]

# INDEX TO VOL. I.

## By A. M.

### PERSONS.

## PLACES.

# INDEX TO VOL. II.

## By A. M.

## PERSONS.

## PLACES.

## ADDENDA ET CORRIGENDA EXTRA—See Page 200.

### Vol. II.—Page 208, Line 20.

Since this was written, our attention has been called to a passage in Stair's Institutes, B. iii., t. 5, sec. 50, which explains the nature of these competing brieves. Colonel Bannatyne married Marion, the daughter of the Laird of Blackwood. In contemplation of these nuptials, her father conveyed his estate to the Colonel "and the heirs, to be procreate betwixt him and her; which failing, to the heirs of the said Marion Weir by any other lawful husband, which failing, to the heirs of Bannatyne." Colonel Bannatyne died without issue of the marriage. His widow afterwards married Mr William Laurie, by whom she had a son. The question then arose whether, under the above destination, the estate belonged to the heirs of Colonel Bannatyne, or to the son of the second marriage. It was compromised by the son succeeding to the estate, and paying a sum of money to the Laird of Corehouse as the heir of his brother.

Vol. II., p. 418, line 16, for 1660, read 1650; and p. 419, line 15; p. 457, line 22, the same correction. Vol. II., p. 181, line 2, for "p. 26," read "p. 58;" p. 226, line 11, for "William," read "Robert;" p. 402, 2d line from bottom, for "1660," read "1670;" p. 513, line 10, for "1662," read "1626."        G. V. I.

# CONCLUSION.

In bringing this Work to a close, some commentary on the contents of the third—the Appendix Volume—may be allowable.

The article, pp. 1–18, on the agriculture of the Upper Ward, will be found good, having been produced by one of the most enterprising of the tenant-farmers of the Upper Ward of Lanarkshire.

John Taylor, who is reported to have died at Leadhills in the 137th year of his age, has due notice paid both to the story of his life, and the experience of his latter years—as see pp. 19–21.

The Old Bridge of Lanark—the paper, pp. 22–31—as to its structure, and the funds whence raised, is curious and suggestive as to the ways of the people, and the relative importance of places in Scotland at date of its erection.

The Clydesdale Upper Ward Society, which has prospered well, has some curious rules, introduced in paper given at pp. 31, 32; as, that the entrants "must be Protestants," and "must not swear or profane the Sabbath," etc.

The article which is headed "Crawford," pp. 33–35, is the corrected version promised at p. 81, Vol. I.

Leadhills, as noticed by Pennant, in 1782, pp. 35, 36; from the "*Household Words*," August, 1852, pp. 36–43; by J. N., pp. 43–48; and by A. M., pp. 196, 197; has had fair attention, but not more than was due to the locality.

Ordnance Survey results, as to acreage of parishes in the Upper Ward, and occupied as land, roads, villages, water, or railways, are given at p. 49, and in such form as may prove instructive.

The mountain heights, as shown on Ordnance sheets, and the rivers and streams in the Upper Ward, are reported at pp. 50, 51.

Ordnance Survey measurements, as to the soil in its character and extent, houses, domains, works, etc., are fully reported upon, pp. 52–59—and that analysis was laborious.

Census figures, 1755 to 1861, are given at p. 60, for the parishes in the Upper Ward, noting increase or decrease therein; also population of the villages, etc., in the district.

Valuation Roll papers for 1858-9 have been largely made use of in showing the distribution of property, etc., in the Upper Ward; and the results at various dates, given p. 61, may be valuable.

Distribution of property in the various parishes of the Ward occupies pp. 62-79, and will be instructive as to the relative positions of the estate-holders in the district.

Farms—of what value on the Roll, and how placed in the district —will be found reported at pp. 80-98.

Index to properties in the Ward will be found at pp. 99-103.

    „    proprietors, names of,    „    „    103-107.

    „    farms,    „    „    „    108-117.

    „    tenants,    „    „    „    117-126.

In constructing the above pages, it will be seen that, while the number of lines in each page are alike, the entries are in three alphabetical sets, those largest in value taking precedence.

Rent advance on farms, chiefly pastoral, will be found at p. 127; and the increase on those reported between 1857 and 1863 may be suggestive of the prosperity of the flock-master.

Factors on the estates in the Upper Ward, with their addresses, etc., may prove useful to parties seeking "locations" there.

Magnates of the Upper Ward of Lanarkshire are noticed, p. 129, with reference figures, showing the estate or "stake" the parties may have in the district.

Mansion, domain, wood, etc., on the estates; those resident wholly, partially, or non-resident, given in due order, pp. 130, 131.

House, villa, ground, wood, grass park, etc., of the estates of second class size, are shown in pp. 134, 135.

Distribution of estate property in the Ward,    p. 136.

    „    farms leased in the Ward,    p. 137.

Nomenclature of proprietors in the Ward, pp. 138, 139.

    „    large lease-holders in the Ward, p. 140.

The entries in the statistical pages in this volume have numeral references on the margin, which, being consecutive, may be readily found, and are frequently called attention to in the topographic sections of Volumes I. and II.

Page 141 shows the parochial arrangements of the Upper Ward, with the names of the teachers of the parish; the ministers of the Free and U.P. Churches are also given.

At page 142 and 143 an attempt is made to show the agricultural statistics of sixty of the larger farms in the parishes of Crawford, Crawfordjohn, Wiston and Roberton, Symington, Dolphinton, and Carnwath, and such information has been made frequent use of in the topographic text of Volumes I. and II.

At p. 144 are the general statistics of the Ward—perhaps the most suggestive page in this volume.

Culter, Notes on, 145-160, by J. W. B., will prove instructive to those interested in that pretty district; the note as to increase of rents on the Culter-Allers estate, and the memorial as to the teinds of Culter and Kilbucho, may prove also valuable.

Douglas, Notes on, by J. H., pp. 160-166, and those on Douglasdale by J. J., pp. 169-195, are curious, interesting, and were prepared by gentlemen well qualified to report on a district with which they have been long and respectably connected.

Bodinglee farm, tacks of for 1727 and 1794, may prove curious as to the tenure of land in the last century.

"Gold at Leadhills" is an instructive paper.

Addenda et Corrigenda, by G. V. I., are few—pp. 197, 200, and 256.

Indices, pp. 200-256, are extensive, and, it may be, needful in volumes aspiring to prove useful as those of reference.

A. M.

---

The "Items of Inquiry," as originally drawn up for this Work, are reprinted in beginning of this volume, and will show that the field of information looked into was large; and it is trusted that the task undertaken has been faithfully attended to.

*June 30, 1864.*　　　　　　　　　　A. M.

GLASGOW: PRINTED BY THOMAS MURRAY AND SON.